# Unofficial peace diplomacy

Manchester University Press

## Key Studies in Diplomacy

Series Editors: J. Simon Rofe and Giles Scott-Smith

Emeritus Editor: Lorna Lloyd

The volumes in this series seek to advance the study and understanding of diplomacy in its many forms. Diplomacy remains a vital component of global affairs, and it influences and is influenced by its environment and the context in which it is conducted. It is an activity of great relevance for International Studies, International History, and of course Diplomatic Studies. The series covers historical, conceptual, and practical studies of diplomacy.

Previously published by Bloomsbury:

*21st Century Diplomacy: A Practitioner's Guide* by Kishan S. Rana
*A Cornerstone of Modern Diplomacy: Britain and the Negotiation of the 1961 Vienna Convention on Diplomatic Relations* by Kai Bruns
*David Bruce and Diplomatic Practice: An American Ambassador in London, 1961-9* by John W. Young
*Embassies in Armed Conflict* by G.R. Berridge

Published by Manchester University Press:

*Reasserting America in the 1970s* edited by Hallvard Notaker, Giles Scott-Smith and David J. Snyder
*Human rights and humanitarian diplomacy: Negotiating for human rights protection and humanitarian access* by Kelly-Kate Pease
*The diplomacy of decolonisation: America, Britain and the United Nations during the Congo crisis 1960–64* by Alanna O'Malley
*Sport and diplomacy: Games within games* edited by J. Simon Rofe
*The TransAtlantic reconsidered* edited by Charlotte A. Lerg, Susanne Lachenicht and Michael Kimmage
*Academic ambassadors, Pacific allies: Australia, America and the Fulbright Program* by Alice Garner and Diane Kirkby
*A precarious equilibrium: Human rights and détente in Jimmy Carter's Soviet policy* by Umberto Tulli
*US public diplomacy in socialist Yugoslavia, 1950–70: Soft culture, cold partners* by Carla Konta
*Israelpolitik: German–Israeli relations, 1949–69* by Lorena De Vita
*Diplomatic tenses: A social evolutionary perspective on diplomacy* by Iver B. Neumann

# Unofficial peace diplomacy

## Private peace entrepreneurs in conflict resolution processes

Lior Lehrs

MANCHESTER UNIVERSITY PRESS

Published by Manchester University Press
Oxford Road, Manchester M13 9PL

www.manchesteruniversitypress.co.uk

British Library Cataloguing-in-Publication Data
A catalogue record for this book is available from the British Library

ISBN   978 1 5261 4765 3   hardback
ISBN   978 1 5261 8245 6   paperback

First published 2022
Paperback published 2024

Typeset by
New Best-set Typesetters Ltd

# Contents

| | | page |
|---|---|---|
| *List of figures* | | vi |
| *Acknowledgments* | | vii |
| *List of abbreviations* | | ix |
| | | |
| Introduction | | 1 |
| 1 Theoretical framework: private peace entrepreneurs | | 16 |
| 2 Norman Cousins and US–Soviet–British negotiations on a Nuclear Test Ban Treaty, 1962–1963 | | 71 |
| 3 Suzanne Massie and the Cold War during the Reagan era, 1983–1988 | | 117 |
| 4 Brendan Duddy and the negotiations between the Provisional IRA and the British government during the conflict in Northern Ireland, 1973–1993 | | 148 |
| 5 Uri Avnery and his dialogue with the PLO in the context of the Israeli–Palestinian conflict, 1975–1985 | | 206 |
| Conclusions | | 263 |
| | | |
| *Appendix* | | 287 |
| *Index* | | 289 |

# List of figures

1.1 The "broker" in the network system      *page* 20
1.2 Action patterns of PPEs      35
1.3 PPE patterns of influence on the official diplomatic sphere      50
1.4 Variables that determine PPEs' ability to have an influence      58
2.1 President John F. Kennedy with representatives from the American Association for the United Nations, March 1962. Copyright: United Press International      78
2.2 Soviet leader Nikita Khrushchev, Alice Bobrysheva (member of the Soviet Peace Committee), and Candice Cousins (Norman Cousins's daughter), April 1963. Copyright: Norman Cousins Papers, UCLA Library      87
3.1 President Ronald Reagan and Suzanne Massie at the White House, November 1988. Copyright: Ronald Reagan Presidential Library      126
3.2 Soviet leader Mikhail Gorbachev and Suzanne Massie at the White House State Dinner, December 1987. Copyright: Ronald Reagan Presidential Library      132
4.1 Brendan Duddy with former MI6 officer Michael Oatley, April 1998. Copyright: Brendan Duddy's family      155
4.2 The guest room at Duddy's home where the meetings took place during the 1975 talks. Copyright: Lior Lehrs      159
5.1 Meeting between members of the Israeli Council for Israeli–Palestinian Peace and PLO leaders in Tunisia, January 1983. Copyright: Uri Avnery's archive, The National Library of Israel      237
5.2 Cartoon by Ze'ev after the meeting in Tunisia, published in *Haaretz* on 25 January 1983. Copyright: Israeli Museum of Cartoons and Comics in Holon and Ze'ev's daughters, Dorit Farkash-Shuki and Naomi Farkash-Fink      238

# Acknowledgments

It is quite common for people who live in an intractable conflict area to feel that the "conflict" is a natural phenomenon that they have to live with, like an earthquake or storm, and that nothing can be done to change it, especially by ordinary citizens. For this reason, I have always been fascinated by cases involving people who refused to accept this assumption. During my studies in International Relations and the Middle East, I took a special interest in the history of diplomatic contacts and peace efforts that sought to address the Israeli–Arab and Israeli–Palestinian conflicts over the years. The scholarship generally focused on the official sphere, which was often characterized by stalemate and stagnation. But in researching the topic, I noticed that alongside the well-known official negotiations and meditation channels, there had also, over the years, been less-known and less-researched unofficial dialogue channels that were initiated by private actors, some of whom even played critical roles. Against this background, I began to look for similar cases in other conflict areas around the world and thus discovered dozens of cases of "private peace entrepreneurs" in different regions and at different times. This inspired me to devote years of research to this topic, which eventually led to this book. None of this would have been possible without the help and support of many people, and this is a great opportunity to thank them.

I would like to thank Avraham Sela and Arie Kacowicz for their helpful feedback and enriching conversations during my work on this research project, and Dan Miodownik and Galia Press-Barnathan for their endless support, encouragement, and advice. I would also like to express my gratitude to Louis Kriesberg, Daniel Kurtzer, Niall Ó Dochartaigh, Elie Podeh, Ruti Teitel, and Hilde Henriksen Waage for their ongoing support, suggestions, and invaluable assistance. I am indebted to the late Robert Jervis for our inspiring dialogue and his insightful feedbacks. He was a giant of IR, a real intellectual and one of the kindest scholars I have ever met. I also wish to honor the memory of Yaakov Bar-Siman-Tov, who was a teacher and friend, and is sorely missed.

I am grateful to Ronald Zweig, director of New York University's Taub Center, and to the center's administrator, Shayne Figueroa, for their support and hospitality during my postdoctoral fellowship at NYU. A thank you is due to I. William Zartman and Daniel Serwer, from the Johns Hopkins University School of Advanced International Studies (SAIS) Conflict Management Program, and to Sarah Cobb and Susan H. Allen, from George Mason University's Carter School for Peace and Conflict Resolution, for hosting me as a visiting scholar during my research.

This research was also made possible thanks to scholarships and grants, and I am indebted to the Leonard Davis Institute for International Relations at the Hebrew University of Jerusalem and the Harry S. Truman Research Institute for the Advancement of Peace. I wish to thank all the interviewees for their cooperation and insights, and the dedicated archivists in the various archives I have used. Special thanks to Eamonn Downey and the Duddy family for their kind support and help during my research in Northern Ireland.

I also wish to thank Giles Scott-Smith, who followed and supported the process of this book project from the beginning, and Lucy Burns and Robert Byron of Manchester University Press for all their assistance and dedication. Special thanks to Merav Datan for her careful and thoughtful editing.

This work would not have been possible without my dear family and friends, who gave me endless support and had to listen, over and over again, to stories and details about various private peace initiatives, and were required to express interest. I am particularly thankful to my dear *Shmutz* friends," whose longstanding friendship I cherish and whose encouragement was a tremendous resource for me. Above all I would like to thank my parents, Dina and Gideon, for their love and support. I am especially indebted to my mother, who served as a "shadow reviewer" and a source of inspiration for the work, being herself a "peace entrepreneur" who, on the eve of the 1967 Israeli–Arab war, sent a letter to Soviet leader Alexei Kosygin calling on him to act to prevent the war. The war was not prevented, and she is still waiting for a reply.

# List of abbreviations

| | |
|---|---|
| ANC | African National Congress |
| CCNTB | Citizens' Committee for a Nuclear Test Ban |
| ENDC | Eighteen Nation Disarmament Committee |
| ETA | Euskadi Ta Askatasuna |
| FLN | Front de Libération Nationale (National Liberation Front) |
| ICIPP | Israeli Council for Israeli–Palestinian Peace |
| ICJP | Irish Commission for Justice and Peace |
| IDASA | Institute for Democracy in Africa |
| IDF | Israel Defense Forces |
| MHS | mutually hurting stalemate |
| MK | Knesset member |
| NATO | North Atlantic Treaty Organization |
| NIO | Northern Ireland Office |
| NIS | National Intelligence Service |
| NSC | National Security Council |
| PAC | PIRA Army Council |
| PIRA | Provisional Irish Republican Army |
| PLO | Palestine Liberation Organization |
| PNC | Palestinian National Council |
| POW | prisoners of war |
| PPE | private peace entrepreneur |
| PTBT | Treaty Banning Nuclear Weapon Tests in the Atmosphere, in Outer Space and Under Water (the Partial Test Ban Treaty) |
| RUC | Royal Ulster Constabulary |
| SANE | National Committee for a Sane Nuclear Policy |
| SDI | Strategic Defense Initiative |
| SDLP | Social Democratic and Labour Party |
| UN | United Nations |
| WBGS | West Bank and Gaza Strip |

# Introduction

In his play *The Acharnians* (425 BC), Greek playwright Aristophanes told the story of Dikaiopolis – an Athenian citizen who, in the context of the ongoing war with Sparta, tried to promote a discussion at the Athenian citizen assembly about achieving peace. The audience ignored his request and expressed support for the continuation of the war. As a result, Dikaiopolis decided to launch a private appeal to Sparta and indeed concluded a private peace treaty with it.[1] The story of Dikaiopolis is fictional but it represents the real international historical phenomenon of "private peace entrepreneurs" (PPEs), which stands at the center of this book.

PPEs are individual private citizens who, without official authority, initiate channels of communication with official representatives from the opposing side during a conflict, in order to promote a conflict resolution process. Although the history of international and internal conflicts reveals many cases of PPEs, some of whom played a valuable or even critical role in conflict resolution efforts, the literature has not examined this important phenomenon with the full and specialized attention that it deserves, let alone conceptualized the PPE as a distinct international actor. This book aims to fill that gap, both theoretically and empirically. It highlights the ability of private individual citizens – who are not politicians, diplomats, or military leaders – to operate as important and influential actors in international politics in general, and in peace processes in conflict areas in particular.

The chapter presents a definition of PPEs and positions the phenomenon within current theoretical literature, discusses its contribution to various fields, and describes the similarities and differences between PPEs and other theoretical frameworks and actors. It then presents the research questions and methodology, and outlines the structure of the book.

### Definition: private peace entrepreneurs

PPEs have four basic defining characteristics. First, they are private citizens with no official authority.[2] They are neither appointed nor elected to outline, shape, or carry out foreign policy, or to negotiate peace, and they act only in their own name and without an official mandate. In this regard they may be described as self-appointed peace envoys.

Second, PPEs are local peacemakers who belong to one of the disputing sides (a state or ethnic community) in the conflict. In cases of internal conflict, they are members of the national framework in which the conflict is taking place.[3] There have also been cases involving external PPEs – namely, private citizens who do not belong to either of the disputing sides – although such cases are beyond the scope of this study. Internal PPEs are characteristically quite different from external PPEs in terms of resources, acquaintance with the conflict, motivation, legitimacy, and potential role. These two types of PPEs therefore deserve separate analysis, and this research focuses on internal, or local, PPEs. The distinction is similar to that of Wehr and Lederach between the "outsider-neutral" mediator, who has no connection to either side of the conflict, and the "insider-partial" mediator, who is "the mediator from within the conflict."[4]

Third, PPEs initiate channels of communication with official representatives from the other side of the conflict, not with private citizens. The communication might take place directly with leaders or mid- or low-ranking representatives, or through a mediator who has a direct channel to officials on the other side of the conflict.

Fourth, the goal of PPEs' activities is to promote a process of conflict resolution and to influence the official sphere as well as relations between the leaderships of the disputing sides (in this regard the PPE differs from Dikaiopolis). Subject to the conditions and the circumstances of the conflict, their goal might be positioned anywhere along a wide spectrum, from resolving a specific disagreement or an urgent crisis, through creating a channel for negotiation, to drafting a peace agreement.

### Theoretical background

The PPE phenomenon is essentially a unique phenomenon with its own distinct characteristics and patterns that have yet to be adequately analyzed and theorized. It does not accord with any of the concepts postulated in the existing scholarship. This study outlines a special analytical framework for the PPE phenomenon and offers a unique toolkit to discuss and analyze the PPEs' resources, activities, relations with the establishment, and impact on the official sphere. At the same time, a number of research fields and theoretical frameworks that intersect and correspond with the phenomenon can be identified in the literature, and this work seeks to contribute to these areas of research. The study uses relevant elements from these research fields in developing a proposed analytical framework for the PPE phenomenon, and examines differences between PPEs, on the one hand, and various terms and frameworks in the scholarship, on the other.

The PPE phenomenon falls within the sphere of research on unofficial diplomacy. Various scholars in the field of diplomatic studies have identified a process that developed during the second half of the twentieth century and intensified after the end of the Cold War: the patterns of diplomacy changed as new unofficial and non-governmental actors emerged in the diplomatic sphere, and the monopoly over international diplomatic processes previously enjoyed by professional diplomats and foreign ministries weakened. In describing this phenomenon the literature coined terms such as "unofficial diplomacy," "citizen diplomacy," and "new diplomats," and scholars noted that the revolution in the information and communication technology, and the processes of globalization and democratization, played a role in its development.[5] The rise of these actors was described as part of the "democratization of diplomacy" and the transformation from "club diplomacy" to "network diplomacy."[6]

The discussion on these new actors provoked a debate about their importance and influence and became linked to a broader debate on the existence of a crisis in diplomacy. Proponents of the crisis thesis argue that traditional official diplomacy has become obsolete and is nearing its end, while opponents argue that it is more vital than ever and has an impressive capacity for adaptation to change. The controversy also relates to the distinction between an approach that emphasizes the role of the state system in diplomacy, and an approach that posits a global society in which diplomacy operates as multi-centric networks with various types of actors, within which the state system constitutes only one option for engaging in diplomacy.[7]

In parallel, in the field of conflict and peace research, discussions developed around the concept of "track two diplomacy." Montville defined the term as "unofficial, informal interactions between members of adversarial groups or nations with the goals of developing strategies, influencing public opinion, and organizing human and material resources in ways that might help resolve the conflict."[8] Scholars emphasize that track two is not intended to substitute for the official negotiation track (track one) but to support it. Track two encompasses a wide range of activities and encounters between citizens from conflicting sides, and over time scholars have drawn distinctions among various types of track two practices. Agha et al., for example, distinguished between "soft" track two diplomacy, which aims to familiarize each side with the other and change perceptions and relations over the long term, and "hard" track two diplomacy, the goal of which is to produce a proposal for a political agreement and to advance official negotiations. Diamond and McDonald formulated the term "multi track diplomacy" using nine tracks, with various actors and functions in each track, as part of a peacemaking system.[9]

A key component of this literature centers on "problem-solving workshops" that bring together participants from parties to a conflict, preferably with access to decision makers. The workshops are facilitated by an impartial third party, usually a "scholar-practitioner" with expertise in conflict resolution and social psychology, and are aimed at exploring the parties' needs and fears and developing new ideas and solutions. These workshops began in the 1960s, when the leading scholars who initiated and facilitated them – such as John Burton, Herbert Kelman, and Ronald Fisher – also developed the theoretical work on the subject, offering different models and approaches as a basis for their workshops.[10]

While there are some points of intersection between the PPE phenomenon and the track two framework, they are essentially different for several reasons. First, track two refers to a wide range of encounters between private citizens from rival groups, whereas PPEs are not interested in a meeting with private citizens on the other side but in a dialogue with the official leadership, for the explicit purpose of influencing the official sphere and promoting conflict resolution.[11]

Second, PPEs are active players who devote time and energy to their ongoing independent activity, and often pay a price for it, whereas participants in track two "problem solving" workshops are usually invited by a third party and have a limited, temporary, and passive role. The track two literature focuses on how workshops change the participants' perceptions towards the conflict and the rival side, whereas PPEs' pro-peace perceptions and commitment are a pre-existing factor that pre-dated their participation in meetings and motivated them to pursue their PPE efforts in the first place. Moreover, there is usually no significant role for an external third party in PPE activity, as PPEs initiate and facilitate their contacts directly with the rival side. The focus of the two frameworks also differs: while track two scholarship focuses on a process, the research on PPEs focuses on an agent that can become involved in various processes, initiatives, and projects, including track two. In this sense, the track two framework is too limited, revealing only part of the vast and varied picture of unofficial peace diplomacy.

Third, scholars describe track two as a complementary track, designed to support the official track, and the two components are presented as part of a single system aimed at a common goal. However, the PPE prism reveals more complex relations between the unofficial and the official spheres. PPEs often act under conditions of tension and in a manner that clashes with official policy. They might operate under conditions of diplomatic vacuum, with no official dialogue underway, or even under circumstances of war, violence, or an official policy that opposes negotiations. PPEs are not defined by their relationship with the leadership or position vis-à-vis official negotiations; their independent activity stands on its own.

Fourth, the track two literature centers on the more organized, structured, and professional activities and meetings of citizen diplomacy, especially the problem-solving workshops conducted by key scholars in the field, while ignoring the wide range of informal diplomatic initiatives and activities that take place in a more amateurish, private, covert, and unprofessional manner, occasionally without awareness of the theoretical context. In addition, the scholarship on track two and citizen diplomacy tends to see this as a new phenomenon and to focus on contemporary cases, thus ignoring the historical dimension that this study seeks to contribute to the field.

This study on PPEs contributes to literature on the inclusion of civil society in peace processes. Scholars in that field have considered the important role that civil society organizations can play, arguing that there is a link between their inclusion in the peacemaking process and the sustainability of the peace agreement, and offering possible ways to incorporate civil society in functions such as advocacy, facilitation, and monitoring.[12] The study also accords well with the recent "local turn" in the scholarship on peacebuilding, which derives from a critical view of the liberal peacebuilding project that is managed by international actors and, according to this critique, is based on a universal Western model that excludes the local context. The "local turn" emphasizes the potential role of local actors, communities, and organizations in peacebuilding, providing a model for "peace from below" as opposed to top-down liberal peacebuilding.[13] This research, which focuses on the PPE as a local peacemaker, shares and affirms some of the assumptions of the "local turn" approach.

The PPE is a hybrid actor, engaging, on the one hand, in practices from the world of traditional diplomacy, and, on the other hand, in practices from the world of civil society and political activism. The study attempts to bridge the gaps between the two sets of literature, borrowing theoretical tools from these fields for inclusion in the proposed analytical framework. Towards that end, the framework combines elements from the literature on international relations, diplomacy, and negotiations with elements from the literature on social movements and activism in general, and in the field of world politics and peace in particular.

Three important diplomatic practices, well known in the scholarship on negotiations, deserve special attention for their relevance to the discussion on PPEs: mediation, backchannel diplomacy, and use of a special envoy. Many PPEs strive to integrate these diplomatic models in their unofficial activity and to use them as a means of influencing the official diplomatic sphere.

*Mediation* is defined as intervention by a third party, external to the conflict, carried out voluntarily, with the consent of the parties, in order to promote an agreed solution. Scholars emphasize that the mediator should be neutral and impartial. External official mediators can be representatives of a superpower, state, or international organization.[14] PPEs are not mediators in the classic sense, as the disputing sides did not request their involvement and did not necessarily grant them permission to mediate, and, unlike mediators, they are not a "third party." They are local actors who come from within the conflict, and their efforts do not necessarily qualify as mediation. Although the main elements of the orthodox definition do not apply to PPE activities, PPEs may evince some characteristics of the mediator's role. Over the years, the scholarship has developed broader definitions of mediation in order to expand the traditional framework and include new types of mediation, such as "quasi-mediation" and "informal mediation" carried out by private and unofficial actors.[15] Scholars point to changes in the nature of the world's conflicts since the end of the Cold War, from inter-state to intra-state disputes, as a significant reason for the growing role of private peace mediators.[16]

The second practice is *backchannel diplomacy* – an official communication channel conducted in complete confidentiality, without the knowledge of the media or the public. Usually the political and bureaucratic establishment is also unaware, and only a small, exclusive circle of decision makers is involved in the process.[17] Backchannels rely on individuals with close ties to decision makers, who in turn have confidence in them. These individuals are granted the authority to explore a variety of options, with more leeway than "front-channel" talks allow, and to commit to a tentative outline of an agreement. PPEs, as unofficial actors, do not meet the definition of backchannel negotiators, but if their informal channels gain a certain measure of official recognition from decision makers, they can become backchannels. Wanis-St. John acknowledges the possibility of a backchannel that begins as a "freelance" initiative, without official status, and later receives official approval.[18]

The third practice centers on the role of a *special envoy* – a diplomatic emissary sent at the request, and initiative, of a leader for a special diplomatic mission (also known as "ad-hoc diplomacy").[19] It is important to distinguish between PPEs – who act on their own behalf and initiative, operate over time out of an ideological commitment, and can under certain circumstances be integrated into the official sphere – and special envoys, who serve in an official capacity on behalf of decision makers and often come from the establishment.

At the same time, the literature on civil society activism, and especially on "transnational civil society," also has significant relevance to the analysis of PPEs' activity. The scholarship on transnational civil society, a growing field in international relations literature since the end of the Cold War, focuses on transnational movements as global actors engaged in cross-border collective and independent activity, with activists and members from different countries who share common ideas, values, and goals. These transnational movements, coalitions, and networks struggle for various global causes such as human rights, environmental issues, social justice, and arms control. They seek to have an impact on world politics and aim to influence three target audiences: states, international institutions, and civil society.[20] Two central concepts that have developed in this literature deserve mention. The first is the concept of a "transnational moral entrepreneur," which refers to actors (individuals or groups) who work for normative global change. The second is the "transnational epistemic community," a network of cross-border experts whose members share common normative and causal beliefs and work to disseminate ideas and policy prescriptions.[21]

The PPE is an individual citizen, not a transnational movement or a cross-border network, and PPEs' activity centers on a limited diplomatic goal in the context of conflict resolution in the particular geographical area where they live, rather than on global issues. However, because PPEs, like transnational activists, are civil society actors who engage in cross-border action and seek to influence international politics and diplomacy, this study uses insights and concepts from the work on transnational civil society. PPE efforts also overlap somewhat with peace activism, and the study therefore uses tools from research on social movements, particularly peace movements, and contributes to this literature. The discussions on PPEs and on peace activists share certain questions, such as the conditions for effective activism and the unique challenges of civil society activities pertaining to war and peace.[22]

This study on the PPE phenomenon underscores the need for more theoretical attention to the individual private citizen as an international and diplomatic actor. It examines the PPE's agency while addressing the complex dynamic between this agent and the structure.[23] Nearly half a century ago James Eayrs wrote about the "emergence of the individual to a significant role in world politics" and criticized the dominant theory for ignoring the individual as an actor and treating that individual only "as a creature of the state to which he belongs."[24] The research on the PPE phenomenon challenges basic assumptions and thinking patterns in the main international relations paradigms and raises fundamental questions on issues such as authority and representation in international relations and diplomacy.[25]

The study also contributes to the literature on entrepreneurs. The term "entrepreneur" comes from the French word *entreprendre*, meaning "to undertake," and scholars in the field emphasize three main dimensions: innovation, proactiveness, and risk taking. Another important dimension in the literature is opportunities: entrepreneurs strive to identify and take advantage of opportunities. These components are highly relevant for the analysis of PPEs. In addition to research on business entrepreneurs, the literature contains discussions on social entrepreneurs, policy entrepreneurs, and moral entrepreneurs, and this study adds the dimension of entrepreneurs in the field of unofficial peace diplomacy.[26]

Alongside the theoretical aspects, the book makes a historiographical contribution because it sheds light on important figures who have been excluded from the history textbooks, and offers an alternative perspective to traditional narratives concerning the history of the conflicts. It also contributes to historical studies that, while focusing on specific figures who engaged in private diplomacy, do not conceptualize their activity as part of a wider phenomenon.[27] The book's historical dimension seeks to contribute to the evolving field of research on "new diplomatic history," which examines various actors, individuals, and groups who played diplomatic roles in the broader sense, and to the history of "private international relations" as well as the research approach of "peace history," which focuses on the history of ideas, individuals, and groups in relation to the promotion of peace.[28]

## Research design

The book focuses on two research questions. The first relates to the definition of the phenomenon – *who are the private peace entrepreneurs?* – and discusses its boundaries and characteristics. In what way are PPEs and the theoretical characteristics of the phenomenon unique? What resources do they have, and what types of PPEs are there? What are their action patterns and the response patterns of the official establishment? And what are the limits of the phenomenon and the main criticisms leveled against it?

The second research question is about the impact of the phenomenon – *what is the impact of private peace entrepreneurs on the official diplomatic sphere?* To explore this question, the study first examines whether PPEs have any impact, and, if so, how it is expressed and what are the influence patterns of PPEs. In the second stage, it examines which variables and conditions affect the ability of PPEs to influence and play an effective and significant role in conflict resolution processes. In this context, the research analyzes variables at three levels: those related to the PPEs, those related to their peace initiative, and those that are external.

The research combines theoretical discussion with comparative historical analysis, examining four empirical case studies of PPEs from different conflicts and different historical eras and geographical regions:

1. Norman Cousins and the Nuclear Test Ban Treaty negotiations among the United States, the Soviet Union, and the United Kingdom (1962–1963)
2. Suzanne Massie and the Cold War during the Reagan era (1983–1988)
3. Brendan Duddy and negotiations between the Provisional Irish Republican Army (PIRA) and the British government during the conflict in Northern Ireland (1973–1993)
4. Uri Avnery and his dialogue with the PLO in the context of the Israeli–Palestinian conflict (1975–1985)

The case studies come from three conflicts that were at the heart of post-1945 twentieth-century diplomatic history: the Cold War between the United States and the Soviet Union, the Israeli–Palestinian conflict, and the conflict in Northern Ireland. Their examination uses the research method of cross-comparisons, which analyzes a phenomenon through case studies from different historical and geopolitical conditions, provides a broad perspective on a full range of variation, and minimizes biases related to political or national context. The empirical research on the case studies allows for an in-depth process-tracing analysis of the PPEs and their activity and influence by offering a broad empirical field from which to identify similarities and differences and examine various angles and components of the phenomenon.

The case studies differ in terms of several variables, including the period and conflict area, the type of conflict (two cases involve international conflict and two involve a conflict between a state and a non-state actor), the stage in the evolution of the conflict, the types of PPEs and their resources and action patterns, the objective of PPEs' initiatives, and their relations with decision makers. In order to draw valid theoretical conclusions about the variables that shape the effectiveness of the PPEs, the case studies also differ in terms of PPEs' influence patterns and the degree of their impact on the official diplomatic sphere.

The four case studies come from the post-Second World War international historical context, mainly from the early 1960s through the early 1990s. This historical period reflects a transformative stage in the development of the PPE phenomenon, during which an awareness of unofficial diplomacy in the academic, diplomatic, and political discourse began to take shape.

As the end of the Cold War, with the accompanying changes in the international context, is considered a key milestone in the scholarship on private actors in peace diplomacy and international politics,[29] this study focuses on the preceding years in order to trace the evolution of the PPE phenomenon, and its main patterns and practices, at this critical stage.

Another advantage of the selected case studies is that they represent long-term PPE activity in the three examined conflicts, and in fact include a series of initiatives and efforts at different stages, thus allowing for use of the method of "within-case analysis" to identify how the variance in conditions over time affected the outcomes. The comparative historical analysis is based on awareness and sensitivity to the historical context of the various cases, and it allows one to draw generalized conclusions about common characteristics and similarities between PPEs, while also identifying differences and unique conditions in each case.

The analysis of the case studies uses a proposed theoretical framework (to be presented in the first chapter) that offers a unique toolbox for the analysis of PPEs using relevant theoretical tools drawn from various research fields. The study employs the method of a "structural-focused comparison," which is structural because it makes a systemic comparison using general questions examined in each case, and is focused because it centers on particular aspects of the case studies. This method is intended to examine a phenomenon in such a way that the explanations emerging from each case can be combined to formulate a complex and comprehensive theory.

The empirical analysis is based on a wide variety of sources, including official and private archival resources, historical studies, memoirs, biographies, interviews, and media reports. Notably, PPE case studies frequently encounter the problem of lack of resources because of the unofficial and often undocumented nature of their activity. In many cases neither the official governmental archives nor the PPEs themselves maintain records of their activities. Therefore, the case selection was also influenced by the accessibility of primary sources that would allow for an in-depth examination of the PPEs' activity and its consequences. The study sought to combine sources from official state archives with private archival sources and sources pertaining to relevant actors and parties in each case. The research highlights that in order to expose the unofficial and lesser-known layers of diplomacy, it is necessary to expand the scope of sources and use unofficial and private sources alongside the official ones.

The comparative perspective is further broadened by a pool of thirty-six additional control cases that meet the definition of the phenomenon, helping to provide a broad empirical basis for analysis of the PPEs' activities and for the illustration and demonstration of various aspects. The list of cases appears in appendix.

## The structure of the book

The first chapter outlines the analytical framework for examining the phenomenon of PPEs, including their characteristics, activities, and impact. The first part presents a typology of the phenomenon as it relates to the following components: the PPEs' resources, types of PPEs, their action patterns, the official establishment's attitude towards PPEs, and critical arguments against their activities. The second part deals with the PPEs' impact on the official diplomatic sphere, identifies PPEs' influence patterns, and suggests a multivariable system that distinguishes among variables related to PPEs, variables related to their peace initiative, and external variables. This framework is used to analyze the case studies in the subsequent chapters.

Chapters 2–5 present analyses of the case studies, with each chapter offering a brief historical background, a summary of the PPEs' biography and worldview, an analysis of the PPEs' efforts and initiatives, and an examination of their impact on the official diplomatic sphere.

The second chapter analyzes the case of Norman Cousins, editor of the *Saturday Review* and anti-nuclear activist, as an American PPE in the context of the nuclear test ban negotiations (1962–1963). The analysis addresses Cousins's role in establishing the American–Soviet Dartmouth dialogue conferences, his meetings with Soviet premier Khrushchev and US president Kennedy, a proposal he made that served as a basis for Kennedy's American University speech, and his efforts to secure support for the Partial Nuclear Test Ban Treaty.

The third chapter analyzes the case of Suzanne Massie, an American author and expert on Russian culture who strove to promote dialogue and improve relations between the US and the USSR in the context of the Cold War. The chapter examines her PPE efforts and relations with both sides, which included frequent visits to the Soviet Union, meetings with US president Ronald Reagan, and an exchange of messages between the parties, during the years 1983–1988.

The fourth chapter analyzes the case of Brendan Duddy, a businessman from Northern Ireland who served as an intermediary between the British government and the Republican leadership at various times between 1973 and 1993. The analysis focuses on three main stages in Duddy's peace efforts: the backchannel he established during the 1975 truce, mediation initiatives during the first (1980) and the second (1981) Republican prisoners' hunger strikes, and the revival of Duddy's channel in 1990–1993.

The fifth chapter analyzes the case of Uri Avnery, editor of the weekly *Haolam Hazeh*, a Knesset member, and a peace activist, who as an Israeli PPE established and maintained contact with the Palestine Liberation Organization (PLO). The analysis extends from Avnery's first unofficial diplomatic activity in the 1950s and first contact with a PLO official in 1975, through the establishment of the channel between members of the Israeli Council for Israeli–Palestinian Peace (ICIPP) and PLO leaders, to Avnery's meetings with PLO chairman Arafat in the early 1980s.

Drawing on the empirical research, the closing chapter presents a comparative analysis of the PPEs' activities and impact, offering final conclusions and insights. The discussion covers a range of questions and issues, such as the PPEs' influence on the official sphere, their personality profile, their social character, the risk of misperception of their activity, and PPEs as a historical phenomenon.

## Notes

1 Aristophanes, *The Acharnians*, trans. D. Parker (New York: New American Library, 1973).
2 The term "private" in this context refers to their unofficial status and thus may apply to individuals with public status from various fields outside official and governmental circles as well as anonymous citizens.
3 An exceptional case is the "diaspora PPE," who lives abroad but has familial, ethnic, or cultural ties with, or is descended from, one of the disputing sides (see discussion on types of PPEs in chapter 1).
4 P. Wehr and J. P. Lederach, "Mediating conflict in central America," *Journal of Peace Research*, 28:1 (1991), 86–88.
5 R. Langhorne, "The diplomacy of non-state actors," *Diplomacy and Statecraft*, 16:2 (2005), 331–339; B. Hocking, "Privatizing diplomacy?" *International Studies Perspectives*, 5:2 (2004), 147–152; A. F. Cooper and B. Hocking, "Governments, non-governmental organisations and the re-calibration of diplomacy," *Global Society*, 14:3 (2000), 361–376; R. Langhorne, "Current developments in diplomacy: Who are the diplomats now?" *Diplomacy and Statecraft*, 8:2 (1997), 1–15; P. Sharp, "Making sense of citizen diplomats: The people of Duluth, Minnesota, as international actors," *International Studies Perspectives*, 2:2 (2001), 131–150; J. R. Kelley, "The new diplomacy: Evolution of a revolution," *Diplomacy and Statecraft*, 21:2 (2010), 286–305; M. R. Berman and J. E. Johnson (eds), *Unofficial Diplomats* (New York: Columbia University Press, 1977); A. Curle, *Making Peace* (London: Tavistock, 1971), 225–244.
6 J. Heine, "From club to network diplomacy," in A. F. Cooper, J. Heine, and R. Thakur (eds), *The Oxford Handbook of Modern Diplomacy* (Oxford: Oxford University Press, 2013), 54–69; M. Conley and C. Beyerinck, "Citizen diplomacy," in C. M. Constantinou, P. Kerr, and P. Sharp (eds), *The SAGE Handbook of Diplomacy* (London: Sage, 2016), 521–529.
7 B. Hocking, "The end(s) of diplomacy," *International Journal*, 53 (1997–1998), 169–172; B. Hocking, "Catalytic diplomacy: Beyond 'newness' and 'decline'," in J. Melissen (ed.), *Innovation in Diplomatic Practice* (London: Macmillan,

1999), 21–42; A. F. Cooper, "Beyond representation," *International Journal*, 53:1 (1997–1998), 173–178; A. Stemmet, "Globalization, integration and fragmentation: Forces shaping diplomacy in the new millennium," *Politeia*, 21:3 (2002), 18–38; Sharp, "Making sense," 146.

8  J. V. Montville, "The arrow and the olive branch: A case for track two diplomacy," in J. W. McDonald and D. B. Bendahmane (eds), *Conflict Resolution: Track Two Diplomacy* (Washington D.C.: Institute for Multi-track Diplomacy, 1995), 9.

9  J. Davies and E. Kaufman (eds), *Second Track/Citizens' Diplomacy* (Lanham: Rowman & Littlefield, 2002); L. Diamond and J. McDonald, *Multi-track Diplomacy* (West Hartford: Kumarian, 1996); H. Agha, S. Feldman, A. Khalidi, and Z. Schiff, *Track-II Diplomacy: Lessons from the Middle East* (Cambridge, Mass,: The MIT Press, 2003); D. D. Kaye, *Talking to the Enemy: Track Two Diplomacy in the Middle East and South Asia* (Santa Monica: RAND, 2007); P. Jones, *Track Two Diplomacy in Theory and Practice* (Stanford: Stanford University Press, 2015).

10  R. J. Fisher (ed.), *Interactive Conflict Resolution* (Syracuse: Syracuse University Press, 1997); H. C. Kelman and S. P. Cohen, "The problem-solving workshop: A social-psychological contribution to the resolution of international conflicts," *Journal of Peace Research*, 13:2 (1976), 79–90; John W. Burton, "Track two: An alternative to power politics," in John W. McDonald, Jr. and Diane B. Bendahmane (eds), *Conflict Resolution: Track Two Diplomacy* (Washington, D. C.: Center for the Study of Foreign Affairs, 1987), 65–72; N. N. Rouhana, "Interactive conflict resolution: Issues in theory, methodology, and evaluation," in P. C. Stern and D. Druckman (eds), *International Conflict Resolution after the Cold War* (Washington, D.C.: National Academy Press, 2000), 294–337.

11  PPE activity also differs from "track one-and-a-half" diplomacy, defined as meetings between officials from conflicting sides that take place in unofficial settings. See S. A. Nan, "Track one-and-a-half diplomacy," in R. J. Fisher (ed.), *Paving the Way* (Lanham: Lexington Books, 2005), 161–173.

12  A. Wanis-St. John and D. Kew, "Civil society and peace negotiations: Confronting exclusion," *International Negotiation*, 13:1 (2008), 11–36; T. Paffenholz, "Civil society and peace negotiations: Beyond the inclusion–exclusion dichotomy," *Negotiation Journal*, 30:1 (2014), 70, 73; D. Nilsson, "Anchoring the peace: Civil society actors in peace accords and durable peace," *International Interactions*, 38:2 (2012), 243–266.

13  R. Mac Ginty and O. P. Richmond, "The local turn in peace building: A critical agenda for peace," *Third World Quarterly*, 34:5 (2013), 763–783; H. Leonardsson and G. Rudd, "The 'local turn' in peacebuilding: A literature review of effective and emancipatory local peacebuilding," *Third World Quarterly*, 36:5 (2015), 825–839.

14  J. Bercovitch, *Studies in International Mediation* (New York: Palgrave, 2012); C. A. Crocker, F. O. Hampson, and P. Aall (eds), *Grasping the Nettle: Analyzing Cases of Intractable Conflicts* (Washington, D.C.: US Institute of Peace Press, 2005); P. Wallensteen and I. Svensson, "Talking peace: International mediation in armed conflicts," *Journal of Peace Research*, 51:2 (2014), 315–327.

15  L. Kriesberg, "Formal and quasi-mediators in international disputes: An exploratory analysis," *Journal of Peace Research*, 28:1 (1991), 19–27; A. P. Hare, "Informal mediation by private individuals," in J. Bercovitch and J. Z. Rubin (eds), *Mediation in International Relations* (London: Macmillan, 1992), 52–63; C. Turner and M. Wählisch (eds) *Rethinking Peace Mediation* (Bristol: Bristol University Press, 2021).

16  M. Lehti, *The Era of Private Peacemakers* (Cham: Springer, 2018), 1–12.

17  A. Wanis-St. John, "Back-channel negotiation: International bargaining in the shadows," *Negotiation Journal*, 22:2 (2006), 119–144; P. Jones, "Ethical dilemmas of back-channel diplomacy: Necessary secrecy or a secret foreign policy?" *Hague Journal of Diplomacy*, 13:4 (2018), 483–501.

18  Wanis-St. John, "Back-channel," 120–121.

19  G. R. Berridge, *Talking to the Enemy* (New York: St. Martin's Press, 1994), 101–116; H. M. Wriston, "The special envoy," *Foreign Affairs*, 38:2 (1960), 219–237.

20  M. E. Keck and K. Sikkink, *Activists Beyond Borders* (Ithaca: Cornell University Press, 1998); R. Price, "Transnational civil society and advocacy in world politics," *World Politics*, 55:4 (2003), 579–606; A. Klotz, "Transnational activism and global transformations: The anti-apartheid and abolitionist experiences," *European Journal of International Relations*, 8:1 (2002), 49–76; A. M. Florini (ed.), *The Third Force: The Rise of Transnational Civil Society* (Tokyo: Japan Center for International Exchange, 2000).

21  E. Nadelmann, "Global prohibition regimes: The evolution of norms in international society," *International Organization*, 44:4 (1990), 479–526; P. M. Haas, "Introduction: Epistemic communities and international policy coordination," *International Organization*, 46:1 (1992), 1–35.

22  K. Salomon, "The peace movement: An anti-establishment movement," *Journal of Peace Research*, 23:2 (1986), 115–127; D. S. Meyer, "Protest cycles and political process: American peace movements in the nuclear age," *Political Research Quarterly*, 46:3 (1993), 451–479; D. Lieberfield, "Parental protest, public opinion, and war termination," *Social Movements Studies*, 8:4 (2009), 375–392; D. Cortright, "Assessing peace movement effectiveness in the 1980s," *Peace & Change*, 16:1 (1991), 46–63.

23  See A. E. Wendt, "The agent–structure problem in international relations theory," *International Organization*, 41:3 (1987), 335–370.

24  J. Eayrs, *Diplomacy and its Discontents* (Toronto: University of Toronto Press, 1971), 76.

25  P. Sharp, "For diplomacy: Representation and the study of international relations," *International Studies Review*, 1:1 (1999), 53; C. Jönsson and M. Hall, *Essence of Diplomacy* (New York: Palgrave Macmillan, 2005), 98–118.

26  A. M. Peredo and M. McLean, "Social entrepreneurship: A critical review of the concept," *Journal of World Business*, 41:1 (2006), 56–65; A. N. Licht and J. I. Siegel, "The social dimensions of entrepreneurship," in M. Casson, B. Yeung, A. Basu, and N. Wadeson (eds), *The Oxford Handbook of Entrepreneurship* (Oxford: Oxford University Press, 2008), 511–539; A. Nicholls (ed.), *Social Entrepreneurship* (Oxford: Oxford University Press, 2011); M. Mintrom and P.

Norman, "Policy entrepreneurship and policy change," *Policy Studies Journal*, 37:4 (2009), 649–667; M. Kaptein, "The moral entrepreneur: A new component of ethical leadership," *Journal of Business Ethics*, 156:4 (2019), 1135–1150. A study by Oliver-Lumerman et al. on life narratives of Israeli and Palestinian peace activists uses the term "Peace Entrepreneurs," defining it as a subcategory of social entrepreneurs who are "committed to establish[ing] a social venture with the aim of promoting peace activities in a context of extreme intergroup conflict." A. Oliver-Lumerman, T. B. Zilber, H. S. Magadlah, T. Rubel-Lifschitz, and Y. Tabib-Calif, *Peace Entrepreneurs and Social Entrepreneurship* (Northampton: Edward Elgar Publishing, 2021), 2.

27 See, for example, K. L. Stanford, *Beyond the Boundaries: Reverend Jesse Jackson in International Affairs* (Albany: SUNY Press, 1997); A. Bloemendal, *Reframing the Diplomat: Ernst van der Beugel and the Cold War* (Leiden and Boston: Brill, 2018).

28 G. Scott-Smith, "Introduction: Private diplomacy, making the citizen visible," *New Global Studies*, 8:1 (2014), 1–7; R. Summy and M. Saunders, "Why peace history?" *Peace & Change*, 20:1 (1995), 7–38.

29 See, for example, E. F. Babbitt, "The evolution of international conflict resolution: From Cold War to peacebuilding," *Negotiation Journal*, 25:4 (2009), 539–549; R. B. Hall and T. J. Biersteker (eds), *The Emergence of Private Authority in Global Governance* (Cambridge: Cambridge University Press, 2002).

# 1

# Theoretical framework: private peace entrepreneurs

This chapter outlines the theoretical framework of the private peace entrepreneur phenomenon and offers a toolkit to discuss and analyze PPEs' characteristics, activities, and impact. The first part presents a typology of PPEs, outlining their resources, types, and action patterns; the official establishment's attitude towards PPEs; and critical arguments against their activities. The second part examines PPEs' impact on the official diplomatic sphere, identifies their influence patterns, and suggests an analytical framework that distinguishes among variables: those related to the PPEs, those related to their peace initiative, and those that are external. I will use this framework to analyze the case studies in subsequent chapters.

## Part I: typology of private peace entrepreneurs

### The power resources of private peace entrepreneurs

PPEs have no official authority or legal status based on appointment or election. They have no state or intergovernmental organization resources or leverage, and their activity is unofficial and independent. These facts lead us to ask: How do they operate without official sources of power, authority, and legitimacy? What are their alternative resources? And what resources help them influence official processes?

Israeli journalists Nahum Barnea and Shimon Schiffer asked these questions in reference to the *Hudna* (truce) initiative led by Israeli businessman Eyal Erlich and two other Israeli PPEs in 2001. Barnea and Schiffer wondered how "three people with no official status, only good intentions and a lot of time, can initiate a multinational move, and bypass all the players ... who get paid for this job."[1] Historian Tim Pat Coogan posed a similar query about the role of Father Alec Reid in the Northern Ireland peace process. Coogan wrote that he was amazed "how much had been achieved by one man, armoured in nothing but goodness and lonely belief."[2]

These kinds of questions have also been raised in the literature on civil society actors in international politics.[3] Hall and Biersteker point to the development of "private authority" in the international system, which reflects the power of private actors who were not created by states and do not gain support from governments to enjoy patterns of legitimate authority.[4]

The power resources of PPEs are complicated and vague. Because they have no formal or legal basis, PPEs' authority is based on non-material power and legitimacy as they are perceived by other actors. PPEs' authority depends on social meaning and subjective perceptions and is influenced by social and historical context – much like the apostle described by Søren Kierkegaard who cannot prove that he has "divine authority" and needs to "produce that impression."[5]

Identifying the power resources of PPEs is not a simple task, because they are tied to dynamic and flexible terms like trust, reputation, appreciation, and approval. Discussion of these resources also depends on the action patterns of the PPEs and their target audience, as these resources correspond with the different target audiences PPEs wish to influence. These include decision makers on the PPEs' side, the public, the decision makers on the other side, and international actors. In many cases, there is a link between the resources affecting one target audience and those affecting another. However, resources in reference to one target audience are not guaranteed to have the same ability with regard to another target audience, and indeed sometimes a resource that helps with one audience can be a disadvantage in activities aimed at another.

This issue is also related to the analysis in the literature on the resources and skills that mediators in negotiation require; at the end of this section, I will compare the power resources of PPEs with those of external official mediators.

*Resources of knowledge and expertise*

This type of resource is relevant to the activity of non-governmental actors in the international arena. Scholars in the field have argued that expertise and access to information can provide these actors with legitimacy and special status.[6] Scholarship on international mediation has also pointed to skills and knowledge resources that are needed to promote successful mediation, such as good communication skills and an ability to understand the dynamics of conflict.[7]

In reference to PPEs, there is a need to distinguish between two dimensions of knowledge resources. The first concerns the knowledge and expertise resources that PPEs gain and develop during their lives in various spheres of activity that are unrelated to their work as PPEs. These resources depend on the type of PPE, their life experiences, and their professional field. The spectrum of this knowledge can be wide, based not only in the international political arena but also in fields like science, language, culture, economics, religion, and history. These knowledge resources can, under certain conditions, be an important and significant power resource in promoting a private peace initiative. Knowledge resources can also include skills such as negotiating, speaking, communication, and the ability to analyze information.

The second dimension relates to knowledge and expertise resources that PPEs acquire during their peace activities. These emerge from their unofficial diplomatic correspondence, contacts, and meetings with official representatives from the other side of the conflict. When there are no other communication channels available, these resources are especially significant and exclusive. This resource – which is developed through the PPE's activities – in turn facilitates their activities. In the course of their efforts, PPEs are exposed to information about the other side's figureheads, opinions, disagreements, internal processes, sensitivities, and trends. Over time they acquire the abilities and tools that allow them to become familiar with various subjects and perspectives on the rival side, as well as the relations between the disputing parties. When PPEs develop extended and direct contact with officials from the rival side that is based on mutual trust and appreciation, they are exposed to unique information that is not available in public statements and receive immediate reactions to and comments on ideas, proposals, events, and developments.

This information and knowledge can, in some cases, be even more significant and reliable than official and governmental information. Creekmore, in his research on the nuclear crisis of 1994 in North Korea, claims that the assessments of non-governmental groups and scholars who visited North Korea and met with North Korean officials were more accurate than those provided by American and South Korean intelligence officers.[8] Uri Avnery, an Israeli PPE who had had longstanding channels of dialogue with leading figures of the PLO since the mid-1970s, said in 1981 that "Foreign Minister Shamir has important information from his resources. … I permit myself to say that my friends and I have information resources of our own, maybe not much worse."[9]

*Resources of access and networks*

This type of resource is also mentioned in the literature on civil society actors in international politics, with scholars claiming that transnational non-governmental organizations acquire legitimacy through parallel systems of networks with a variety of actors.[10] Lederach, in his research on the role of citizens and communities in peacebuilding, shows the importance of "web making" – establishing relations and networks – in this process.[11]

Access to and networks with key persons and power circles can generate important power resources for PPEs. Although a complicated and elusive element, such access has a crucial importance. It is a dynamic, incremental, and evolutionary resource: relations can change over time and networks develop gradually, as one contact leads to another contact and access to one circle influences and promotes access to other circles. The development and evolution of network systems of PPEs are thus a dominant variable in PPEs' activities. I highlight four circles of access and networks here:

1. *Access to decision makers and other official actors on the side of the PPEs.* This is a crucial resource in the PPE's efforts to promote a transition to the official sphere. The circle of "decision makers" is wide and complex, and access in some cases is only to one specific official actor.
2. *Access to officials on the rival side.* Officials can come from different levels and ranks – from low-ranking officials to the main leader – and the contact can be direct or indirect (through a mediator). In many cases there is a link between these first two types of networks: if PPEs have access to decision makers on their side, this access can be an important power resource in the eyes of their partners on the rival side because they are perceived as being close to the power circles. At the same time, access to the rival side can be portrayed among the decision makers as a power resource of PPEs because it shows acquaintance with the other side and an ability to serve as an envoy or a mediator with its leadership.
3. *Access to actors in the domestic arena.* PPEs can have networks in various circles and fields, such as the economy, the media, and civil society, as well as religious institutions. Under certain conditions these networks can be a basis for establishing contact with powerful and influential actors in the political and diplomatic sphere or influencing the general public.
4. *Access to international actors.* Some PPEs develop networks with actors and power circles around the world during their personal or professional lives. Sometimes, networks from a specific field (such as economics, for example) lead to networks in the diplomatic field. Contacts with international actors can also serve as a basis for establishing an indirect channel with the rival side, in cases where no direct channel is available. Networks in the international arena can create a negative perception in public opinion towards the PPEs, presenting them as "external agents" – especially when these contacts do not enjoy public legitimacy. On the other hand, they can also give PPEs a certain prestige, at least for some audiences. Finally, decision makers will find it difficult to ignore PPEs who have influence over leaders of states with special importance, and in these cases may even want to take advantage of such influence.

According to the terminology of network theory, PPEs act as "brokers" bridging between "structural holes" and creating links between network clusters that would otherwise remain disconnected. The power of the brokers depends on their unique location in the network system and not on their internal characteristics, and is based on the fact that they have unique networks, referred to as "bridging ties."[12]

The brokers' position gives them significant social capital with a high potential for power and impact ("brokerage-power").[13] Goddard argues that the brokers' position in the network system gives them three important advantages. First, they have strategic flexibility, giving them more options and opportunities for action and the ability to access different systems and mediate between actors. Second, cultural innovation gives them a better ability to develop new and novel ideas and to combine different ways of thinking and behaving. The third advantage is diffusion, which is the ability to bridge various cultural and lingual worlds and transfer ideas between networks while adjusting them to the target audiences.[14]

This resource – that is, of access and contacts – requires two final comments. First, in addressing the question of the perception, or misperception, of access, it is important to note that because PPEs have no official status, the perception of their network system and their access to decision makers – whether positive or negative – has a crucial impact on their efforts. In some cases, the perception can be wrong, based on an incorrect impression

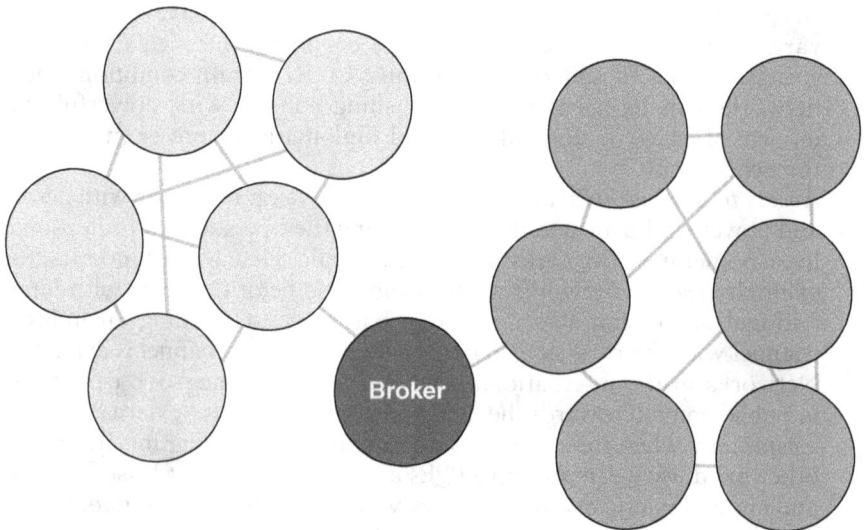

Figure 1.1 The "broker" in the network system

or interpretation, and this can have important implications for the initiative. This aspect is unique to the sphere of unofficial diplomacy and it deserves special attention.

The second comment concerns the fact that PPEs can obtain an important advantage of accessibility-related resources when they have contact with "unrecognized" non-state actors. These are actors with which the official state government has no direct official diplomatic communication, and refuses to recognize. These situations pose a major challenge for the official diplomatic system, and PPEs' access to such actors gives the official establishment an unconventional and non-binding way to dialogue.

This is relevant in cases of negotiating with paramilitary organizations. Scholars distinguish in these processes between "practical tactical negotiation," which deals with finding solutions for specific crises such as a hostage kidnapping, and "strategic political negotiation," which focuses on long-term political agreement.[15] States fear that a public, official, and direct negotiation with these organizations would give these actors legitimacy and endanger the credibility of the government in light of its public statements promising not to negotiate with them.[16] The history of this phenomenon reveals many cases of PPEs who had channels of communication with unrecognized paramilitary non-state actors: for example, Willie Esterhuyse with the African National Congress (ANC; South Africa), Brendan Duddy with the PIRA (Northern Ireland), Padma Ratna Tuladhar with Maoist guerrillas (Nepal), Stella Sabiiti with the Uganda National Rescue Front II (Uganda), Menachem Froman with the Palestinian organization Hamas (Israel–Palestine), and José María Portell with the Basque group Euskadi Ta Askatasuna (ETA; Spain).

*Value-based resources*

These resources are based on components such as values, principles, ethics, and norms – comparable to the "moral authority" the literature uses, for example, in describing power resources of transnational civil society actors such as human rights organizations. Moral authority depends on the perception that these actors represent the public interest and that they are not motivated by private interests but are working to promote normative goals.[17] Also the literature on mediation refers to resources of moral authority and "soft power." Scholars indicate, for example, credibility and prestige as important resources and discuss the need for the mediator to be perceived as impartial, reliable, and independent.[18]

In discussing PPEs' moral and spiritual resources, I distinguish here between three main types:

1. *Religious authority.* PPEs with religious status have power resources that can help them in their activities. Religious authority can provide

PPEs with the image of a reliable actor with pure intentions, one who is not motivated by personal or narrow political interests. It can also grant public or communal backing to the peace efforts. Scholars in peace research argue that the unique social status of religious leaders allows them to play a potential role in the process of peacemaking.[19]

2. *Intellectual authority.* Intellectual resources can provide PPEs with a spiritual status, portraying them as actors with a deep and wide perspective who work out of honest concern in the public's interest – at times even with a "prophetic" dimension. Scholars point to resources used by intellectuals acting in the political sphere, such as "symbolic capital," expertise, academic or professional reputation, and perceived independence from any powerful forces. The intellectual authority relates also to the discussion on the term "public intellectuals," that is, academics, scientists, intellectuals, or writers who deviate from their professional role and address the public arena to promote a political and social agenda.[20]

3. *Ideological authority.* Resources relating to the dimension of values, ideology, and worldview can also play a role in PPE activity. PPEs can be perceived as actors motivated by values and moral commitment, acting above private interests. This perception can provide their actions with a certain legitimacy, even among those who disagree with their views. This can be seen, for example, in reactions to the private peace mission of American PPE George Logan to France in 1798 in light of the fear of a war between France and the US. After the initiative, the American politician John Dickinson defined Logan as a citizen who loves his country and has "boundless benevolence." Also William Codman, who disagreed politically with Logan, claimed that Logan had "essentially served his country."[21] An example can also be seen in a letter sent by the Israeli Foreign Ministry to its representatives in 1966, against the background of the world journey of Israeli PPE Abie Nathan. Even though the ministry had some concerns about his trip and his meetings, it demanded he was treated with respect, "the way treating a figure that was published due to its mission of good intentions."[22]

Ideological and moral authority resources can also play an important role in relations with the rival side. The perception on the other side of the PPE as committed to resolving the conflict, disagreeing with the government's position, and working to change the official policy can serve as a significant power resource. "It gives you a lot of power," explains Israeli PPE Ron Pundak, "it tells them: we and you share the same goal and we want to get there ... it pushes them to be more flexible."[23] We saw this in American PPE Jesse Jackson's visit to Iraq in 1990. The Iraqi president Saddam Hussein accepted Jackson's request for a gesture while clarifying: "I am doing it only for you, not for Bush! I have no appreciation for him, but I have for you."[24] As soon as PPEs are portrayed on the other side as political partners who want to find a common ground, not as one conspiring against them, they receive a special status. At the same time, however, by positioning themselves too close to the rival's views, PPEs may damage their ability to influence decision makers on their own side, as officials may question their reports and information, wondering if they are reliable or biased because of their political views.

### Instrumental and tactical power resources

PPEs' nonconventional characteristics provide them with tactical resources that, in some conditions and circumstances, give them important advantages over official diplomats. I specify four main elements of these:

1. *Secrecy.* As private citizens with no official status, PPEs can promote their peace efforts secretly, without raising questions or suspicions. While travel, meetings, and visits of official leaders or diplomats attract media attention and raise questions and expectations that could damage a diplomatic move, PPEs can travel, conduct meetings, exchange messages, and promote diplomatic moves without media attention or exposure to actors outside of the secret circle. In many cases PPEs are unknown to the public. In cases where they are public figures, their movements raise no suspicions because they are those of private citizens – related to personal activity and not to diplomacy. This ability can be a crucial element in diplomatic initiatives.

    Scholars emphasize the importance of secrecy as a condition for successful negotiation and stress that early public or media exposure can put the negotiations at risk, harden parties' positions, and even lead to the collapse of the negotiation process. Secrecy provides the parties a larger maneuvering space, a freer and more open dialogue in which the threat of being trapped in public statements or commitments is absent. It also excludes spoilers that could endanger the negotiations, and avoids political and public pressure and the influence of the ongoing events. Secrecy also prevents the risk of the exaggerated expectations and rumors that emerge around leaders' summits or negotiation rounds and which can lead to failure and disappointment. Wanis-St. John argues that in order to address the conditions of uncertainty in the peace process, negotiations should be done under the "fog of peacemaking."[25] This element is relevant in cases where PPEs promote secret efforts, but not necessarily in cases of PPEs' public efforts (see discussion below on the PPE's action patterns).

2. *Deniability.* Because PPEs are private citizens without official position, decision makers can use them to explore new ideas, deliver messages, or exchange views with the rival side while keeping a distance from them. This ensures that in the case of a leak or a failure, they can deny any connection and argue the PPEs acted independently. This is an important advantage, and one that official diplomats cannot provide. Marion Creekmore, who accompanied Jimmy Carter on his private peace mission to North Korea in 1994, used this argument when trying

to convince the US president Bill Clinton's administration to use Carter: "If he were successful, the administration could claim credit; if he failed … the administration could distance itself from this initiative."[26]

3. *Openness and creativity.* The channels of PPEs are informal, non-binding, and located outside official diplomatic protocol rules and frameworks. As such, they can facilitate open and creative dialogue in which all ideas can be raised without fear. Such dialogue allows thinking "outside the box" and discussing options that official actors cannot. The official system often suffers from structural weaknesses that undermine actors' ability to develop and freely discuss new and creative ideas on controversial political issues. During violent conflict, any debates on solutions and concessions are regarded as sensitive and controversial within public and political discourse. Often, therefore, official systems have no apparatuses or forums to think and discuss them.

   PPEs try to fill this intellectual vacuum. Klein and Malki, for example, argue that the taboo in Israel on the issue of a possible political solution for Jerusalem prevented governmental bodies from dealing with the topic and preparing to negotiate on the subject. Thus, at "the moment of truth," they had no choice but to use ideas and materials provided by unofficial and non-governmental actors.[27] Furthermore, ideas developed within the PPEs' sphere of activities are based on dialogue with representatives from the rival side and on feedback PPEs have received from them. This interactivity provides an important advantage over the development of ideas within a single-nation brainstorming group or think-tank.

4. *Continuity.* When political and diplomatic systems have a high rate of turnover – with frequent changeover of ministers, ambassadors, and advisors – PPEs, as stable actors with the advantage of continuity of personal relations, experience, and knowledge, are a major power resource. Many PPEs have devoted long years of their life to their peace efforts. Often, officials recognize that their term is short and want to use actors with long-term acquaintance with the field, seeing the PPEs as an important resource to that end. Paffenholz, in her research on the role of civil society in peace processes, claims that peace organizations with longstanding experience and work in the field can serve as an "institutional memory" of the process.[28]

### Public status

In certain conditions, resources related to public status and presence in the media are also useful for PPEs. These resources refer to a status the PPEs have developed and gained during their life, and one that is often related to fields or professions quite apart from their peace efforts. Public status can refer to the domestic arena or to international public opinion. This status, which is of particular importance in PPEs' public efforts, can provide their initiative with publicity and public backing. It can also be helpful in secret efforts, as an important public status can give PPEs leverage, influencing official actors. In some cases, famous PPEs will establish public organizations that give them backing and a public framework for their work. Frederik van Zyl Slabbert and Alex Boraine, for example, formed the Institute for Democracy in Africa (IDASA); Uri Avnery and his colleagues founded the ICIPP; and Hubert Herring founded the Committee on Cultural Relations with Latin America.

The ability of PPEs who have a powerful public status to use the media in advancing their peace efforts is an important aspect of this resource. Lieberfeld argues that "media outreach" and having media partners are important conditions for the success of peace organizations.[29] We see this in the phenomenon of "celebrity diplomacy," when famous public figures, mainly from the music and film industries, use their exposure and access to the media to promote political, social, and diplomatic goals in the global arena.[30]

*Power resources: between PPE and an external mediator*

Given the points of convergence between the activity of PPEs and that of external official mediators, it is helpful to compare these two types of actors in terms of power resources. The main difference is that external mediators represent a state (in many cases a superpower) or an international organization, with the accompanying political, economic, and military resources. They can use these resources in their mediation efforts as tools to threaten and punish or to incentivize and compensate. In addition, the process of official mediation is part of a common course in international diplomacy, with a well-known set of rules and diplomatic elements that give the mediator certain advantages – which are absent in the work of PPEs. But, at the same time, PPEs have, as stated, alternative unofficial power resources that help them, and in certain conditions and contexts they have more advantages than the external official mediators.

External mediators also have resources such as knowledge, networks, moral authority, tactical means, and public status, but these are different in their essence from those of PPEs because they are based on official sources related to a state or international organization. This includes, for example, information from official intelligence and governmental research bodies, official diplomatic network systems, and public status that is based on a formal position.

Comparative analysis shows that the balance of advantages and disadvantages between these two types of actors varies according to case and context. For example, PPEs usually have an advantage when it comes to secrecy or the question of flexibility; but external mediators have an advantage concerning the ability to help the parties to "save face" or to use sticks and carrots. The comparison also depends on the type of conflict. Kriesberg argues, for example, that in internal conflict between a government and a non-state actor, the government usually opposes an external mediator becoming involved, claiming this would be intervening in an internal problem. In such a case, an unofficial mediator would have an advantage.[31]

This discussion relates to Wehr and Lederach's distinction between "outsider-neutral" mediator and "insider-partial" mediator. They argue that the former is based on neutrality while the latter is based on trust relations (using the Spanish term *confianza*) with the disputing parties. This difference between types is similar to Max Weber's distinction between rational-legal authority and traditional authority. According to Wehr and Lederach, the parties' willingness to accept internal mediators derives from trust based on personal relations. But it is also based on knowing that these mediators are part of the conflict, and thus at the end of the negotiation process will remain in the conflict area and live with the consequences of their actions. They emphasize that while every mediation process needs trust, this element is a central criterion in the internal mediator model.[32] Other scholars point to the importance of "insider mediators" in internal conflicts, arguing that in this kind of conflict, local unofficial actors are better able than official national or international actors to influence paramilitary organizations and promote steps such as a ceasefire.[33]

This distinction also relates to the debate in the literature on the mediator's neutrality as a condition for successful mediation. Scholars differ on this. Some argue that a mediator has to be neutral – an objective actor "from Mars" – in order to be accepted by the parties and an effective mediator. Other scholars posit that biased mediators also play an important role if they have the resources that the parties perceive as important and the influence to push the parties to make concessions towards agreement. Biased mediators, according to this approach, have interests in the conflict but are still able to promote a process that will be considered fair by the parties.[34]

PPEs are not neutral actors who come "from Mars"; they belong to one of the parties and have clear ideological positions and opinions about the main topics on the negotiation table. But they are in a unique position, one that often allows them to be perceived by the parties not as neutral, but as an honest actor whose goal is to resolve the conflict and not just for the interests of one side. Also, in some cases decision makers on the PPE's side perceive an advantage in using the PPE as an internal actor, rather than an external third party because the latter has its own political interests and motives; the involvement of the external actor in the process thus transforms the negotiations into a more complex game between three parties. Furthermore, mediation by an external third party forces decision makers to expose their proposals and bargaining positions to this external actor, with possible political consequences. In the case of mediation through PPEs, on the other hand, the content of the negotiations would not reach international actors, only internal actors whom the decision makers trust.

## Types of private peace entrepreneurs

PPEs come from different fields and life experiences and various personal, professional, social, and political backgrounds. Different types of PPE will obtain different resources and tools, which will have an impact on their actions and effectiveness. In this section, I discuss and analyze seven main PPE prototypes, the unique power resources of each prototype, and the limitations, criticism, and dilemmas relevant to each prototype.

### Journalist PPEs

PPEs from the media world obtain resources during their professional lives that they can use in their peace efforts, for example unique knowledge of the conflict, the rival side, and domestic and international politics (knowledge resources). The mediation efforts of Basque journalist José María Portell, between Spain and ETA, were based on his longstanding work and expertise on ETA and on the conflict in the Basque country.[35] Journalist PPEs can also have access to power circles in their country and abroad (access resources), prestige and credibility (moral authority), and public status. Finally, they also use the privileges that come with the work of journalists to promote their PPE activity (tactical resources). For example, the meeting between Israeli journalist Uri Avnery, the editor of the weekly *Haolam Hazeh*, and PLO chairman Yasser Arafat in July 1982 in Beirut during the First Lebanon War was possible because of Avnery's official invitation from the Israel Defense Forces (IDF) Spokesperson's Unit, which was granted to all newspaper editors in Israel. Avnery used it when he was investigated by the police over that meeting.[36]

The work of journalists interfaces with the world of politics and diplomacy, and scholars have referred to the meeting points between these spheres. Geyer claims that journalists have become the "new diplomats" because they meet with unusual actors, such as dictators and leaders of paramilitary organizations, with whom official diplomats will not or cannot meet.[37] And Gilboa coined the term "media broker diplomacy" in reference to the ability of journalists to serve as intermediaries in conflicts.[38]

But sometimes the roles of journalist and PPE clash. Dilemmas over secrecy arise when, as a journalist, one needs to push for publication, while, as a PPE, one needs to maintain secrecy to protect secret efforts and to publish only when it contributes to the cause of the activity. American PPE Norman

Cousins, the editor of *Saturday Review*, did not report in real time on his meeting with the Soviet Union leader Nikita Khrushchev in 1963 – despite it being an event with significant media importance – to avoid damaging his diplomatic secret mission. He exposed the details of the meeting only after Khrushchev left office, explaining that he had not reported on it because he had gone on this mission "not as journalist but as private emissary."[39] There were also multiple cases of meetings between Avnery and PLO officials in which he was asked not to publish, and he kept his promise, even when such a major "scoop" could have helped his newspaper. PLO leaders have mentioned their appreciation of this fact.[40] On the other hand, journalists can use their media platform and their public stage as a vital tool that other PPEs lack (tactical resource). American journalists Harry Ashmore and Bill Baggs, for example, used their access to the public when they decided in September 1967 to expose the details of their peace initiative with North Vietnam after they felt it was scuttled by the Johnson administration.[41]

Journalist PPEs can be criticized and accused of not being objective or of turning into the story itself instead of being the reporter of the story. However, it should be stressed that PPE journalists such as Cousins, Avnery, Ashmore, and Baggs were known as journalists with a clear political position – without trying to appear neutral – who combined journalist work with social and political activism.

## Business leader PPEs

This type of PPE is located in the seam line between the business world and the diplomatic world. Their motive for action can be a combination of ideology and economic and professional interests, when the continuation of conflict could damage and threaten their business and peace could bring economic dividends. This relates to the scholarship on trade and mutual economic dependence as tools to promote peace and the potential role of the private sector and the business community in peace processes.[42]

PPE business leaders enjoy certain resources. Their economic status and capabilities can be helpful in their PPE activity (tactical resources). In South Africa, for example, many meetings with the ANC that took place in various countries were possible due to economic assistance from the company Anglo-American PLC of the PPE Gavin Relly.[43] The work of these PPEs is often accompanied by a flexible schedule allowing them to work on their unofficial peace efforts. The Israeli PPE Eyal Erlich, a businessperson who led the "*Hudna* initiative," claimed that his work provided him with a "valuable resource: time, without it I would not have been able to deal with advancing the *Hudna*."[44]

In addition to this, some PPEs with senior business status have access to decision makers and power circles not only in their country, but also on the rival side and around the world (access resources). One example is German

PPE Albert Ballin, who was the director of the Hamburg America Line. His mediation efforts between Germany and England before the First World War were based on his access to German emperor Wilhelm II and other key persons in official German circles, as well as to British decision makers.[45]

The life experiences of PPE business leaders also give them special skills in negotiations, crisis management, and communication (knowledge and expertise resources). Also, in certain conditions and contexts, their economic success and the importance of their company to the national economy provide them with the resources of reputation, legitimacy, moral authority, and public status. Anthony Bloom, a PPE from South Africa, claimed "[W]e could be dismissed as politically naive, but we ran large businesses – we couldn't be accused of treason."[46] On the other hand, business leaders can face criticism that their incentive is based on private economic interests and, furthermore, their businesses can pay a heavy price as a consequence of their diplomatic endeavors.

### Religious leader PPEs

Religious leaders can play an important role in conflict resolution, especially in societies with high religious commitment and in conflicts in which the religious dimension plays an important role. The religious status of these PPEs can be an important resource in relations with various actors and audiences – on both their side and the rival side (access resources). Archbishop Jaime Gonçalves from Mozambique, for example, together with the Sant'Egidio Community, was able to gain the trust of both parties in the civil war: the Mozambique Liberation Front (the government's party) and the Mozambican National Resistance.[47] These PPEs can use their religious resources also to gain access to, and influence over, violent non-state actors that official actors cannot, or are not willing to, communicate with, especially with religious groups.

Religious PPEs can use special tools and resources related to their spiritual status. Little uses the term "hermeneutic of peace" to refer to the use of religious texts, practices, and rituals by religious actors to promote peace efforts.[48] Some of these PPEs, for example, add prayers to their meetings: Father Alec Reid, a religious PPE who facilitated communication channels in Northern Ireland, would sometimes open the meetings with a prayer; Rabbi Menachem Froman conducted a common prayer with a Muslim audience during his meeting in 1997 with Hamas leader Sheikh Ahmad Yassin; and during the visit of Jesse Jackson to Syria in 1984, some of the meetings started with a prayer by Christian and Muslim religious leaders who joined him for the mission.[49]

Religious leaders also obtain unique skills of persuasion, communication, and expression (knowledge resources), and sometimes achieve a high public status. It should also be mentioned that a few PPEs, such as George Logan

(United States), Richard Cobden (the United Kingdom), and Hendrik van der Merwe (South Africa), belong to the Quakers, also called "the Friends Church," a religious community founded during the seventeenth century which shares a pacifist worldview.[50]

### "Former official" PPEs

Decision makers or official diplomats who have ended their official position can try to return to the diplomatic sphere as a PPE. Scholars claim that unofficial diplomats who were once in an official role have important advantages that can be very useful.[51] PPEs who were former officials bring significant resources. First, they have deep knowledge of the diplomatic world and practices and diplomatic skills (knowledge resources). Second, they have obtained a wide networks system during their professional lives (access resources). For example, Alon Liel served as an official Israeli diplomat in Turkey during the 1980s and his contacts in Turkey played a role in establishing his unofficial dialogue with Syria. Also, as PPE, Nimrod Novik used the networks in the US and in Egypt that he had gained during his official position as advisor to the Israeli leader Shimon Peres as prime minister and as foreign minister. "I felt," Novik explained, "that I have an asset in my hand and to waste it will be a crime to my children and grandchildren."[52]

Third, "former official" PPEs have prestige and public status. This element is particularly crucial when the PPE is a former high-ranking leader. The best example is former US president Jimmy Carter and his peace initiative with North Korea in 1994. Joel Wit, Daniel Poneman, and Robert Gallucci, who served in official positions during this period, wrote that Carter brought with him "critical assets," one of them being "the unique status and stature of a former president of the United States."[53] The visit of a former president to a state that the US has no diplomatic relations with has dramatic implications – even without official approval.

Cooper published a study on former leaders as unofficial diplomats, referring to the practice as "diplomatic afterlife." He argued that these are hybrid actors who combine tools they gained as being part of the traditional state club with tools from the world of transnational non-governmental diplomacy. According to Cooper, this phenomenon bridges between "public authority" and "private authority" and between classic leadership and innovative leadership.[54]

### Scholar PPEs

Some PPEs are scholars, academics, or intellectuals who have left the "ivory tower." An example of "public intellectuals,"[55] these individuals use their tools to get involved in the unofficial diplomatic sphere and promote conflict resolution in their conflict area. Various scholars have written on the potential role of academics in the field of conflict resolution.[56] These PPEs use the vital resources they have to advance their peace efforts. For example, their unique academic resources (knowledge resources) often include expertise on the other side of the conflict (such as PPE Professor Herring, who was an expert on Latin America) or on conflict resolution (such as PPE Professor Hendrik van der Merwe, who was an expert in the field of conflict resolution and peace studies). They can also use the academic cover in their peace efforts, which enables comfortable and non-formal settings for meetings with the rival side's representatives that would be difficult to facilitate in a different context (access and tactical resources). In Israel, for example, where the law prohibits meetings with the PLO but permits them as part of academic conferences, the "academic hat" allows Israeli PPEs to meet with PLO officials in academic forums.[57]

Academics also enjoy special prestige and reputation and some moral and intellectual authority that can assist them in their activity. De Villiers defined Esterhauyse as one of the main symbols of "the Africaner nationalism in the academic community,"[58] a fact that provided him with vital resources. PPE Judah Leon Magnes is another example. His position as the first president of the Hebrew University provided him with a special national and international status. Even though he had no official role in the Zionist institutes and his views were very controversial in the Jewish community, he was considered an important actor in the diplomatic sphere by all parties involved, because he was, as Sand defined him, one of the main "seniors of the first academics generation."[59]

## Politician PPEs

Political public figures, such as parliament members or politicians, who promote a private peace initiative have unique tools, but also face challenges and difficulties.

Politician PPEs can be defined as PPEs so long as they are not elected or nominated to an official position that authorizes them to negotiate or conduct foreign policy. The main difference between them and other PPEs is that, besides their peace activity, they are also involved and competing in the political sphere and some of them are part of the parliament.

This type of PPE has important resources and advantages. One of their critical resources, which other PPEs lack, is their political power and the ability to use it for their peace efforts. The private diplomacy of British PPE Richard Cobden with France while he was a Member of Parliament in 1859 is an example. Cobden was a key figure in the Radicals Party, which was a small but important element in the government's coalition and vital for its stability – a fact that provided Cobden with leverage on Prime Minister Palmerstone.[60] Politician PPEs also have parliamentarian tools that can be useful. Israeli members of the Knesset (such as Mattityahu Peled) used their parliamentarian immunity to meet with PLO officials when the law prohibited these meetings; Alex Boraine, a PPE who was a parliament member in South Africa, and established a dialogue with the ANC, said that at various times his counterparts from the ANC used the fact that he was a parliament member and asked him to raise questions or topics for discussion in Parliament.[61]

The participation of politician PPEs in the political game provides them with relevant knowledge resources and access to decision makers. Membership in parliament can be a significant power resource in establishing contact with the other side, proving that the PPE has some public political backing. In some cases, the rival side would prefer to talk with an elected representative than with a business leader or an intellectual, assuming they have more influence. Mahmoud Abbas, a PLO leader, noted that the PLO valued contact with Knesset members, and that the PLO hoped their Israeli counterparts in unofficial meetings would incorporate in the Knesset.[62] The public status of politician PPEs is also a useful resource. For example, Alex Boraine and Frederik van Zyl Slabbert's status as former parliament members in South Africa and founders of IDASA assisted them in generating a powerful public reaction to their public peace meeting with ANC officials in Dakar in 1987.

Politician PPEs' participation in a transnational ideology creates a common basis that can be used as a bridge to representatives on the rival side who share the same ideology. George Logan, an American PPE who traveled to France, is one example: he was a member of the pro-French Democratic Society in Philadelphia known for his support of the ideas of the French revolution. Another example is Nepalese PPE Padma Ratna Tuladhar: the fact that he was a left-wing politician helped him in establishing contact with Maoists guerrilla groups.[63]

At the same time, politician PPEs have unique difficulties deriving from their political identity, an identity that could assign their initiative a certain political label. While this can be advantageous, it often has a negative impact on the attitude towards the initiative and its public image. The initiative can be portrayed as part of a cynical political game influenced by narrow political interests. For example, when Jesse Jackson, during his campaign in the Democratic Party presidential primaries in the US, initiated a private mission to Syria to release an American soldier held hostage there, many argued he was motivated by his desire to attract voters.[64]

### Diaspora PPEs

PPEs in the diaspora live outside the conflict area but are part of the nation or community involved in a conflict and choose to interfere and promote peace efforts from abroad. Scholars argue that diaspora communities serve in many cases as "peace spoilers," but they can also play a positive role in peace processes. They can, for example, use their access to decision makers in the "hosting state" or in their approach to international public opinion or organizations. They can also facilitate dialogue forums when it is difficult or impossible to establish them in the conflict area.[65]

The geographical location of diaspora PPEs provides them with important resources, but it can also cause challenges. Their main advantage is that they have more opportunities to meet and interact with various actors or can visit countries that are inaccessible to citizens from the "mother country." An example of this is Nahum Goldmann, president of the Jewish World Congress and a US citizen, who led his own independent private diplomacy, outlining a wide network of connections and relationships across the world: in the West, the Soviet bloc, and Arab countries. In the 1950s, Joe Golan, his advisor on Arab affairs, helped him to establish contacts in the Arab world.[66]

Goldmann's diplomacy often clashed with official Israeli diplomacy. We see this tension, for example, in the Israeli reaction to Goldmann's meeting with King Hassan II of Morocco in 1969. Israel prime minister Golda Meir claimed she did not need another Foreign Minister in her government, and Goldmann responded that he owed reports only to the Jewish people and not to Golda Meir.[67] Goldmann's US citizenship was helpful when Egypt invited him to a meeting in 1970, as the decision in the Khartoum Arab summit of 1967 prohibited contact with Israelis. By meeting with an American Jew, Nasser could argue he had not breached the decision.[68]

However, the interference of a PPE from the diaspora can also be perceived as rude and meddlesome by local leadership and the public. An example of this is the Israeli leadership's response to Goldmann's peace initiative in 1970. Meir attacked Goldmann publicly and advised him to "stay in Israel for a while, live our life, go down to the border settlements and outposts, and only afterwards criticize us and preach to us."[69]

PPEs living in a country that is the rival side in the conflict have certain advantages, such as their deep acquaintance "from the inside" with the country and its public, and sometimes the ability to contact and influence decision makers. Mohamed Rabie, an American-Palestinian professor, mediated between the PLO and the US administration; and Niall O'Dowd, an American-Irish journalist, mediated between Sein Fein, in Northern Ireland, and the US administration. Both of them had an impressive access to the leadership of both parties and were able to promote diplomatic moves.

### Minority PPEs

PPEs who belong to an ethnic minority group connected to the other side of the conflict can use their unique resources as a possible "ethnic bridge." They know the state and the society from the inside, yet share political, social, and cultural ties with the rival side. Abdulwahab Darawshe, for example, is an Israeli-Arab politician who served as a Knesset member. Darawshe served as an intermediary between Israel and the PLO in the 1980s and later between Israel and Syria in 1994. He attempted to use his access to the leadership on both sides to promote a dialogue between them.[70]

In concluding this discussion of PPE types, I should mention that in some cases PPEs belong to more than one prototype. Niall O'Dowd, for example, was a journalist PPE but also a diaspora PPE; Jesse Jackson was both a politician PPE and a religious leader PPE; Uri Avnery was a journalist PPE and also a politician PPE.

Along with the above-mentioned main prototypes of PPE, we can also distinguish between two main categories of PPE with regard to their attitude towards the official establishment. The first is *dissident peace entrepreneurs*, who challenge and publicly attack the official leadership and its policy. The second category is *complementary peace entrepreneurs*, who hope to assist and supplement official diplomacy without publicly criticizing the policy makers. Pundak outlines a differentiation similar to the one I use between these two categories, suggesting we distinguish between actors who extend the edge of the envelope from inside and those who are working pushing the envelope from outside.[71] Rabie used a similar image, arguing that in the initiative he led with William Quandt between the US and the PLO in 1988, they acted as "insiders working from the outside rather than outsiders trying to get inside."[72]

PPEs also differ in their ideology and worldview. They share the goal of resolving conflict and promoting peace but are motivated by different worldviews. Some PPEs have a strong national worldview, while others have a more universal cosmopolitan perspective. Some PPEs have a strong religious background and commitment, while others have no religious sentiment or are even anti-religion. Some PPEs are pacifist, while others are very far from pacifism. And some PPEs have a liberal and capitalist ideology, as opposed to PPEs who hold socialist and communist beliefs. PPEs are typically interested in politics and many of them are active in other political or social issues along with their peace activity.

### Action patterns of private peace entrepreneurs

In this section, I distinguish between three main action patterns of PPEs: secret action aimed towards decision makers, public action towards public opinion, and action through a third party.

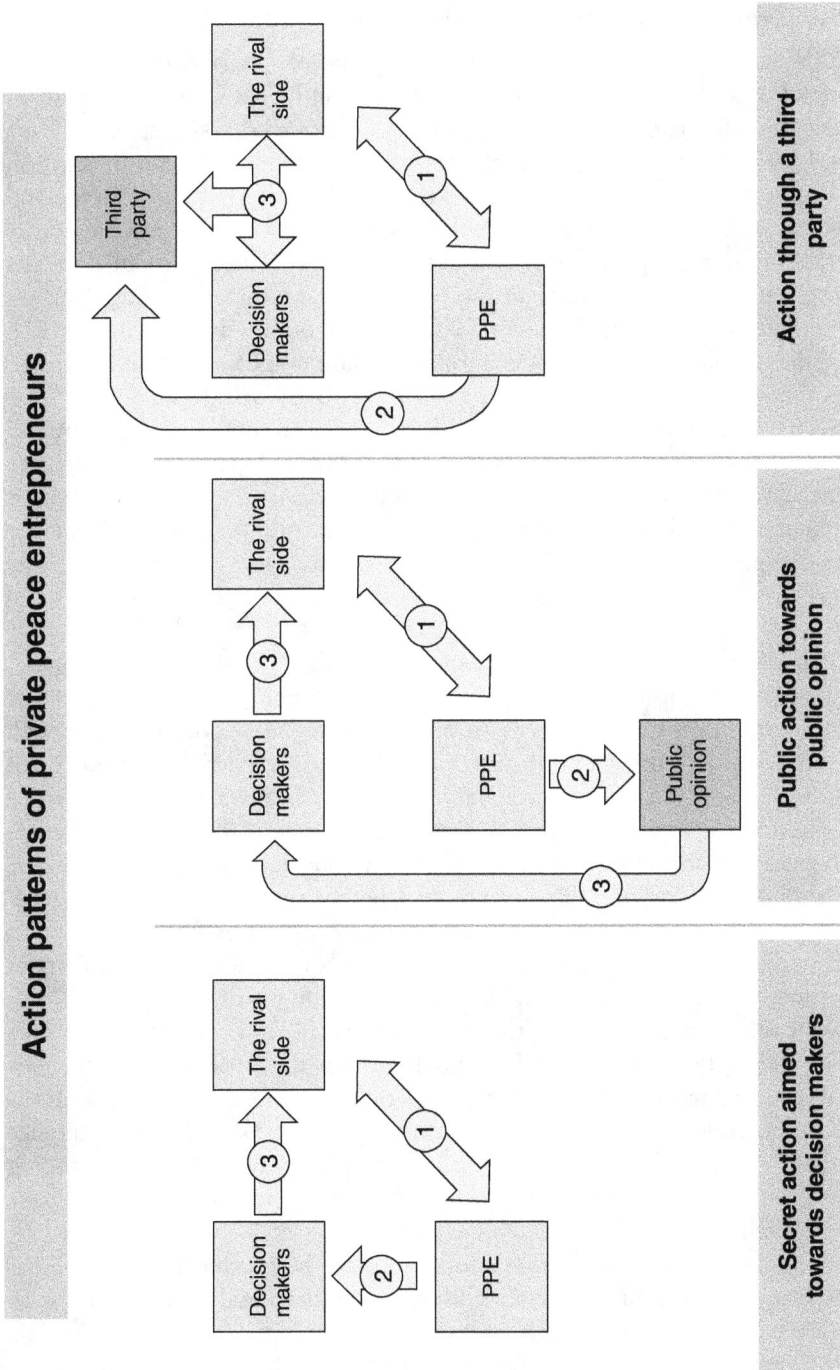

Figure 1.2 Action patterns of PPEs

*Secret action aimed towards decision makers*

In this action pattern, PPEs combine elements of external mediator with those of official negotiator, working secretly to influence decision makers on both sides and promote diplomatic moves in the official policy sphere. Given this, I use theoretical tools from the literature on negotiation and mediation in analyzing this pattern. PPEs hope that, with their power resources and contacts with the rival side, they will be able to convince the official actors on their side to support and promote the initiative. The two main elements in this pattern are dialogue with the rival side and efforts targeting decision makers on the PPE's side. The goal is to move from the unofficial sphere to the official sphere, to turn their unofficial channel into an official channel, or to receive a mandate to serve as a special envoy or intermediary.

Secrecy is a central dimension in this pattern, and the unofficial character of the PPE's channels is a crucial aspect of the effort to keep them confidential. If there are no official channels of communication between the parties or a stalemate in official talks, then a diplomatic vacuum forms and PPEs enter with the goal of filling it. Their peace efforts can serve, using the analogy of the human body, as "collateral veins" that are produced by the body in order to bypass a blockage in the vessels.

This pattern can be significant, especially in the "pre-negotiation" phase. The pre-negotiation phase starts when at least one of the parties in the conflict considers negotiation as an option and signals about it, or through an initiative of a third party; and it ends when the parties agree to open official negotiations or when one of them withdraws from support of negotiation. It is a period in which the parties move from unilateral steps to a joint search for shared solutions. In the phase of pre-negotiation, the parties hold unbinding talks to explore whether there is a possible agreed-upon basis for opening direct official negotiations.[73] The PPEs can play an important role at this stage, and their channels can be used to implement the functions that stand at the heart of pre-negotiations.

We can distinguish among the efforts of the PPEs in this action pattern in various ways: between PPEs who focus on the process and relations between the parties, and PPEs who focus on the content of the negotiations and on possible solutions. This distinction can also be seen as the difference between more passive PPEs, who aim to serve as a channel for exchanging messages, and more active PPEs, who interfere in the content and propose specific solutions.

Putnam describes official negotiations as a "two-level game": the negotiators need to negotiate simultaneously with their international partners and with domestic groups at home. He argues that the "win-sets," that is, the possible negotiating outcomes that could be accepted by domestic constituencies, influence and shape the negotiation process.[74] PPEs are not authorized to negotiate, and usually they do not receive instructions from decision makers. But they want to shift the initiative into the official sphere, and in order to do that, this pattern requires them to evaluate the "win-set" of the decision makers on their side based on their information, analysis, and public statements. In this action pattern, the PPEs' ability to work secretly in a non-formal and non-binding way is an important advantage for decision makers, offering them a tool with low risk. The level of trust between the PPE and the decision makers is especially crucial in this action pattern. Officials need to be confident that the PPEs will deliver the messages intact, without interfering in the content, and that they will not expose the details or leak the information to the media.

The main disadvantage for PPEs in this action pattern is their dependency on the decision makers' willingness to support and promote their initiative. The official actors must be ready and able to endorse PPEs' efforts and to integrate them into the official sphere. The main dilemma in this context is what PPEs should do when they face strong and decisive resistance by the official decision makers: should they stop their secret efforts and wait for a change of position or of leaders, or should they move to a different action pattern?

This action pattern pushes PPEs to behave as a complementary PPE, acting from within the existing framework and not deviating too far from official policy lines or challenging decision makers. PPEs need to be careful not to publicly criticize the official leaders and to keep information confidential to avoid damaging the initiative and to prove they are reliable and trustworthy. In cases of "success," the PPEs need to acknowledge that they will not necessarily gain public credit or gratitude for their secret activities, at least in the short term. Indeed, in some cases, PPEs' ability to use this action pattern again could be damaged by exposing their role to the public.

### Public action towards public opinion

In this strategy, PPEs integrate elements of negotiator and activist and use public peace entrepreneurship to influence public opinion in order to pressure decision makers to change official policy or promote a change in leadership. The media dimension has a crucial role in this pattern. Along with contacting the rival side, PPEs approach the public and try to change opinions and rally support for their initiative.

Here, PPEs face challenges similar to those faced by peace movements, which makes the literature on these movements useful in analyzing this pattern. Carter argues that the difficulties faced by peace campaigns, led by civil society organizations, derive from the fact that they challenge the fundamental idea of promoting national security only by military means.[75] In many cases, especially during periods of warfare and violence, various actors in the public discourse and in the media blame peace activists for being too naive or not patriotic enough, or for caring only about the rival side. Many peace movements prefer not to establish contacts with the other side, fearing it will damage their public support and push them out of the political consensus. In general, public peace entrepreneurship, like every public peace campaign, challenges the public discourse, especially during an ongoing conflict. It undermines the assumption that only the government can deal with issues of security and foreign policy and challenges the demand to stand behind the government and not criticize it during an ongoing conflict.[76]

At the center of this pattern is a strategy that can be termed the "doubting" strategy. Scholars in the literature on international non-governmental human rights organizations, and transnational moral entrepreneurs, show that a main tool of these actors is the strategy of "shaming": that is, pointing to a government's behavior that is considered a breach of a moral obligation in order to embarrass its leaders and push for internal and external pressure to change the policy.[77] The doubting strategy of PPEs, however, aims to create cracks in hegemonic perceptions and beliefs about the conflict and plant seeds for alternative thinking.

According to Bar-Tal, a society in intractable conflicts develops a "conflictive ethos" that is based on social beliefs that help it cope with the conflict. This includes societal beliefs about self-victimhood, a positive collective self-image of a moral and peace-seeking society, and de-legitimization and de-humanization of the opposing side. This ethos points to the opponent as the one responsible for the conflict and objecting to compromises.[78] PPEs try to undermine and challenge the "conflictive ethos" and to raise questions about the beliefs that have become, during the course of the conflict, inter-subjective understandings with wide support among the public. PPEs try to challenge the perception of the conflict as predestination and the gaps between the parties as unbridgeable, and to fight against "social facts" that determine that "there is no partner" on the other side, presenting a "mirror image" in which one side is peace seeking and the other side is a warmonger. While the shaming strategy highlights the gaps between the rhetoric and the practice of governments on human rights and moral issues, the doubting strategy explores the mismatch between rhetoric and self-identity as "peace seeking" and a policy which in practice is the opposite.

The doubting strategy also wishes to change the "enemy image" and undermine societal beliefs about the rival side. Enemy image is a collective perception concerning the other side that develops during a conflict, growing to a point where it is very hard to change and it becomes a major obstacle in the conflict resolution process. Enemy image includes theoretical, emotional, and normative elements regarding the rival side. It often goes together with attribution errors and misperceptions, such as a tendency to explain the rival side's behavior as the result of its basic character and not due to circumstances or external influence, or to see the enemy as a unitary actor and ignore internal differences.[79] Scholars argue that conflict resolution and reconciliation require changing stereotypical attitudes towards the enemy and legitimizing and humanizing the other side, including recognizing its needs.[80] PPEs want to expose the public to the human aspects of the "enemy" – to promote a more complicated and nuanced perception and reveal the other side's internal differences, and possible changes.

In addition to this, the doubting strategy has the positive aspect of PPEs' desire to plant seeds for alternative thinking about the option of negotiation and the possibility of an agreement. It addresses one of the elements in Zartman's ripeness theory: that is, the need for the perception of a "way out" among parties, a sense that a negotiated solution is possible (I will provide a full discussion of the ripeness theory in the second part of the chapter).[81] Scholars have difficulty explaining exactly how to develop and promote this element in conditions of ongoing conflict, hostility, and lack of communication between parties. PPEs play a role in this by trying to promote alternative discourse, policy, and thinking patterns that recognize the possibility of negotiation. This aspect overlaps with elements Kelman and Lieberfeld mention in relation to the potential impact of track two, that is, a "sense of negotiation possibility" and a "belief that at least some elements on the other side are interested in a peaceful solution."[82] The doubting strategy is thus a public and visible pattern that focuses on public perceptions and opinion. This action pattern is usually more complicated and difficult to achieve in the short term, and is especially challenging if decision makers oppose the initiative and try to thwart it. This pattern often contradicts official policy, but there are also cases in which PPEs' public activities go hand in hand with official peace efforts.

### Action through a third party

In this action pattern, PPEs seek to promote peace efforts through external actors who may have leverage over the disputing parties. Besides the contact with the rival side, the PPEs approach an external actor to use its power resources, in this way overcoming their own lack of official power resources. The external actor can be a state, a superpower, or an international organization (global or regional), with influence on both sides, an interest in the conflict resolution process, and the potential coercion ability and resources of carrots and sticks.[83] PPEs hope that the fruits of their private diplomacy can serve the external international actor, who can support and promote their initiative. This pattern is similar to Keck and Sikkink's "boomerang effect," which refers to transnational activists who, feeling that channels to the state are blocked, bypass their government and approach international partners to create external pressure.[84]

The goal of this pattern is for the external actor to adopt the initiative, or parts of it, and work to promote it, in this way bringing the PPE's activities into the official diplomatic sphere. The advantage in this pattern is that an international actor with powerful official resources can significantly contribute to the PPE's efforts. But the main problem is that PPEs could face harsh criticism for "inviting" pressure from outside and for pushing to involve an external actor to change the policy of the government on their side. In this pattern, PPEs are required to have, in addition to the contact with the rival side, international networks and access to key figures and diplomatic circles around the world. And finally, they must have the ability to convince all of these to support their efforts and to endorse – and promote – their initiative.

### The official establishment's reaction to PPE activity

At the heart of the phenomenon of PPEs stands the complex relationship between them and the official establishment on their own side. This relationship is shaped by a structural tension: that is, between the subversive nature of PPEs' activity and the assumption that promoting conflict resolution depends on the ability to influence official actors who, in turn, are able and authorized to promote such a process. This dynamic and complicated relationship has received insufficient attention in the literature on track two and citizen diplomacy.

In the sections below, I identify three main response patterns in the official establishment's attitude towards PPEs: resistance, indifference, and endorsement.

#### Resistance

The establishment is almost instinctively inclined to resist this kind of unofficial activity. Gopin claims that "governments are allergic to any diplomatic efforts other than official ones," and Ashmore writes about "professional institutional snobbery that is often expressed as automatic resentment of outsiders – 'amateurs' – meddling with official business."[85] This pattern of resistance refers to active opposition translated into operative actions against the PPE. The level of resistance might vary by case – from weak denunciation of a PPE's initiative to decisive steps to thwart it – and it might employ any of a variety of tools.

In some cases, the establishment might make use of its own legal system, including legislation, investigations, and indictments against the PPE. Uri Avnery, for example, faced a criminal investigation after his meeting with

PLO chairman Yasser Arafat in 1982; Abie Nathan was convicted and sent to an Israeli prison in 1989 because of his meeting with PLO officials; the US administration threatened to take legal measures against Jesse Jackson after his visit to Cuba in 1984; and Padma Ratna Tuladhar was arrested in Nepal due to meetings he had with Nepalese Maoists.[86]

In Israel, meetings between Israeli PPEs and PLO representatives that had been taking place since the mid-1970s sparked a major public debate, which included demands to put the PPEs on trial. But the legal authorities asserted that these meetings were not against the law. In 1983, Yitzchak Zamir, the Israeli attorney-general at the time, declared it was not possible to prosecute Israelis who met with Arafat so long as there was no proof that classified information was transmitted or that any other action that might jeopardize Israeli security took place during the meetings. "These meetings perhaps damage the state's image but not its security," Zamir claimed.[87] The legal framework changed in 1986, however, after the Israeli parliament passed a new law prohibiting Israeli citizens from having contact with representatives of a group identified by the government as a terrorist organization.[88] According to this new legislation, there was no need to prove that the meeting caused damage to the state's security; the fact that the meeting had taken place was enough for a conviction. This law – which led to investigations, indictments, prosecutions, and the jailing of two Israelis[89] – was revoked in January 1993 after Yitzhak Rabin's government came to power.

In the US, legislation was passed after George Logan's 1798 peace mission to France prohibiting any American citizen without official authority from maintaining "any correspondence or intercourse with any foreign government or any officer or agent thereof, with intent to influence the measures or conduct of any foreign government or of any officer or agent thereof, in relation to any disputes or controversies with the United States or to defeat the measures of the United States."[90] This law, the "Logan Act," still exists today (with minor modifications), and while it has come up in political and legal discourse on many occasions, it has never been used as the basis for a conviction.[91]

In the United Kingdom there were efforts to thwart meetings between British citizens and Sinn Féin leaders by using anti-terrorism legislation to prohibit these leaders from entering Britain.[92] In Spain, various mediation efforts between the government and the Basque organization ETA were regarded by the authorities as a crime under Spanish anti-terrorism laws.[93] In South Africa voices demanded the prosecution of citizens who met with the ANC, but this did not happen.[94]

Another tool that has been used against PPEs is restrictions on movement. In the 1960s, North Vietnam was on a US list of countries that American citizens were not allowed to visit using an American passport, which the

State Department used as a tool against PPEs, among others, who traveled to Vietnam. In February 1966, the passports of Staughton Lynd, Herbert Aptheker, and Tom Hayden were revoked after they returned from meetings in Hanoi (including a meeting with Pham Van Dong, North Vietnam's prime minister), claiming they damaged proper management of the foreign policy.[95] In Israel as well legal measures have been taken against PPEs who traveled to countries considered "enemy states." In 1967, Abie Nathan was jailed because he had flown his private plane to Egypt.[96]

Yet another tool that has been used against PPEs is a request to the official authorities of a third country to assist in thwarting PPEs' activity. The United States, for example, asked the Netherlands to prevent George Logan from continuing to France in 1798; in 1962 Israel informed the French authorities of Joe Golan's contacts with the Algerian Front de Libération Nationale (National Liberation Front; FLN), which resulted in his being declared a *persona non grata* in France.[97]

Officials have often made use of discursive tools in their fight against PPEs. One example is a discourse of contempt, which aims to decrease the initiative's apparent importance, undermine the PPE's credibility, and present discussion of the issue as ridiculous and unnecessary. For example, after the revelation of the meetings channel that PPE Moshe Amirav had opened with Palestinian representatives, Israeli prime minister Yitzchak Shamir described the endeavor as a "not very serious story of a man who, out of foolishness or naiveté, became entangled in talks with PLO members."[98] After Ashmore and Baggs exposed their dialogue with Hanoi and the official messages they delivered from Washington, the State Department responded mockingly that Ashmore perhaps had an "understandable personal feeling" that his channel was at the center of the stage, but he actually had no "significant role" and was only "a very very small part" in the large picture.[99]

Another type of discursive tool is to depict the PPE's activity as a disruptive and irresponsible invasion into a professional and official area, one that undermines official policy and possibly sabotages ongoing negotiations or political efforts behind the scenes. Such a claim, for example, was leveled against Jesse Jackson when he decided to travel to Syria in 1984 in an attempt – which ultimately succeeded – to release an American soldier who was being held hostage there. US government officials claimed that Jackson's initiative could damage the delicate negotiations underway on this issue.[100] Also, in the case of John Sayre in Nicaragua, State Department officials considered that his efforts, rather than leading to peace, caused more damage to it, and argued that peace is "too volatile to be left to the people" and is a "job for professionals."[101]

The most extreme discursive tool is the discourse of betrayal, which entails accusing the PPE of abandoning loyalty to the state or the group and "crossing the line" to the other side. In South Africa, for example, Defence Minister Malan and other senior officials accused Alex Boraine and his fellow PPEs who met with the ANC of being disloyal and unpatriotic.[102] Similarly, Logan's peace mission to France was described by Federalist Party members and the Federalist press as a treasonable plot.[103]

## Indifference

Decision makers sometimes respond to PPE initiatives by choosing a middle ground that appears as an ambiguous option that neither opposes nor supports or encourages the PPE's activity. In these cases, the officials do not attempt to thwart the private initiative – indeed, they might even agree to be a passive recipient of the PPE's reports – yet they maintain a distance from the initiative and avoid giving any signals that might be interpreted as indicating consent.

A good example is the Israeli government's attitude towards Alon Liel's activity. At the beginning of his peace initiative, Liel was told that Prime Minister Sharon opposed negotiations with Syria but that as a private citizen Liel could do as he wished. Liel regularly updated the Foreign Affairs Ministry after each meeting he had with his Syrian contacts, and the ministry officials responded as "passive listeners," that is, they recorded his reports without adding questions or asking him to deliver messages on their behalf.[104]

Similar activities took place in South Africa. Willem de Klerk – the brother of Fredrik de Klerk, a senior National Party leader who became president in 1989 – joined an unofficial meeting channel with the ANC and updated his brother. While Fredrik de Klerk told his brother that these meetings were against party policy and that he did not want to know anything about them, Willem de Klerk insisted and sent him written feedback after every meeting. "I am not going to respond to your letters," Fredrik de Klerk said to his brother, "but thanks very much, I'm most grateful." Later Fredrik told his brother that these reports helped him realize "that a quantum leap is necessary and ... that it's not that risky."[105]

The boundaries of this pattern of response are blurred, with some cases located in grey areas. It is often difficult to determine whether policy makers' indifference is closer to "passive opposition" or to "silent consent." The distinction between "knowing" and "consenting" is also a relevant question in this context. The issue surfaced during the "Goldmann affair" in Israel in 1970. PPE Nahum Goldmann, who was president of the World Jewish Congress, reported to Prime Minister Golda Meir that he had received an invitation to meet as a private citizen with Egypt's President Nasser in Cairo. Goldmann made it clear that he was not seeking official permission to go. He merely wanted to inform the prime minister because doing so was an Egyptian request and because he regarded it as a "friendly obligation."[106]

Meir and Foreign Minister Abba Eban challenged the logic of the distinction, and Meir insisted on bringing the issue to the government, where she told ministers that Goldmann was seeking authorization to meet Nasser. The government eventually declared that it did not authorize Goldmann to conduct this mission, "neither by saying explicitly that he is representing the government, nor by implying it from the fact that the Israeli government was requested to permit it and gave him permission."[107] Israel's ambassador in Rome raised the same dilemma before the secretary-general of the Foreign Ministry in 1958 concerning the activity of Joe Golan. The ambassador wrote that Golan gave him reports on his meetings and he avoided expressing any response – positive or negative – on Golan's activities. But he was worried that Golan would interpret this as an approval of his activities.[108]

It is important to emphasize that the policy of indifference can easily shift towards one of the other patterns of response. British prime minister Palmerston, for example, changed his attitude towards Richard Cobden's initiative with France in 1859 from indifference to endorsement, and Israeli prime minister Shamir changed his attitude towards Moshe Amirav's unofficial channel with the Palestinians in 1987 from indifference to resistance.

### Endorsement

A response pattern of endorsement means that the decision makers support PPEs' efforts and choose to use them and their activity infrastructure as a tool to promote a policy of conflict resolution. As US vice-president Al Gore stated, referring to Jimmy Carter's private peace mission to North Korea in 1994, "Let's make lemonade out of this lemon."[109] In these cases the unofficial sphere of the PPEs' activity spreads into the official and governmental spheres. Patterns of endorsement might vary in the level of official "utilization" and involvement or extent of the role that decision makers allow PPEs to play in the official processes. Endorsement can be specific and temporary, or it can be more significant and for the long term. Decision makers can use PPEs as envoys or intermediaries, or they can use their ideas and proposals. I will elaborate on this in the section on influence patterns of PPEs in the second part of this chapter.

### Challenges and criticism

PPE initiatives tend to provoke lively public debates and often spark criticism against the PPEs. In this section I consider the main arguments against the PPE phenomenon presented by critics in public discourse.

The first argument is that these private actors have no formal or moral authority or mandate to negotiate. Because they represent no one except themselves, they have no legitimacy to interfere in foreign policy. They were not elected or nominated, which raises questions about their moral source of authority and legitimacy.

The second argument is that meeting with enemies provides them with a propaganda tool and legitimacy without any concrete concessions or changes in policy. This argument is raised especially in cases of meetings with leaders of "rogue states" or violent non-state actors. These actors – who are refused recognition by official governments and often many other actors in the international community – are seeking international legitimization. Carter, for example, was accused of giving legitimacy to dictatorships and repressive regimes through his meetings with dictators such as the leaders of North Korea and Haiti.[110] In another case, Eliyahu Ben-Elissar, head of the Foreign Affairs and Defense Committee in the Knesset, argued in 1983 that Arafat was "using his meetings with Israelis for the purpose of propaganda."[111] Leaders from Ireland and the Social Democratic and Labour Party also claimed that Sinn Féin used the activity of the PPE Father Reid to emerge from political isolation.[112]

A counter-argument to this criticism claims that these meetings, which are viewed by both sides, send a message to the public on both sides. Avnery claims, "when you are meeting with the enemy, also your enemy is meeting with its enemy." The Israeli public saw Israelis meeting with Arafat – their worst enemy – but at the same time the Palestinians saw their leader meet with Zionists – their worst enemy. This sends the Palestinian public a message that not all Zionists are terrible and it may be possible to start a dialogue with them.[113] The fact that the PLO officials who met with Avnery and other PPEs, such as Said Hammami and Issam Sartawi, were harshly criticized by some Palestinians, and eventually murdered by a radical Palestinian organization as a result of these meetings, reinforces that these meetings were not a one-way street. The participation of the PLO officials gave the meetings legitimacy, and they paid a price for this message. The PPE Alex Boraine raised another counter-argument referring to his meetings with the ANC, saying that it was the other way around: they decided to meet with the ANC because it already had legitimacy after existing for seventy-five years and having strong support in South Africa.[114]

A third argument is that this activity is not democratic; it bypasses the elected government and damages its ability to conduct a unified policy. It sends the rival side, and the world, mixed signals and confuses messages on official policy. On the other hand, the counter-argument is that were PPEs to pretend to represent the government, then it becomes very problematic; but if they are acting only as private citizens in a democratic society and are clear about this, it is legitimate. Some may even argue that PPE activity is part of the right and the duty of civil society in democracy.

The fourth argument is the claim that PPEs do not have official information – that is, military intelligence information or diplomatic knowledge about other secret channels – that is relevant to the dialogue with the rival side. On the other hand, as I mentioned in the discussion on power resources, PPEs' longstanding and direct contact with the other side provides them with unique alternative knowledge resources that can sometimes be more accurate than intelligence agencies' information. Another critical argument in this context is the lack of professional tools needed in negotiations, such as legal and diplomatic expertise.[115]

The fifth argument concerns the risk that the initiative of the PPEs will lead to developments that go counter to their intentions and damage the goal of peace. Agha et al. claim that track two can have "unexpected results."[116] The exposure of the initiative can push the establishment to react with steps thwarting the initiative and can lead to escalation. Another possibility is that a disappointed reaction from the rival side – rejection, public denial, or a failure in the talks – can send a negative message to the decision makers and the public that can be fatal to the PPE's efforts.

## Part II: the influence of private peace entrepreneurs

This section addresses the question of indicators for assessing the influence of the activities of private peace entrepreneurs and presents the analytical framework I will use to explore the question. Towards this end, let us first review the discourse on this issue in related fields of study.

Within the literature on unofficial and track two diplomacy, scholars use different approaches to the question of influence. This dimension is termed "transfer" or "dissemination."[117] Some scholars doubt the potential of this phenomenon to have an influence. Bercovitch, for example, argues that unofficial intervention represents an ineffective model of mediation, while Eban described private diplomacy as yielding "so meager a harvest" that even "a negotiator of limited skill and wisdom who can commit his government is likely to be more effective than a man of great virtuosity who lacks that mandate."[118] Scholars have also cast doubt on the ability of track two workshops to contribute to conflict resolution and generate concrete results.[119] Other scholars (such as Hoffman, Saunders, and Berman and Johnson) have argued that citizen diplomacy has an influence but it is indirect, longterm, and not measurable.[120] Scholars in the field of track two diplomacy have underscored that it cannot be measured using the indicators that apply to official diplomacy, given that the objectives differ, and that its effectiveness should be assessed according to the goal established by the participants, which is not necessarily to influence the official track.[121] Scholars have identified a number of distinctions relevant to this question, including the distinction between "internal effectiveness" (influencing participants in the talks) and "external influence" (influencing the conflict), or between the "micro objectives" of track two and "macro-goals."[122] Likewise, there is disagreement in the literature regarding the target audience of track two: decision makers or the political culture and general public.[123]

Prominent scholars in the field have proposed various criteria. Agha et al. proposed five indicators: the readiness of the two sides to sit together; agreement on a common frame of reference; attainment of substantive agreements; the establishment of informal contacts and networking; and the dissemination of new ideas. Chigas proposed indicators such as changed attitudes about the other and the conflict, improved communication, relationships and trust, and impact on conflict institutionalization. Kelman posited an indicator to assess whether the activities contributed to the creation of a "political atmosphere" favorable to negotiation as well as negotiating cadres and yielded input that informed political thinking and decision making. Lieberfeld identified various sources of potential influence, including reinforcement of the sense among decision makers that negotiations are possible, as well as a shift in public opinion and electoral politics. Cuhadar has argued that analyses of the influence of track two diplomacy should examine not only the outcome of negotiations but also the influence on the negotiating process in the transmission of information, skills, perspectives, and insights to official institutions and the official negotiation track.[124]

Similarly, the literature on international mediation also includes debates on indicators for the assessment of success.[125] Some scholars distinguish between objective, "measurable" criteria – such as whether the mediation led to dialogue or agreement, or helped reduce violence – and subjective indicators – such as whether the mediator and parties were satisfied with the mediation process.[126] The Haass success index proposes an operational definition whereby mediation is deemed successful if it led to considerable and positive change in the parties' interaction, partially successful if it led to dialogue, of limited success if it led to a ceasefire, and a failure if it had no influence on the conflict or the parties.[127]

Scholars in the field of mediation have underscored the difficulty of identifying the role of the mediator in the success or failure of the process, and of separating the mediator's role from other variables. Some have also emphasized that mediation should be assessed in accordance with both its starting point and the objectives defined by the parties and the mediator.[128] In addition, there are those who claim that the outcome of mediation should be assessed not only by whether an agreement was signed but also by exploring the question of whether the best possible agreement was reached, that is, whether the agreement was durable over time, and whether it was fair to both sides and equally beneficial.[129]

Scholars in the field of transnational civil society and peace movements have also addressed this question, which is relevant especially to the discussion on private peace entrepreneurs who operate openly with the aim of influencing the public. Scholars in these fields have distinguished among various target audiences in terms of influence, including governments, international institutions, global civil society, and public and media discourse.[130]

Against this background I will now describe the approach adopted in this study for the purpose of analyzing the influence of private peace entrepreneurs, as well as the premises underlying this approach and the main differences between this and other approaches.

First, it should be underscored that the phenomenon at the heart of this study is unique, and its characteristics differ both from those of other civil society activities such as track two or peace movements, and from those of similar diplomatic activities such as international mediation. Accordingly, the question of influence and "success" also has to be addressed differently and separately.

Because this phenomenon is located at the point of convergence between unofficial civil society activity and official diplomatic activity, the question of influence will be addressed by drawing on relevant tools from both spheres, alongside new tools that relate specifically to the phenomenon of private peace entrepreneurs. As noted, the literature on track two diplomacy encompasses a wide range of activities that differ in terms of key variables, including their objectives and the identity of participants, and therefore the use of uniform indices for such different types of activity would compromise the study and distort the findings. This study is based on the premise that one cannot use the same tools to assess and analyze an encounter between students from rival parties to a conflict, the purpose of which is educational, and an encounter between a private peace entrepreneur and official representatives of the rival party, the purpose of which is diplomatic and political. Problem-solving workshops, too, need to be assessed differently from PPE activities because the aim of such workshops is to change participants' perspectives, which is not relevant to an analysis of PPEs' objectives.

Second, this study does not employ a dichotomous perspective that differentiates between "success" and "failure." Instead it presumes that the phenomenon and its implications are far more complex and intricate, and that the question of "success" entails judgment on the part of the observer. As such, the discussion here examines whether there is any influence on the official diplomatic sphere and aims to identify the *patterns of influence* that represent aspects of actual influence by PPE activity in the unofficial sphere on talks, developments, and steps taken in the official sphere.

This approach recognizes that different patterns of influence can operate simultaneously.

Third, this study aims to enhance insights and refine conclusions regarding points of convergence between the official and unofficial spheres. Many studies that address the influence of track two on track one employ only general and vague concepts such as "change in political culture" or "creating a sense of possibility," whereas this study aims to propose more operational tools in order to better assess and more clearly define channels of influence between PPE activities and events and developments in the official sphere. These tools require in-depth empirical analysis of the official and unofficial spheres as an integrated whole, as well as cross-correlation between sources from both spheres and an in-depth empirical examination of micro-level events (conversations, meetings, letters) to identify the "fingerprints" of PPE activity in the official political and diplomatic spheres. The model used here for the patterns of influence proposes "rigid" indicators representing channels of influence that are as clearly defined as possible, minimizing the need for interpretation and estimation.

### Patterns of influence by PPEs on the official sphere

This study identifies eight possible patterns of influence by PPEs on the official diplomatic sphere.

#### Influence through mediation

This pattern refers to cases in which PPEs influence the official diplomatic sphere by playing the role of mediator between parties to a conflict. The theoretical literature on international mediation identifies a large array of strategies and roles in conflict mediation. In analyzing this pattern of influence I employ five key roles of mediation identified in the literature:[131]

1. *Communicator* – assisting in the exchange of messages, opinions, and information between the parties. In this capacity the PPE provides a passive channel of communication, serving as a go-between for the parties without actually intervening substantively.
2. *Facilitator* – creating the space and conditions for a meeting and a channel for direct dialogue between the parties. In this capacity the PPE helps the parties coordinate and lay the foundation for direct talks. This role relates to the concept of "procedural strategies" by which the mediator is involved in outlining the framework of the negotiating process with respect to elements such as the nature of meetings and the agenda of each meeting, among others.[132]
3. *Formulator* – proposing and promoting formulas for a solution or assisting in the formulation of messages and agreements. This is a more active

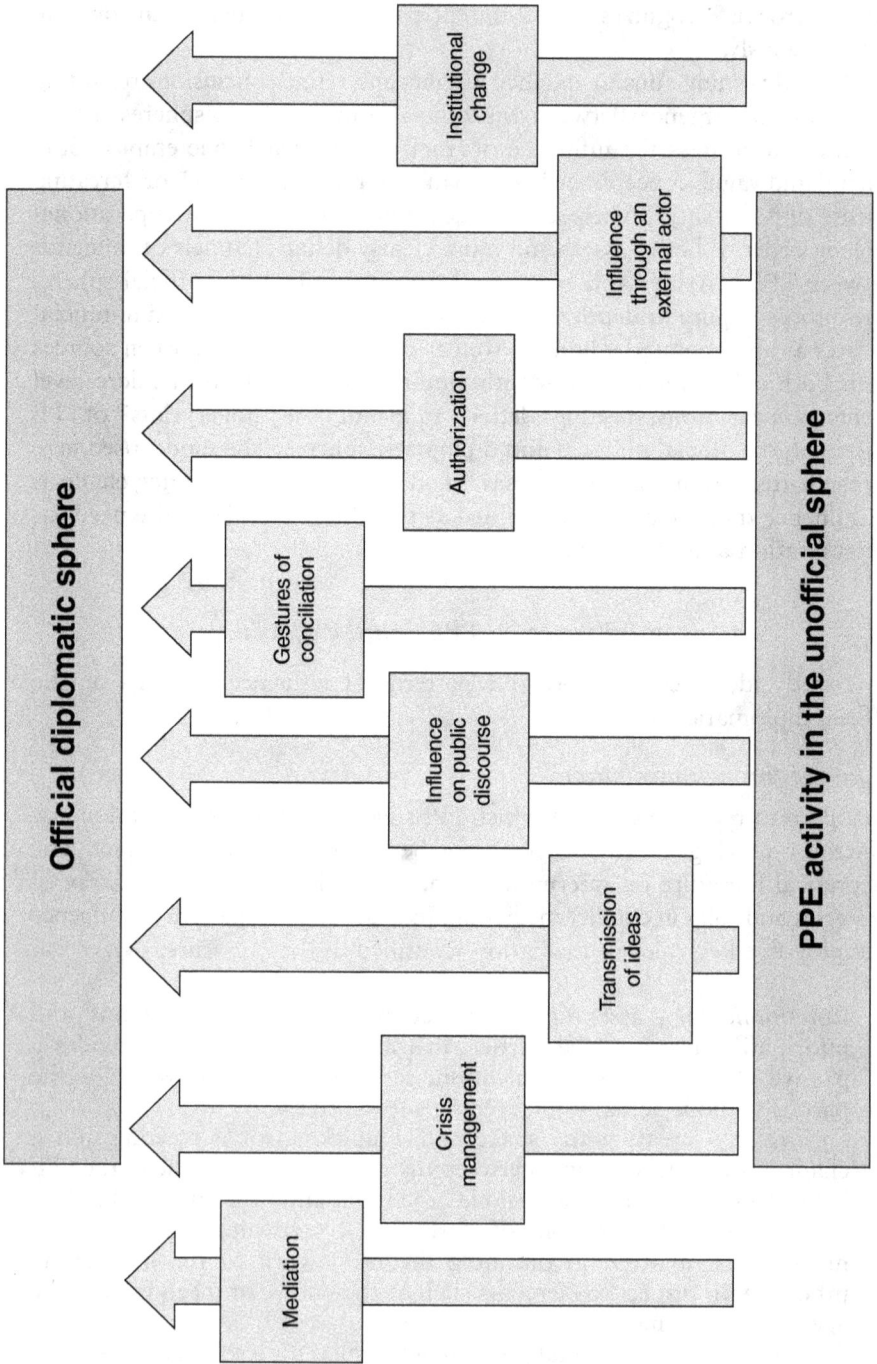

Figure 1.3 PPE patterns of influence on the official diplomatic sphere

role in which the PPE is involved in the substance of negotiations and proposes topics for discussion, reframing of the issues, and potential resolution of disagreements.

4. *Psychoanalyst* – helping the parties deal with the psychological and emotional dimensions of the conflict in order to build trust and change perceptions as well as the "enemy image."[133] This element did not appear in traditional definitions of the mediator's role in the literature, but over the years awareness has increased regarding the psycho-social dimensions of conflicts and their importance in the negotiating process. In this capacity the PPE is not involved in the process or substance, but rather in the removal of emotional and psychological barriers that emerged during the course of the conflict.[134] In this context the PPE aims to correct misunderstandings, change misperceptions, uncover unknown characteristics of the rival party, address the collective fears and concerns of each side, and build trust and mutual respect between the parties. This role is particularly important in cases of intractable and protracted conflict, which tend to be prolonged, violent, and complex.[135]

5. *Manipulator* – using resources of power to advance negotiations through incentives and compensation or threats and sanctions.[136] This role refers primarily to official mediators with significant resources of political, military, and economic power that can function as a carrot or stick in the negotiating process. The PPE does not have these power resources but, under certain conditions, does have alternative "soft" resources that can provide incentives or apply pressure on the parties in order to advance negotiations.

## *Influence through crisis management*

This pattern of influence relates to the unique and complex circumstances of an international crisis that require means of management that the PPEs undertake. An international crisis, as defined in the literature, is a situation characterized by severe threat to important national interests and values or to national reputation, by time pressure and a growing risk of escalation, or by the possibility of deterioration to a violent confrontation.[137] The International Crisis Behavior project defines international crisis as a change in the nature and rise in intensity of a hostile interaction that threatens stability and poses a challenge to the international system, with an increasing likelihood of military confrontation. Under these circumstances, PPEs can play a very important part by contributing to the management and resolution of the crisis. Successful crisis management, according to Dixon's definition, occurs when the efforts lead to agreed understandings that, if only temporarily, resolve or eliminate at least some of the problems at the heart of the crisis.[138] It should be underscored that crisis management differs from conflict resolution in that the former is aimed at resolving an immediate crisis and preventing escalation, rather than seeking long-term solutions or addressing the roots of a conflict.[139]

In this pattern of influence, during a crisis, under conditions of tension, risk of escalation, and lack of communication between the rival parties, the PPE seeks to provide a vital channel of communication for the transmission of messages, easing of tension, and advancement of a solution to the crisis. Such activities can make a significant contribution. Many scholars have highlighted the contribution of official or unofficial channels of communication during a crisis, which can take the form of assisting the parties by reducing uncertainty, preventing misunderstandings, and reaching an agreement that will end the crisis, among other means.[140]

The decision by PPEs to pursue emergency measures during a crisis usually stems from their sense that official actors are not working to resolve the crisis or that they chose to follow a course that could lead to confrontation. A salient characteristic of this pattern is the PPEs' effort to challenge the underlying "game of chicken" as game theory terms it, which typifies international crises – that is, a situation in which the fear of losing face prevents cooperation and leads parties to defect.[141] The very act of approaching the other side might look like a concession, and neither side wants to appear as if it is conceding. Such obstinacy can lead to confrontation. Under these circumstances, the fact that an initiative to end the crisis originates with a private actor can provide both sides with the ladder they need to "climb down from the tree" without losing face, allowing each side to claim that it did not blink first as it did not approach the other. This resource corresponds with Morgan's argument that parties to a crisis find it easier to respond to initiatives proposed by a mediator or to concede to a third party than to concede to their rival.[142] There are two additional characteristics worth noting in this context. First, the distinction on which a PPE's initiative is based – between the government and the public and between the official position and that of the PPE – makes it easier for the other side to respond to the initiative and to accept that it is based on good intentions. Second, when a crisis requires an immediate response, the fact that the PPE's existing network of contacts with the other side can be activated instantly is an important advantage.

*Influence through the transmission of ideas*

This pattern of influence focuses on developing and disseminating ideas and on their influence on official diplomatic processes. During the initial phase, the PPE's activities and meetings with representatives of the other side serve as a factory for ideas with the characteristics of a cross-border epistemic community. These activities can generate proposals, concepts, or solutions, which Adler terms "units of variation."[143] During the second phase, the ideas formulated by the PPE take on a life of their own and spread to other arenas. The dissemination of new ideas can take place in a number of ways: through transmission to the public, political, or media discourse, or through transmission to the official system on the PPE's side, the rival side, or a third side. The process might be dynamic, going from one arena to another, and sometimes one of the official actors adopts the idea and acts to advance it. During the third phase the idea is incorporated into the official sphere and becomes part of the diplomatic talks, official statements, or proposals for negotiation, and occasionally it is even translated into agreements and facts on the ground. At this stage the idea becomes a point of reference to which state officials must respond, regardless of whether they want to adopt it or thwart it. The transmission of ideas to the official sphere is not necessarily immediate and in fact could take a long time. During this process, an idea might change and grow or acquire new interpretations that were not part of the original concept.

*Influence on public discourse*

This pattern refers to situations in which the PPE acts publicly to enlist public support for negotiations and urge the public and various domestic actors to take action in this regard. In this pattern the initiative elicits a substantial public response, which manifests in various ways and spheres of activity. The public initiative can influence public opinion, social movements, the media, and the public sphere in several ways: by changing public discourse and creating a "discursive opposition"; by producing "news slots" on dialogue and negotiations at a time when violence and confrontation dominate the media; by influencing the process of "agenda setting" so that the option of a political solution receives more attention and is ascribed more importance in the media or public discourse; or by influencing the political balance of considerations regarding risk versus reward.[144]

PPEs can influence public discourse, among other means, by becoming an independent source of information and interpretation or by promoting extensive media coverage that compels the official establishment to respond. They might also supplement their efforts with activities such as demonstrations, petitions, and press conferences. It is important to bear in mind that official responses to public pressure do not necessarily correlate with the expectations or aspirations of the PPE. In some cases, they might conform to the spirit of the initiative, and in other cases they might conflict with the PPE's intent and actually be aimed at subduing public pressure and criticism.

*Influence through gestures of conciliation*

The aim of this pattern of influence is to address a mutual lack of trust that impedes the parties' transition to a peace process. Many scholars argue that a conflict resolution process requires a minimal or sufficient degree of trust. This assumption reflects a dilemma, as Kelman describes, whereby the rival parties cannot launch a peace process without some measure of mutual trust, but they cannot build trust without embarking on such a process.[145] In this pattern, the PPE aims to resolve the dilemma through the promotion of "gestures of conciliation."

Mitchell identifies four types of conciliation gestures:

1.  *Concession* – announcing a retreat from a publicly declared bargaining position.
2.  A *symbolic* gesture aimed at conveying willingness to begin a process of conciliation.
3.  *Tension-reducing measures* entailing an action or statement aimed at eliminating or reducing dangers and concerns in situations of confrontation that could escalate.
4.  *Confidence-building measures* in the form of unilateral measures aimed at building trust and demonstrating the lack of hostile intention towards the other party.[146]

These measures are also associated with Osgood, who, in the context of the Cold War, proposed the Graduated Reciprocation in Tension-reduction model comprising a series of unilateral initiatives and gestures aimed at reducing mistrust and preventing escalation.[147] Such measures and gestures can help change perceptions as well as the "enemy image," increase domestic pressure on the other side to respond by making a concession or reciprocal gesture, or even serve as a starting point for a peace process. Under certain circumstances, however, the gesture might be perceived as propaganda or a sign of weakness, and fail.[148] Gestures of conciliation are to a large extent an element of "public diplomacy" and are often accompanied by a media dimension that helps disseminate the message. They might constitute what Dayan and Katz term a "transformative media event" in which a historical turning point is reflected in a media event.[149]

In this pattern of influence, the PPE is aware that lack of trust between the parties impedes their transition to a conflict resolution process, and therefore aims to remove this obstacle by promoting measures to build trust and break the deadlock. There are three ways by which PPEs can promote gestures of conciliation:

1.  Approaching leaders on the other side to encourage them to initiate a gesture of conciliation. This may draw on two resources. First, PPEs are very familiar with the perspectives and impressions vis-à-vis the other side among their own public, and often among decision makers as well, and this familiarity helps them devise a framework for the gesture that is suited to the target audience and its concerns and sensitivities. Second, the other side is aware of the PPEs' domestic struggle against official

policy. Therefore, and because PPEs present their request as a tool that can influence the domestic balance of considerations and reinforce the position of those who share their view, their initiative carries weight that an official initiative does not and is seen as more credible than an official initiative. At the same time, however, PPEs are constrained because they cannot officially offer anything in exchange for the gesture or guarantee a positive response on the part of their government.

2. Approaching officials on the PPEs' side to encourage them to initiate a gesture towards the rival side. Here the PPEs' main resource is their familiarity with the leadership on the other side as well as its needs and problems, and this helps them formulate a suitable framework for the gesture.

3. PPEs with access to officials on both sides can correlate gestures and promote mutual measures that provide a return for gestures taken by each side. This is similar to the "IFU" tactic ("I will make a concession if you will make one first") presented by Mitchell.[150]

### Authorization of PPEs

This pattern constitutes the ultimate, ideal scenario for PPE activity. In this pattern of influence, PPEs report to official actors regarding the unofficial channel they have created, as well as the substance and conclusions that have emerged in their talks. Subsequently this channel receives official "accreditation" and is transformed into an official channel of negotiations. The timing of the PPEs' report to officials varies by case. It might take place when the channel is created or at a later stage when it has yielded results. "Accreditation" of the channel occurs when official actors adopt it and redirect and oversee it as an official channel, integrating their own representatives into the channel or granting an official mandate and issuing instructions to the PPE.

In this pattern the PPEs' unofficial channel might evolve as a backchannel and its unofficial nature can help it remain clandestine. There might be a transitory phase between the PPE reporting to the official establishment and their authorization. The duration of this period varies by case, and during this time officials are aware of the PPEs' activities but the latter lack official authorization and receive no official instructions. This phase is somewhere between a response pattern of "indifference" and one of "endorsement" on the part of the establishment, and it is sometimes difficult to identify the dividing line. Likewise, the granting of "official accreditation" might be a gradual process.

### Influence through an external actor

This pattern of influence is based on the third action pattern of PPEs. It combines involvement by an external actor and PPE activities outside the context of relations between parties to the conflict. These activities translate into influence on the official sphere through a PPE's inclusion of an external actor – a state or an international organization. The PPEs report to external actors regarding their contacts and the meetings they have held, their outcomes, and the ideas and proposals that have emerged from their unofficial channels, which the external actor then uses to transfer the activities to the official sphere. The external actors' role in this pattern is based on their official status, their sources of leverage to influence the process, and their network of contacts with the parties to the conflict. When the initiative comes from an important international actor, it is harder for the parties to ignore or reject it, and it requires them to respond within the official diplomatic sphere. The external actor can be involved at various stages of the PPE activity: at the start of the process, by assisting in establishing contact with representatives of the rival side or providing a facility or funding for the meetings, or at later stages, after the talks through the PPE's unofficial channels have made significant progress. In this pattern the external actors' characteristics and power resources are of great importance: Does the external actor represent a superpower or a small state? What is the nature of relations between the external actor and the two parties to the conflict? Are the parties prepared to accept the external actor's involvement? Does the external actor have previous experience in mediation efforts between the parties?

### Changes in institutional procedures

This pattern refers to PPE influence on procedural changes in the institutions of the parties to the conflict. In this pattern the peace efforts of the PPE require the parties to respond, which in turn leads to domestic structural changes such as the creation of a new decision-making forum or apparatus, or the convening of a committee or special session within existing institutions. These measures might involve a state or a non-state actor such as a paramilitary organization. The pattern is particularly applicable when conditions of diplomatic stalemate or vacuum prevail and there is no official dialogue. Under such circumstances unofficial PPE-initiated channels constitute a new and innovative development, requiring institutions on both sides to make structural or conceptual changes so as to decide how to respond to these developments.

### Multivariable system for the analysis of PPE activity

Drawing on the typology presented in this chapter, I wish to propose a theoretical-analytical framework by which I will examine the variables that affect PPEs' ability to promote their efforts and influence the official diplomatic sphere. This framework is based on the research hypothesis that PPE activity is affected by variables that correspond with three levels of analysis: variables related to the PPE, variables related to the initiative, and external variables. Using a set of variables that correlate with these different levels, I will examine which of the variables played a significant part in the PPEs' patterns of influence and how various conditions affected the outcome of their activities. Analysis of the case studies using this framework will allow us to draw conclusions regarding the variables and the conditions under which PPE activity can be most effective and influential.

## Variables related to the PPE

The variables at this level of analysis refer to the PPEs themselves and to their characteristics and resources. The variables proposed at this level are based on the typology presented in the previous section.

1. Type of PPE – to which category of PPE do they belong?
2. The PPE's network system – what resources of access and contacts do they have?
3. The PPE's knowledge resources – what resources of knowledge, expertise, and experience do they have?
4. The PPE's value-based resources – what moral, spiritual, and ideological resources do they have?

## Variables related to the initiative

The variables at this level of analysis relate to the nature of activity and characteristics of the initiative advanced by the PPE.

1. *Secrecy vs. publicity and the action pattern.* Was the activity carried out clandestinely or publicly? What was the action pattern? This variable relates both to the question of secrecy and to the target audience of the initiative.
2. *The objective of the initiative.* What were the substance and main objective of the initiative? This variable relates to the question of whether the main objective of the initiative was modest and focused or ambitious and comprehensive. It is used to assess a number of elements, including the following: Was the initiative focused on a single issue, or was it aimed at reaching agreement on a wide range of issues? Was the initiative intended to resolve an immediate crisis in the near term, or did it aim to promote long-term change? Was it focused on an objective related to process (such as opening a channel for direct negotiations) or to substance (such as reaching an agreement on arms control)? And did the issue on which the initiative focused constitute an important and sensitive matter of national security for the parties, or was it a "soft" issue of lesser importance?
3. *Correlation with official policy.* Did the objective of the initiative accord with or conflict with official policy? This variable is used to assess

**Variables related to the inititative**
1. Secrecy/publicity, action pattern
2. The objective of the initiative
3. Correlation with official policy
4. Direct or indirect contact

**External variables**
1. Characteristics of the conflict
2. Ripeness
3. Leaders' positions and domestic conditions
4. Parallel channels
5. Internal agents

**PPEs' influence on the official diplomatic sphere**

**Variables related to the PPE**
1. Type of PPE
2. Network system
3. Knowledge resources
4. Value-based resources

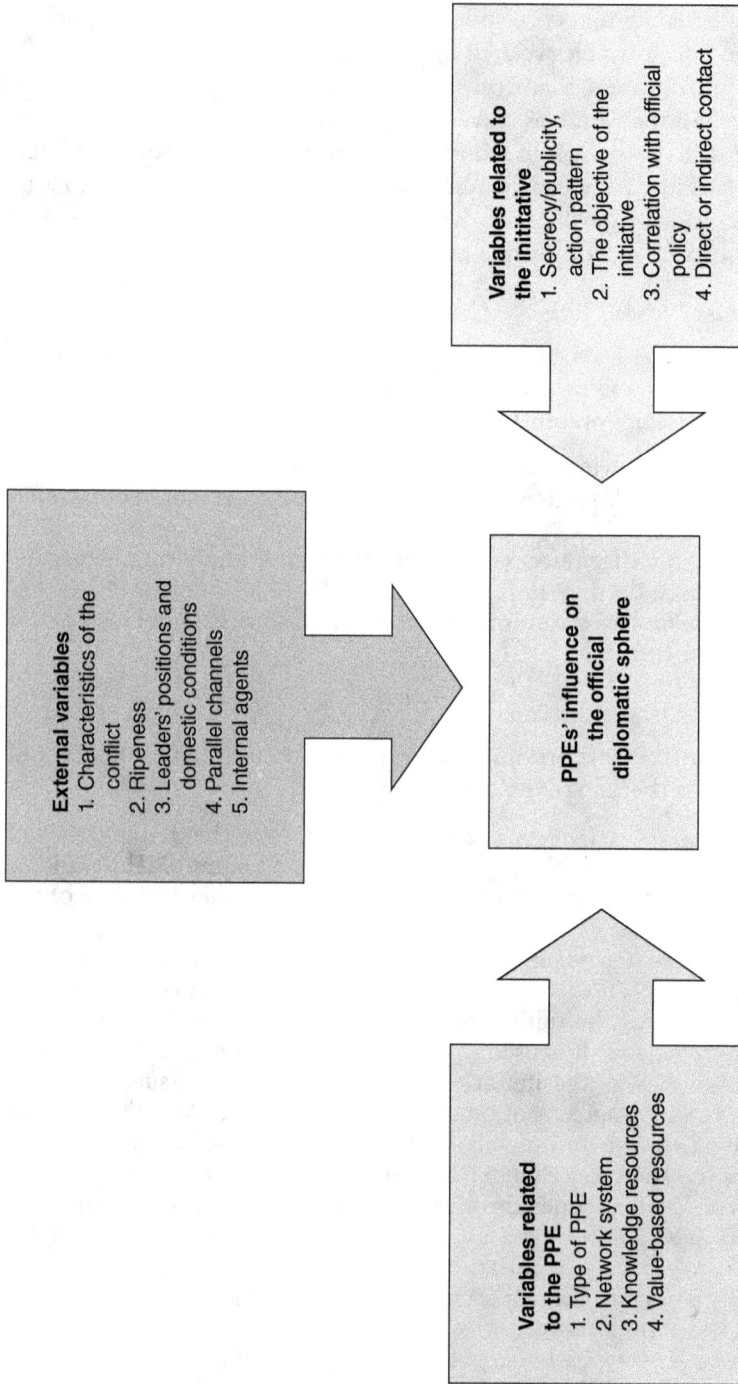

**Figure 1.4** Variables that determine PPEs' ability to have an influence

whether the objective of the initiative was in line with or complementary to the official policy positions of decision makers, or whether it conflicted with them and defied official state policy. This variable also relates to the distinction between a "complementary peace entrepreneur" and a "dissident peace entrepreneur."

4. *Direct or indirect contact.* What is the nature of the unofficial channel that underpins the initiative? This variable relates to the channel of communication on which the PPE's initiative is based, and it is used to assess how direct and accessible the channel is to senior echelons on both sides. Is the PPE's channel of communication accessible to leaders on both sides? Does the PPE's unofficial channel include high-ranking or low-ranking official representatives from the rival side? Was it indirect, relying on the assistance of a mediating actor?

*External variables*

This level of analysis concerns external variables that are not related to PPEs or their initiative, but rather to conditions related to the conflict, the leaders, the domestic arena on each side, and the regional and international arenas. These variables reflect influential factors that are relevant to any analysis of peace initiatives or mediation efforts, whether official or unofficial. The variables are of supreme importance in all aspects of peace initiatives, and their impact deserves careful assessment. I have selected the following variables for the analysis at this level:

1. *Characteristics of the conflict.* This variable relates to a series of factors and characteristics that reflect the nature of relations between the parties and affect the likelihood that negotiation and mediation efforts will be effective. In this context there are a number of criteria and characteristics that have been identified in the literature as having an influence on the parties' willingness to accept mediation and on the likelihood of success, and which are also applicable to an analysis of the influence of PPEs:
   i.   What is the nature of the conflict, and what is the balance of power between the parties? Is it an inter-state conflict, a domestic conflict, or a conflict between a state and a non-state actor?
   ii.  What was the level of intensity of the conflict at the time of the PPE's initiative? At what stage in the evolution of the conflict was the initiative launched? Did it take place under conditions of escalation and violence, or under conditions of tension and conflict but without violence?
   iii. Do the parties maintain diplomatic relations? What is the history of their relationship? Did they have peaceful, cooperative relations in the past? Were there periods of conflict and periods of negotiation between them in the past?
2. *Ripeness.* Did the salient conditions identified by ripeness theory exist? This approach highlights the importance of timing for peace initiatives

and aims to identify the conditions and circumstances necessary for advancing a conflict resolution process or initiating mediation or negotiations. Zartman identified three key elements that constitute necessary – but not sufficient – conditions for the resolution of a conflict:

i. Both parties perceive themselves to be in a "mutually hurting stalemate" (MHS) – that is, they see themselves as deadlocked and unable to end the conflict through military victory, and they regard the existing situation as painful and taking an unacceptable toll. Often this perspective is informed by a catastrophic event or a sense of pending catastrophe. Escalation and crisis can contribute significantly to fostering ripeness.[151] This concept also corresponds with arguments in the literature regarding the influence of "political shock" on the emergence of conditions for the resolution of a prolonged conflict.[152] Zartman emphasizes that MHS includes both subjective and objective elements, but that the conditions for ripeness are subjective. According to him, subjective ripeness can occur at various stages of the conflict.[153] An external mediator can play a part in cultivating the perceptual element of the parties' ripeness. Developments in the international arena might also have an impact.

ii. Both parties believe that there is a "way out" – that is, they sense that it is possible to reach an agreeable solution through negotiations and that the rival side is prepared to do so. They do not have to identify a specific solution, only a sense that both parties share a willingness to search for a possible solution.

iii. Each side has a "valid spokesperson" – that is, a strong leadership recognized as representing each side and able to ensure that an agreement would be honored and implemented. Zartman notes that this is an essential element, albeit of lesser importance than the first two elements.[154]

This approach has generated debates and disputes regarding the concept of ripeness, with various scholars presenting different arguments and highlighting different elements. Kriesberg argues that the condition for ripeness is a belief on both sides that it is necessary to enter into negotiations, although he also points out that sometimes parties are interested in negotiating but not necessarily in reaching an agreement. According to him, the belief might stem from domestic or external pressure, a difficult and unbearable status quo situation, or potential benefits.[155] Stedman, who examined which actors must develop the MHS perspective as a condition for ripeness, identifies two types of actors: the first comprises actors who serve as a "patron" for one of the parties to the conflict, with a monopoly over assistance to the "client" (external actors), and the second comprises military actors on both sides (internal actors).[156] Lieberfeld has pointed out the need for leaders to recognize that they have no alternative partner to an agreement.[157]

3. *The position of leaders and the domestic conditions.* What was the position of leaders on both sides? How did domestic actors and

developments influence the situation? This element refers to domestic variables on each side and examines their influence on PPE activity. The main variable is the leadership on both sides, which constitutes a key player with decisive influence. The analysis of this variable relates to leaders on both sides of the conflict during the stage at which the PPE was operating, and it will examine their worldview, political situation, and extent of domestic legitimacy, as well as the totality of circumstances and conditions under which they operated. The discussion will address the leaders' positions regarding the conflict, the opposing side, resolution of the conflict generally, and the PPE peace efforts specifically.

Scholars in the field have identified the leadership as a decisive variable and examined the influence of cognitive factors – such as the leaders' belief systems, learning processes, and sensitivity to public opinion – on peace initiatives and processes.[158] Some scholars have argued that a change in leadership can create conditions that facilitate the pursuit of a new initiative or revision of policy, which in certain cases can advance peace processes.[159] The literature also addresses the influence of domestic factors – such as political developments, pressure groups, and public opinion – on peace negotiations.[160]

4.  *Parallel channels of communication.* Were there parallel channels of communication or parallel peace initiatives? Did developments along other channels influence the initiative? Did the PPE's unofficial channel constitute an exclusive channel of communication?

    This variable is based on the premise that, alongside variables related to the conflict and the parties, ripeness for progress along the PPE's unofficial channel also depends on parallel or competing channels between parties to the conflict. These might include efforts by various mediators or channels between various actors in the same conflict or in another conflict that is related to and affects the parties (termed "interlocking conflicts").[161] Under certain circumstances, stalemate or failure in one channel can facilitate progress in a parallel channel, while in other situations positive developments in one channel can facilitate talks in another channel. We can identify three salient situations in relation to this variable:

    i.   An unofficial channel initiated by the PPE under conditions of diplomatic vacuum, when there are no official diplomatic relations or other official or unofficial channels of communication between the parties. In such cases the PPEs have an advantage because there are no competing channels, although there are also dangers inherent in a situation that depends on only one channel of communication.

    ii.  An unofficial channel initiated by the PPE under conditions of no official diplomatic relations between the parties, yet in parallel with mediation efforts by other domestic or external, official or unofficial actors, between the same parties, or with the participation of other parties engaged in the conflict. The literature addresses the topic of the existence of several parallel channels of mediation and identifies disadvantages and advantages in that. On the one hand, a multiplicity of channels can undermine the process by generating tension or confusion or fueling competition among the various channels, or by leading to "channel shopping" whereby each side uses a number of channels to seek the most favorable terms. On the other hand, under certain circumstances parallel channels can complement one another, with each channel having a different function.[162]

iii. An unofficial channel initiated by the PPE under conditions of official diplomatic relations and official channels between the parties, with the PPE channel usually having been opened during a stalemate or crisis in official relations. In these cases the relevant questions are whether the channels are linked, how the messages transmitted through these channels differ, whether the participants of each channel are aware of the competing channels, and how official actors view the PPE channel – whether they see it as a complementary effort that can assist them or an act of sabotage that undermines official channels.

5. *Internal governmental agents.* Did the PPE have a "government outpost" or an "agent inside the establishment" who played a part in promoting the PPE's initiative? This variable refers to the existence of an actor in the official establishment who supports a PPE's outlook and the advancement of their initiative. Such agents provide the PPE with a "foothold" in the official arena, and they can contribute in a number of ways, including facilitating access to decision makers, persuading actors in various official fora, or adapting the initiative to the political arena. The degree of involvement and support for the PPE's initiative on the part of the internal agent varies by case. It can be substantial and proactive – comparable to the role of a "mentor" as Agha et al. termed it[163] – or less substantial and more passive. Scholars in the literature on social movements have discussed the need to create alliances with partners inside the establishment.[164]

In conclusion, this chapter has presented a theoretical framework that will serve as a basis for analysis of the case studies in the next chapters. It has described characteristics of the PPE phenomenon and offered a typology of their types, resources, activities, and relations with the establishment. The chapter has proposed a multivariable system for the examination of PPEs' influence on the official sphere, which subsequent chapters will use in order to analyze the impact of PPEs' activity in the case studies.

## Notes

1 N. Barnea and S. Schiffer, "Three little errors," *Yedioth Ahronoth* (4 January 2002).

2 T. P. Coogan, *The Troubles* (Boulder: Roberts Rinehart, 1996), 404.

3 Price, "Transnational civil society," 582.

4 R. B. Hall and T. J. Biersteker, "The emergence of private authority in the international system," in R. B. Hall and T. J. Biersteker (eds), *The Emergence of Private Authority in Global Governance* (Cambridge: Cambridge University Press, 2002), 5.

5 J. Golomb, *In Search of Authenticity* (London: Routledge, 1995), 60–61.

6 Price, "Transnational civil society," 587–559; D. Stone, "Introduction: Global knowledge and advocacy networks," *Global Networks*, 2:1 (2002), 1–12.

7 O. R. Young, *The Intermediaries* (Princeton: Princeton University Press, 1967), 87–90; B. S. Mayer, *Beyond Neutrality* (San Francisco: Jossey-Bass, 2004), 220–221.

8 M. Creekmore, *A Moment of Crisis* (New York: Public Affairs, 2006), 290.

9 U. Avnery, *My Enemy, My Friend* (Tel-Aviv: Bitan, 1989), 246.

10 A. Hudson, "NGOs' transnational advocacy networks: From 'legitimacy' to 'political responsibility'?" *Global Networks*, 1:4 (2001), 342.

11 J. P. Lederach, *The Moral Imagination* (Oxford: Oxford University Press, 2005), 75–86.

12 S. P. Borgatti and V. Lopez-Kidwell, "Network theory," in J. Scott and P. J. Carrington (eds), *The SAGE Handbook of Social Network Analysis* (London: Sage, 2011), 40–42.

13 R. S. Burt, "Structural holes and good ideas," *American Journal of Sociology*, 110:2 (2004), 349–399.

14 S. E. Goddard, "Brokering change: Networks and entrepreneurs in international politics," *International Theory*, 1:2 (2009), 262–268.

15 A. P. Schmid and P. Flemming, "Quantitative and qualitative of kidnapping and hostage negotiation," in G. O. Faure and I. W. Zartman (eds), *Negotiating with Terrorists* (London: Routledge, 2010), 49.

16 D. G. Pruitt, "Negotiation with terrorists," *International Negotiation*, 11:2 (2006), 382–383; P. Jones, "Talking with al Qaeda: Is there a role for track two?" *International Negotiation*, 20:2 (2015), 177–198.

17 T. Risse, "The power of norms versus the norms of power: Transnational civil society and human rights," in A. M. Florini (ed.), *The Third Force* (Tokyo: Japan Center for International Exchange, 2000), 186; Hall and Biersteker, "The emergence," 14; Kelley, "The new diplomacy."

18 J. Bercovitch and R. Jackson, *Conflict Resolution in the Twenty-first Century* (Ann Arbor: University of Michigan Press, 2009), 35–36; Young, *The Intermediaries*, 84–85.

19 C. F. Alger, "Religion as a peace tool," *Global Review of Ethnopolitics*, 1:4 (2002), 94–109; D. Little, *Peacemakers in Action* (Cambridge: Cambridge University Press, 2007), 429–448; R. S. Appleby, "Religion as an agent of conflict transformation and peacebuilding," in C. A. Crocker, O. Hampson, and P. Aall (eds), *Turbulent Peace* (Washington, D.C.: United States Institute of Peace Press, 2001), 827.

20 B. A. Misztal, *Intellectuals and the Public Good* (Cambridge: Cambridge University Press, 2007), 13–36, 21–28; S. Sand, *Intellectuals, Truth and Power* (Tel Aviv: Am Oved, 2000), 18–22.

21  F. B. Tolles, "Unofficial ambassador: George Logan's mission to France, 1798," *William and Mary Quarterly*, 7:1 (1950), 5, 19.

22  Israel State Archive (hereafter ISA), MFA 3835/1, Telegraph from the Foreign Ministry, 9 March 1966.

23  Interview with Ron Pundak, 25 December 2009.

24  Stanford, *Beyond the Boundaries*, 2. Hussein is referring to US president George H. W. Bush.

25  Wanis-St. John, "Back-channel," 125–129; On secret diplomacy see: C. Bjola and S. Murray (eds), *Secret Diplomacy* (New York: Routledge, 2016).

26  Creekmore, *A Moment of Crisis*, 60.

27  M. Klein and R. Malki, "Israeli–Palestinian track two diplomacy," in E. Kaufman, W. Salem, and J. Verhoiven (eds), *Bridging the Divide* (Boulder: Lynne Rienner Publishers, 2006), 119.

28  Paffenholz, "Civil society," 74.

29  Lieberfeld, "Parental protest," 384–385.

30  See A. F. Cooper, *Celebrity Diplomacy* (Boulder: Paradigm Publishers, 2008).

31  L. Kriesberg, "Coordinating intermediary peace efforts," *Negotiation Journal*, 12:4 (1996), 348.

32  Wehr and Lederach, "Mediating conflict," 87–88.

33  S. Mason, *Insider Mediators* (Berlin: Berghof Foundation, 2009); Wanis-St. John and Kew, "Civil society," 24.

34  See P. J. Carnevale and S. Arad, "Bias and impartiality in international media-tion," in J. Bercovitch (ed.), *Resolving International Conflicts* (London: Lynne Rienner, 1996), 39–53; S. Touval, *The Peace Brokers* (Princeton: Princeton University Press, 1982), 10–16.

35  R. P. Clark, *Negotiating with ETA* (Reno: University of Nevada Press, 1990), 84.

36  Avnery, *My Enemy*, 14.

37  G. A. Geyer, "Journalists: The new targets, the new diplomats, the new intermedi-ary people," in R. Schmuhl (ed.), *The Responsibilities of Journalism* (Notre Dame: University of Notre Dame Press, 1984), 72, 75.

38  E. Gilboa, "Media-broker diplomacy: When journalists become mediators," *Critical Studies in Media Communication*, 22:2 (2005), 99–101.

39  N. Cousins, "Notes on a 1963 visit with Khrushchev," *Saturday Review* (7 November 1964), 16.

40  Avnery, *My Enemy*, 21, 55, 211.

41  See H. S. Ashmore and W. C. Baggs, *Mission to Hanoi* (New York: G. P. Putnam's Sons, 1968), 5–7, 62–80; "Journalist says peace talks chance scuttled by LBJ," *Miami News* (18 September 1967).

42  G. Ben-Porat, "Business and peace: The rise and fall of the new Middle East," *World Political Science Review*, 1:1 (2005), 43; N. Golan-Nadir and N. Cohen, "The role of individual agents in promoting peace processes: Business people and policy entrepreneurship in the Israeli–Palestinian conflict," *Policy Studies*, 38:1 (2017), 21–38; A. Gerson, "Peace building: The private sector's role,", *American Journal of International Law*, 95:1 (2001), 102–119.

43  D. Lieberfeld, "Evaluating the contributions of track-two diplomacy to conflict termination in South-Africa, 1984–1990," *Journal of Peace Research*, 39:3 (2002), 370.
44  Eyal Erlich, *Hudna* (Tel Aviv: Aryeh Nir, 2005), 18.
45  L. Lehrs, "A last-minute private peace initiative: Albert Ballin's mediation efforts between Germany and Britain, 1908–1914," *Hague Journal of Diplomacy*, 13:4 (2008), 297–322.
46  Lieberfeld, "Evaluating," 370.
47  I. Msabaha, "Negotiating an end to Mozambique's murderous rebellion," in I. W. Zartman (ed.), *Elusive Peace* (Washington, D.C.: Brookings Institution, 1995), 204–230.
48  Little, *Peacemakers*, 438–440.
49  A. Hass, "Rabbi Froman visited Sheikh Yasin: Good chances for a truce in the war between the peoples," *Haaretz* (15 October 1997); Little, *Peacemakers*, 72; Stanford, *Beyond the Boundaries*, 95–98.
50  See M. B. Weddle, *Walking in the Way of Peace* (Oxford: Oxford University Press, 2001); C. H. M. Yarrow, *Quaker Experiences in International Conciliation* (New Haven: Yale University Press, 1978).
51  V. Stoica, "Is there a new diplomacy in the latter half of 20th century?" *Studia Universitatis Babes-Bolyai – European Studies*, 1–2 (1996), 192; Sharp, "Making sense," 141.
52  Interview with Nimrod Novik, 1 January 2009.
53  J. S. Wit, D. B. Poneman, and R. L. Gallucci, *Going Critical* (Washington, D.C.: Brookings Institution Press, 2004), 242.
54  A. F. Cooper, *Diplomatic Afterlives* (Malden: Polity Press, 2015), 1–18, 156–171.
55  Misztal, *Intellectuals*, 21–28.
56  J. Ramoneda, P. Vilanova, W. Salem, and E. Kaufman (eds), *Breaking the Wall* (Barcelona: Center of Contemporary Culture, 2005); P. Wallensteen, "The strengths and limits of academic diplomacy: The case of Bougainville," in K. Aggestam and M. Jerneck (eds), *Diplomacy in Theory and Practice* (Malmö: Liber, 2009), 258–281.
57  Agha et al., *Track-II*, 137.
58  D. Lieberfeld, "Contributions of a semi-official pre-negotiation initiative," in R. J. Fisher (ed.), *Paving the Way* (Lanham: Lexington Books, 2005), 108.
59  Sand, *Intellectuals*, 155.
60  N. C. Edsall, *Richard Cobden* (Cambridge, Mass.: Harvard University Press, 1986), 332.
61  A. Boraine, *A Country Unmasked* (Oxford: Oxford University Press, 2000), 24; H. Shibi, "MK Peled told the police: I have immunity," *Yedioth Ahronoth* (1 October 1987).
62  M. Abbas, *Through Secret Channels* (Reading: Garnet Publishing, 1995), 89–90.
63  Tolles, "Unofficial ambassador," 8; Mason, *Insider Mediators*, 7.
64  Stanford, *Beyond the Boundaries*, 291.
65  J. Bercovitch, "A neglected relationship: Diasporas and conflict resolution," in H. Smith and P. Stares (eds), *Diasporas in Conflict* (Tokyo: UN University,

2007), 21, 26; Y. Shain, "The role of diasporas in conflict perpetuation or resolution," *SAIS Review*, 22:2 (2002), 115–144.

66  T. Segev, "The Joe Golan affair," *Haaretz* (29 December 2005).

67  S. Segev, *The Moroccan Connection* (Tel Aviv: Matar, 2008), 158.

68  M. Chazan, "Goldmann's initiative to meet with Nasser in 1970," in M. A. Raider (ed.), *Nahum Goldmann* (Albany: Suny Press, 2009), 311.

69  Chazan, "Goldmann's initiative," 309–310.

70  Abbas, *Through Secret*, 54–57.

71  Interview with Ron Pundak.

72  M. Rabie, *U.S.–PLO Dialogue* (Gainesville: University Press of Florida, 1995), 157–158.

73  I. W. Zartman, "Pre-negotiation: Phases and functions," *International Journal*, 44 (1988), 237–253; J. Rothman, *Developing Pre-negotiation Theory and Practice* (Jerusalem: Davis Institute, 1989), 5–19.

74  R. D. Putnam, "Diplomacy and domestic politics: The logic of two-level games," *International Organization* (1988), 433–437.

75  A. Carter, *Peace Movements: International Protest and World Politics since 1945* (London and New York: Longman, 1992), 262–264.

76  Carter, *Peace Movements*, 262–267; Lieberfeld, "Parental protest," 383.

77  Risse, "The power of norms," 188; Keck and Sikkink, *Activists Beyond Borders*, 23–24.

78  D. Bar-Tal, "From intractable conflict through conflict resolution to reconciliation: Psychological analysis," *Political Psychology*, 21:2 (2000), 351–365.

79  J. G. Stein, "Psychological explanations of international conflict," in W. Carlsnaes, T. Risse, and B. A. Simmons (eds), *Handbook of International Relations* (London: Sage, 2002), 292–308; R. Holsti, "Cognitive dynamics and images of the enemy," in J. C. Farrell and Asa P. Smith (eds), *Image and Reality in World Politics* (New York: Columbia University Press, 1967), 16–39.

80  Stein, "Psychological explanations," 301; Bar-Tal, "From intractable conflict," 357–358.

81  I. W. Zartman, "Ripeness: The hurting stalemate and beyond," in P. C. Stern and D. Druckman (eds), *International Conflict Resolution after the Cold War* (Washington, D.C.: National Academy Press, 2000), 228–229.

82  Lieberfeld, "Evaluating," 358; H. C. Kelman, "Evaluating the contributions of interactive problem solving to the resolution of ethnonational conflicts," *Peace and Conflict*, 14:1 (2008), 38.

83  C. R. Mitchell, *The Structure of International Conflict* (Basingstoke: Macmillan, 1981), 286–313; C. A. Crocker, F. O. Hampson, and P. Aall, *Taming Intractable Conflicts* (Washington, D.C.: United States Institute of Peace Press, 2004), 21–43.

84  Keck and Sikkink, *Activists beyond Borders*, 12–13.

85  M. Gopin, *Holy War, Holy Peace* (New York: Oxford University Press, 2002), 46; H. S. Ashmore, "An exercise in semi-diplomacy: The case of Vietnam," in M. R. Berman and J. E. Johnson (eds), *Unofficial Diplomats* (New York: Columbia University Press, 1977), 140.

86  Avnery, *My Enemy*, 20; A. Nathan, *Abie Nathan* (Tel-Aviv: Poalim, 1998), 167–179; Stanford, *Beyond the Boundaries*, 134; Little, *Peacemakers*, 81; Mason, *Insider Mediators*, 7.

87  G. Lior, "The position of Zamir: Meetings with Arafat – not a crime," *Yedioth Ahronoth* (11 September 1983).

88  M. Bar-On, *In Pursuit of Peace: A History of the Israeli Peace Movement* (Washington, D. C.: United States Institute of Peace Press, 1996), 213–216.

89  Bar-On, *In Pursuit*, 214–216; D. Meridor, "Reply of the Minister of Justice on Israelis' meetings with the PLO," *Knesset Papers* (30 May 1989); Interview with David Ish Shalom, 8 September 2008.

90  D. F. Vagts, "The Logan Act: Tiger or sleeping giant?" *American Journal of International Law*, 60:2 (1966), 268.

91  Vagts, "The Logan Act," 271–280; M. V. Seitzinger, *Conducting Foreign Relations without Authority: The Logan Act* (Washington, D. C.: Congressional Research Service, 2015).

92  G. Adams, *Hope and History* (Kerry: Brandon, 2003), 17.

93  Clark, *Negotiating with ETA*, 228–229.

94  Lieberfeld, "Evaluating," 368.

95  M. Hershberger, *Traveling to Vietnam* (Syracuse: Syracuse University Press, 1998), 32–34, 51–54, 66, 69, 98, 138; S. Lynd and T. Hayden, *The Other Side* (New York: New American Library, 1967), 190.

96  Bar-On, *In Pursuit*, 201.

97  Tolles, "Unofficial ambassador," 11; J. Golan, *Pages from a Diary* (Jerusalem: Karmel, 2005), 323–326.

98  Y. Rabiyia and B. Barzel, "Nusseibeh was on his way to a lecture when he was attacked by four masked persons and was injured," *Yedioth Ahronoth* (22 September 1987).

99  Ashmore and Baggs, *Mission to Hanoi*, 82; H. Smith, "U.S. denies charge Johnson negated peace initiative," *New York Times* (19 September 1967).

100  "Jackson not sure he will visit Syria," *New York Times* (28 December 1983); Stanford, *Beyond the Boundaries*, 90–91.

101  C. F. Howlett, "Neighborly concern: John Nevin Sayre and the mission of peace and goodwill to Nicaragua, 1927–28," *The Americas*, 45:1 (1988), 43.

102  Boraine, *A Country*, 27; Lieberfeld, "Evaluating," 367.

103  Tolles, "Unofficial ambassador," 9–10, 22.

104  Interview with Alon Liel, 9 February 2009.

105  Lieberfeld, "Contributions," 114–115; A. Sparks, *Tomorrow is Another Country* (London: Heinemann, 1995), 80.

106  Y. Ben-Porat, *Dialogues* (Jerusalem: Edanim, 1981), 36.

107  Chazan, "Goldmann's initiative," 307.

108  ISA, MFA 3767/63, Israel's ambassador in Rome to the secretary-general, 26 June 1958.

109  S. S. Harrison, *Korean Endgame* (Princeton: Princeton University Press, 2002), 218.

110  B. I. Spector, "Deciding to negotiate with villains," *Negotiation Journal*, 14:1 (1998), 49.

111 "The government will discuss today a proposal to prohibit meetings with Arafat," *Haaretz* (23 January 1983).

112 R. Alonso, "Pathways out of terrorism in Northern Ireland and the Basque country: The misperception of the Irish Model," *Terrorism and Political Violence*, 16:4 (2004), 704.

113 Interview with Uri Avnery, 28 February 2014.

114 Boraine, *A Country*, 27.

115 Young, *The Intermediaries*, 109–110; Agha et al., *Track-II*, 163.

116 Agha et al., *Track-II*, 164–166.

117 See Jones, *Track Two Diplomacy*, 85–100.

118 Rouhana, "Interactive conflict," 332; A. Eban, *The New Diplomacy* (New York: Random House, 1983), 386; J. Bercovitch, "A case study of mediation as a method of international conflict resolution: The Camp David experience," *Review of International Studies*, 12:1 (1986), 43–65.

119 Rouhana, "Interactive conflict," 326; Kaye, *Talking*, 3; Lieberfeld, "Evaluating," 355.

120 H. Saunders, "When citizens talk: Nonofficial dialogue in relations between nations," in John W. McDonald, Jr. and Diane B. Bendahmane (eds), *Conflict Resolution: Track Two Diplomacy* (Washington, D. C.: Foreign Service Institute, 1987), 81–87; M. Hoffman, "Defining and evaluating success: Facilitative problem-solving workshops in an interconnected context," *Global Society: Journal of Interdisciplinary International Relations*, 9:2 (1995), 150–67; M. R. Berman and J. E. Johnson, "Afterword," in M. R. Berman and J. E. Johnson (eds), *Unofficial Diplomats* (New York: Columbia University Press, 1977), 263; N. N. Rouhana, "Unofficial intervention: Potential contributions to resolving ethno-national conflicts," in J. Melissen (ed.), *Innovation in Diplomatic Practice* (London: Palgrave, 1999), 111–132.

121 Rouhana, "Unofficial intervention," 125; D. Chigas, "Negotiating intractable conflicts," in C. A. Crocker, F. O. Hampson, and P. Aall (eds), *Grasping the Nettle: Analyzing Cases of Intractable Conflicts* (Washington, D. C.: United States Institute of Peace Press, 2005), 151.

122 R. J. Fisher, "Introduction," in R. J. Fisher (ed.), *Paving the Way* (Lanham: Lexington Books, 2005), 5; Rouhana, "Interactive conflict," 294–337.

123 A. Schiff, "'Quasi track-one' diplomacy: An analysis of the Geneva process in the Israeli–Palestinian conflict," *International Studies Perspectives*, 11:2 (2010), 97–99.

124 Agha et al., *Track-II*, 194–195; Chigas, "Negotiating," 137–149; H. C. Kelman, "Contributions of an unofficial conflict resolution effort to the Israeli–Palestinian breakthrough," *Negotiation Journal*, 11:1 (1995), 21–23; Lieberfeld, "Evaluating," 358–359; E. Cuhadar, "Assessing transfer from track two diplomacy: The cases of water and Jerusalem," *Journal of Peace Research*, 46:5 (2009), 652.

125 M. Kleiboer, "Understanding success and failure of international mediation," *Journal of Conflict Resolution*, 40:2 (1996), 361–362; L. Kriesberg, "Varieties of mediating activities and mediators in international relations," in J. Bercovitch (ed.), *Resolving International Conflicts* (London: Lynne Rienner, 1996), 219–220; Bercovitch and Jackson, *Conflict Resolution*, 45–46.

126 J. Bercovitch, "Introduction," in J. Bercovitch (ed.), *Studies in International Mediation* (Houndmills: Palgrave Macmillan, 2002), 17; Bercovitch and Jackson, *Conflict Resolution*, 45–46.

127 J. Bercovitch and A. Houston, "The study of international mediation," in J. Bercovitch (ed.), *Resolving International Conflicts* (London: Lynne Rienner, 1996), 19.

128 Kleiboer, "Understanding success," 361–362.

129 P. T. Hopmann, *The Negotiation Process and the Resolution of International Conflicts* (Columbia: University of South Carolina Press, 1996), 28–30.

130 Klotz, "Transnational activism," 49–76; Keck and Sikkink, *Activists beyond Borders*, 25–26; Summy and Saunders, "Why peace history?" 12–18.

131 J. Bercovitch, J. T. Anagnoson, and D. L. Wille, "Some conceptual issues and empirical trends in the study of successful mediation in international relations," *Journal of Peace Research*, 28:1 (1991), 7–17; J. B. Stulberg, *Taking Charge/ Managing Conflict* (New York: Lexington Books, 1987), 31–35; I. W. Zartman and S. Touval, "International mediation: Conflict resolution and power politics," *Journal of Social Issues*, 41:2 (1985), 27–45; K. Aggestam, "Quasi-informal mediation in the Oslo channel: Larsen and Holst as individual mediators," in J. Bercovitch (ed.), *Studies in International Mediation* (Houndmills: Palgrave Macmillan, 2002), 57–79.

132 Bercovitch and Houston, "The study," 29–30.

133 Aggestam, "Quasi-informal," 68–69.

134 D. Bar-Tal and E. Halperin, "Socio-psychological barriers to conflict resolution," in D. Bar-Tal (ed.), *Intergroup Conflicts and Their Resolution* (New York: Psychology Press, 2011), 217–224.

135 On intractable conflicts see P. T. Coleman, "Intractable conflict," in M. Deutsch and P. M. Coleman (eds), *The Handbook of Conflict Resolution* (San Francisco: Jossey-Bass, 2001), 428–450.

136 Zartman and Touval, "International mediation," 39–40.

137 O. Holsti, "Crisis management," in L. Pauling (ed.), *World Encyclopedia of Peace – Vol. 1* (Oxford: Pergamon Press, 1986), 212; Young, *The Intermediaries*, 10; J. Wikenfeld et al., "Mediating international crises: Cross national and experimental perspectives", *Journal of Conflict Resolution*, 47:3 (2003), 281; P. Williams, *Crisis Management* (London: M. Robertson, 1976), 24.

138 W. J. Dixon, "Third-party techniques for preventing conflict escalation and promoting peaceful settlement," *International Organization*, 50:4 (1996), 656–657.

139 Wikenfeld et al., "Mediating international crises", 281–284.

140 Williams, *Crisis Management*, 190; Young, *The Intermediaries*, 35–38.

141 K. A. Oye, "The conditions for cooperation in world politics," in R. J. Art and R. Jervis (eds), *International Politics* (New York: Longman, 2000), 83–96.

142 T. C. Morgan, *Untying the Knot of War* (Ann Arbor: University of Michigan Press, 1994), 126.

143 E. Adler, "The emergence of cooperation: National epistemic communities and the international evolution of the idea of nuclear arms control," *International Organization*, 46:1 (1992), 104.

144 Klein and Malki, "Israeli–Palestinian," 112; G. Wolfsfeld, *Media and the Path to Peace* (Cambridge: Cambridge University Press, 2004), 35–36; D. A. Scheufele and D. Tewksbury, "Framing, agenda setting, and priming: The evolution of three media effects models," *Journal of Communication*, 57:1 (2007), 11; Lieberfeld, "Evaluating," 358–359.

145 H. Kelman, "Building trust among enemies: The central challenge for international conflict resolution," *International Journal of International Relations*, 29:6 (2005), 644; D. W. Larson, "Trust and missed opportunities in international relations," *Political Psychology*, 18:3 (1997), 713, 724.

146 C. Mitchell, *Gestures of Conciliation* (New York: St. Martin's Press, 2000), 96–101.

147 C. E. Osgood, *Alternative to War or Surrender* (Urbana: University of Illinois Press, 1962).

148 Larson, "Trust," 719–720; Mitchell, *Gestures of Conciliation*, 165–166.

149 D. Dayan and E. Katz, *Media Events* (Cambridge, Mass.: Harvard University Press, 1992), 147–187.

150 Mitchell, *Gestures of Conciliation*, 104.

151 See I. W. Zartman, *Ripe for Resolution* (New York: Oxford University Press, 1989), 263–266.

152 B. D. Mor, "Peace initiatives and public opinion: The domestic context of conflict resolution," *Journal of Peace Research*, 34:2 (1997), 205.

153 Zartman, "Ripeness," 229–232.

154 Zartman, "Ripeness." For critiques of this theory, see M. Kleiboer, "Ripeness of conflict: A fruitful notion?" *Journal of Peace Research*, 31:1 (1994), 109–116.

155 L. Kriesberg, *International Conflict Resolution* (New Haven: Yale University Press, 1992), 144–146.

156 S. J. Stedman, *Peacemaking in Civil War* (Boulder: L. Rienner Publishers, 1991), 235–238.

157 D. Lieberfeld, *Talking with the Enemy* (Westport: Praeger, 1999), 90–92.

158 A. L. George, "The operational code: A neglected approach to the study of political leaders and decision-making," *International Studies Quarterly*, 13:2 (1969), 190–222; D. Lieberfeld, "Political leadership, peacemaking and post-conflict reconciliation: Xanana Gusmão and East Timor," *Leadership*, 14:1 (2018), 58–82.

159 Stedman, *Peacemaking*, 241–242; Lieberfeld, *Talking*, 88–90, 122–123.

160 Putnam, "Diplomacy"; Kleiboer, "Understanding success"; 364–366; Mor, "Peace initiatives."

161 L. Kriesberg, "Interlocking conflicts in the Middle East," *Research in Social Movements, Conflicts and Change*, 3 (1980), 99–119.

162 Kriesberg, "Coordinating intermediary," 341–352; Wanis-St. John, "Back-channel," 137; C. A. Crocker, F. O. Hampson, and P. Aall, "Rising to the challenge of multiparty mediation," in C. A. Crocker, F. O. Hampson, and P. Aall (eds), *Herding Cats* (Washington, D.C.: United States Institute of Peace Press, 1999), 665–699.

163 Agha et al., *Track-II*, 4–5.

164 M. Giugni, *Social Protest and Policy Change* (Lanham: Rowman & Littlefield, 2004), 5; Lieberfeld, "Parental protest," 376.

# 2

# Norman Cousins and US–Soviet–British negotiations on a Nuclear Test Ban Treaty, 1962–1963

While no individual can dictate policy, no individual should exempt himself from the attempt to do so."

*Norman Cousins*[1]

## Introduction

The Nuclear Test Ban Treaty negotiations, which involved the United States, the Soviet Union, and Britain, were a complex process that took many years and touched on security, political, economic, and scientific interests and considerations. Various international actors (France, Germany, and China) and developments that took place in diverse Cold War arenas also influenced the negotiating process. Within this multi-dimensional international tangle, Norman Cousins – an American journalist and social activist – started working to stimulate and motivate diplomatic moves and to be integrated as an actor into the international events and developments that led, in July 1963, to the conclusion of the Treaty Banning Nuclear Weapon Tests in the Atmosphere, in Outer Space and Under Water (the Partial (or Limited) Test Ban Treaty – PTBT or LTBT, respectively). This chapter will look at Cousins's role and involvement in the process as a case study of a private peace entrepreneur. The chapter is based on archival material from the John F. Kennedy Library, Cousins's papers at the University of California, Los Angeles library, and the Archives of the Archdiocese of Mechelen-Brussels in Belgium, as well as memoirs and secondary sources on the Kennedy administration, US–USSR relations, and negotiations on a nuclear test ban during this period.

In 1972, about a decade after his mediation initiative between Kennedy and Khrushchev, Cousins published a book detailing the initiative and his role in the process,[2] but historically the literature on the negotiations leading to the PTBT has paid only marginal attention to Cousins's role.[3] More recently, though, Cousins's political and diplomatic activities have begun to receive attention in scholarly research on American peace activism during the Cold War.[4] Interestingly, a 2013 documentary on Kennedy's Cold War policy placed a great deal of emphasis on Cousins's peace initiative.[5]

## Historical background

The year 1954 may be taken as marking the start of a global public discourse on the need for the superpowers to reach an agreement limiting or putting an end to nuclear testing. The discussion was sparked by nuclear tests that the United States conducted in the Marshall Islands in March 1954, which resulted in heavy environmental damage and physical harm from radioactive fallout to American soldiers who participated in the tests, a nearby crew of twenty-three Japanese fishermen, and residents of adjacent islands. The incident sparked international protests and led many public figures – including Indian prime minister Jawaharlal Nehru, scientist Albert Einstein, and Pope Pius XII – to call for an end to nuclear testing.[6]

In March 1958 the Soviet Union declared that it was suspending nuclear testing and urged the other nuclear-capable states to do so as well. A month later US president Dwight D. Eisenhower wrote to Soviet leader Nikita Khrushchev, offering to sponsor an international conference of scientific experts from both sides who would give consideration to the monitoring and oversight system necessary to verify an agreement banning nuclear tests. The experts' conference opened on 1 July 1958, in Geneva and concluded with a report outlining the conditions for a viable and effective verification system that could identify violations of the agreement. Following the conference of experts, the three nuclear powers – the United States, Soviet Union, and Britain – agreed to enter into negotiations on a nuclear test ban, and these began on 3 October in Geneva. Concurrently all three states also declared a moratorium on nuclear testing.[7]

The talks in Geneva soon exposed deep divisions over the necessary verification mechanisms, with the United States presenting a series of reservations it had regarding the conclusions of the experts' report. In late 1959 the leaders of the United States, Soviet Union, Britain, and France agreed that they would convene a summit in May 1960 to pursue talks on the issue. On the eve of this summit, however, an American U-2 spy plane in Soviet airspace was shot down, which triggered a crisis in bilateral relations. Although the summit did convene, it was quickly brought to a close. Similarly, the talks between the delegations in Geneva continued, but the Eisenhower administration came to an end without any real progress having been achieved.[8]

In 1961 President Kennedy entered office, and efforts to achieve a treaty continued. In April 1961 the United States and Britain presented the Soviets with a draft treaty that called for twenty annual on-site inspections in every nuclear-capable state, although at the talks in Geneva they announced that they would also agree to twelve inspections. The Soviets rejected the Western powers' proposals. During the negotiations, the United States stressed that in order to ensure a verification and monitoring regime that could identify underground tests and distinguish them from earthquakes, it would be necessary to have on-site inspections. The Soviet Union was resistant, however, and voiced concerns that the presence of foreign inspectors on its soil could provide a cover for Western espionage. The dispute over verification also surfaced during the Kennedy–Khrushchev summit in Vienna in June 1961.[9]

Lack of progress in the negotiations and tension between the superpowers over Berlin led to a declaration by the Soviet Union (in August 1961) and later by the United States (in September 1961) that it was rescinding its moratorium and renewing nuclear testing.[10] In an effort to break the deadlock, the United States and Britain proposed a partial ban based on an agreement that would prohibit testing in the atmosphere without reference to underground testing. The Soviets initially rejected the proposal, but in November they announced that they would agree to a partial ban on the condition that both sides commit themselves not to conduct underground tests until an agreement had been reached on complete nuclear disarmament. The West opposed this proposal and refused to commit to a moratorium without verification after the Soviet Union suspended the 1958 moratorium. At this stage the talks in Geneva reached a crisis point, and the last meeting within this forum took place in January 1962, after 353 rounds of talks.[11]

In October 1962 the international community was rocked by the discovery of Soviet nuclear missiles in Cuba and the dramatic inter-superpower crisis that ensued, during which the fear of nuclear war became more real than ever.[12] The crisis exacerbated mutual suspicion between the two sides, while simultaneously underscoring the need to cooperate in order to address the nuclear threat. After the crisis was resolved, Kennedy and Khrushchev had an exchange of letters in which they called for progress towards a test ban treaty, and two closed-door meetings were held between Soviet deputy foreign minister Vasily Kuznetsov and the US envoy to Geneva, Arthur Dean – on 30 October and 7 November – but they were unable to make progress on a test ban. On 27 November 1962, Khrushchev sent British prime minister Harold Macmillan a letter making it clear that he would not agree to on-site inspections on Soviet territory. Following the Cuban missile crisis, Khrushchev faced fierce criticism over his policy both domestically and from China, and the assessment in the United States was that the Soviet Union was not interested in pursuing a treaty at that time.[13]

## Norman Cousins: life story and worldview

Norman Cousins was born in the United States, in the state of New Jersey, on 24 June 1915. After graduating from Columbia University, he began a career as a journalist. In 1940, at the age of twenty-five, he was appointed executive editor of the *Saturday Review of Literature* and an editor-in-chief two years later.[14] For years Cousins worked in three arenas concurrently. First, as an editor and writer, Cousins produced editorials that drew attention and had an impact, and these were supplemented by a series of books in which he laid out his worldview. The second arena was his public activity, which he pursued through civil society organizations and the promotion of humanitarian projects. The third arena involved dealing with decision makers and leaders – in the United States, in the Soviet Union, and throughout the world.

On 18 August 1945, shortly after the bombing of Hiroshima and Nagasaki, Cousins published one of the most famous editorial essays in American history. Under the title "Modern Man is Obsolete," he argued that nuclear weapons signaled the end of an age in human history and the beginning of a new era that would have repercussions for all aspects of the fabric of human life. Cousins asserted that "man's survival on earth is now absolutely dependent on his ability to avoid a new war."[15]

Cousins expanded his essay into a book, which became a bestseller in the United States and was translated into many languages.[16] The atom bombs that were dropped on Japan left a strong impression on Cousins, and in 1949 he began promoting a project named "Moral Adoptions," which provided aid to four hundred Japanese children orphaned by the bombings. Later, in 1953, he led another project in which Japanese girls injured during the bombing received medical care in the United States.[17] Cousins and his wife also adopted a girl from Hiroshima.[18]

In his writings, Cousins repeatedly warned against the nuclear threat and critiqued the American public discourse on this issue for focusing on questions of supremacy and rivalry rather than solutions or moral aspects. He tried to persuade the public that since the advent of the nuclear age the rules of the game had changed, and that the security of the United States no longer depended on military supremacy and continuous armament, but rather on putting a stop to the arms race and reaching an agreement on arms control and peace.[19]

The events of August 1945 also clarified Cousins's position regarding the need for world government and fueled his struggle for this cause. "The need for world government was clear long before August 6, 1945," he argued, "but Hiroshima and Nagasaki raised that need to such dimensions that it can no longer be ignored."[20] Cousins regarded the principle of federalism as the basis for world order. He argued that this principle did not aim to eliminate differences but rather to prevent them from becoming violent conflicts. Accordingly, he regarded the weakness of the United Nations (UN) as a contributing factor to the crises and wars that erupted after 1945, and he called for a stronger UN with legislative and enforcement powers, and for the revision of its charter.[21]

Cousins translated his worldview into action. In October 1945 he was part of a group of about fifty American public figures who convened a conference in which they called for a federal world government. In February 1947 several organizations united to form an organization whose platform advocated "a world government with limited powers, adequate to prevent war" – the United World Federalists. In 1952 Cousins was appointed as president of the organization.[22]

In 1956 Cousins became increasingly active in the area of nuclear testing. That year a group of scientists presented him with an analysis regarding the human harm resulting from radioactive fallout. In addition to using his magazine as a tool to raise public awareness of the issue,[23] Cousins became involved in establishing an umbrella organization in the United States that would lead the public campaign against nuclear testing. In June 1957, the National Committee for a Sane Nuclear Policy (SANE) was founded, with Norman Cousins and Clarence Pickett serving as its first chairmen. SANE began to lead a large-scale campaign that included newspaper ads (usually written by Cousins), demonstrations, petitions, press conferences, and congressional lobbying. The organization began to attract growing numbers of activists, and founded branches throughout the United States. By the summer of 1958 it had 25,000 members.[24]

SANE's activities included monitoring events and responding to international developments. Following the 1958 Soviet announcement that it had suspended nuclear testing, Cousins called on the American administration to take a similar initiative and declare an immediate cessation of American nuclear testing. In August 1958, after the United States suspended nuclear testing, Cousins and Pickett sent President Eisenhower a telegram commending this move and calling for progress on a test ban treaty. When official talks opened in Geneva, SANE intensified its activities, establishing an information center in New York and launching an initiative to produce a statement, signed by public figures (including Albert Schweitzer, Eleanor Roosevelt, and Martin Luther King), which called on the delegates in Geneva to conclude a treaty.[25] Notably, towards the end of the 1950s SANE was accused of engaging in communist activities, and Cousins responded with a counter-campaign aimed against any association of the organization with communist elements. Some of the measures he took towards this end sparked a backlash of internal criticism against him.[26]

Cousins supplemented his public anti-nuclear campaign with efforts to engage international actors. In early 1957 he approached Dr. Albert Schweitzer – an intellectual, physician, and Nobel Peace Prize laureate – urging him to issue a public call against nuclear testing. Dr. Schweitzer agreed, and in April 1957 he delivered remarks that resonated widely with global public opinion. Subsequently the two maintained a special relationship that lasted over the years.[27] Through his activities Cousins also developed a relationship with Indian prime minister Nehru and published a book about their discussions.[28] Other contacts within Cousins's international network included British philosopher Bertrand Russell, who was active in the nuclear disarmament campaign, Filipino diplomat Carlos Romulo, and Masatoshi Matsushita, Japan's envoy to the Nuclear Test Ban Treaty talks.[29]

Cousins also focused on the administration in Washington and tried to build a relationship with the various presidents and influence their policies. His first contact with Dwight Eisenhower was in 1951, when Eisenhower, a NATO commander, wrote to Cousins in response to an editorial in his magazine *Saturday Review*.[30] Evidently Eisenhower had been following Cousins's writings. Similarly, Arthur Larson, an aide to Eisenhower, claimed that during a meeting with Eisenhower in August 1956, the president, after querying whether he read the *Saturday Review*, had shown him an editorial by Cousins on the hydrogen bomb, adding that the article had left a deep impression on him.[31]

Cousins wrote to Eisenhower throughout the latter's presidential terms and often received a response. But his efforts to develop a dialogue on the nuclear issue ran into barriers posed by Lewis Strauss, chairman of the Atomic Energy Commission, who was strongly opposed to Cousins's views and concerned about their influence on the president. Thus, for example, Cousins's request to meet with the president to brief him on the meeting with Dr. Schweitzer was declined, as was his proposal that the president hold a discussion on nuclear testing with a group of scientists who were not participating in governmental nuclear programs. After Strauss's departure the situation changed, and Cousins's access to the president improved. The two corresponded in May 1959 regarding Cousins's proposal for a presidential lecture on world law; met in August 1959 to discuss Cousins's visit to the USSR; corresponded in March 1960 about nuclear arms control; and met in New York in September 1960.[32]

Under the Kennedy administration, a special relationship developed between Cousins and the White House. Throughout Kennedy's presidency (1961–1963), the two frequently exchanged letters on a range of issues, with Cousins offering Kennedy suggestions, copies of articles he had authored, draft texts for speeches, or information. Kennedy requested that Cousins write to him directly when he deemed it appropriate, and he typically responded to these letters.[33] The Kennedy–Cousins correspondence included exchanges about US efforts to convey information on nuclear testing to the public in the Soviet Union (November 1961); exchanges about US policy in Congo and Laos (January–February 1962); and statistical information from Cousins to Kennedy regarding the results of surveys on the American public's attitude towards the UN (March–April 1962).[34]

The correspondence between Cousins and the White House reveals that the Kennedy administration indeed followed Cousins's writings. In one letter, for example, Kennedy added a handwritten note telling Cousins that he had enjoyed reading his article on Laos in the "excellent" magazine he edited.[35] In another instance, Pierre Salinger, White House press secretary during the Kennedy administration, sent Cousins a letter commending him on an article he had written regarding US–USSR relations and adding his own reaction to the article, which he asked that Cousins not share with others.[36] Moreover, Cousins and Kennedy met on a number of occasions: in March 1962 Cousins participated in a meeting between the president and representatives from the American Association for the United Nations, and in April 1962 Cousins and his wife were dinner guests at the White House.[37] McGeorge Bundy, Kennedy's national security advisor, related in 1991, after Cousins's death, that the relationship between Cousins and Kennedy was "unusually direct and personal for a notable editor and modern President" and "the President liked and respected Norman ... they shared a deep common concern about the search for peace." According to Bundy, Kennedy always wanted to know Cousins's current view on issues such as the UN, arms control, and relations with Khrushchev.[38]

## The beginning of Cousins's PPE activities

Cousins's activities naturally led him to promote contact with the USSR as well. In 1954 American peace movements began drawing attention in the Soviet Union. Unlike Stalin, Khrushchev ascribed importance to Western "peace forces" and was open to dialogue between the USSR and these forces. In 1955 the Soviet embassy in Washington prepared an internal report surveying the history of the public campaign in the United States against nuclear testing, and an official Soviet article published in 1958 cited Cousins.[39]

On 30 January 1959, a group of American public figures – including Cousins – sent a letter addressed to Kennedy, Khrushchev, and Macmillan calling for serious negotiations on a test ban treaty. Khrushchev sent a

**Figure 2.1** President John F. Kennedy with representatives from the American Association for the United Nations, March 1962; Norman Cousins is third from the right, behind Kennedy

response arguing that the American position on inspections was impeding negotiations.[40] Later, in early 1961, SANE sent a letter to the leaders of the United States, USSR, UK, and France, and this time, too, Khrushchev sent a response, explaining that he supported a test ban treaty and viewed disarmament as the cardinal problem facing the world, and expressing hope that the activities of SANE would bear fruit.[41]

On 8 March 1961, Cousins sent Khrushchev a letter seeking clarification of the Soviet position on various issues related to disarmament and to a test ban treaty. Cousins sent Khrushchev similar letters with lists of questions on other occasions as well. On at least one occasion Khrushchev replied to these questions in a lengthy and detailed letter, explaining to Cousins that although there were ideological differences between the countries, it was possible to work together to promote peace – "you can work for peace without becoming a communist. And we can work for peace without becoming capitalists."[42] In August 1961, following the Soviet declaration that it was lifting its moratorium, Cousins sent Khrushchev a letter criticizing his decision.[43]

Cousins tried repeatedly to secure a visa to visit the Soviet Union, but his requests were consistently denied until 1958, when he was invited to deliver a series of lectures in the Soviet Union. Underpinning the invitation was a cultural exchange agreement that the US and USSR had signed in January 1958. The visit took place (in coordination with the State Department) in June 1959, and while in the Soviet Union Cousins met with a variety of figures and organizations, including leaders of the Soviet Peace Committee and the writers' union.[44] Alice Bobrysheva, a member of the Soviet Peace Committee, wrote that in June 1959 she was asked to organize a meeting between the Committee and Cousins, towards which end she received biographical information and details about his positions and activities. She was surprised to discover that Cousins had spoken out fiercely against the Soviet Union, including against the Soviet intervention in Hungary in 1956 and the use of the Peace Committee as a Soviet propaganda tool. Bobrysheva claimed that at the time the Peace Committee only worked with communists from other countries who supported Soviet policy, and she therefore found it hard to understand the decision to invite an "anti-Soviet" figure to meet with the Committee. In retrospect she wrote that the decision had been taken at the highest echelons of the Communist Party, and in her view the knowledge that President Eisenhower supported the visit influenced this decision.[45]

Following his visit to the Soviet Union, and after meeting with President Eisenhower, Cousins launched the Dartmouth Conferences, a platform for unofficial American–Soviet meetings, which began in 1960 and continued even after the end of the Cold War. The Eisenhower administration and the State Department supported the idea, and it later received approval from the Soviet side as well. The project was intended to infuse substance into the cultural exchange agreement signed between the two states, and during the conferences participants discussed a range of issues, including arms control, aid to developing states, and measures to promote relations between the two states and societies.[46] According to Voorhees, Cousins was "the heart of the Dartmouth Conference" and the dialogue it facilitated "was a result of his vision and efforts."[47]

Cousins had proposed the project at a meeting with the Soviet Peace Committee, whose members then conveyed the proposal to the Soviet leadership. In November 1959 they informed him that they had received approval and suggested holding the first meeting as soon as possible. The approval was possible thanks to support from Khrushchev and the Central Committee of the Communist Party. During preparatory discussions in advance of the conferences, Soviet delegates proposed that the meetings be held between representatives of the Soviet Peace Committee and leaders of American peace groups. According to Bobrysheva, the Soviet side had a hard time accepting the concept of a "private citizen" as understood in the capitalist world. Cousins, however, insisted that the participants not be acting as representatives of governmental institutions, but rather participating in their capacity as individuals. On the American side, Cousins led the work of compiling the list of participants for the first conference, while on the Soviet side participants were chosen by the Peace Committee and approved by the leadership, with Khrushchev's involvement in selecting the head of the Soviet delegation.[48]

The first conference took place in October 1960 at Dartmouth College in New Hampshire. The American delegation was headed by Cousins and Professor Philip Mosely, an expert in Soviet studies, while the Soviet delegation was headed by Aleksander Korneichuk, a member of the Central Committee of the Soviet Communist Party and a close associate of Khrushchev.[49] According to Bobrysheva, Cousins and Korneichuk quickly formed a special bond, which was the key to the success of the first conference.[50] After the conference, members of the Soviet delegation visited Cousins at his home and met his family.[51] Upon returning to the Soviet Union, the delegates delivered a detailed report on the conference to the Peace Committee leadership and the Communist Party Central Committee. They also reported on the event at a public conference in Moscow attended by journalists, academics, and students. In his remarks at this conference, Korneichuk emphasized Cousins's role as the initiator and organizer of the project.[52]

The second conference took place on the Crimean Peninsula in the Soviet Union in May 1961, shortly before the scheduled summit between Kennedy and Khrushchev in Vienna. The two sides used the meeting to transmit messages in advance of the summit: American participants conveyed messages they had received from the Kennedy administration regarding the president's expectations of the summit to their Soviet counterparts, and a Soviet delegate relayed messages about Khrushchev's aims with respect to the summit to an American colleague at the conference.[53]

The participants at the Dartmouth Conferences often reported on the discussions to Washington or Moscow.[54] Soviet archives, for example, have revealed a detailed report on the second conference that had been prepared for Khrushchev by the Soviet delegates, and which included summaries of analyses that had been presented by Cousins.[55] Through such reports the Soviet leadership learned about Cousins and his positions. Moreover, in parallel to the conferences, a dialogue developed between Cousins and his Soviet counterpart, Korneichuk. When the Soviet Union announced that it would be resuming nuclear testing, in August 1961, Cousins wrote to Korneichuk urging him to persuade his leadership to overturn this decision. Korneichuk rejected Cousins's request and, in his response, defended the Soviet policy.[56]

The third conference took place in Andover, near Boston, in October 1962. The Soviet delegation was headed by Evgeny Fedorov, secretary-general of the Soviet Academy of Sciences and the Soviet delegate to the talks in Geneva, and Yuri Zhukov, a leading Soviet journalist. The conference took place in the shadow of the Cuban missile crisis, with both sides deciding to continue the discussions despite the dramatic events. The Soviet delegation had had some internal division in this regard, until its members consulted with the Soviet ambassador to Washington, Anatoly Dobrynin, who advised that they continue the conference as planned.[57]

During the conference there emerged an initiative that reflects the interface between the unofficial and official at these conferences. The initiative was launched in light of the presence of Father Felix Morlion, president of the Pro Deo University in Rome and a close associate of the pope,[58] who had been invited by Cousins on the basis of his efforts to promote a dialogue between the Vatican and Moscow. In reaction to reports about the Cuban missile crisis, participants raised the possibility of Pope John XXIII intervening and calling for the withdrawal of military shipments as well as a lifting of the embargo. Conference participants on both sides conveyed this proposal to the leaders of the two states: Cousins contacted President Kennedy's advisor Ted Sorensen, who discussed the idea with the president, and the Soviet delegates relayed the proposal to Moscow. Khrushchev expressed support, while Kennedy welcomed the pope's intervention but refrained from issuing a call referring to the embargo. The initiative led to a public declaration by the pope that addressed all of Kennedy's requirements and was submitted in advance for approval by both sides. The pope's call did not have a significant impact on the crisis, but the incident attests to the potential of the Dartmouth Conferences to be at the center of an international diplomatic initiative.[59]

Cousins sought to promote another initiative during the conference, proposing that the delegations publish a joint statement in which they would recommend a ten-day moratorium on action and the establishment of a UN commission to examine the facts immediately and formulate recommendations to resolve the crisis. The Soviet side responded with a counter-proposal, suggesting that a declaration be issued calling for a meeting between Kennedy and Khrushchev. As the parties were unable to reach an agreement, the conference concluded without a joint statement.[60]

## First Cousins–Khrushchev meeting, December 1962

In November 1962 Cousins received a telephone call from the Soviet ambassador to Washington, Dobrynin, inviting him to meet with Khrushchev in

Moscow on 14 December. The background to the invitation was a suggestion by Father Morlion that Cousins be used as a mediator between Rome and Moscow. During the Andover conference, Father Morlion had spoken with two Soviet delegates, telling them that he had reason to believe that the Vatican would accept Cousins as a mediator for contact with the Soviet Union and offering to arrange a meeting between Cousins and Khrushchev after he had met with the pope. Father Morlion recounts that when he asked the Soviet delegates whether they trusted Cousins, "Their answer was the first authentic human manifestation of really profound friendship."[61] The Soviet delegates expressed openness to the idea but said they would respond officially only after returning to Moscow. Dobrynin's phone call to Cousins attests to Moscow's acceptance of the initiative. In a confidential memorandum to the pope and the Kennedy administration in November 1962, Father Morlion explained that the selection of Cousins as a mediator stemmed from his being a "unique case" who had earned Khrushchev's personal confidence on the basis of his peace activism and his books. The memorandum further claimed that Cousins was perceived in Moscow as a typical "leader of a new peace loving generation" who was committed to "the human family and the cause of peace."[62]

Cousins reported on the planned visit to White House press secretary Pierre Salinger,[63] who spoke about it with the president and informed Cousins that the White House had no objection to the visit. Cousins was even invited to Washington to meet with Senior White House aide Ralph Dungan and later with President Kennedy. At the White House meeting, Kennedy spoke with Cousins about the need to establish peaceful relations with the Soviet Union and reduce tension between the countries, pointing to a test ban treaty as an immediate possible measure. But he also argued that the Russian leadership was suspicious and opposed to the minimal inspections needed for such an agreement. Kennedy further asked Cousins to impress upon Khrushchev the seriousness of his intention to improve relations: "I'm not sure Khrushchev knows this, but I don't think there's any man in American politics who's more eager than I am to put Cold War animosities behind us and get down to the hard business of building friendly relations."[64]

After a brief visit to Rome and a meeting with Vatican representatives,[65] Cousins arrived in Moscow, where he met with various Soviet representatives and colleagues from the Dartmouth Conferences, and was invited to attend a speech by Khrushchev at the Supreme Soviet.[66] Zhukov told Cousins about the tension between China and the USSR, and about the criticism Khrushchev was receiving in the aftermath of the Cuban missile crisis. He emphasized that Khrushchev's policy towards the West was being put to the test. Korneichuk repeatedly underscored Khrushchev's interest in reaching agreements with the West that would justify his conduct in Cuba and policy of peaceful coexistence, noting also that Khrushchev was interested in putting an end to the arms race, among other reasons because he wanted to direct resources to domestic economic goals.[67] When Khrushchev and Cousins eventually met, they conversed for more than three hours on a wide range of issues.[68]

Their meeting began on a personal note, with Khrushchev asking Cousins to tell him about his family and wondering why his daughters had not joined him on his trip. Later Khrushchev spoke with Cousins openly about issues such as the Soviet Union's economic problems, the transformation of the state's Communist Party into a destructive bureaucratic system, and his feelings about China's harsh criticism of him. Khrushchev's remarks during the meeting indicate that he was well aware of Cousins's activities and the Dartmouth Conferences. He mentioned the three conferences that had taken place up till then and jokingly said, "Everybody speaks now well to me of America. Do you know what you have done?" Khrushchev also told Cousins that he had received a report about the discussions at Andover, and his impression was that "real work is done for peace."[69]

Part of their discussion focused on the question of Vatican–Soviet relations, and in this context the two discussed the possibility of creating a channel for dialogue between the parties, as well as the Vatican's demand that the Soviet Union release Ukrainian archbishop Josyf Slipyj, who had been in a Soviet prison since 1947. The latter part of their conversation touched on US–USSR relations: Khrushchev emphasized his interest in improving relations between the states, and said that towards this end he would agree to meet the president "more than halfway." He asserted that the immediate measure needed was a treaty to ban nuclear testing. Khrushchev made it clear that the Soviet Union was not opposed to inspections and was prepared to accept "reasonable inspection," arguing that it was possible to reach an agreement on this matter that would satisfy both sides. Cousins reported during the conversation that in his view Kennedy was very interested in a test ban treaty, and that there was no one in American politics more interested in ending the Cold War. Cousins also mentioned his ideas about strengthening the UN as a mechanism to ensure world peace, but Khrushchev was skeptical, claiming that he regarded the UN as a tool in the hands of the US, and that he would not agree to UN intervention in his country. At the end of the discussion Khrushchev gave Cousins handwritten messages of greeting intended for President Kennedy and Pope John XXIII on the occasion of Christmas.[70]

Cousins then left the Soviet Union for the Vatican, where he met with the pope and presented him with Khrushchev's Christmas greeting. Upon his return to the United States, Cousins sent Khrushchev a letter with a summary of his conversation with the pope and a medallion he had received from the pope. Likewise, he sent Kennedy a detailed memorandum on his visit as well as the message of greetings from Khrushchev.[71]

## Deadlock in official negotiations and preparations for another visit

A few days after Cousins's visit, Khrushchev sent President Kennedy a dramatic letter in which he declared that "for the noble and humane goal of ceasing nuclear weapon tests," he was willing to meet the president "halfway" on the controversial issue of inspections. Khrushchev noted that during the meeting between Arthur Dean and Vasily Kuznetsov on 30 October, Dean had said that the US would agree to two to four on-site inspections annually on Soviet territory, and on this basis Khrushchev expressed his willingness to agree to two to three inspections annually. This was a significant declaration of consent to on-site inspections on Soviet territory; the letter marked a shift from the position stated in Khrushchev's letter to Macmillan in November 1962, in which he had voiced objection to this condition.[72] The Kennedy administration viewed the letter favorably, as an indication of genuine Soviet interest in proceeding towards a treaty. At the same time, however, the letter exposed differences in the two states' interpretations of the Dean–Kuznetsov conversation, which before long erupted in a crisis. Kennedy, in his response to Khrushchev, welcomed the new proposal but asserted that Dean had not expressed consent to two to four annual inspections – but rather to eight to ten – pointing out that this was a significant compromise relative to the original position, which called for twelve to twenty inspections.[73] Kennedy's position on the matter was also influenced by his assessment that it would be hard to secure Senate support for an agreement that required only a small number of annual on-site inspections.[74]

The controversy over the number of on-site inspections was also at the heart of talks that took place in New York among delegates of the United States, the Soviet Union, and Britain in January 1963, and of the Eighteen Nation Disarmament Committee (ENDC) talks that took place in Geneva in February 1963,[75] where the parties reached a deadlock. The Soviet delegates voiced strong disappointment with the American response to their proposal, going so far as to publicly expose recent correspondence between Kennedy and Khrushchev so as to persuade international public opinion of the validity of their stance. At the talks themselves, the Americans proposed a compromise of six to seven annual inspections, but the Soviets categorically rejected this proposal, emphasizing that they would not agree to additional concessions beyond those contained in their own proposal. At this stage various international actors began to express concerns that the talks might collapse, dashing any hopes of reaching an agreement.[76]

In parallel to these developments, Cousins's contacts with officials in the US administration, the USSR, and the Vatican led to another visit to the Soviet Union. In January 1963, Cousins was invited to a meeting with the Soviet ambassador to Washington, who informed him that following their meeting, Khrushchev had decided to release Archbishop Slipyj as a gesture to the pope.[77] After the archbishop's release, Cousins continued to provide a channel for the exchange of messages between the USSR and the Vatican, specifically in the context of two incidents that clouded the relations between the parties, and following which Cousins conveyed clarifications from the Vatican to Khrushchev and Dobrynin.[78] In light of the success of the archbishop's release, Cousins was again approached by the Vatican for a mission in the USSR – to secure the release of the archbishop of Prague, Josef Beran, who was also imprisoned in the Soviet Union. Subsequently, Cousins initiated meetings with Dungan and Secretary of State Rusk regarding the possibility of another visit to the Soviet Union. Rusk informed Cousins of the state of negotiations, expressing his concerns about the talks collapsing. He explained the misunderstanding over the number of annual inspections and suggested that Cousins convey the seriousness of US intentions to Khrushchev and propose to him that the negotiations focus on all issues except this one, and that after negotiations had been completed, the two leaders – Kennedy and Khrushchev – would meet and reach an agreement on this issue.[79]

After the meeting with Rusk, Cousins met again with Ambassador Dobrynin and conveyed a request to meet once again with Khrushchev. Before long the Soviet ambassador contacted Cousins and informed him that a meeting with Khrushchev had been scheduled for 12 April.[80] According to Alice Bobrysheva, this meeting was possible thanks to Dobrynin and the leaders of the Soviet delegation at the Dartmouth Conferences.[81] At the meeting that later took place between Dobrynin and Robert Kennedy – the president's younger brother and the attorney-general in the Kennedy administration – Dobrynin reported to Kennedy about plans for the meeting between Cousins and Khrushchev and asked him about the nature of relations between Cousins and President Kennedy.[82]

Once it was known that Cousins was expected to meet again with Khrushchev, the White House set up a meeting between Cousins and President Kennedy. On 12 March they had an eighty-minute conversation during which the president reviewed the background of the dispute over inspections, underscoring that the most important mission now was to convince Khrushchev that Kennedy was genuinely interested in reaching an agreement and to put an end to the threat of nuclear war.[83] After their meeting, the two continued to correspond. In a letter to the president, Cousins discussed the two main points he was committed to presenting to Khrushchev: first, to emphasize that it would be a mistake to interpret the misunderstanding over inspections as a sign that the US was not interested in an agreement; second, to attest that there was no one in American politics who believed more strongly than Kennedy in the need to cultivate peaceful relations with the Soviet Union. Kennedy wished Cousins success in his travels and expressed appreciation for his efforts. The two also discussed Cousins's public activity, and Kennedy praised these efforts but suggested that at this stage the campaign focus on educating and informing the public about nuclear testing, and that it refrain from mobilizing public support for a treaty until a genuine breakthrough in negotiations had been achieved. Kennedy pointed out that efforts in the public arena would become especially important once the treaty had been submitted to the Senate for ratification.[84]

On the eve of Cousins's departure for the Soviet Union, Kennedy contacted him by telephone and emphasized the administration's hope of breaking the deadlock. Kennedy again asked that Cousins try to persuade the Soviet leader that there had been "an honest misunderstanding" and that rather than debate conflicting versions, they should pave the way to a fresh start. On his way to the Soviet Union, Cousins stopped in Rome, where he met with senior Vatican officials and received an official copy in Russian of a new papal encyclical on peace to deliver to Khrushchev.[85]

## The second meeting between Khrushchev and Cousins

The second encounter between Khrushchev and Cousins took place on 12 April 1963. Cousins first arrived in Moscow with his two daughters, and after meeting with colleagues from the Dartmouth Conferences, he and his daughters were flown to the city of Sochi, along the coast of the Black Sea, and from there driven to Khrushchev's retreat in the city of Gagra. The meeting began in a spirit of camaraderie and light conversation. Khrushchev told Cousins that he came to the Black Sea dacha whenever he needed to contemplate important problems or write important speeches. Khrushchev also gave his guests a tour of his home and played a game of badminton with Cousins and his daughters. Cousins was impressed by Khrushchev's state of health and physical fitness, which differed from what the media had been reporting.[86]

After the tour, Cousins's two daughters were ushered to the swimming pool, while the two men sat down to a long conversation with the company of an interpreter and a minute taker. First they briefly addressed matters relating to Soviet–Vatican relations – the release of Archbishop Slipyj, a request to release Archbishop Beran,[87] and the papal encyclical on peace – but most of their conversation focused on US–Soviet relations and the test ban treaty negotiations.

Figure 2.2 Soviet leader Nikita Khrushchev, Alice Bobrysheva (member of the Soviet Peace Committee), and Candice Cousins (Norman Cousins's daughter), April 1963; Bobrysheva is on the left and Cousins is in the middle

Cousins began his remarks by pointing out that he had come not on an official mission, but as a private citizen. Nevertheless, he explained, Kennedy had asked him to try to clarify the misunderstanding that had occurred over the US position on the issue of on-site inspections. Khrushchev questioned how this could be seen as a misunderstanding, when both Jerome Wiesner, Kennedy's science and technology advisor, at his meeting with Fedorov, and Dean, at his meeting with Kuznetsov, had presented this as the official American stance. He then presented Cousins with his version: following the Cuban missile crisis, he had seen a real opportunity to promote a treaty, and had therefore approached the members of his government and persuaded them to accept the American condition of three annual on-site inspections, although from the Soviet perspective this was not necessary. The assumption had been that accepting this condition would make it possible to conclude a treaty. But after informing the Americans of the Soviet agreement, he was stunned to discover that their condition had changed, that they were now demanding eight inspections, and now Khrushchev felt humiliated and deceived. In this context he also pointed to the criticism he had received from the Chinese leadership, which called him naive and attacked his policy of coexistence with the West.[88]

Cousins, stressing that President Kennedy admired both Dean and Kuznetsov, suggested that they not enter into a pointless debate about the discussion that had taken place between the two, but rather see it as an honest misunderstanding and make a fresh start. Cousins also tried to convince the Soviet leader that Kennedy was serious and his intentions genuine. As evidence, Cousins told Khrushchev that he and other representatives of civil society organizations working to promote a test ban treaty had shared their plans for a public campaign with the president, who had taken an interest and even offered suggestions. "It seemed to me inconceivable that he would have encouraged this public campaign if he had publicly advocated a test ban only for propaganda purposes, as the Soviet press had charged."[89] In addition, Cousins showed Khrushchev one of the flyers they planned to use for the campaign. He then explained that Kennedy could not receive Senate support for the treaty on the basis of only three annual inspections.[90]

During the meeting Cousins presented the suggestion Rusk had raised – namely, that the talks in Geneva focus on the other issues, aside from on-site inspections, and that after agreement had been reached on those issues, the two leaders would meet again to resolve the dispute in this matter. Khrushchev rejected the proposal, explaining that he felt he had been misled and he would not agree to return to his government and request additional flexibility. Moreover, he asserted, if any change were to take place in the Soviet stance, it would be in the other direction – towards withdrawal of its consent to three inspections per year. Khrushchev told Cousins that he was under pressure from military and nuclear scientific circles, which were calling for an additional series of tests, and added that he was thinking of granting authorization. The possibility of renewed testing gravely concerned Cousins: "You've broken my heart. If this opportunity is missed, there may never be another." Cousins argued that if the Soviet Union resumed testing, the United States would respond in kind and the situation would escalate: "None of this adds either to American or Russian security."[91]

Cousins tried to present Khrushchev with another argument, recalling that during the Cuban missile crisis a Soviet spokesman had announced that no missiles had been stationed in Cuba – a statement that turned out to be untrue – and on this basis he proposed that one misunderstanding cancel the other. Finally, after a lengthy discussion of the issue, Khrushchev agreed to accept Kennedy's explanation and turn over a new leaf. At the same time, however, he stressed that the ball was now in the American court and it depended on the US response: "You can tell the President I accept his explanation of an honest misunderstanding and suggest that we get moving. But the next move is up to him."[92]

The two also discussed the American proposal for a bilateral agreement on authors' rights of copyright. Khrushchev presented his negative impression of the state of American culture, claiming that the United States had become a nation of television viewers and comic book readers. Cousins tried to correct this impression by presenting data about reading and the consumption of culture in the United States and describing the educational television networks.

Cousins also told Khrushchev that when speaking before various audiences about promoting peace with the Soviet Union, he was often asked how one could speak of peace when Khrushchev had announced that he would "bury" the United States. To this Khrushchev replied that what he had meant was that the capitalist system in the United States itself – not the Soviet Union – would bury the country: "The workers in your society will bury the system." He pointed out that although he was fiercely critical of the capitalist regime in the United States, he had great admiration for the American people. Towards the end of the meeting, Khrushchev reiterated his support for a policy of peaceful coexistence between the two superpowers. He asserted that Stalin had been wrong to isolate the Soviet Union from the rest of the world, noting that many in both countries tended to stress differences, but that it was necessary to speak about common interests as well: "The two most powerful countries in the world could find some way to live in peace, but the next move was up to the United States."[93]

When their six-hour conversation came to a close, Cousins thanked Khrushchev and returned to the United States. Glenn Seaborg, chairman of the Atomic Energy Agency under Kennedy, later wrote that the conversation between Cousins and Khrushchev "did more than explain history – it helped to make history."[94]

## Between the second meeting and the treaty: Kennedy's speech

On 22 April 1963, Cousins arrived in Washington to brief President Kennedy on his visit to the Soviet Union. He informed the president that Khrushchev had felt deceived after persuading his government to agree to three inspections per year, and that he was under heavy pressure to adopt a more hardline policy. Kennedy told Cousins that over time he was discovering how difficult it was to maintain communication on the important issues even with allies of the United States, let alone the Soviet Union. Ironically, according to the president, he and Khrushchev were in the same political position of wanting to prevent a nuclear war but having to deal with hardliners, and he stressed that lack of progress strengthened the opponents on both sides, who then reinforced each other.

Cousins asserted that the issue of a test ban had become the watershed issue that would determine the fate of Khrushchev's policy of coexistence with the West: successful negotiations would prove that his policy had borne fruit, whereas failure would provide a foundation for the Chinese to criticize his policy and for the perpetuation of propaganda against him within the Soviet Union. Cousins argued that Khrushchev was at a critical juncture and that the stalemate could lead to the end of negotiations and to a Soviet shift towards closer relations with China, and added that a high-level Chinese delegation was planning to visit Moscow in June. President Kennedy was glad to hear that Khrushchev had agreed to make a fresh start and could empathize with his domestic problems, but wondered how they could overcome the dispute. Cousins explained that Khrushchev was now waiting for the Americans to take the initiative, and offered two suggestions. First, the United States could accept the conditions proposed by the Soviet Union and agree on a treaty for a trial period of months. His second suggestion was to make a public call for an end to the Cold War, proposing a "breathtaking new approach toward the Russian people" and offering a "fresh start in American—Russian relationships." Kennedy said that he would think about this and requested that Cousins prepare a memorandum on the issue.[95]

According to Sorensen, President Kennedy had nearly lost hope by the spring of 1963, but the message that Khrushchev had conveyed to Cousins, an additional message relayed by a Soviet scientist at a conference in London, and the Senate decision to suspend atmospheric nuclear testing had helped him maintain some measure of hope.[96] After his meeting with Kennedy, and at the president's request, Cousins met with Dungan; Llewellyn Thompson, the former US ambassador to Moscow; William Foster, chief of the Arms Control and Disarmament Agency; and Adrian Fisher, Foster's deputy. Cousins found these figures to be receptive and came away with the impression that they were determined to find a path to a breakthrough.[97]

Following his visit to the White House and as requested, Cousins sent a letter to President Kennedy in which he elaborated on his proposal. On 30 April 1963, he wrote "It seems to me that you ought to beat Mr. K to the punch. The moment is now at hand for the most important single speech of your Presidency. It should be a speech which, in its breathtaking proposals for genuine peace, in its tone of friendliness for the Soviet people and its understanding of their ordeal during the last war, in its inspired advocacy of the human interest, would create a world groundswell of support for American leadership."[98] Cousins expressed concern that during his speech at the upcoming meeting of the Soviet Communist Party Central Committee, scheduled for May, Khrushchev would announce a fundamental change in Soviet policy, towards closer relations with China and increasing confrontation with the West. He argued that a speech by Kennedy along the lines proposed would make it more difficult for Khrushchev to deliver a speech that was hostile to the United States, would shift the ball to the Soviet court, and would compel Khrushchev to continue the dialogue with the United States.[99]

Cousins's letter had a tremendous impact on President Kennedy, who relayed it to Ted Sorensen with instructions to write a speech along the lines proposed by Cousins. Sorensen then invited Cousins to Washington, informing him that the president was interested in incorporating suggestions raised by Cousins at their meeting and in his letter into his upcoming speech at American University on 10 June. The Soviet Communist Party meeting had been postponed until June, and the president's speech at the University seemed the most appropriate forum for the purpose. Sorensen asked Cousins to provide him with ideas for the speech, and on 1 June Cousins presented him with a draft speech, explaining that it addressed both Khrushchev and the American public.[100] In an April 1964 interview, Sorensen stated that one of the main sources of inspiration for this speech by Kennedy was Cousins's letter to the president.[101] It should be noted that while Cousins was included in the process of drafting the speech, Kennedy excluded many administration officials who would normally have been involved in drafting a speech that addressed foreign relations. Only a select few were privy to the process, and the draft was shared with Defense and State Department officials only two days before it was to be delivered.[102]

In parallel, Cousins maintained channels of communication with the Soviets and continued trying to persuade them not to abandon the efforts to reach an agreement. He sent a letter to Khrushchev thanking him for his hospitality and briefing him about the meeting at the White House. He conveyed that he had presented Khrushchev's position regarding recent developments to the president, and that the president had been understanding, expressing the hope that the talks continue and an agreement could be reached. Cousins again urged Khrushchev not to abandon his policy of pursuing peace because of an unfortunate misunderstanding, emphasizing that the president had expressed a genuine interest in bridging the divides and reaching an agreement. Cousins asked that Khrushchev conduct a direct dialogue with Kennedy before reaching "hard conclusions" about the possibility of achieving an agreement. To underscore the fact that his remarks had President Kennedy's backing, Cousins wrote that he had presented the letter to Kennedy to ensure that it indeed accorded with his views.[103]

In addition, Cousins met with Dobrynin and explained to him that Kennedy's intentions were genuine and he very much wanted a treaty. He said that Kennedy had promised him to invest a great deal of effort to break out of the stalemate, and he asked that the ambassador relay this fact to the leadership in Moscow. Dobrynin was pleased to hear this but made it clear that, in light of the recent crisis and developments in his country, it would be difficult for him to convey such a message to Moscow regarding the president's intentions unless he could point to something specific to back it up. At this stage Cousins attempted, once again, to promote his private proposal that there be a trial period for a test ban, as an interim arrangement on the path to a long-term agreement. He believed that this approach could help the parties overcome their disagreement as well as their domestic political problems. Under his proposal, the parties would agree to a trial period of six months during which all the elements of a regime banning nuclear testing would be implemented, with a minimal number of on-site inspections (two). At the end of this period the two sides would have clearer answers as to the existing points of dispute and the conditions for reaching an agreement would be more favorable. In presenting the idea to Ambassador Dobrynin, Cousins stressed that this was his own proposal as a private citizen. He argued that if the Soviet Union believed that a small number of inspections would suffice, then the trial period would validate its position. The ambassador took an interest in the proposal.[104]

Cousins also met with members of Kennedy's administration to discuss his proposal. He prepared a detailed memorandum for the president, explaining that such an arrangement could be implemented by presidential order, with no need for Senate ratification. In terms of informing the public, he suggested explaining that, given the treaty's importance for security, it was necessary to have a trial period to test the system before submitting the treaty for Senate ratification.[105] Kennedy's national security advisor, Bundy, informed Cousins that his proposal had been examined but the administration had identified two key problems with it. First, the trial period would not provide an opportunity to examine inspection capabilities because presumably the Soviets would not conduct any tests or violate the treaty during this period. Second, the proposal did not resolve the dispute over the number of on-site inspections, and a trial period was not expected to change the parties' position in this regard.[106] In response to the administration's reservations, Cousins replied that he, too, did not expect the Soviets to violate the treaty during the trial period. In his view, however, this did not necessarily mean that the detection equipment could not be tested, as during this time the Soviet Union would experience many natural earthquakes and this would provide an opportunity to test the means of differentiating between natural earth movements and those that resulted from nuclear testing. Furthermore, he pointed out, his proposal was meant as a tool to maintain the dialogue while Khrushchev was preparing for the Chinese delegation's visit and the Soviet Communist Party meeting in June, and to ensure that the window of opportunity did not close in the meantime.[107]

At the official level, Kennedy, Macmillan, and Khrushchev were engaged in correspondence at this time. Kennedy and Macmillan proposed sending high-level officials to Moscow for backchannel talks in another attempt to break the deadlock. Khrushchev's response conveyed his sense of despair and strong doubts about possibilities for progress, and he once again laid the blame with his counterparts in the West for rejecting his proposal on the matter of on-site inspections. At the same time, though, he expressed a willingness to receive the delegates in Moscow. The parties then agreed that the officials would arrive in Moscow in mid-July, and Khrushchev warned against the repercussions of another failure.[108]

On 10 June 1963, the plan that had taken shape in Cousins's mind during his travels between Washington and Moscow came to fruition, as President Kennedy, speaking at American University, delivered a speech that was unprecedented in its approach to relations with the Soviet Union. He called for a reassessment of the US's basic assumptions and a reexamination of the approach to the Soviet Union and the Cold War, urging that people reject the view of peace as an unattainable, unrealistic goal, in favor of a more practical perspective that recognized that peace could only be achieved through a gradual and complex process involving a series of measures and agreements, rather than any magic formula. He cautioned against a distorted view of the other side – a view that ignored the Russian people's achievements and acts of courage – and called for the pursuit of measures to improve relations between the two blocs, such as strengthening the UN, establishing a direct line of communication between the superpowers, and pursuing arms control measures. In closing, Kennedy remarked that it was necessary to make a fresh start in the talks on a nuclear test ban treaty, and he expressed hope that the high-level negotiations in Moscow would soon yield a treaty. As a show of good faith, he declared that the United States would not conduct atmospheric nuclear tests so long as other states refrained from doing so as well.[109] According to Sorensen this was "the first Presidential speech in eighteen years to succeed in reaching beyond the cold war" and Seaborg described it as Kennedy's supreme effort to cut through the walls of mistrust between East and West.[110]

A comparative analysis between the draft speech Cousins had prepared for Kennedy[111] and his letters to the administration, on the one hand, and President Kennedy's speech at American University, on the other, can help us identify which of Cousins's ideas were incorporated into the official speech. For example, the discussion of "genuine peace" at the start of Cousins's draft appears in Kennedy's speech as well, and some of the sentences are even identical or only slightly modified. Another element that appeared in Cousins's draft (and in his letter to Sorensen) as well as Kennedy's speech was the claim that war is not inevitable or beyond human control, and that problems created by human beings can be resolved by human beings. Another example is a proposal by Cousins – which appeared in both his memorandum to Kennedy and his draft proposed speech – to refer to the heavy price paid by the Soviet Union during the Second World War. Such a reference did indeed appear in the official speech.

On the day of the speech, Kennedy's advisor Schlesinger telephoned Cousins to discuss it. After the call, Cousins wrote to Schlesinger to thank him for the call, stating that the speech "met the demands of the situation brilliantly and inspiringly. This is the stuff of which historical change is made."[112] He wrote to Kennedy as well, saying that "it was that rare event when a man speaks both to the moment and to the next generation. The first calls for courage, the second for vision. You had both."[113] The president thanked Cousins for his remarks.[114]

The Soviet response to Kennedy's American University speech was positive. Khrushchev described it as "the best speech by any president since Roosevelt," and the Russian press published the full text of the speech.[115] The Soviets also responded to the speech with a number of gestures, such as abandoning the fifteen-year-old practice of jamming Western radio broadcasts – and foremost among them *Voice of America* – across the USSR, and in talks that took place shortly after the speech they agreed, for the first time after consistently objecting, to inspections by the International Atomic Energy Agency at the Agency's reactors. Furthermore, in the aftermath of the speech the two sides agreed to establish a permanent line of communication, and on 20 June 1963, in Geneva, delegates of the United States and the Soviet Union signed what came to be known as the Hot Line Agreement. The most significant element of the Soviet response, however, was presented by Khrushchev at a speech in Berlin on 2 July, when he proposed a partial test ban treaty that – in contrast to his past position – would not be conditional on a moratorium on underground nuclear testing. At the same time, he proposed pursuing a non-aggression pact between NATO states and Warsaw Pact states in order to improve the international atmosphere.[116]

The date of Kennedy's speech corresponded with the timeframe proposed by Cousins – before the meeting of the Soviet Communist Party and on the same day that the Chinese delegation arrived in Moscow. As Cousins had predicted, the Chinese delegation bore a letter – the content of which was released to the international press – in which China demanded that the communist world adopt a more hardline position towards the West, and condemned Khrushchev for his weakness and for seeking coexistence with capitalism. At this stage Khrushchev had to choose between Washington and Beijing, and his decision to reprint Kennedy's speech in the Soviet press, and not to publish the Chinese letter, symbolized his choice to continue pursuing efforts to reach an agreement with the United States, rather than cultivate closer relations with China.[117] Fursenko and Naftali argue that in late April 1963, after returning to Moscow from his vacation by the Black

Sea, Khrushchev convened his senior party officials and minister of defense, and informed them of decisions that pointed to a strategic choice of pursuing relations with the United States: a willingness to agree to a partial test ban treaty (banning testing in the atmosphere, outer space, and undersea) if it turned out that a complete ban was unachievable, and a willingness to remove the question of Berlin from the agenda and not make a treaty conditional on the resolution of this issue. This position remained classified until Khrushchev publicly announced it in July 1963.[118]

Cousins stayed in touch with Khrushchev after Kennedy's speech as well. On 24 June he sent the Soviet leader a statement of support for a test ban treaty signed by American business leaders, and argued that Kennedy's leadership was having an impact on American public opinion on this issue and that there could be no doubt about the sincerity of US intentions regarding the achievement of a treaty.[119] On 17 July, Cousins sent Khrushchev a draft article he had written about their April 1963 meeting – which he had kept secret and on which he had not reported in real time – saying that he would welcome comments and corrections. He added that he believed the article could help Americans better understand the problems facing Khrushchev in negotiating a test ban treaty (the article was published only after Khrushchev left office in late 1964).[120]

Khrushchev's public statement sparked hopes regarding the anticipated negotiations in Moscow. Although a partial test ban would not address all the problems related to nuclear testing, it would provide a practical solution, allowing the parties to reach an agreement by circumventing the highly disputed question of on-site inspections. Such an agreement also had advantages at the domestic level for the United States, as it was expected to draw broader support in the Senate than a complete ban would have done. On 15 July 1963, the talks opened in Moscow, with William Averell Harriman, former US ambassador to Moscow, representing the United States, Foreign Minister Andre Gromyko representing the Soviet Union, and Lord Hailsham serving as the British delegate. On 25 July the three representatives signed the Treaty Banning Nuclear Weapon Tests in the Atmosphere, in Outer Space and Underwater, also known as the Partial Test Ban Treaty.[121]

Thus, after hundreds of nuclear tests and innumerable rounds of negotiations, the parties managed to achieve a historical, and the first significant, agreement on arms control between the superpowers. Many saw this as a potential turning point in relations between the states; British delegate Hailsham, for example, described the treaty as the greatest step forward in international relations since the start of the Cold War.[122] After the agreement was signed, Kennedy sent Cousins a dispatch about the treaty, in which he had written, "To Norman Cousins, with warm regards, JF Kennedy."[123]

### After the treaty: Cousins enlists in public campaigning

The ties between Cousins and the Kennedy administration continued and
grew even stronger after the treaty had been signed, as they joined efforts
in the struggle to enlist Senate support and mobilize American public opinion
in favor of the treaty. Cousins met with Schlesinger during this period and
discussed establishing an ad-hoc citizens' group to promote Senate ratification.
He also met with Rusk, Harriman, Deputy National Security Advisor Carl
Kaysen, and Senator Humphrey to discuss the details of the campaign. On
7 August 1963, the White House hosted a meeting between the leaders of
a newly established body – the Citizens' Committee for a Nuclear Test Ban
(CCNTB) – and President Kennedy and other administration officials. Kennedy
thanked Cousins for establishing the organization and outlined the difficulties
they were expected to encounter in the campaign to achieve a two-thirds
Senate majority for ratification of the treaty. Cousins spoke on behalf of
the CCNTB, pointing out that it had members from all spheres of life with
diverse political views, and that its objective was to reflect American public
support for the treaty. President Kennedy proposed various ideas and areas
of activity for the organization, as well as additional possible members who
might be invited to join, and he promised to personally approach some of
the figures he had nominated.[124]

After the meeting Cousins prepared and presented the White House with
a series of letters in the president's name, addressed to various figures, primarily
prominent business leaders, inviting them to join the campaign. The letters
noted that the president was striving to reach a Senate majority of four-fifths,
going beyond the necessary two-thirds, and that Cousins would be in touch
with them to discuss the issue.[125] Cousins and the CCNTB played an important
role in the public debate that took place during the leadup to Senate ratification. Cousins participated in a number of televised debates with Dr. Edward
Teller, who was leading the campaign against the treaty. He also testified
before the Senate Foreign Relations Committee. The day before his testimony
he spoke with Kennedy, who gave him some advice. During his subsequent
testimony, Cousins spoke about his meeting with Khrushchev and called
on the Senate to ratify the treaty.[126]

Cousins chaired the advisory council to the CCNTB, overseeing its activities
and publications, which included statements to the press, media interviews,
and the dissemination of informational brochures, among other measures.[127]
The Kennedy administration was extremely appreciative of Cousins's tireless
activity, and on 30 August National Security Advisor Bundy wrote to Cousins
to convey the president's deep appreciation for his and the CCNTB's efforts.[128]

The goal became a reality on 24 September 1963, when the Senate ratified
the PTBT by a majority of 80 to 19. A few days later Sorensen wrote to

Cousins, thanking him for his "excellent job on the test ban treaty," expressing the hope that they would have many more opportunities to work together. Sorensen also invited Cousins's suggestions for an upcoming speech by Kennedy.[129] On 7 October 1963, a month and a half before his assassination, President Kennedy sent a letter to Cousins, thanking him and expressing his personal appreciation for the efforts he and his colleagues in the committee had led. Kennedy wrote, "The committee made a real contribution in developing better understanding of the purpose of the treaty, and your initiative with the group was essential. ... We have many tasks ahead in seeking to establish a more peaceful and orderly world, and I look forward to working with you in our common endeavor toward that goal."[130]

## Analysis and conclusions: the impact of PPE Cousins on the official sphere

### *Influence patterns*

Historian Lawrence Wittner had the following to say about Cousins's role in the process that led to the PTBT:

> Although Kennedy and Khrushchev certainly deserve considerable credit for their willingness to back the treaty, the remarkable role of Cousins in fostering it should not be forgotten. He had helped to launch the crucial worldwide movement, mobilizing prominent individuals such as Stevenson, Schweitzer, and Nehru; creating and encouraging organizations such as SANE; and arousing worldwide public opposition to nuclear tests. Furthermore, he became a key figure in the diplomatic maneuvering that led directly to the U.S.–Soviet agreement on an atmospheric nuclear test ban.[131]

McGeorge Bundy, Kennedy's national security advisor, had the following to say in a 1991 eulogy for Cousins:

> I saw close up how Norman's insistence that we must go forward on these matters, in early 1963, became an important force in the process that led from the initially gloomy aftermath of the Cuban missile crisis, first to Kennedy's speech at American University expressing a new hope for Soviet–American peace, and then onward to the treaty that stopped most of the world's atmospheric nuclear testing. As Kennedy might have put it, this success had a hundred fathers, and Norman was surely one of them, because you can truly say that without him it might not have happened."[132]

In his study on the Dartmouth Conferences, Voorhees concluded that Cousins had provided Khrushchev and Kennedy with an important communication channel, which helped thaw Cold War relations and without which achievement of the PTBT would, at the very least, have taken longer.[133] Pietrobon argued that Kennedy's use of Cousins was one of "the most successful use[s] of a 'citizen diplomat' during the Cold War."[134]

Which influence patterns were at work in Cousins's activity as a PPE?

Cousins was able to achieve *influence through mediation* between the United States and the Soviet Union; his mediation efforts earned recognition from both states, and he successfully managed to mediate at the highest official level: between Kennedy and Khrushchev. Cousins's mediation efforts included the role of a *communicator* in that he transmitted messages relating to negotiations on a test ban treaty between the two sides. Cousins also relayed messages between the Soviet Union and the Vatican as well as between the United States and the Vatican. He physically carried documents between the parties, including Christmas greetings from Khrushchev to Kennedy and the pope.

In his capacity as a mediator, Cousins also played the part of a *formulator*, as demonstrated by his proposal to agree on a test ban treaty for a trial period, which he presented to Kennedy and Bundy as well as Soviet ambassador Dobrynin. Furthermore, he incorporated aspects of the role of a *psychoanalyst* in his mediation efforts. Evangelista claims that Cousins's meeting with Khrushchev in April 1963 was particularly important in paving the way to an agreement and that it served two purposes: to persuade Khrushchev that Kennedy was interested in an agreement, and to make it clear that for domestic political reasons, Kennedy was unable to accept the Soviet terms regarding the number of on-site inspections.[135] Another element was Cousins's effort to change Soviet perceptions of the United States and present positive aspects of American society. On the American side, Cousins tried to shatter the perception of the Soviet Union as a single uniform entity and to make the administration aware of the domestic constraints facing Khrushchev. In his conversations with Kennedy, Cousins managed to convey the complexity of Khrushchev's domestic situation and even inspire a sense of empathy and shared destiny. Thanks to the direct, personal relationship he had established with the Soviet leader, Cousins had the ability to convey Khrushchev's impressions and feelings to the American administration.

In his capacity as a *facilitator*, Cousins had a leading role in establishing the Dartmouth Conferences as an unofficial channel between the two states. When acting as a mediator between officials in Washington and Moscow, however, he did not focus on facilitating: the official channel was not producing results at the time and it did not appear that another meeting would resolve the issue. Yet the parallel channel between the Vatican and Moscow, provided by Cousins, did incorporate this element: Cousins spoke with each side about creating a channel of communication between their respective representatives since there was no official channel available at the time. Notably, Cousins, as an unofficial mediator, lacked official state resources that could have provided leverage in acting as a *manipulator*, but he did try to exert pressure on the parties by warning of possible scenarios if they squandered the opportunity to reach an agreement. He pointed out to Khrushchev, for example, that this might be the last opportunity to conclude a treaty, and he warned Kennedy that Khrushchev might abandon his policy of peaceful coexistence and shift Soviet policy closer to that of China.

Another dimension was Cousins's influence through *gestures of conciliation.* His initiative led to one of the most significant conciliatory gestures in the history of the Cold War, namely President Kennedy's speech at American University. The speech was Cousins's idea – proposed at a meeting with Kennedy and further developed in a letter – and shortly thereafter it became a reality. Cousins outlined the objectives of the speech, recommended a timetable for its delivery, and prepared a draft that contributed substantively to the official speech. Cousins's efforts also led to gestures of conciliation between the Soviet Union and the Vatican, with the former deciding to release the archbishops Slipyj and Beran from Soviet prison. Likewise, Khrushchev's letters of greeting to Kennedy and the pope constituted a gesture of conciliation that occurred as a result of Cousins's mission.

Cousins's influence was also evident in the *transmission of ideas* from the unofficial sphere to the official sphere. These included his proposal to ban testing for a trial period, an idea that generated discussions within official bodies on both sides, as well as the ideas and terms he formulated that trickled into President Kennedy's official speech.

In parallel to his efforts behind the scenes, Cousins also operated in the public sphere and had an *influence on the public discourse* in the US and around the world. He contributed through articles and books, interviews and lectures, public campaigning, and a network of international contacts. Cousins also sought to change the "enemy image" in the United States and challenge what the public believed about the Soviets (the "doubting strategy"). One such example is the article he wrote about his meeting with Khrushchev in April 1963. In addition to reporting on their meeting, Cousins described aspects of the Soviet leader's human side that were unknown to the American reader. Accompanying the article were photos of "Grandpa" Khrushchev playing with Cousins's daughters and engaging in a game of badminton with Cousins. The body of the article also reported on jokes that the Soviet premier had told, a tour of his summer home, and the sports he practiced.[136]

After the PTBT had been signed, Cousins led a large-scale public campaign for its ratification in coordination with the White House. Other patterns of influence are also evident in Cousins's activities. He engaged in *influence through crisis management,* for example by participating in crisis management efforts during the Cuban missile crisis (October 1962), and through his efforts to resolve the US–USSR crisis surrounding their misunderstanding about the number of on-site inspections (April 1963). His attempt to secure the pope's assistance in calming the atmosphere during the Cuban missile crisis exemplifies the pattern of *influence through an external actor*.

### Variables related to the PPE

In examining this issue, it is important first to address two separate aspects of Cousins's life as a whole: his position as a journalist and the editor of an important magazine, and his role as a social activist and the leader of two civil society movements. Each position brought with it resources, advantages, and assets alongside disadvantages and limitations. As a journalist, Cousins had accumulated substantial resources and developed an expertise on various political issues; he traveled the world, met with international leaders, and enjoyed the advantages of public respect and a wide readership. He was careful to separate his role as a journalist from his activities as a PPE, and therefore did not report in real time about his meeting with Khrushchev, for example, even though it would have been a significant media event, because he did not wish to sabotage the very process he was trying to promote.

Cousins's efforts as a social activist affiliated with SANE and the United World Federalists provided him with public activism tools, a broad network of contacts, an arena in which to cultivate expertise on subjects such as nuclear testing, and public recognition of his standing as a prominent leader of campaigns on relevant issues. Cousins drew admiration for his peace efforts as well as recognition in the form of various prizes, including the Eleanor Roosevelt Peace Award (1963), the United Nations Peace Medal (1971), and the Niwano Peace Prize. Yet there were also disadvantages to being affiliated with these movements, which had their critics among the establishment as well as the general public. During the 1950s, for example, as the United States was cracking down on individuals suspected of having communist ties, charges of having communist connections were leveled against the movements to which Cousins belonged, which undermined their public standing. An August 1955 report by the State Department's Security Office noted that Cousins had close ties with a number of "left of center" groups.[137] Because of concerns about such criticism, Cousins, a fierce opponent of communism himself, waged a campaign against individuals in his own movements who had any affiliation with the communist movement.

The main resources that served Cousins in his efforts were the following.

1. *Access and network system.* Underpinning Cousins's ability to influence the official sphere was the network of contacts and the trust he had

built among decision makers in the United States, the Soviet Union, and the Vatican.

On the American side, there developed a relationship of mutual respect and trust between Cousins and Kennedy. It began with letters from Cousins to Kennedy and his staff on matters of foreign policy. Kennedy responded to some of the letters, asking Cousins to write to him directly when he deemed it appropriate, and the two met on a number of occasions. Cousins's meetings with Soviet figures, particularly Khrushchev, and his visits to the Soviet Union provided a highly significant power resource in his relations with Kennedy. These contacts effectively opened the door of the Kennedy administration to Cousins, as the officials were eager to receive details and reports about his meetings. Cousins's second visit to the Soviet Union, in April 1963, constituted an important turning point in his relations with the Kennedy administration, after which they began to cooperate more closely and Kennedy became quite accessible to Cousins.

The gradual process of relationship building between Cousins and the Kennedy administration is illustrated by a December 1961 letter from Sorensen's assistant to Cousins, in response to a request to meet. The assistant informed Cousins that Sorensen did not meet with private individuals or organizational representatives, and that his job was to advise the president rather than work with individuals who had ideas about implementing the president's plans.[138] Between 1961 and 1963, however, Cousins and Sorensen formed a strong relationship, to the extent that Sorensen drew on Cousins's assistance in drafting the president's speeches. From Cousins's files we know that his special relationship with Kennedy administration officials, such as Bundy, Dungan, and Sorensen, lasted for years, even after Kennedy's assassination and after these officials had left their posts.[139]

On the Soviet side, the relationship began with Cousins's first visit, in 1959, and continued with the Dartmouth Conferences, while in parallel he maintained a correspondence with Khrushchev. In addition to the relations that formed between Cousins and Soviet delegates to the Dartmouth Conferences, in time Cousins also established a relationship with Dobrynin, the Soviet envoy to Washington, and the network he built ultimately led to his meeting with Khrushchev. Furthermore, in the course of leading the Dartmouth Conferences, Cousins built relations of trust and deep respect with the Soviet delegates, relations that included visiting them at home, meeting their families, and exchanging letters.[140] The impact of these special relations is illustrated by the words of Alice Bobrysheva, a Soviet participant in the project:

The great gift I received from the first Dartmouth Conference, and which I proudly cherished for the following 30 years, was my association with Norman Cousins. ... Meeting Norman Cousins was like opening a window onto a wider world, with more issues to think about and resolve than I had previously confronted. He introduced me to a wider range of solutions. Every meeting with him in the 30 years that followed that first meeting left me enriched by his ideas, his energy and his dedication to improving life on our planet.[141]

The Soviet delegates to the Dartmouth Conferences reported to the Soviet leadership, which meant that Khrushchev was aware of the meetings and of Cousins's role in the process. The initiative that led to Cousins's first meeting with Khrushchev began at the conference in Andover, and the Soviet consent to the meeting was built on the trust that had developed between Soviet delegates to the conferences and Cousins. Voorhees claims that the Soviet participants' familiarity with Cousins and the fact that they trusted him contributed more to his securing an invitation to meet with Khrushchev than did his activities and writings over the years.[142] Another factor was the special relations that Cousins developed with Dobrynin and Boris Karpovich of the Soviet Embassy to the United States. According to Bobrysheva, Cousins's second meeting with Khrushchev was facilitated by Ambassador Dobrynin and the heads of the Soviet delegation to the Dartmouth Conferences.[143]

Cousins's relations with the Soviet Union were also shaped by his contacts with the American administration and the Vatican. His first visit to the Soviet Union (1959) was made possible largely because the Soviets were aware that it had Eisenhower's support. On the eve of his second visit to the Soviet Union (1962), the Soviets became aware of Cousins's ties with the Vatican, and the Vatican's idea of using him as a mediator was an indication of the trust he enjoyed at the Vatican. At the time, the Soviet government was interested in establishing ties with the Vatican, which made Cousins's relationship with the Vatican an important power resource in the process. The Soviets were also aware of Cousins's relations with President Kennedy. In particular, they knew of his meetings at the White House and that Kennedy had asked him to convey messages, and these factors constituted an important power resource for Cousins in his interactions with the Soviet Union.

Cousins's connection with the Vatican began with the friendship that formed between him and Father Morlion, and the Vatican's choice of Cousins as a mediator was based on Father Morlion's recommendation as well as Cousins's network of Soviet contacts. Flamini argues that from the Vatican's perspective, Cousins's lack of official standing was another factor that made him suitable for the mission because it meant that should the contacts with the Kremlin fail, there would be no official repercussions and the Vatican could deny any involvement.[144] In addition to the above, Cousins had an international network of contacts that included leading figures such as Dr. Schweitzer, Indian prime minister Nehru, and various government officials in Japan.

2. *Knowledge resources.* As a prominent journalist and expert in foreign policy, Cousins was a respected figure both among the public and in government circles. In this area he indeed had unique knowledge resources. Kennedy and his staff followed Cousins's writings and took an interest in his articles.

Cousins also had important knowledge resources that derived from his contacts with the Soviet side, at a time when such contacts were rare. His testimony before the Senate Foreign Relations Committee is illustrative: after hearing this testimony, Senator Frank Carlson observed that he did "not know of anyone who has spent more time studying the Russian problems than Mr. Cousins. He has been over there; he has visited them. He has written about them."[145] Cousins himself stated at the outset of his testimony that he had no "scientific or military competence" but he had had the opportunity to visit the Soviet Union and to spend time with Khrushchev, and "in the course of such visits I was able to make a number of contacts and develop information which I believe has a bearing on the matter before us."[146] Another unique resource Cousins had was his familiarity with the domestic political situation on both sides – the United States as well as the Soviet Union. This resource enabled him to determine how much leeway there was in the parties' positions and the potential for agreement. Cousins ascribed much importance to this element, incorporating proposals and suggestions that were intended to address it.

3. *Value-based resources.* On the American side, Cousins built on the fact that ideologically he was on common ground with Kennedy, who viewed him as an ally in this sense as well as a partner on a number of issues, foremost among which were US–USSR relations, the achievement of a test ban treaty, and the important role of the UN. Although their positions sometimes differed, the two shared a basic outlook that allowed Kennedy to support and encourage Cousins in his efforts, while also making it possible for Cousins to consult with Kennedy about his movement's public campaigning, to take his advice into account, and to persuade Khrushchev of the president's sincerity.

On the Soviet side, Moscow acknowledged Cousins's efforts on behalf of the peace movement in the United States, especially his role in the campaign against nuclear testing. This dimension granted Cousins tremendous moral authority and helped foster an image of him in Soviet eyes as an American who was committed to the goals of peace, an end to the arms race, and an end to nuclear testing, as someone who was acting to pursue these goals and was not afraid to criticize official American policy on these matters.

Soviet leaders were also aware of Cousins's critical point of view. According to Fursenko and Naftali, in 1961 Khrushchev learned about Cousins's criticism of CIA assessments regarding the Soviet Union. According to them, this gave the Soviets the impression that Cousins was an "independent-minded critic."[147] The same impression is illustrated by a letter of August 1963 to Cousins from Boris Karpovich of the Soviet Embassy in Washington, in reaction to an article by Cousins about the PTBT that appeared in the *Washington Post*. Karpovich wrote that Cousins's article exemplified "an objective, non-partisan approach" that he believed was missing from the American discourse about the treaty.[148]

In a report he prepared in November 1962, Father Morlion concluded that Cousins had earned Khrushchev's trust on the basis of his writings and peace activism.[149] According to Flamini, it was Cousins's role as leader of the Dartmouth Conferences and his efforts to promote disarmament that provided the credentials necessary to make him eligible for a meeting with Khrushchev.[150] The fact that Khrushchev chose to reply to the letters he received from Cousins and SANE reflects the importance he ascribed to their work and to dialoguing with them. In this context it should be noted that, conversely, Cousins also never hesitated to criticize or attack Soviet policy in its various forms, and he would even do so during his meetings with Soviet delegates. He was critical, for example, of the Soviet decision to resume nuclear testing, of the Soviet intervention in Hungary, and of the activities of the Communist Party in the United States and of manifestations of anti-Semitism in the Soviet Union. This was helpful in terms of the American administration's perception of him.

## Variables related to the initiative

1. *Secrecy/publicity and the action pattern.* Cousins was meticulous about maintaining absolute secrecy and a clear division between his work as a journalist or social activist and his activities as a PPE. His meetings with Khrushchev remained a secret even though they would have made a remarkable story that any American journalist would want to report. Only in November 1964 did Cousins publish a detailed account of his second meeting with Khrushchev in his magazine. He never revealed real-time information about his meetings with President Kennedy or

members of the administration, nor did he disclose details to which he had been privy regarding contacts with the Soviet Union. By maintaining secrecy, Cousins cultivated the parties' trust, which helped him promote his initiative. Nonetheless, once a test ban had been achieved, Cousins shifted from backchannel measures to public activity aimed at promoting public support for the treaty, and at this point he did reveal that he had visited the Soviet Union, using this fact as a power resource to influence public opinion.

2. *The goal of the initiative.* Cousins's initiative focused on a distinctly identifiable, specific issue relating to the crisis that negotiations on a nuclear test ban treaty had reached. An ideologue and idealist, Cousins held a radical, nearly utopian, worldview as to the world order, but at the same time he elected to focus his initiative on a particular issue that, at that moment, posed a major barrier to progress in superpower relations. He was hoping to promote a process that, though limited, would be seen as achievable and meaningful. Evidently Cousins was capable of differentiating between the long-term strategic vision and the immediate tactical effort required. American diplomat Yale Richmond, who was involved in promoting cultural relations with the Soviet Union, described Cousins as "an idealist, a doer, a pragmatist – a rare combination."[151] Although Cousins did discuss broader issues, including the structure of the UN, with various players on both sides, the attention these issues received was supplementary to the initiative. In his contacts with Eisenhower, too, Cousins managed to enlist the administration's support for the Dartmouth Conferences – as a targeted goal without strategic political implications – but his efforts to shift the president's position on more substantive matters, such as a moratorium on nuclear testing, were not as successful.

3. *Correlation with official policy.* Cousins's initiative correlated with the official policy of the Kennedy administration and did not challenge the president's positions. Cousins was quite familiar with the positions on both sides and knew how much leeway they had, and he purposefully worked within the existing constraints while simultaneously searching for ways to break through them. It is noteworthy that Cousins deliberately adopted this approach, even though his views on certain issues, such as the degree of inspection needed for a test ban treaty, did not overlap with the official position.

In advance of each visit to the Soviet Union, Cousins made a point of ensuring that the White House did not object to his plans. In January 1964, for example, at a meeting with Rusk, the possibility of another visit to the Soviet Union came up, and Cousins made it clear that it was important for him to make sure that his private activities did not clash with official policy or official efforts of which he was unaware.[152]

4. *Direct or indirect contact.* Cousins's initiative was based on personal, direct dialogue with the two leaders – Kennedy and Khrushchev – which made it possible to circumvent problems and barriers in their communication at the bilateral level. Cousins provided a safe, direct, short-term method for the leaders to exchange messages and views. Sachs claims that Kennedy and Khrushchev understood the importance of their private communication, "outside the glare and distortions of the media," adding that in this respect Cousins served as an "informal go-between" who helped Kennedy improve communication with Khrushchev.[153] The United States and the Soviet Union did, of course, have official communication channels, but Cousins's ability to meet personally and in parallel with both leaders, and to mediate directly and immediately between them, was remarkable and, in the diplomatic landscape of the time, unique.

## External variables

1. *Characteristics of the conflict.* Cousins operated within the context of an international conflict between two superpowers that had diplomatic relations and official communication channels, but under the conditions of a cold war, an arms race, ideological confrontation, and spheres of rivalry and competition across the world – between the Western bloc and the Soviet bloc.

2. *Ripeness.* The Cuban missile crisis of October 1962 brought the Cold War to a boiling point and created the sense that the superpowers were on the verge of an abyss, that maintenance of the present situation posed tremendous threats. The two superpowers acknowledged that the ongoing nuclear armament and proliferation were creating global instability and would take a heavy toll and usurp many resources. This may be seen as an expression of the perception of a *mutually hurting stalemate.* Various actors on both sides pointed to the emergence of this conclusion in the aftermath of the Cuban missile crisis. Carl Kaysen of the National Security Council (NSC) wrote in an internal memorandum that the crisis had exposed the superpowers' common interest in curtailing potential conflicts, and Kennedy's advisor, Sorensen, claimed that the Cuban missile crisis had spotlighted the American interest in a peaceful resolution and helped promote the perception of disarmament as a necessity rather than a dream.[154] Likewise, on the Soviet side, Oleg Troyanovsky, an advisor to Khrushchev, stated that the events of October 1962 had a "tremendous educational value for both sides and both leaders," who realized that the threat of nuclear annihilation was real, and that they needed to establish more stable and constructive superpower relations.[155] According to Zubok and Harrison, following the Cuban missile crisis Khrushchev shifted his approach "from existential deterrence

through bluff and brinkmanship towards regulation of the nuclear arms race."[156]

3.  *The leaders' positions and the domestic conditions.* Both leaders – Kennedy and Khrushchev – believed as a matter of principle in adopting arms control measures to address the issue of nuclear testing. They both had to deal with domestic pressures and circumstances that shaped the contours of their policy, but their basic stance remained in favor of a treaty.

    Even as a senator and presidential candidate, Kennedy had spoken out in favor of arms control and in support of a treaty banning nuclear testing. As early as 1956, he had declared that the United States should lead a global effort to put an end to nuclear testing.[157] During the 1960 election campaign, Kennedy asserted that the "catastrophic arms race" was generating deadly atmospheric pollution, promoting nuclear proliferation, and would eventually lead to global annihilation.[158] In his speech as president at the UN General Assembly in September 1961, Kennedy reiterated this position and called for negotiations on a comprehensive plan for complete and total nuclear disarmament, underscoring that the first step should be a nuclear test ban treaty: "This can be done now. Test ban negotiations need not and should not await general disarmament."[159]

    Khrushchev, too, supported such an agreement – subject to certain conditions – both because he recognized the cost of the nuclear arms race and in light of the crisis with China and the Soviet interest in developing warmer relations with the United States as a step towards enhancing its international status and isolating China. Khrushchev hoped that such a treaty could lead to additional agreements between the superpowers on other issues, including the question of Germany and a non-aggression pact between NATO and the Warsaw Pact states. In addition, he believed that by concluding a treaty and improving relations with the United States, the Soviet Union would be able to reallocate resources for the betterment of its economy.[160] Accordingly, Cousins was able to operate under "comfortable" conditions and benefit from both leaders' support for the issue he sought to advance. He found that both leaders were receptive to his efforts and demonstrated a willingness to listen. This is a highly significant and helpful element. Kennedy was also open to the use of informal and nonconventional diplomacy and had used this tool on various occasions.[161]

    With regard to the domestic conditions, on the American side Kennedy's conduct during the Cuban missile crisis reinforced his public stature in the United States and gave him more domestic leeway. In the eyes of the public he had "defeated" the Soviet Union and knew how to protect

American interests, which, reciprocally, created new opportunities for him and gave him room to initiate new political measures in US–USSR relations.[162] On the Soviet side, in the aftermath of the Cuban missile crisis, Khrushchev became the target of growing criticism across the communist world, while on the domestic front he grew weaker. Yet these factors also fueled his need for a political success, in the form of a treaty with the United States, in order to prove to his critics that the policy of coexistence with the West was fruitful, and in the hope that such a development would lead to agreements on other issues. Moreover, because he was keen to conclude a treaty, Khrushchev was willing to accept a partial ban and to delink the issue of nuclear testing from other bilateral disputes.

4. *Parallel channels of communication.* The issue of a test ban treaty had been a core topic of discussion in negotiations among the United States, the Soviet Union, and Britain since 1958. It was discussed at the negotiations in Geneva, at the ENDC, in correspondence between the leaders, and at additional diplomatic gatherings, among other fora, but these invariably reached a deadlock. As such, Cousins's initiative was not aimed at creating an exclusive communication channel between two parties that were refusing to speak, nor did it introduce an issue that was beyond the scope of official discussions. His initiative emerged against the background of unproductive diplomatic channels of communication and fruitless official initiatives by various actors, at a particular moment in time when it met a crucial need, by taking steps and thinking "outside the box" – thereby reinvigorating both the process and the parties, preventing the talks from collapsing completely, and salvaging the historic opportunity to conclude a treaty. Paradoxically, it was precisely after the Cuban missile crisis had alerted the two sides to the importance of the issue, when the conditions had become ripe for progress, that the diplomatic efforts reached a deadlock and diplomats at the various fora dedicated to the issue despaired of the process. Consequently, both sides then became more willing to listen to and accept assistance from an unconventional and unofficial actor.

5. *Internal governmental agents.* Through his efforts, Cousins was able to make new allies who would support his cause within the ruling establishment on both sides. On the American side, senior administration officials such as Bundy and Sorensen became supportive of Cousins's initiative at some point, took an interest in his proposals, and helped him from within the establishment – all with the backing of President Kennedy. On the Soviet side, Cousins earned the support of various officials, including Korneichuk and Bobrysheva, and in time Dobrynin as well, who contributed to his efforts from within Soviet institutions.

# Notes

1   G. Warner and M. Shuman, *Citizen Diplomats* (New York: Continuum, 1987), 187.

2   N. Cousins, *The Improbable Triumvirate: John F. Kennedy, Pope John, Nikita Khrushchev* (New York: W. W. Norton, 1972).

3   See, for example, G. T. Seaborg, *Kennedy, Khrushchev, and the Test Ban* (Berkeley: University of California Press, 1981).

4   J. Voorhees, *Dialogue Sustained: The Multilevel Peace Process and the Dartmouth Conference* (Washington, D.C.: United States Institute of Peace Press, 2002); L. S. Wittner, *Resisting the Bomb* (Stanford: Stanford University Press, 1997); A. Pietrobon, "The role of Norman Cousins and track II diplomacy in the breakthrough to the 1963 Limited Test Ban Treaty," *Journal of Cold War Studies*, 18:1 (2016), 60–79.

5   *JFK: A President Betrayed*. Cory Taylor, Agora Productions, 2013. DVD.

6   K. Oliver, *Kennedy, Macmillan, and the Nuclear Test-Ban Debate, 1961–63* (Houndmills: Macmillan Press, 1998), 4; Wittner, *Resisting*, 1–2; Seaborg, *Kennedy*, 3–4; M. Evangelista, *Unarmed Forces* (Ithaca: Cornell University Press, 1999), 47.

7   Oliver, *Kennedy*, 6–10; Seaborg, *Kennedy*, 11–13; Evangelista, *Unarmed Forces*, 60–62; H. K. Jacobson and E. Stein, *Diplomats, Scientists, and Politicians: The United States and the Nuclear Test Ban Negotiations* (Ann Arbor: University of Michigan Press, 1966), 45–53.

8   Seaborg, *Kennedy*, 14–25; Oliver, *Kennedy*, 10–15; Evangelista, *Unarmed Forces*, 62–69; A. F. Dobrynin, *In Confidence* (New York: Times Books, Random House, 1995), 39–42.

9   Seaborg, *Kennedy*, 59; Oliver, *Kennedy*, 21; Jacobson and Stein, *Diplomats*, 276–277; Dobrynin, *In Confidence*, 43–46, 99–100; W. Taubman, *Khrushchev* (New York: Norton, 2003), 493–500; J. See, "An uneasy truce: John F. Kennedy and Soviet–American Détente, 1963," *Cold War History*, 2:2 (2002), 167–168.

10  Jacobson and Stein, *Diplomats*, 280–283; Seaborg, *Kennedy*, 57–59, 81–82, 89; Oliver, *Kennedy*, 30, 36; Evangelista, *Unarmed Forces*, 71–72.

11  Oliver, *Kennedy*, 35, 54–56; Seaborg, *Kennedy*, 86, 121–122; Jacobson and Stein, *Diplomats*, 411.

12  On the crisis see J. G. Blight and D. A. Welch, *On the Brink: Americans and Soviets Reexamine the Cuban Missile Crisis* (New York: Noonday Press, 1990).

13  Oliver, *Kennedy*, 135–143; Jacobson and Stein, *Diplomats*, 425–426, 431–432.

14  The magazine's name was later shortened to "*The Saturday Review.*" On the history of Cousins's life see R. Keenan, "Norman Cousins," in D. W. Whisenhunt (ed.), *Encyclopedia USA – Vol. 17* (Gulf Breeze: Academic International Press, 1992), 2–5.

15  N. Cousins, *Present Tense: An American Editor's Odyssey* (New York: McGraw-Hill, 1967), 120–130; N. S. Katz, *Ban the Bomb: A History of SANE, the Committee for a Sane Nuclear Policy, 1957–1985* (New York: Greenwood Press, 1986), 1–2.

16  N. Cousins, *Modern Man is Obsolete* (New York: The Viking Press, 1945); L. S. Wittner, *One World or None: A History of the World Nuclear Disarmament Movement through 1953* (Stanford: Stanford University Press, 1993), 66–67; Warner and Shuman, *Citizen Diplomats*, 163.

17  Cousins, *Present Tense*, 324–352; Wittner, *Resisting*, 12; A. Pierobon, "Humanitarian aid or private diplomacy? Norman Cousins and the treatment of Atomic Bomb victims," *New Global Studies*, 8:1 (2014), 121–140.

18  Cousins, *Present Tense*, 283.

19  Cousins, *Present Tense*, 186–189, 246–247, 290, 370–371, 426, 478.

20  Katz, *Ban the Bomb*, 2; Cousins, *Present Tense*, 132–133.

21  Cousins, *Present Tense*, 189–192, 127–128, 162–165, 187–192, 407–408; N. Cousins, *In Place of Folly* (New York: Harper, 1961), 120–141.

22  Katz, *Ban the Bomb*, 4–13.

23  Cousins, *Present Tense*, 266–272, 274–280, 289–291, 369–371, 423–431, 477–508.

24  Katz, *Ban the Bomb*, 21–44; Wittner, *Resisting*, 12, 51–59.

25  Katz, *Ban the Bomb*, 32–38.

26  Wittner, *Resisting*, 325–329; Katz, *Ban the Bomb*, 45–64.

27  Katz, *Ban the Bomb*, 16–17; Wittner, *Resisting*, 30–32; N. Cousins, *Albert Schweitzer's Mission: Healing and Peace* (New York: W. W. Norton, 1985), 143–300.

28  N. Cousins, *Talks with Nehru* (New York: J. Day, 1951).

29  Wittner, *Resisting*, 84, 101; Wittner, *One World*, 308; Cousins, *Albert Schweitzer's Mission*, 157–166, 186–189, 195–198, 201–202, 205–208.

30  N. Cousins, *The Pathology of Power* (New York: W. W. Norton, 1987), 74; Voorhees, *Dialogue Sustained*, 25.

31  A. Larson, *Eisenhower* (New York: Scribner, 1968), 172–173.

32  Wittner, *Resisting*, 142–143, 368–369; Cousins, *Albert Schweitzer's Mission*, 243–244, 246–252; Cousins, *The Pathology*, 74–82.

33  John F. Kennedy Library (hereafter JFKL), White House Central Subject Files (hereafter WHCSF) 579, Cousins to Kennedy, 6 September 1962.

34  JFKL, WHCSF 579, Kennedy to Cousins, 28 November 1961; Cousins to Kennedy, 18 January 1962; Cousins to Kennedy, 26 January 1962; Cousins to Kennedy, 21 March 1962; Salinger to Cousins, 27 March 1962; O'Brien to Harvey, 27 March 1962; JFKL, President's Office Files (hereafter POF) 13, Kennedy to Cousins, 1 February 1962; JFKL, POF 8, Cousins to Kennedy, 12 April 1962; Kennedy to Cousins, 23 April 1962.

35  JFKL, WHCSF 579, Kennedy to Cousins, 5 April 1961.

36  JFKL, WHCSF 579, Salinger to Cousins, 3 August 1962.

37  Norman Cousins Papers (hereafter NCP), 1206/3, N. Cousins, "Notes of the Meeting with the President, 13 March 1962"; Cousins to Kennedy, 12 April 1962; JFKL, POF 13, Cousins to Kennedy, 28 May 1962; Evelyn Lincoln to Cousins, 1 June 1962.

38  JFKL, WHCSF 659, M. Bundy, "For Norman Cousins, 29 January 1991."

39  Wittner, *Resisting*, 103–105.

40  Evangelista, *Unarmed Forces*, 62–63.

41 Wittner, *Resisting*, 344; Cousins, *Albert Schweitzer's Mission*, 255–258; NCP, 1219/5, Khrushchev to Cousins and Pickett, 8 February 1961.

42 Wittner, *Resisting*, 344–345; Cousins, *Albert Schweitzer's Mission*, 258–266; NCP, 1219/5, Cousins to Khrushchev, 4 March 1961; Cousins to Khrushchev, 8 March 1961, Cousins to Khrushchev, 4 January 1962.

43 Evangelista, *Unarmed Forces*, 74 n116.

44 Wittner, *Resisting*, 105, 314; Voorhees, *Dialogue Sustained*, 26; Cousins, *Present Tense*, 291–302; A. Bobrysheva, *Thanks for the Memories* (Dayton: Kettering Foundation Press, 2003), 5–7; Cousins, *Albert Schweitzer's Mission*, 243–244.

45 Bobrysheva, *Thanks*, 5.

46 Voorhees, *Dialogue Sustained*, 25–30, 335; Cousins, *Present Tense*, 400–401; Cousins, *The Pathology*, 74–75; P. D. Stewart and H. H. Saunders, "The Dartmouth Conference: The first 50 years," in M. Gilmore and P. Dallas (eds), *The Dartmouth Conference* (Dayton: Kettering Foundation, 2010), 7; Bobrysheva, *Thanks*, 15–20. Alongside the Dartmouth Conferences, American and Soviet representatives also met within the framework of the Pugwash conferences, which began in 1957, at which scientists and researchers from various countries met to discuss issues related to arms control.

47 Voorhees, *Dialogue Sustained*, 22.

48 Bobrysheva, *Thanks*, 7–8, 14–16; Voorhees, *Dialogue Sustained*, 28–31.

49 Voorhees, *Dialogue Sustained*, 28–29, 30–35; Bobrysheva, *Thanks*, 16–17, 23–31, 49; Cousins, *Albert Schweitzer's Mission*, 252–254; Stewart and Saunders, "The Dartmouth," 8–9.

50 Bobrysheva, *Thanks*, 17.

51 Voorhees, *Dialogue Sustained*, 34; Bobrysheva, *Thanks*, 32.

52 Bobrysheva, *Thanks*, 36; Voorhees, *Dialogue Sustained*, 35.

53 Voorhees, *Dialogue Sustained*, 35–46, 342; Cousins, *Present Tense*, 401–410; Bobrysheva, *Thanks*, 38–44.

54 Y. Primakov, "Reminiscing on the Dartmouth Conference," in M. Gilmore and P. Dallas (eds), *The Dartmouth Conference* (Dayton: Kettering Foundation, 2010), 1; Voorhees, *Dialogue Sustained*, 333–345; National Archive, Department of State Central Files, Central Decimal File 1960–1963, 511.61/11–1860, Memorandum of Conversation, 18 November 1960.

55 Voorhees, *Dialogue Sustained*, 42–43; A. Fursenko and T. Naftali, *One Hell of a Gamble* (New York: W. W. Norton, 1997), 126–127.

56 Voorhees, *Dialogue Sustained*, 46; Bobrysheva, *Thanks*, 46.

57 Cousins, *The Improbable*, 13–18; Voorhees, *Dialogue Sustained*, 46–53; Cousins, *Present Tense*, 411–417; Bobrysheva, *Thanks*, 39–40, 45–55; Stewart and Saunders, "The Dartmouth," 15; Taubman, *Khrushchev*, 583.

58 See K. Schelkens, "Vatican diplomacy after the Cuban Missile Crisis: New light on the release of Josyf Sliypyj," *Catholic Historical Review*, 97:4 (2011), 694–695.

59 Cousins, *The Improbable*, 13–19, 44–46; Voorhees, *Dialogue Sustained*, 51–52; Archives of the Archdiocese of Mechelen-Brussels (hereafter AAMB) 20/4, Memorandum for John XXIII and John F. Kennedy, 8 November 1962; JFKL, POF 65, Salinger to the President, 30 October 1962; Schelkens, "Vatican

diplomacy," 696. R. Flamini, *Pope, Premier, President* (New York: Macmillan, 1980), 56–58.

60  Voorhees, *Dialogue Sustained*, 50–51; Bobrysheva, *Thanks*, 53.

61  Memorandum for John XXIII; Cousins, *The Improbable*, 20–21; Salinger to the President, 30 October 1962; Schelkens, "Vatican diplomacy," 696–697; Voorhees, *Dialogue Sustained*, 51–52.

62  Memorandum for John XXIII; Cousins, *The Improbable*, 20–21.

63  JFKL, POF 65, Salinger to the President, 30 November 1962; Salinger to the President, 16 November 1962.

64  Cousins, *The Improbable*, 21–25; R. Reeves, *President Kennedy* (New York: Touchstone Books, 1994), 439–440.

65  Schelkens, "Vatican diplomacy," 699–700.

66  NCP 1219/8, Cousins to Fedorov, 21 December 1962; Cousins to Bobryshova, 21 December 1962; Cousins to Ivanov, 21 December 1962; Cousins, *The Improbable*, 32–37; AAMB 20/4, Report of the Meeting between Mr. Nikita Khrushchev and Mr. N, 14 December 1962; Report for President John F. Kennedy, 17 January 1963.

67  Cousins, *The Improbable*, 32–35; Report for President John F. Kennedy, 17 January 1963.

68  On the conversation between Cousins and Khrushchev, see Cousins, *The Improbable*, 38–57; Report of the Meeting between Mr. Nikita Khrushchev and Mr. N; Report for President John F. Kennedy, 17 January 1963; Reeves, *President Kennedy*, 440; NCP 1206/8, Cousins to Bykov, 21 December 1962. Khrushchev used his regular interpreter, but Cousins asked and received permission to use Oleg Bykov, who had participated in the Dartmouth Conference, as an interpreter.

69  Report of the Meeting between Mr. Nikita Khrushchev and Mr. N.

70  Report of the Meeting between Mr. Nikita Khrushchev and Mr. N; Cousins, *The Improbable*, 47–57; Schelkens, "Vatican diplomacy," 700–702; Taubman, *Khrushchev*, 583; M. F. Leffler, *For the Soul of Mankind* (New York: Hill and Wang, 2007), 161; Flamini, *Pope*, 66.

71  Cousins, *The Improbable*, 58–66; NCP 1219/5, Cousins to Khrushchev, 21 December 1962; Khrushchev to Pope John XXIII, 15 December 1962; Schelkens, "Vatican diplomacy," 702–704; Flamini, *Pope*, 66–67; JFKL, POF 8, Cousins to Kennedy, 28 December 1962; Report for President John F. Kennedy, 17 January 1963.

72  Taubman, *Khrushchev*, 583; Oliver, *Kennedy*, 146.

73  Oliver, *Kennedy*, 146–147; T. C. Sorensen, *Kennedy* (New York: Harper & Row, 1965), 728; A. M. Schlesinger, *A Thousand Days: John F. Kennedy in the White House* (London: Deutsch, 1965), 896.

74  Oliver, *Kennedy*, 146, 169; Seaborg, *Kennedy*, 181; Voorhees, *Dialogue Sustained*, 62.

75  ENDC was a forum that was established under UN auspices and included NATO and Warsaw Pact members, as well as neutral states. It served as a framework for talks on a nuclear test ban treaty.

76  Oliver, *Kennedy*, 148–160; Taubman, *Khrushchev*, 584.

77  Cousins, *The Improbable*, 67–73; Schelkens, "Vatican diplomacy," 705–706.

78  NCP, 1219/5, Cousins to Khrushchev, 14 February 1963; Cousins, *The Improbable*, 74–76; NCP, 1206/8, Cousins to Dobrynin, 15 February 1963.

79  Cousins, *The Improbable*, 77–79.

80  Cousins, *The Improbable*, 79; JFKL, POF 16, Cousins to Kennedy, 2 April 1963; Voorhees, *Dialogue Sustained*, 63.

81  Bobrysheva, *Thanks*, 56.

82  "Memorandum for Attorney General Kennedy to President Kennedy, 3 April 1963," *Foreign Relations of the United States 1961–1963 Vol. VI* (Washington: GPO, 1996), 262.

83  Wittner, *Resisting*, 418; JFKL, POF 16, Cousins to Kennedy, 13 March 1963; Sorensen, *Kennedy*, 728; M. R. Beschloss, *The Crisis Years: Kennedy and Khrushchev, 1960–1963* (New York: Edward Burlingame Books, 1991), 586; L. S. Wittner, "Looking back: Norman Cousins and the Limited Test Ban Treaty of 1963," *Arms Control Today*, 42 (2012), www.armscontrol.org/act/2012-12/looking-back-norman-cousins-limited-test-ban-treaty-1963 (accessed 19 April 2022).

84  Cousins to Kennedy, 13 March 1963; Cousins to Kennedy, 2 April 1963; JFKL, POF 16, Kennedy to Cousins, 15 March 1963; Wittner, *Resisting*, 418.

85  Cousins, *The Improbable*, 79–81; N. Cousins, "The outstretched hand," *Saturday Review* (13 February 1965), 20–21; Flamini, *Pope*, 92.

86  Cousins, *The Improbable*, 81–89; Bobrysheva, *Thanks*, 56, 58; NCP 1206/5, Cousins's notes on the meeting with Kennedy, 22 April 1963.

87  Archbishop Beran was released in May 1963 as a result of Cousins's efforts.

88  Cousins, *The Improbable*, 95–97; Taubman, *Khrushchev*, 585; Reeves, *President Kennedy*, 510–511.

89  Cousins's notes on the meeting with Kennedy; Cousins, *The Improbable*, 92–95.

90  Cousins, *The Improbable*, 95, 100; Reeves, *President Kennedy*, 511.

91  Cousins's notes on the meeting with Kennedy; Cousins, *The Improbable*, 98–99; A. Fursenko and T. Naftali, *Khruschev's Cold War: The Inside Story of an American Adversary* (New York: Norton, 2006), 518; JFKL, POF Presidential Recordings, Tape no. 82; NCP, 1220/1, Cousins's notes on 1963 visit with Khrushchev, 22 April 1963.

92  Cousins, *The Improbable*, 99, 101; Cousins's notes on 1963 visit.

93  Cousins's notes on the meeting with Kennedy; Cousins, *The Improbable*, 101–109.

94  Seaborg, *Kennedy*, 207.

95  On the meeting see: Cousins, *The Improbable*, 111–117, 122; Tape 82; Cousins's notes on the meeting with Kennedy; Seaborg, *Kennedy*, 212; R. Schlesinger, *White House Ghosts* (New York: Simon & Schuster, 2008), 130; Reeves, *President Kennedy*, 511–512; Oliver, *Kennedy*, 184; Fursenko and Naftali, *Khruschev's Cold War*, 519–520.

96  Sorensen, *Kennedy*, 729.

97  Cousins, *The Improbable*, 119–121; Cousins's notes on the meeting with Kennedy.

98  JFKL, Sorensen Papers, 36, Cousins to Kennedy, 30 April 1963.

99  Cousins to Kennedy, 30 April 1963; Oliver, *Kennedy*, 184; Sorensen, *Kennedy*, 730; Wittner, *Resisting*, 420; Schlesinger, *White House*, 130; Reeves, *President Kennedy*, 511–512.

100  Cousins, *The Improbable*, 122–123; Wittner, *Resisting*, 420; Fursenko and Naftali, *Khruschev's Cold War*, 520; Oliver, *Kennedy*, 184; Sorensen, *Kennedy*, 730; JFKL, Sorensen Papers, 36, Cousins to Sorensen, 1 June 1962; JFKL, Kennedy Oral History Program, Theodore C. Sorensen, "Recorded interview by Carl Kaysen, 15 April 1964."

101  Sorensen, "Recorded interview," 71; see also: Sorensen, *Kennedy*, 730.

102  Sorensen, *Kennedy*, 730–731; Oliver, *Kennedy*, 184–185; Schlesinger, *White House*, 130–131; Leffler, *For the Soul*, 182; J. D. Sachs, *To Move the World* (New York: Random House, 2013), 72; T. O. Windt, "John F. Kennedy," in K. Ritter and M. J. Medhurst (eds) *Presidential Speechwriting* (College Station: Texas A&M University Press, 2003), 100.

103  NCP, 1219/5, Cousins to Khrushchev, 30 April 1963.

104  Oliver, *Kennedy*, 177; JFKL, WHCSF 659, Cousins to Kennedy, 26 April 1963; NCP, 1206/8, Cousins to Dobrynin, 29 April 1963.

105  Cousins to Kennedy, 26 April 1963.

106  JFKL, WHCSF 579, Bundy to Cousins, 7 May 1963.

107  JFKL, WHCSF 579, Cousins to Bundy, 16 May 1963.

108  Seaborg, *Kennedy*, 207–211; Oliver, *Kennedy*, 169–178; Sorensen, *Kennedy*, 729; Schlesinger, *A Thousand Days*, 898–899.

109  Seaborg, *Kennedy*, 213–216; Reeves, *President Kennedy*, 513–514; Sorensen, *Kennedy*, 730; See the speech: http://www.jfklibrary.org/Asset-Viewer/ BWC7I4C9QUmLG9J6I8oy8w.aspx (accessed 25 March 2021).

110  Sorensen, *Kennedy*, 730; Seaborg, *Kennedy*, 216.

111  NCP, 1206/6, Speech draft for Kennedy's American University speech.

112  JFKL, WHCSF 579, Cousins to Salinger, 10 June 1963.

113  JFKL, POF 16, Cousins to Kennedy, 11 June 1963.

114  JFKL, POF 16, Evelyn Lincoln to Cousins, 17 June 1963.

115  Sorensen, *Kennedy*, 733; Reeves, *President Kennedy*, 516; Seaborg, *Kennedy*, 218; Schlesinger, *A Thousand Days*, 904; Fursenko and Naftali, *Khruschev's Cold War*, 525; Taubman, *Khrushchev*, 602.

116  Sorensen, *Kennedy*, 733; Windt, "John F. Kennedy," 100; Cousins, *The Improbable*, 124–126; Seaborg, *Kennedy*, 218; Schlesinger, *A Thousand Days*, 904–905; Oliver, *Kennedy*, 192–193.

117  Reeves, *President Kennedy*, 509, 513; Cousins, *The Improbable*, 124–125; Fursenko and Naftali, *Khruschev's Cold War*, 527; Cousins, *Albert Schweitzer's Mission*, 298.

118  Fursenko and Naftali, *Khruschev's Cold War*, 520–521.

119  Cousins, *Albert Schweitzer's Mission*, 298–299.

120  NCP, 1219/5, Cousins to Khrushchev, 17 July 1963.

121 Oliver, *Kennedy*, 194–205; Taubman, *Khrushchev*, 603; Sorensen, *Kennedy*, 734–736.

122 V. Mastny, "The 1963 Nuclear Test Ban Treaty: A missed opportunity for detente?" *Journal of Cold War Studies*, 10:1 (2008), 3; See, "An uneasy truce," 183–186.

123 Reeves, *President Kennedy*, 549; Katz, *Ban the Bomb*, 84; JFKL, WHCSF 579, E. Christine Camp to Cousins, 5 September 1963.

124 JFKL, WHCSF 579, Norman Cousins Statement on Test Ban Treaty, 7 August 1963; JFKL, POF 100, Citizens Committee for A Nuclear Test Ban; Cousins, *The Improbable*, 127–136; Wittner, *Resisting*, 426–428; Sorensen, *Kennedy*, 739; Katz, *Ban the Bomb*, 84; Sachs, *To Move*, 113–114; Seaborg, *Kennedy*, 264–265.

125 JFKL, POF 16, Cousins to Evelyn Lincoln, 15 August 1963; Cousins to Evelyn Lincoln, 19 August 1963.

126 "Testimony of Norman Cousins," in Nuclear Test Ban Treaty: Hearings before the Committee on Foreign Relations, United States Senate, 88th Congress, August 1963 (Washington, D.C.: U.S. Govt. Printing Office, 1963), 706–712; Cousins, *The Improbable*, 144–148; Seaborg, *Kennedy*, 276.

127 Wittner, *Resisting*, 428; JFKL, Sorensen Papers 53, P. B. Zucker, "Nuclear Test Ban Treaty Ratification Public Relations Program, 6 August 1963."

128 JFKL, WHCSF 579, Bundy to Cousins, 30 August 1963.

129 NCP 1213/7, Sorensen to Cousins, 28 September 1963.

130 JFKL, WHCSF 579, Kennedy to Cousins, 7 October 1963. In early October 1963 Cousins attended a gathering at the White House that included members of Congress and White House staff, who met to celebrate the Senate ratification of the treaty. See Cousins, *Albert Schweitzer's Mission*, 299–300.

131 Wittner, "Looking back."

132 Bundy, "For Norman Cousins."

133 Voorhees, *Dialogue Sustained*, 65.

134 Pietrobon, "The role," 61.

135 Evangelista, *Unarmed Forces*, 85.

136 See Cousins, "Notes on a 1963 visit."

137 Wittner, *Resisting*, 158.

138 NCP, 1213/7, Sitrin to Cousins, 11 December 1961.

139 See NCP, 1197/3; NCP 1213/7; JFKL, Dungan Papers, 14.

140 See NCP 1219/8; Voorhees, *Dialogue Sustained*, 34, 52.

141 Bobrysheva, *Thanks*, 28.

142 Voorhees, *Dialogue Sustained*, 63, 346.

143 Bobrysheva, *Thanks*, 56.

144 Flamini, *Pope*, 66.

145 "Testimony of Norman Cousins," 711.

146 "Testimony of Norman Cousins," 706.

147 Fursenko and Naftali, *One Hell of a Gamble*, 347.

148 NCP, 1206/8, Karpovich to Cousins, 30 August 1963.

149 Memorandum for John XXIII.

150 Flamini, *Pope*, 64.
151 Voorhees, *Dialogue Sustained*, 401. See also Pietrobon, "The role," 78.
152 NCP, 1206/7, Cousins's notes on a visit in the White House, 23 January 1964.
153 Sachs, *To Move*, 72.
154 See, "An uneasy truce," 165; Sorensen, *Kennedy*, 726.
155 V. M. Zubok and H. M. Harrison, "The nuclear education of Nikita Khrushchev," in J. L. Gaddis, P. Gordon, E. May, and J. Rosenberg (eds), *Cold War Statesmen Confront the Bomb* (Oxford: Oxford University Press, 1999), 160.
156 Zubok and Harrison, "The nuclear education," 161, 164–165.
157 Schlesinger, *A Thousand Days*, 453.
158 P. Nash, "Bear any burden? John F. Kennedy and nuclear weapons," in J. L. Gaddis,, P. Gordon, E. May, and J. Rosenberg (eds), *Cold War Statesmen Confront the Bomb* (Oxford: Oxford University Press, 1999), 123–124.
159 See Kennedy's 1961 speech: https://2009–2017.state.gov/p/io/potusunga/207241.htm (accessed 25 March 2021).
160 See, "An uneasy truce," 177–178; Mastny, "The 1963 Nuclear," 24–25; Fursenko and Naftali, *Khruschev's Cold War*, 507–508; Wittner, *Resisting*, 423–424; Leffler, *For the Soul*, 187–188.
161 Kennedy used, for example, the French journalist Jean Daniel as an unofficial envoy to Cuba, see: W. M. LeoGrande and P. Kornbluh, *Back Channel to Cuba: The Hidden History of Negotiations between Washington and Havana* (Chapel Hill: University of North Carolina Press, 2015), 42–43, 76–78.
162 See, "An uneasy truce," 166; Beschloss, *The Crisis*, 577, 600.

# 3

# Suzanne Massie and the Cold War during the Reagan era, 1983–1988

I felt that her frequent travels to the Soviet Union had revealed to her undercurrents of great power. ... Suzanne Massie gave a glimpse of a different Soviet reality from the one I read about in my secret briefing papers.

George Shultz, US Secretary of State 1982–1989[1]

## Introduction

The 1980s were a turning point in the history of the Cold War. They began under a shadow of growing tension and hostility, and concluded with a transformation of superpower relations. During this critical period, Suzanne Massie – an American writer and expert on Russian culture and history – developed contacts with officials in Washington and Moscow, and worked to promote dialogue and improve relations between the countries.

This chapter examines the activity and influence of Massie as a PPE during the years 1983–1988. It explores her relations with both sides, which included frequent visits to the Soviet Union and meetings with US president Ronald Reagan. The chapter is based on archival materials from the Ronald Reagan Presidential Library, memoirs by relevant actors, an interview with Suzanne Massie, media reports, and historical studies.

The official historiography of Reagan's Cold War policy does not pay much attention to Massie's activities. Although memoirs by Reagan and his secretary of state, George Shultz, did mention her role, the landmark publication in this context was a 2010 book by James Mann – *The Rebellion of Ronald Reagan* – a significant portion of which is devoted to Massie's influence.[2] In 2013, Massie published a book that presents her story.[3] Massie's role has also been recognized in Russia, where a documentary film about her, titled *Better to Light a Candle*, was produced in 1991.[4]

## Historical background

In 1979, after the détente of the 1970s in US–USSR relations, the Cold War again became evident as the two superpowers reentered a cycle of escalatory activity. It began with the Soviet invasion of Afghanistan in December 1979, which led to a US boycott of the 1980 Olympic Games in Moscow and a grain embargo against the Soviet Union. This was followed by the closure of the Soviet consulate in New York and the American consulate in Kiev, as well as a suspension of cultural and scientific exchanges.[5]

In January 1981, Ronald Reagan was inaugurated as the US president, and the new administration embarked on a large military buildup. Between 1981 and 1985 it increased the defense budget by 7 percent annually. In addition, Reagan launched the Strategic Defense Initiative (SDI), an ambitious research project aimed at developing a space-based anti-missile defense system. The administration also decided to deploy American medium-range missiles in Western Europe as a response to Soviet SS-20 missiles in Eastern Europe. These steps were accompanied by harsh rhetorical attacks against Moscow, a prominent example of which was Reagan's description of the Soviet Union as an "evil empire" during a 1983 speech.[6] The US also increased its active support for anti-Communist forces in the developing world.[7]

The question of the policy towards the Soviet Union created a division within the Reagan administration between a more pragmatic camp, led by Secretary of State Georg Shultz, and the hardliners, led by National Security Advisor Bill Clark and Secretary of Defense Casper Weinberger. Reagan had a reputation as a hawk and staunch anti-communist, but during his first term he gradually shifted towards Shultz's stance.[8] Against the background of growing tension during the early 1980s, the parties held numerous rounds of arms control talks in Geneva, which included discussions on strategic arms reduction and intermediate-range nuclear forces, but they were unable to reach any agreement.[9]

On the Soviet side, the early 1980s were characterized by deep political, social, and economic crises. Soviet leader Leonid Brezhnev died in November 1982. His successor, Yuri Andropov, died in February 1984, and the next leader, Konstantin Chernenko, died in March 1985. The Soviet economy and industry were in a state of decline, the agricultural situation was desperate, and the technological gap with the US was widening. In addition, the Soviet army had faced heavy losses in Afghanistan, and the Solidarity movement in Poland was challenging the Communist regime. New forces in the Soviet system began calling for dramatic reform and a change in domestic and foreign policy. One of these was Mikhail Gorbachev, who would lead the Soviet Union during the second half the 1980s.[10]

In the early 1980s the tension between the two countries intensified, reaching its highest level since the Cuban missile crisis of 1962. Gorbachev asserted that "never, perhaps in the postwar decades, was the situation in the world as explosive and hence, more difficult and unfavorable, as in the first half of the 1980s."[11] The year 1983 was a peak moment, marking the combination of various developments. In March 1983, Reagan delivered his "evil empire" speech and announced the launch of SDI. In September 1983, after entering Soviet airspace, Korean Air Lines Flight 007 was shot down by Soviet fighter jets, resulting in the death of 269 passengers and crew, including a US congressman. Reagan described this as "an act of barbarism."[12] In November 1983, NATO conducted a military exercise ("Able Archer 83"), which led the Soviets to suspect that NATO forces might actually be planning a surprise nuclear attack. Former CIA director Robert Gates described the event as "one of the potentially most dangerous episodes of the Cold War."[13] Later that month, the first Pershing II missiles were deployed in West Germany, leading the Soviet Union to halt arms control talks with the US and to deploy more missiles in Eastern Europe.[14]

### Suzanne Massie: life story and worldview

Suzanne Massie (née Rohrbach) was born in New York City, on 8 January 1931, to Swiss parents. Her father, who worked for the Swiss foreign service, was stationed in the United States at the time. Her mother had lived in Russia for a few years as a teenager during the First World War; having traveled there in 1914 to spend the summer with the family of a friend of her father, she was unable to leave when the war broke out and for its duration. Massie's mother introduced her to Russian culture. Massie graduated Vassar College and worked for a while for *Time* magazine. After marrying, Massie shelved her career and worked as a housewife, devoting much of her time to her son, who had been diagnosed with hemophilia.[15]

In 1958, Massie decided to learn Russian and took a course in an adult education program, where her teacher described her as a "Russian soul." Massie's connection to Russia continued to develop as her husband Robert Massie, a writer and former intelligence officer, worked on a book about the Russian czar Nicholas and his wife Alexandra (who also had a son with hemophilia) and she assisted in the research and editing. Their work on the book led the Massies to travel to Leningrad in 1967. This first visit marked the beginning of a long friendship between Massie and Russia. In 1968 the couple moved to Paris for four years, during which time Massie continued to study Russian and visited the Soviet Union twice a year, developing contacts and networks of Russian friends, particularly poets, artists, and intellectuals. Massie felt at home in Russia: "There is no rational explanation for this mysterious attachment I felt," she explained, "or why it seemed I had found a family that I had never known existed."[16] Massie's special interest in Russia drove her to write her own book, about five Russian poets from Leningrad – *The Living Mirror* – which was published in 1972.[17] A subsequent book – *Land of the Firebird: The Beauty of Old Russia* – which focused on Russian history and culture before the Communist revolution, was published in 1980.[18] The latter was a great success, garnering Massie some publicity in the US, and subsequently she was invited to give lectures in various forums, including military institutions.[19] Although she was an independent researcher, in 1985 she became a fellow of the Harvard Russian Research Center. She also served on the board of the International League for Human Rights.[20]

Massie's position and views on the Soviet Union were based on a fundamental distinction between the regime and the people, and she described herself as "fiercely anti-Soviet–pro-Russian people."[21] She aimed to reveal the unknown and the unseen aspects of Russia, beyond the "enemy image," and to portray a more complex picture of the rival side. "I very much like to explain to Americans the human side," she stated in a 1985 interview; "the Russians are human beings."[22] She encouraged greater contact and more frequent encounters between Americans and Russians, and saw in her efforts an opportunity to "share my love for both America and Russia" and "to bring them to a better relationship with each other as fellow human beings."[23]

Massie had harsh criticism of the US foreign policy establishment. She found its approach towards the Soviet Union "limiting and in many instances just plain wrong," and blamed the bureaucrats for being locked in their political science models and devoted to the status quo. According to Massie, the establishment was dominated by "hardliners and Kremlinologists who had viewed the Soviet Union as an implacable foe for decades," and their views "contrasted diametrically" with hers.[24] Massie was not involved in politics or activism, and despite developing close ties with President Reagan, she described herself as an independent "leaning toward conservative democrat." She emphasized that all her efforts followed from her own initiative as a private citizen, as she believed that she could make a contribution: "My father had taught me to believe that every citizen has a responsibility to act. So on my own, I acted."[25]

## The beginning of Massie's PPE activities

Massie started to reach out to official circles in the US in 1972, after her request for a visa for another trip to Russia was refused without explanation.

She spoke with various senators, hoping they could help, but to no avail. She also approached the State Department, but they refused to assist her. Only in 1980 did help arrive – from her networks in the military. Major Tyrus W. Cobb, a professor at West Point Military Academy (who had met Massie when she participated in a seminar), was planning to visit the Soviet Union and asked Massie for a few copies of her book to pass along to Soviet officials. After he returned, Cobb told Massie that one of the officials who received her book had suggested that she contact a specific person at the Soviet Embassy in Washington. Massie phoned the embassy and was invited to meet with Valentin Berezhkov. This was her first meeting with a Soviet official.[26]

In late 1982, Massie again phoned Berezhkov and he invited her to dinner with his wife at their home. "In those cold war days," Massie claimed, "this was an extraordinary invitation." During the dinner, Massie told the story of her visa request, while Berezhkov listened and took notes. Massie said jokingly that in any other country, she would have received a medal for the books she had written on Russia. Towards the end of the evening, Berezhkov took out a copy of Massie's book and asked her to sign it for Andropov. Massie agreed and signed, adding "with hope for the future of the great Russian land," omitting any reference to the Soviet Union.[27]

In February 1983, Berezhkov telephoned Massie and informed her that he had received confirmation from Moscow that she could visit anytime she wanted. But her application process still did not go smoothly. After she informed Berezhkov of the problems she was facing, he suggested that she meet with Georgy Arbatov, director of the Soviet think-tank USA Institute,[28] who would soon be visiting the US. Massie agreed and subsequently was invited to a reception at the Soviet mission to the UN in New York, where Berezhkov introduced her to Arbatov. Her exchange with Arbatov indicated that he was aware of the issue, and he acknowledged that Massie had been having "some trouble" with the bureaucrats. "I have too," he added, and asked Massie to apply again. She tried again and this time her application was approved.[29]

Massie traveled to the Soviet Union in September 1983. Although she was pleased to be returning to Russia after such a long struggle for a visa, her visit occurred at a time of high tension between the countries – shortly after the Soviets had shot down the Korean airliner, which in turn had led to a suspension of flights to Moscow. Nonetheless, Massie found a flight via Paris and arrived as planned. Her trip was different from previous visits as this time she had contacts with official circles. In Moscow, Massie was invited to the USA Institute, where she met with Berezhkov and Vitaly Zhurkin, one of the deputy directors of the institute. They discussed the relations between the countries, and Massie heard harsh words about Reagan from the two Soviet representatives, who asserted that he was seeking war and wished to destroy the Soviet Union. They repeatedly referred to Reagan's characterization of the Soviet Union as an "evil empire." Massie suggested that they look at Reagan's deeds, rather than his words, and proposed a resumption of cultural exchanges, but they expressed unwillingness to consider this possibility so long as US missiles were deployed in Europe.[30]

Massie was told that Arbatov, the institute's director, could not meet with her, so she asked to meet with his first deputy, Rodomir Bogdanov, who was also a KGB representative. She had heard from Cobb that Bogdanov was a powerful figure, and in order to gain access she claimed she had a message for him from Cobb. At their meeting, Massie stressed the need for dialogue between the countries and proposed renewing their cultural exchange, but Bogdanov rejected the idea. They talked about the Korean Air Lines incident and the evolving crisis, and Massie received a very alarming message from Bogdanov: "You don't know how close war is," he claimed.[31] Bogdanov's words of warning shocked Massie and stayed with her, as did other troubling remarks made by ordinary people whom she encountered during her visit. A French diplomat in Moscow told her about the exceptional "psychosis of war" in the Soviet media. As Massie was leaving Moscow, she felt obligated to do something: "My deep conviction grew that it was a dangerous time ... and that I must somehow speak out about what I had seen and experienced in the Soviet Union ... and voice my belief that we had to begin some kind of discourse with the Soviets again as soon as possible."[32]

### Massie's first meeting with Reagan and her mission to Moscow, 1984

Massie was eager to make contact with the Reagan administration so as to report on the troubling message she had heard in Moscow and urge a renewal of the dialogue. "My message," she said, "was Fire! Fire!" Employing her networks in Washington, Massie met with a few senators, including Bill Cohen of Maine (her home state), whom she had known for many years. Cohen reached out to his old friend Robert McFarlane, who had just been appointed national security advisor in October 1983, to suggest a meeting with Massie.[33] This was an important development as it marked the first time Massie was granted access to the White House.

At her meeting with McFarlane, Massie told him about her recent visit to the Soviet Union. She shared her concerns and her belief in the urgent need to defuse the tension, suggesting a new cultural agreement as a possible first step. McFarlane took a strong interest in her briefing and asked her to prepare a memorandum on the issue. When they met again to discuss her report, McFarlane emphasized the need for some form of dialogue with the Soviets and his keen interest in showing them that the administration was not hostile. Massie proposed that he send her to Moscow to promote negotiations on a cultural agreement: "If you send me, they'll know you're not hostile."[34]

Massie's proposal came at a critical juncture. This was a dangerous moment, marked by high tension, a lack of constructive communication, and fear that any miscalculation could lead to a war. Anatoly Dobrynin, the Soviet ambassador to Washington, later noted that at this point all the contacts he had long established with the White House were broken.[35] By late 1983, leading figures in the Reagan administration had come to believe that there was an urgent need to open new channels with the Soviets in order to defuse tension and change the Soviet perception of Reagan. They were receptive to using informal channels and pursued a few efforts in this direction. McFarlane supported the use of unofficial intermediaries, but Shultz was less enthusiastic. According to Jack Matlock, senior director for European and Soviet Affairs on the NSC staff, several private citizens with contacts in the Soviet Union had offered their help at that point, and they were asked only to inform their contacts that the administration wanted to restart negotiations. Massie, however, was in his view "suited for a more specific task."[36]

On Christmas Eve 1983, Matlock telephoned Massie and gave her a green light to go to Moscow, as she had suggested, to explore the possibility of renewing the cultural exchange. It was agreed that she would be traveling as a private citizen rather than an official envoy. She was, however, invited to Washington to meet with McFarlane and Matlock to prepare for the visit.[37] According to Mann, there were a few advantages for the Reagan administration in using Massie's informal mission. First, an official proposal would be immediately dismissed by the Soviets as an American effort to divert attention from the US deployment of missiles in Europe, whereas Massie was a private citizen, and Moscow therefore would not expect her to justify the Reagan administration's actions. Second, Massie's unofficial channels would allow her to circumvent the two senior Soviet officials – Ambassador Dobrynin and Foreign Minister Andrei Gromyko – who oversaw contact with the US, and whom the NSC regarded as obstacles who would oppose the resumption of dialogue.[38] McFarlane believed that reengaging with the Soviets on less contentious issues could pave the way forward. Matlock argued that renewing the exchange programs would allow the US to engage with the next generation of Soviet leaders, and that meetings between Soviet citizens and Americans would undermine negative stereotypes.[39] Before leaving for Moscow, Massie asked to meet with the president, explaining that her message would be more credible if she could say that it came directly from him, and that it would help her persuade the Soviets to change their opinion of Reagan. McFarlane gave his consent.[40]

Massie met with Reagan on 17 January 1984. The day before this meeting, Reagan had delivered a public speech signaling a change in attitude towards the Soviet Union. His speech emphasized the common interests of the two countries and the need to reduce the risk of war and the level of armaments.[41] At their meeting, Massie praised Reagan's speech and discussed various aspects of Russia, emphasizing the difference between the Russians and the Soviet leaders. She talked about the need to broaden contacts between the citizens of both sides. Towards the end of the meeting, Massie asked Reagan if she could mention in Moscow that she had met with him and that he planned, if reelected, to continue the policy of seeking to improve relations during his second term. Reagan gave an affirmative answer: "Yes, if they want peace, they can have it."[42] Although McFarlane confirmed to Massie that she could make it known that she had met the president, she revealed the real reason for her visit, and meeting with the president, only to her family and closest friends, telling everyone else that she was traveling for research. McFarlane informed Soviet ambassador Dobrynin of Massie's trip, indicating that the White House would be interested in receiving a report from her when she returned.[43] Before leaving, Massie wrote to Reagan, thanked him for the meeting, and told him that she would be returning to the US on his birthday (6 February) and hoped to bring him some good news as a present.[44]

In Moscow, Massie met with Berezhkov and Zhurkin from the USA Institute. She talked about Reagan's speech, and related what he had said at the end of their meeting. Zhurkin said that the speech amounted to empty words so long as the US was continuing to deploy missiles, and told Massie that she was an honest woman who was being used by an "evil man." Massie tried to convince them that Reagan's intentions were real: "I have looked into the president's eyes. I believe he is genuine." Massie also met a few times with Bogdanov. He knew the reason for her visit and told Massie that he was reporting their conversations "to the top." Bogdanov reemphasized the Soviet lack of trust in Reagan and rejected the idea of renewing cultural exchanges, arguing that the US would present it as a victory. Massie recounted Reagan's words to her as evidence of his desire for peace and insisted that the countries needed to resume talks, adding that culture could be a first step. Bogdanov explained to Massie that for the purposes of the visit they had granted her the status of a "tourist" – rather than a "guest of the embassy" – in order to convey their disapproval of the administration alongside their approval of her private visit. Bogdanov strongly criticized US ambassador Arthur Hartman, and Massie came to the conclusion that the Soviets' openness to private channels might stem from the difficulties they were facing in communications with the embassy. Eventually, at their final meeting,

Bogdanov informed Massie that the Soviet Union officially agreed to resume cultural talks.[45]

After returning home, Massie telephoned McFarlane and Matlock to report on the trip. A few days after Massie's visit, Andropov died and Chernenko was appointed to replace him. Against this background, Reagan wrote to Massie, referring to the "great change" that had occurred, and expressed hope that her visit "was all you wanted it to be."[46]

Massie was invited to have lunch with the president in the Oval Office on 1 March 1984, to discuss the new leadership and her impressions from the visit. At their meeting she told Reagan that her being able to say that she had personally met the president "made a great deal of difference." She described the disagreement she had had with her Soviet hosts regarding Reagan's speech, and her efforts to attest to his desire for peace. She also reported that the Soviets had agreed to renew cultural talks and had suggested that, as an initial overture, Shultz reach out to Dobrynin, and she stressed the need to act quickly. Massie emphasized the importance of cultural cooperation and offered a few ideas in this context. Reagan and Massie also discussed the possibility of a leaders' summit, which Massie urged Reagan to pursue, arguing that he was a "great communicator" and "could charm" the Soviets.[47] Reagan mentioned the meeting in his diary, adding that Massie was "a remarkable woman with some great insight on the Russians," and that she reinforced his "gut feeling" that it was time for him to meet with Chernenko.[48] The next day, Reagan met with his senior advisors and discussed ways to proceed towards a meeting with Chernenko.[49] The Soviet leader, however, was ill and weak. He died a year after entering office, without having met Reagan. Nonetheless, the parties resumed official cultural negotiations in 1984 and eventually reached a cultural agreement, which Reagan and the subsequent Soviet leader – Mikael Gorbachev – signed in December 1985.[50]

## Massie's growing role during the Reagan–Gorbachev era, 1984–1988

After the Massie–Reagan meetings of early 1984, before and after Massie's mission to Moscow, the two stayed in touch and exchanged letters. In August 1984 Massie sent Reagan an article she had written, and Reagan replied, stating that he had enjoyed the article.[51] After Reagan's victory in the November 1984 elections, Massie wrote to congratulate him, emphasizing that she was always at his service if she could be useful in any way in improving relations with the Soviet Union. Reagan, in response, expressed his appreciation for "the help you have given us in moving our relations with the Soviet Union toward a more constructive course," and added that

**Figure 3.1** President Ronald Reagan and Suzanne Massie at the White House, November 1988

he had asked McFarlane and Matlock to stay in touch with her so that "we can continue to benefit from your advice."[52]

During Reagan's second term, and following Gorbachev's appointment as Soviet leader (in March 1985), relations between Massie and Reagan grew stronger and her influence increased. Throughout these dramatic years, Massie's PPE activity consisted of her contacts with Reagan, which took place via meetings (a total of seventeen), phone calls, and letters, and with other administration officials, as well as her numerous visits to Russia and meetings with Soviet officials. Massie helped Reagan understand the Russians, reported on her trips, provided advice, and exchanged messages between the parties.

In a 1992 interview, McFarlane explained that he had introduced Massie to Reagan for three reasons: her "profound knowledge" of Russian history and culture; her approach, which focused on the human dimension and was therefore more relatable for Reagan than geopolitical analysis; and the fact that she was a realist and, even though she loved the Russian people, had no illusions about the Soviet system. "She's a bit of a performer," he added, "and they related that way. Their personalities are similar."[53] According to Mann, McFarlane also hoped that Massie would help moderate Reagan's hawkish views.[54]

In 1985 the administration began preparing for the possibility of a first leaders' summit. At the time, Reagan had very superficial knowledge of the Soviet Union and had never met a Soviet leader. As part of the preparation, in June the administration began providing Reagan with briefing papers and arranging meetings with experts. Against this background, Reagan also consulted with Massie, who had just returned from a two-month visit to the Soviet Union.[55] Reagan and Massie spoke by phone in August and met at the White House in September.[56]

Before their meeting, Massie had written to the president about her last visit, emphasizing the "significant change" in the Soviet Union: "Never, in the almost 20 years I have known the Soviet Union, have I seen anything quite like it." The purpose of her visit had been to conduct research for her new book, which focused on the Pavlovsk Palace, but she had also met with officials and ordinary citizens. "I saw a broad spectrum of people both humble and mighty," thanks to the "many and varied contacts I have built up there over so many years." Massie had taken notes on her conversations with officials and wished to present them to Reagan. She knew that the Soviets were aware of her contact with the president and believed that they had used the meetings to communicate messages "through personal sources rather than official sources." During her visit, Massie also received a personal message from Gorbachev through Arbatov: she had previously sent Gorbachev two of her books, and the Soviet leader asked Arbatov to thank her for the books and for her "noble work."[57]

A meeting between Reagan and Massie was scheduled for 3 September 1985, before her departure for another visit to Russia. The aim of the meeting was to discuss the countries' relations in anticipation of a summit planned for November in Geneva. Archival documents prepared in advance of the meeting reveal the friendship that had developed between Reagan and Massie and indicate that Reagan, with McFarlane's support, had pushed for the meeting. One internal paper indicated that "this is important to the President – he likes Suzanne very much," and another memorandum explained that "given their friendship" the talking points were brief. The questions in the talking points centered on Massie's analysis and suggestions regarding the summit, in light of her knowing the Russians "so well."[58] In his diary entry regarding the meeting, Reagan described Massie as an "authority on the Soviet Union."[59] In addition to Reagan, Vice-President George Bush, McFarlane, and Matlock also participated in the meeting.

During the meeting, Massie underscored that the Soviet Union was not a monolith, discussed the Russian character, and elaborated on Gorbachev and the differences between him and "the old Kremlin dinosaurs." She briefed Reagan on a meeting she had held with the director of the All-Union Agency on Copyrights (VAAP),[60] who had laid out the Soviet agenda for the summit, presenting the Soviet views on the central issues, including Afghanistan, human rights, and the cultural agreement. With regard to the leaders' upcoming summit, Massie advised Reagan that because he had been in power longer than Gorbachev and was more secure in terms of domestic support, he could afford to be magnanimous.[61]

On the eve of the Geneva summit, Massie wrote to Reagan from Leningrad, describing a sense of hope for improved relations with the US that she had identified in Russia, and conveying her best wishes for the summit. Reagan, replying by way of the American consul in Leningrad, told Massie that he was reading her "magnificent book," which he had brought with him to the summit: "I'm really enjoying it, and it has also helped for the forthcoming meeting."[62] At the time Reagan was reading Massie's book on Russian history, and during a discussion with his advisors in Geneva a day before the summit he referred to the book, pondering what had happened to all the small shopkeepers who had resided in St. Petersburg in 1830.[63]

During this period Gorbachev was hinting at a strategic shift in the Soviet position. At the summit, he agreed to a 50 percent reduction of strategic nuclear weapons, and in January 1986 he publicly called for the abolition of nuclear weapons by 2000. Although their disagreement over SDI was still a significant obstacle, Reagan and Gorbachev did start to build a respectful and constructive relationship at this summit.[64]

The letters that Massie and Reagan exchanged after the summit and after she returned to the US reflected their shared perception that this was a moment of opportunity for change. Reagan wrote that he felt it might be "a point of beginning" and reported on a good chemistry with Gorbachev. Massie reinforced the president's impression and expressed her conviction, based on "many conversations, experiences, and observations of my months in Leningrad," that "this is an extraordinarily important historic crossroads in our relations."[65] But in parallel, voices in the security establishment raised doubts about the capability of the Soviets to change and whether the new leadership really represented fundamentally new thinking, and warned Reagan not to trust Gorbachev.[66] Massie criticized these voices, claiming they were "imbued with Cold War mentality" and "remained lost in their fixed ideas, convinced that nothing could ever change."[67]

Massie's references in her letter to her recent visit drew Reagan's interest and led to two meetings at the White House, on 20 May and 6 June 1986.[68] Reagan subsequently described her in his diary as "the greatest student I know of the Russian people."[69]

A major aspect of Massie's discussions with Reagan over the years was the spiritual transformation underway in the Soviet Union and the growing role of religion. She argued that the topic was a blind spot for US officials because they dealt only with Soviet bureaucrats. Reagan, as a religious person, was especially interested in this aspect and considered it a key for change. He frequently asked Massie about the religious dimension and, following the summit, informed her that Gorbachev had twice mentioned God and even cited a biblical verse.[70]

Massie also underscored Gorbachev's domestic constraints and the tension between him and those in the Soviet establishment who opposed his policy – in a manner reminiscent of Cousins's explanations to Kennedy regarding the struggle between Khrushchev and Soviet hardliners. After his June meeting with Massie, Reagan wrote in his diary that in her view Gorbachev and the "old guard" were in conflict and "I believe this is true."[71] Massie argued that this dynamic highlighted the importance of exchanging messages directly with Gorbachev, rather than through the Soviet bureaucracy.[72]

In her capacity as "Reagan's window on the Soviet Union" – in Mann's words – Massie exposed him to Russian culture and language and taught him terms and proverbs, as well as the correct pronunciation of Gorbachev's name.[73] The best-known example is her introduction, in September 1986, of the Russian proverb *doveryai no proveryai* ("trust but verify"), which she suggested he memorize and use in his talks with the Soviets. Shortly thereafter, at the Reagan–Gorbachev Reykjavík summit of October 1986, Reagan indeed invoked this proverb. He subsequently repeated the phrase on many occasions, including his speech at the signing of the Intermediate-Range Nuclear Forces Treaty in December 1987, after which Gorbachev observed, "You repeat that at every meeting."[74]

Massie also cultivated a relationship with the president's wife, Nancy Reagan. In advance of their May 1986 meeting, Massie suggested to Reagan that his wife join the discussion. In her book Massie explained the logic behind this offer: "If I were Nancy, I would want to take a look at any woman he was talking to about anything." Nancy accepted and, from that point, sometimes joined Reagan's meetings with Massie. On a few occasions Massie and the Reagans had private lunches at the White House. Massie and Nancy also met alone and maintained direct contact through letters and phone calls.[75]

In the spring of 1986, Massie asked McFarlane to connect her with Secretary of State George Shultz, and they met three times during 1986 and 1987. Shultz, on the one hand, opposed channels that were not controlled by the State Department and was more skeptical than the president regarding Massie's claims about a spiritual and religious revival in Russia. On the other hand, Shultz found great value in Massie's experience and felt that she revealed angles of the Soviet Union that he could not find in intelligence reports.[76]

In August 1986, a crisis erupted between the superpowers. After the FBI arrested Gennadiy Zakharov, a Soviet physicist and UN employee, on charges of espionage, the KGB arrested American journalist Nicholas Daniloff. Negotiations on a deal to resolve the crisis then ensued.[77] In the midst of these developments, Massie, having just returned from the Soviet Union, paid a visit to Washington, where she met separately with Matlock, Reagan, and Shultz. She criticized the decision to arrest Zakharov, querying who had made it as Reagan and Shultz were on vacation. Massie's meetings in Washington (22–23 September) took place amidst a growing debate within the administration, and among the public, on the deal under negotiation. In her discussions with Reagan and Shultz, Massie sought to convince them that Gorbachev was probably not behind the arrest of Daniloff, as he too had been on vacation, and she expressed support for the deal. She urged them not to push Gorbachev too far, as he was under tremendous pressure from hardliners "who want to stop this process of improvement."[78]

In her frequent contacts with Reagan and Shultz, Massie offered to help by providing an informal, secret backchannel, as she had for the cultural agreement in 1984: "I believe that Russians trust me and that I could make a contribution," she wrote to Reagan. She also argued that as a woman she had advantages because everybody thinks "women don't know anything" and it is easier to avoid the media. In Massie's assessment, moreover, the Soviets occasionally "favored unleaked personal messages" because their proposals were often leaked and appeared in the media.[79] Even though official communication between the countries had improved since her first mission in 1984, the parties continued to use Massie occasionally for the covert exchange of messages between Washington and Moscow. According to former CIA analyst John McLaughlin, the use of Massie as a secret emissary "perplexed and annoyed" Reagan's foreign policy team.[80]

Among the diverse range of Soviet contacts and networks developed by Massie over the years, her two main contacts in official circles were Bogdanov, the first deputy director of the USA Institute and a KGB official, and Igor Filin, executive sectary of the Peace Committee, former first secretary of the Soviet Embassy, and also a KGB official. According to Massie, they were part of a group of senior KGB officers who supported Gorbachev and were pushing for change.[81] Over the years the USA Institute engaged in meetings with Americans and track two forums (such as Dartmouth Conferences) and supported Gorbachev's new thinking.[82]

Massie's channel was used in early 1987 to convey a message from Gorbachev to Reagan. Bogdanov, in delivering the message to Massie, stressed that it should go directly to Reagan, rather than via Frank Carlucci, the new national security advisor. The message requested US assistance in facilitating a national reconciliation in Afghanistan, in exchange for Soviet help in other regional conflicts and progress on arms reduction. Massie requested a meeting with Reagan, delivered the message, and discussed it with Shultz as well. Reagan and Shultz decided not to proceed with the Soviet proposal. Shultz was critical of the exchange through Massie's channel, describing it as "another instance of the confusion that multiple, unofficial channels create."[83]

Another example involved discussions about a subsequent summit. At their summit in Geneva, Reagan and Gorbachev had agreed to hold the next two summits in Washington and Moscow, respectively. Yet the Soviets failed to respond to follow-up American inquiries regarding a summit in the US. Massie raised the subject with Bogdanov during her visit to Moscow in January 1987, and he replied that Gorbachev could not travel to the US because he would be killed. Massie reported on Bogdanov's concern to Reagan when they met in February 1987, and the president – referring to Massie having "dropped [a] bomb" – noted in his diary that he did not find the warning outlandish as the KGB was capable of such action. Nevertheless, Reagan insisted on holding a summit in the US and empowered Massie to convey a direct message to Gorbachev, inviting him to Washington to continue their face-to-face dialogue and promising that he would travel to Moscow the following year. In March 1987, Massie visited Moscow and personally conveyed the message to Vitaly Gussenko, a close advisor to Gorbachev. Gussenko telephoned her the next day to confirm delivery to Gorbachev and, on both their behalves, "expressed feelings of gratitude" for the message. Upon her return, Massie reported to Carlucci and Reagan.[84] In December 1987 Gorbachev did indeed visit Washington. Massie was invited to the State Dinner for the Gorbachevs at the White House, where she had the chance to meet the Gorbachevs. Raisa Gorbachev, while shaking her hand, said to Massie in Russian, "It is a wonderful book."[85]

On another occasion, Massie served as an informal envoy in the service of Nancy Reagan. Nancy told Massie that the Soviet Union had denied her son's request for a visa. Massie, after raising the issue with officials in Moscow, learned that Gorbachev had not known about this, and that it had to do with sanctions against all ABC network personnel in response to the television series *Amerika*, which was considered offensive to the Soviet Union. Nonetheless, officials in Moscow assured Massie that Reagan's son was welcome to visit whenever he wanted.[86]

In her memoirs, Massie explained that she had tried to influence and persuade both parties: in Moscow she defended Reagan, while in Washington she explained Gorbachev's perspective. "I wasn't only pushing Reagan," she wrote, "but the Russians, too, trying to move them toward each other, trying to explain things to the Russians that would help them understand Reagan – and vice versa – in a way that wasn't so blind and stereotyped."[87]

**Figure 3.2** Soviet leader Mikhail Gorbachev and Suzanne Massie at the White House State Dinner, December 1987

## Challenges and the end of Massie's activity

As Massie's influence grew, so too did the opposition to her efforts within the administration. Her detractors sought to curtail her access to the president. An influential factor in this context was the nomination of Carlucci as the new national security advisor in late 1986. Whereas McFarlane had facilitated Massie's role, and his successor John Poindexter had demonstrated support, Carlucci was more suspicious and demanded to be present at any meeting between Massie and Reagan.[88] In March 1987 the NSC delivered a still-classified intelligence document that evidently concluded that Massie could unwittingly be used by the KGB to influence Reagan.[89] The NSC document did not bar Massie's access to Reagan but it did signal an internal government campaign against her. An April 1987 memorandum to Carlucci from Fritz Ermarth, a Soviet specialist at the NSC, reveals another aspect of the campaign: after Massie had written to Reagan on 13 April 1987, suggesting that they meet so she could report on her recent visit to Russia, Ermarth drafted a proposed reply from the president that aimed to "discourage future visits." Ermarth acknowledged that Reagan would probably find his draft unfriendly, but he argued that if Reagan replied "with his natural style" it would encourage "future requests for access." Ermarth's proposed letter stated that Reagan was unable to meet Massie and suggested that she brief Carlucci or a member of his staff, or send a detailed report.[90] Reagan did not approve the letter and Massie was invited to meet with him in May 1987.[91]

In preparation for Reagan's meetings with Massie, Carlucci drafted memoranda that incorporated responses and counter-arguments to her views and claims. In February 1987, for example, after Massie had sent a letter to Reagan criticizing the US decision to expel Soviet diplomats, and in advance of a meeting between the two, Carlucci presented the president with arguments about the necessity of the decision and recommended that he convey these points to Massie.[92] On another occasion in advance of a scheduled Reagan–Massie meeting, Carlucci wrote that Russia's spiritual revival, on which Massie was so keen, also has negative aspects.[93] The memoranda surrounding Massie's visits to the White House during the tenures of Carlucci (1987) and Colin Powell (1988) as national security advisors reflect efforts to restrict her time with the president to ten or twenty minutes. They indicate that the national security advisors would suggest breaking after the allocated time, and that Massie "may find the time allocation somewhat limiting."[94]

Opposition to Massie within the establishment was also fueled by the fact that Massie's influence was beginning to draw media attention. The press was reporting on her meetings with the president as well as her impact on his views. The *New York Times* described Massie as "a Russian expert who has the President's ear," and *Time* magazine – in an article on the softening of Reagan's position on Russia – referred to her as a "writer with whom Reagan developed a particular rapport."[95] The campaign against Massie also formed part of an internal debate in Washington over relations with the Soviets. Within the security establishment, the arms control talks were a source of criticism and concern regarding Reagan and his policy, particularly after the Reykjavík summit, and Massie was perceived as influencing Reagan to be more dovish.[96]

In addition, in early 1987 Massie suggested that her unofficial role be replaced with an official position. The ambassador to Moscow was about to leave, and on the advice of friends in Washington, Massie wrote to Reagan informing him of her interest in the job. Reagan, surprised, replied that he had no idea she "would be interested in being 'Our Man' in Moscow," adding that he saw her as a "trusted advisor" and hoped she woyld continue to be. The new ambassador was already selected at that point. In her memoirs Massie wrote of her embarrassment at having broken "my rule of never asking him for anything." The idea of Massie as a candidate for ambassador – an idea also raised in the media and by some senators – triggered anger in the State Department and might have exacerbated the hostility towards Massie in the establishment. Carlucci wrote to Reagan that "she clearly wants to play a representational role herself."[97]

Referring to the forces fighting against her, Massie explained that bureaucrats wished to preserve the status quo, and "anyone from the outside who had different views was, by their very nature, suspicious, threatening, and, like a virus, to be excluded or neutralized." Massie argued she was "unconventional" and "a rare woman in that virtually all-male world," whereas the president's advisors wanted to exercise exclusive influence and limit access by anybody else.[98]

Despite the challenges, Massie continued to meet with Reagan until the end of his presidency. During Reagan's historical visit to Moscow in the spring of 1988, Massie's influence was evident: she had advised the president to talk about the contribution of the Soviet women, and Reagan did precisely that on various occasions throughout the visit.[99] Their last meeting in the White House took place in August 1988, when Massie reported to Reagan on the reactions she had heard in Moscow following his visit and on a conversation she had had with Raisa Gorbachev. Reagan and Massie met for the last time in 1990, when Reagan visited Leningrad as a former president, and Massie gave Reagan and Nancy a tour of Pavlovsk Palace. During the 1990s, after the end of the Cold War, Massie was engaged in various cultural and humanitarian projects in Russia. When Reagan died in 2004, Nancy invited Massie to the state funeral. Massie, who was visiting Russia, took a special flight in order to attend.[100]

## Analysis and conclusions: the impact of PPE Massie on the official sphere

### *Influence patterns*

Author James Mann highlighted Massie's role, arguing that she "made a bigger impression upon the president of the United States than the reporting and analysis of the Central Intelligence Agency." He stressed that she met Reagan more often than any other private citizen outside of governmental circles, and claimed that "at a couple of junctures" she played a more significant role than that conveyed by the official historiography.[101] Journalist Christopher Lydon also saw great importance in Massie's activity, describing her as "the woman who ended the Cold War" thanks to "the almost unimaginable persuasive power that she brought to bear on Ronald Reagan."[102] The US ambassador to Moscow, John Huntsman, said in 2017 that there are lessons to be learned from Massie's story: "Private citizens can play a role, just as Suzanne did."[103]

McFarlane argued that Massie "educated Reagan on the difference between the Russian people and the Soviet government," and made him take an interest in the human dimensions of Russia.[104] Likewise, scholars David Reynolds and Robert Ivany pointed out Massie's contribution in changing Reagan's perception of the Russians and in developing his ability to relate to, and empathize with, them.[105] Scholar Michael Schaller claimed that Massie gave Reagan "the kind of folksy reassurance he needed" to justify to himself his engagement with the country he had described as the "evil empire."[106] Others, however, have disputed these arguments regarding Massie's impact on Reagan. Matlock, for example, considered Massie a "marginal figure" who had no influence on policy.[107] Journalist Nicholas Daniloff described Massie's influence as "notable" but argued that other factors – the roles of Nancy Reagan and Margaret Thatcher as well as Soviet politics under Gorbachev – would have changed Reagan's policy towards the Soviet Union even without Massie's contribution.[108] It should be noted that although the parties used Massie to exchange messages, her impact on official diplomatic communication and negotiation was limited.

Which influence patterns were at work in Massie's activity as a PPE? Massie was employing *influence through mediation* as she traveled between Washington and Moscow and met with American and Soviet officials, seeking to sway them and improve their relations. An important element in these efforts was her role as *communicator*, exchanging messages and proposals, including a Soviet message about Afghanistan and an American message about Gorbachev's visit to Washington. Massie also played the role of a *psychoanalyst*, exposing each side to the perspective of the rival side, clarifying misperceptions, and seeking to change the "enemy image." She introduced Reagan to the human dimensions of Russia and highlighted the changes and internal differences on the Soviet side: "My most significant contribution," she claimed, "was offering him a deeper understanding of the Russian people, humanizing them so that he no longer viewed them as faceless communists."[109] Other mediation roles were less significant but sometimes relevant: Massie helped as a *formulator*, suggesting ways of communicating with the Soviets; although she could not be described as a *facilitator*, as she did not facilitate meetings between officials on both sides, she did facilitate a number of cultural cooperation projects; and she used certain tools as a *manipulator*, warning of the possibility of escalation to war, or of the growing strength of Soviet hardliners.

Massie also exerted *influence through the transmission of ideas*. She promoted the idea of renewing cultural negotiations as a first step, and that idea served as a basis for her 1984 mission to Moscow. She also introduced Reagan to various concepts that were later translated into the official diplomatic discourse. His use of the Russian proverb "trust, but verify" and his reference to the role of Soviet women are examples. Massie's suggestions to Reagan also produced *influence through gestures of conciliation* as she advised him on ways to approach and build trust with Gorbachev and the Soviet Union. She was also involved in *influence through crisis management* by helping the parties emerge from the escalating crisis in late 1983, and through her discussions with administration officials during the Daniloff–Zakharov crisis.

### Variables related to the PPE

Massie, as a writer and an expert on Russian culture and history, was a scholar PPE. Her professional path brought her to the Soviet Union and gave her the opportunity to visit frequently and develop networks in Russia. Her research and publications provided her with important symbolic capital and resources that helped her in her PPE activity.

As a PPE and a woman, Massie faced unique gender-related challenges because she operated within an all-male world. There were almost no women in senior positions at the State Department,[110] in the security establishment or the White House (except for Nancy Reagan), or on the Soviet side. At various meetings and White House gatherings, Massie was the only woman in the room. She was strongly aware of the gender dimension in her experience as PPE and referred to it numerous times in her book. It reinforced her sense of being an outsider and contributed to her characterization in governmental circles as "romantic" and not serious.[111] Massie was told by a lecture agent, when she started to give lectures, that "men do not like to hear about politics from women," and in her memoirs she wrote that when the media asked about her meetings with the president, she "deliberately trivialized" herself and replied that they discussed culture, explaining that "culture is permitted to a woman, after all."[112] But Massie also found advantages in being a woman PPE, mainly in her ability to maintain a "low profile," and she told Shultz that women could be especially useful in secret informal diplomacy, as the media would not suspect them.[113]

The main power resources in Massie's activities were the following:

1.  *Access and network system.* On the American side, Massie developed contacts with senators and military officers in the 1970s, and in 1983 she gained access to the White House. Senator Cohen connected her with McFarlane, and McFarlane introduced her to the president. Massie and Reagan developed a special relationship that continued from their first meeting in 1984 until the end of Reagan's presidency, during which time they met on seventeen occasions and exchanged letters and phone calls. An archivist in the Reagan Library told Massie that she had more "face time" with Reagan on Russia than anyone else except for his

advisors.[114] Their relationship evolved into a friendship: Massie wrote to Reagan on his birthdays and after his surgery, and Reagan wrote to Massie when her grandson was born, and on a few occasions personally telephoned her.[115] Massie also formed a relationship with Nancy Reagan and had a few private lunches with the Reagans. Senior officials joined some of Massie's meetings with the president, and occasionally she had separate meetings with Shultz. After Carlucci was appointed national security advisor, there were some efforts to reduce Massie's access to Reagan, but their contact continued.

Massie's initial access to the White House became possible thanks to her knowledge, approach to Russia (her focus on human dimensions and realism), and networks in Washington (McFarlane reportedly received recommendations from two senators he respected) as well as Russia.[116] Her continuing access to Reagan was based on his appreciation of her expertise, his interest in her analysis and advice, and her ongoing visits to, and meetings in, Russia.

On the Soviet side, Massie developed wide networks with people from various fields, but her first meetings with Soviet officials were in the early 1980s: first with Berezhkov thanks to Cobb, who facilitated the contact, and later Berezhkov introduced her to Arbatov (USA Institute). During the second half of the 1980s, her main contact persons in official circles were Bogdanov (USA Institute) and Filin (Peace Committee), both from the KGB, and she also met with Gussenko, Gorbachev's advisor. She had indirect contact with Andropov (who approved her visa) and with Gorbachev, and she had brief exchanges with Gorbachev and his wife, Raisa Gorbachev.[117]

Massie's access to Soviet officials was based on two elements. One was her scholarly work, as her books were valued by the Soviets. The transmission of her book, through Cobb, led to her contact with Berezhkov, and copies also reached Andropov and Gorbachev. The second element was her contacts in Washington. At an early stage her contact with Cobb helped her gain access to Soviet officials – first to Berezhkov and then to Bogdanov, and later the well-known fact of her meetings with the president was helpful in terms of opening doors in Moscow. According to Massie, the Soviets believed that she was honest in her efforts, and that she was not working for any government.[118]

2. *Knowledge resources.* Massie had unique knowledge resources that helped her as a PPE. Her knowledge of Russian history and culture, and her fluent Russian, provided her with useful tools in both Russia and the US. She also had good communication and articulation skills, and she knew how to tell a story. McFarlane referred to Massie as Scheherazade – "weaving a web of stories ... to build Reagan's interest."[119] These

skills helped her spark Reagan's curiosity and draw his attention. Her briefings on Russian people and culture "seemed to interest him more than the strategic power calculations of his experts in the Department of State and Department of Defense," according to Daniloff.[120] Massie also developed knowledge resources through her contacts in Washington and Moscow, which deepened her understanding of the main issues, the views of each side, and developments behind the scenes. Massie's frequent travels to Russia gave her an advantage over specialists who did not visit it. She had unique access to the Russian public thanks to her vast and diverse networks, which gave her insights into the perspective of "the man in the street," as Reagan termed it in a letter to Massie.[121]

3. *Value-based resources.* Massie had a unique point of view, which helped her on both sides. On the one hand, she had a special interest in and passion for Russian culture and people. She devoted her life to studying Russia, and this proved an important resource in building contacts and trust with the Soviet side. On the other hand, Massie drew a clear distinction between the Russians and the Communist regime, emphasizing her criticism and negative view of the Soviet system. She was also on the board of the International League for Human Rights, and participated in protests in front of the Soviet Embassy in support for dissidents.[122] This aspect helped Massie in establishing contact with the White House. McFarlane stressed that Massie loved the Russian people but was "a realist about communism" and had "no illusions about the damage done by the Marxist–Leninist authoritarian political system."[123] In addition, the fact that Massie was known as a writer and scholar, and not as a political activist or member of a political party or movement, helped her establish a more objective image. However, she was occasionally perceived in official circles as having a romanticized view of the "Russian soul."[124]

## Variables related to the initiative

1. *Secrecy/publicity and the action pattern.* Massie kept the details of her meetings with Reagan, and her discussions and backchannel missions in Moscow, confidential. Neither the media nor the public knew about her 1984 mission in real time or about the messages she delivered between the two countries. In time, however, the media began reporting on Massie's meetings with Reagan, and McFarlane told Massie that she could mention having met with the president. Massie used her research as a cover to explain her visits to the Soviet Union and meetings at the White House. She revealed the full account of her PPE activity only in the book she published in 2013.

2. *The goal of the initiative.* Massie's first mission had the specific goal of renewing cultural exchanges as an initial step. It centered on a topic

that was not extremely sensitive relative to others: in Massie's words to Bogdanov, "the only thing we can agree on is mothers and culture."[125] Her subsequent efforts did not focus solely on one issue, but rather formed part of the broader aim of improving the relationship and dialogue between the parties. Massie usually focused on relatively tactical steps that could assist the rapprochement process during the Reagan–Gorbachev era, and not on promoting a specific outline of agreement or a detailed strategic political vision.

3. *Correlation with official policy.* Massie's PPE efforts were always in line with Reagan's policy, and she never publicly criticized the administration's policy on the Soviet Union. Nor did she seek to promote a goal that conflicted with official policy. However, in the internal debate between dovish and hawkish camps within the administration, Massie sided with the more moderate voices. Over time she grew more confident in her contacts with Reagan and Shultz and allowed herself to express critical views, for example regarding the American ambassador to Moscow or the American decision to expel Soviet diplomats.

4. *Direct or indirect contact.* In contrast to Cousins, Massie did not have direct contact with the leader on each side. On the American side she developed direct and close contact with the US president, whereas on the Soviet side she had access to mid-level Soviet officials who conveyed her messages to the Soviet leaders.

## External variables

1. *Characteristics of the conflict.* Massie operated within an international conflict between two superpowers that maintained official diplomatic relations, but under conditions of political and ideological rivalry, an arms race, and competition for influence around the globe. During the period under review, the parties' bilateral relations were marked by numerous disputes (on issues such as arms control, SDI, and human rights), crises (such as the Korean airliner incident and the Daniloff–Zakharov crisis), and conflicts in various parts of the world, including Europe, Latin America, and the Middle East.

2. *Ripeness.* Massie's 1983 initiative took place against a background of growing tension and a combination of events that brought the parties to the brink of war. The danger of this war scare contributed to a perception, among various actors on both sides, of a *mutually hurting stalemate* and of an urgent need to change the superpowers' relations. According to Nate Jones, "the 1983 War Scare served as the fulcrum that pivoted US–Soviet relations from the worst days of the Cold War to their best cooperation since World War II."[126] Massie's proposal of embarking on an informal mission to the Soviet Union came at a time when the Reagan

administration was already looking for ways to renew the dialogue, as illustrated by Reagan's conciliatory speech the day before his first meeting with Massie. Gorbachev's policy and new thinking reinforced the signs of ripeness in the US and encouraged the emergence of the second element in the ripeness theory: the perception that there is a way out. The 1983 crisis had an impact on the Soviet side too, and 1984 saw the first signs of change vis-à-vis the US. This process intensified with Gorbachev's appointment. The 1986 Chernobyl disaster, which occurred during the Gorbachev era, was an important milestone that strengthened the Soviets' sense of urgency surrounding arms control agreements with the US.[127]

3. *The leaders' positions and the domestic conditions.* On the American side, Reagan's tone and policy regarding the Soviet Union shifted in 1984, and his strategy during his second term differed significantly from that of his first.[128] Massie's involvement began just as Reagan was aiming to renew the dialogue with the Soviets. At the time an internal debate was taking place within the administration between the moderate camp, led by Shultz, and the hardliners, led by Weinberger. Reagan was shifting towards Shultz, and McFarlane's appointment reinforced this trend. Reagan believed that having demonstrated US military strength during his early years in office, could now take steps towards negotiating and peacemaking from a position of strength. It is also notable that alongside his anti-communist stance and hawkish reputation, Reagan strongly believed in the abolition of nuclear weapons, and he was optimistic about changing the US relationship with the Soviet Union, especially during the Gorbachev era.[129] Reagan was also popular and politically strong at this point. His 1984 reelection marked one of the biggest victories in US history, and it provided him with a strong mandate and the public legitimacy to promote bold moves. But Reagan still faced internal opposition within his administration and his party over the issue of negotiations with the Soviets, as well as political fallout during 1986–1987 from the Iran-Contra affair.[130]

On the Soviet side, the first half of the 1980s were marked by instability, with four leaders in twenty-six months as well as social and economic crisis. Chernenko ruled for only thirteen months and suffered from ill health, but he supported Brezhnev's détente policy, and promoted the first steps of American–Soviet reengagement.[131] Gorbachev's positions represented a dramatic shift and new thinking on domestic and foreign affairs. He was eager to build new relations with the US, defuse the tension, and stop the arms race. These were not mere tactical changes; rather, they reflected a strategic vision aimed at modernizing Soviet foreign policy, preventing the catastrophe of war, and diverting resources to domestic needs. Gorbachev, who faced opposition within the Soviet establishment, replaced and dismissed several potential rivals in order to achieve full control over matters of policy.[132]

4. *Parallel channels of communication.* The US and the Soviet Union had official relations and communication channels. But in the early 1980s, in light of growing tension, their contact diminished and almost no high-level talks took place. Reagan never met with his Soviet counterpart during his first term. These tensions peaked in late 1983, when the Soviets suspended the arms control talks. Civilian contacts were almost nonexistent, as the cultural exchange programs had been frozen since 1979. It was under these conditions that Massie initiated her first mission, and they compelled the administration to accept informal channels and emissaries. Another example of an unofficial channel with Moscow during these years was that of Lawrence Horowitz, an assistant to Senator Edward Kennedy.[133] The situation changed during the Reagan–Gorbachev era as official contacts and negotiations increased, and Reagan and Shultz met with their Soviet counterparts. But the parties still found value in the use of unofficial channels, such as Massie's, in order to circumvent bureaucracy, as well as certain official actors, and to guarantee secrecy.

5. *Internal governmental agents.* Massie had important allies in the official US establishment. Cobb helped her open doors and reach Soviet officials, and McFarlane was instrumental in granting her access to the White House.[134] The governmental opposition she faced after McFarlane was replaced illustrates his significant role. Over time, Reagan himself became a governmental ally who supported Massie and sought to maintain contact with her. Massie noted that she received more support and respect from military officials than civilian bureaucrats, especially in the State Department.[135] On the Soviet side, Massie's two main allies – Bogdanov and Filin – came from the USA Institute and the Peace Committee, and both were KGB officials.

## Notes

1 G. Shultz, *Turmoil and Triumph* (New York: Charles Scribner's Sons, 1993), 720.
2 J. Mann, *The Rebellion of Ronald Reagan* (London: Penguin, 2010).
3 S. Massie, *Trust but Verify: Reagan, Russia and Me* (Rockland: Maine Authors Publishing, 2013).
4 C. Lydon, "Agent of influence," *The Atlantic*, 271:2 (1993), 28.
5 R. S. Newell, "International responses to the Afghanistan crisis," *The World Today*, 37:5 (1981), 172–181.

6 R. Reagan, "Remarks at the Annual Convention of the National Association of Evangelicals in Orlando, Florida," 8 March 1983, The Reagan Foundation and Institute: www.reaganfoundation.org/library-museum/permanent-exhibitions/berlin-wall/from-the-archives/remarks-at-the-annual-convention-of-the-national-association-of-evangelicals-in-orlando-florida/ (accessed 19 April 2022).

7 R. G. Patman, "Reagan, Gorbachev and the emergence of 'new political thinking,'" *Review of International Studies*, 25:4 (1999), 580–582; J. Matlock, *Reagan and Gorbachev* (New York: Random House, 2004), 11–13, 38–39, 59–60; J. Wilson, *The Triumph of Improvisation* (Ithaca: Cornell University Press, 2014), 71–73.

8 Wilson, *The Triumph*, 63–64, 74, 85–86; B. Miller and Z. Rubinovitz, *Grand Strategy from Truman to Trump* (Chicago: University of Chicago Press, 2020), 157–158; R. M. Gates, *From the Shadows* (New York: Simon and Schuster, 2011), 278–292.

9 Matlock, *Reagan and Gorbachev*, 38–46.

10 J. Santore, "The Soviet crisis of the early 1980s and Mikhail Gorbachev's rise to power," *Socialism and Democracy*, 6:2 (1990), 1–15; P. Shearman, "New political thinking reassessed," *Review of International Studies*, 19:2 (1993), 139–158; Patman, "Reagan, Gorbachev," 577–601.

11 N. Jones, *Able Archer 83* (New York: The New Press, 2016), 108.

12 R. Reagan, "Address to the Nation on the Soviet Attack on a Korean Civilian Airliner," 5 September 1983, The Reagan Library: www.reaganlibrary.gov/archives/speech/address-nation-soviet-attack-korean-civilian-airliner (acccessed 19 April 2022).

13 Gates, *From the Shadows*, 266–273; D. Oberdorfer, *The Turn* (New York: Simon & Schuster, 1991), 51–68; Wilson, *The Triumph*, 76–78; On Able Archer 83 see Jones, *Able Archer 83*; L. Scott, "November 1983: The most dangerous moment of the cold war?" *Intelligence and National Security*, 35:1 (2020), 131–148.

14 Oberdorfer, *The Turn*, 67–68.

15 Mann, *The Rebellion*, 68–69; Massie, *Trust but Verify*, 13–15; S. Kozuharov, "Suzanne Massie," *St. Petersburg Times*, White Nights 2004, 5; Interview with Suzanne Massie, 15 January 2021.

16 Mann, *The Rebellion*, 69–70; Massie, *Trust but Verify*, 15–16, 22–31; Lydon, "Agent of influence," 28, 30.

17 S. Massie, *The Living Mirror: Five Young Poets from Leningrad Comp* (Garden City: Doubleday, 1972).

18 S. Massie, *Land of the Firebird: The Beauty of Old Russia* (New York: Simon and Schuster, 1980).

19 Mann, *The Rebellion*, 70–71; Massie, *Trust but Verify*, 32–33, 45–47.

20 Lydon, "Agent of influence," 28; "A Russian expert who has the President's ear," *New York Times* (26 September 1985).

21 Massie, *Trust but Verify*, 48, 300; "A Russian expert".

22 "A Russian expert"; Interview with Suzanne Massie.

23 Massie, *Trust but Verify*, 19, 40.

24 Massie, *Trust but Verify*, 18, 52.

25  Massie, *Trust but Verify*, 16, 18; Interview with Suzanne Massie.
26  Massie, *Trust but Verify*, 35, 41–43, 54–56; Mann, *The Rebellion*, 70–71.
27  Massie, *Trust but Verify*, 57–58; Lydon, "Agent of influence," 30.
28  The USA Institute, later renamed the Institute of USA and Canada, was founded by the Soviet Academy of Sciences in 1967. See G. Arbatov, *The System* (New York: Times Books, 1992), 295–328; J. Phillips, "Unmasking Moscow's: 'Institute of the U.S.A,'" *Heritage Foundation* (17 December 1982).
29  Massie, *Trust but Verify*, 59–62; Mann, *The Rebellion*, 72. Massie was later informed that Andropov had received the book with her inscription, and had personally approved her visa request (Massie, *Trust but Verify*, 68).
30  Massie, *Trust but Verify*, 62–69; Mann, *The Rebellion*, 73–74. Berezhkov left his position in Washington and moved back to Moscow in 1983.
31  Massie, *Trust but Verify*, 69–71; Mann, *The Rebellion*, 75–76.
32  Massie, *Trust but Verify*, 69–71, 74, 77–78; Mann, *The Rebellion*, 76.
33  Massie, *Trust but Verify*, 80–82; Mann, *The Rebellion*, 76; Lydon, "Agent of influence"; Interview with Suzanne Massie.
34  Massie, *Trust but Verify*, 85–87; Mann, *The Rebellion*, 76.
35  Gates, *From the Shadows*, 258; Dobrynin, *In Confidence*, 478.
36  Matlock, *Reagan and Gorbachev*, 91–92; Mann, *The Rebellion*, 79, 83.
37  Massie, *Trust but Verify*, 90; Mann, *The Rebellion*, 82; Matlock, *Reagan and Gorbachev*, 92–93.
38  Mann, *The Rebellion*, 82–83; N. Daniloff, "Trust but verify: Reagan, Russia, and me by Suzanne Massie (review)," *Journal of Cold War Studies*, 18:4 (2016), 225–228.
39  Wilson, *The Triumph*, 80.
40  Massie, *Trust but Verify*, 95; Mann, *The Rebellion*, 84.
41  See Matlock, *Reagan and Gorbachev*, 80–87; Mann, *The Rebellion*, 679–680.
42  Massie, *Trust but Verify*, 98–101; Mann, *The Rebellion*, 84; R. Reagan, *The Reagan Diaries* (New York: Reagan Presidential Libraries, 2007), 213.
43  Massie, *Trust but Verify*, 101; Interview with Suzanne Massie.
44  Ronald Reagan Presidential Library (hereafter RRPL), Presidential Handwriting File (hereafter PHF) 8/116, Massie to Reagan, 20 January 1984.
45  Massie, *Trust but Verify*, 103–113, 132; Matlock, *Reagan and Gorbachev*, 93.
46  Massie, *Trust but Verify*, 114–115; RRPL, PHF 8/116, Reagan to Massie, 15 February 1984.
47  Massie, *Trust but Verify*, 115–128.
48  Reagan, *The Reagan Diaries*, 222.
49  Reagan, *The Reagan Diaries*, 223.
50  Massie, *Trust but Verify*, 114; Shultz, *Turmoil and Triumph*, 606. In November 1984, after Reagan's reelection, the Soviets decided to renew the arms control talks that had been suspended in November 1983.
51  RRPL, PHF 10/139, Massie to Reagan, 1 August 1984; Reagan to Massie, 21 August 1984.
52  RRPL, PHF 10/151, Massie to Reagan, 8 November 1984; Reagan to Massie, 11 December 1984.

53 Massie, *Trust but Verify*, 368–369; Lydon, "Agent of influence," 28, 30; Mann, *The Rebellion*, 84.

54 Mann, *The Rebellion*, 67.

55 Matlock, *Reagan and Gorbachev*, 132–135; Mann, *The Rebellion*, 90; R. Ivany, "Empathy: The cornerstone of leadership," *Leader to Leader*, 93 (2019), 24–28; Wilson, *The Triumph*, 97.

56 Reagan phoned Massie to thank her for the get-well letter she had sent following his surgery in July. RRPL, PHF 1/11, Massie to Reagan, 28 July 1985; Massie, *Trust but Verify*, 159–162.

57 RRPL, PHF 1/11, Massie to Reagan, 10 August 1985; Massie, *Trust but Verify*, 159, 166.

58 RRPL, PHF 1/11, Hall to Matlock, 6 August 1985; Hall to Proctor, 6 August 1985; Matlock to Martin, 8 August 1985; Matlock to McFarlane, 19 August 1985; Memorandum from McFarlane, 30 August 1985.

59 Reagan, *The Reagan Diaries*, 350.

60 On VAAP see E. Muravina, "Copyright transactions with Soviet authors: The role of VAAP," *Loyola Entertainment Law Journal*, 11 (1991), 421–451.

61 Massie, *Trust but Verify*, 164–173; Matlock, *Reagan and Gorbachev*, 134; Lydon, "Agent of Influence," 28; Daniloff, "Trust but verify," 226.

62 RRPL, PHF 14/209, Massie to Reagan, 27 October 1985; Reagan to Massie, 15 November 1985; Massie, *Trust but Verify*, 181–182.

63 Oberdorfer, *The Turn*, 143; Mann, *The Rebellion*, 65–66; Matlock, *Reagan and Gorbachev*, 134.

64 B. Farnham, "Reagan and the Gorbachev revolution: Perceiving the end of threat," *Political Science Quarterly*, 116:2 (2001), 236; Wilson, *The Triumph*, 98–101; Miller and Rubinovitz, *Grand Strategy*, 161–163.

65 RRPL, PHF 14/224, Reagan to Massie, 10 February 1986; RRPL, Coordination Office, NSC: Records (hereafter CC-NSC) 12, Massie to Reagan, 12 March 1986.

66 Wilson, *The Triumph*, 94–95, 98; Mann, *The Rebellion*, 102–103, 135, 139–140.

67 Massie, *Trust but Verify*, 300.

68 RRPL, CC-NSC 12, Matlock to Mcdaniel, 24 March 1986; Memorandum by Poindexter, 16 May 1986.

69 Reagan, *The Reagan Diaries*, 412.

70 Massie, *Trust but Verify*, 99–100, 126–128, 134–156; Mann, *The Rebellion*, 87–88; Reagan to Massie, 10 February 1986; Reagan, *The Reagan Diaries*, 412; M. E. Malinkin, "Reagan's evolving views of Russians and their relevance today," *Wilson Center* (1 December 2008); Wilson, *The Triumph*, 97–98.

71 Reagan, *The Reagan Diaries*, 417.

72 Massie, *Trust but Verify*, 213–214.

73 Mann, *The Rebellion*, 85; Massie, *Trust but Verify*, 209.

74 Oberdorfer, *The Turn*, 261; Massie, *Trust but Verify*, 230–233; Mann, *The Rebellion*, 65.

75 Massie, *Trust but Verify*, 243–244; Massie to Reagan, 12 March 1986. Nancy Reagan, in a retrospective interview with Mann, described Massie as "pushy" (Mann, *The Rebellion*, 65).

76  Shultz, *Turmoil and Triumph*, 720; Massie, *Trust but Verify*, 304–305; Daniloff, "Trust but verify," 227.

77  See Matlock, *Reagan and Gorbachev*, 197–211.

78  Shultz, *Turmoil and Triumph*, 746; Massie, *Trust but Verify*, 222–223, 311–312; Mann, *The Rebellion*, 97–98; RRPL, CC-NSC 13, Poindexter to the President, 19 September 1986.

79  RRPL, CC-NSC 14, Massie to Reagan, 6 February 1987; Massie, *Trust but Verify*, 312, 316.

80  J. McLaughlin, "The real Ronald Reagan," *SAIS Review of International Affairs*, 30:1 (2010), 150.

81  Massie, *Trust but Verify*, 270–286.

82  Shearman, "New political thinking," 139–158; Arbatov, *The System*, 295–328.

83  Massie, *Trust but Verify*, 275–276, 315–316, 325–326; Shultz, *Turmoil and Triumph*, 872–873; Wilson, *The Triumph*, 129.

84  Massie, *Trust but Verify*, 248–249, 258, 276; Reagan, *The Reagan Diaries*, 478; RRPL, CC-NSC 14, Massie to Reagan, 13 April 1987; Carlucci to Reagan, 30 April 1987; M. C. Quinn, "Reagan–Dobrynin meeting: Plans for next summit?" *United Press International*, 7 April 1986; Interview with Suzanne Massie; Mann, *The Rebellion*, 112–114.

85  Massie, *Trust but Verify*, 264; E. Kastor and D. Radcliffe, "The night of the peacemakers," *Washington Post* (9 December 1987).

86  Massie, *Trust but Verify*, 247; Massie to Reagan, 13 April 1987; Reuters, "Soviet refuses to allow visit by Ron Reagan Jr," *New York Times* (10 January 1987).

87  Massie, *Trust but Verify*, 169.

88  Mann, *The Rebellion*, 106–107; Massie, *Trust but Verify*, 301–302.

89  RRPL, Lisa R. Jameson Files (hereafter LRJF) 1, NSC Intelligence Document, 2 March 1987; Mann, *The Rebellion*, 107–108; Massie, *Trust but Verify*, 299.

90  RRPL, LRJF 1, Massie to Reagan, 13 April 1987; Ermarth to Carlucci, 23 April 1987.

91  Mann, *The Rebellion*, 110; RRPL CC-NSC 14, Ermarth to Green, 27 April 1987.

92  RRPL CC-NSC 14, Massie to Reagan, 6 February 1987; Carlucci to Reagan, 17 February 1987.

93  Carlucci to Reagan, 30 April 1987.

94  RRPL, LRJF 1, Carlucci to Reagan, 2 October 1987; RRPL, CC-NSC 17, Memorandum from Powell, 10 March 1988.

95  "A Russian expert"; B. Seaman, "Has Reagan gone soft?" *Time* (13 October 1986).

96  Mann, *The Rebellion*, 107; Massie, *Trust but Verify*, 299–300; Wilson, *The Triumph*, 84–85.

97  Massie to Reagan, 6 February 1987; Massie, *Trust but Verify*, 287–291; Carlucci to Reagan, 17 February 1987.

98  Massie, *Trust but Verify*, 295–299.

99  Malinkin, "Reagan's"; Oberdorfer, *The Turn*, 298; Massie, *Trust but Verify*, 330, 346. Massie conveyed another message from Moscow to Reagan on 11

March 1988, and was later informed that the administration had responded through official channels. She also joined eleven senators in a visit to the Soviet Union in April 1988. See: Mann, *The Rebellion*, 282–285; RRPL, LRJF 1, Ermarth to Powell, 31 March 1988.

100 Reagan, *The Reagan Diaries*, 636; RRPL, CC-NSC 18, Powell to Reagan, 1 August 1988; D. O'Connell, "At first, small miracles," *Hemalog*, 5:2 (1994), 16–19; Kozuharov, "Suzanne Massie"; Massie, *Trust but Verify*, 352, 357–359, 371–372.

101 Mann, *The Rebellion*, 63–66; J. Mann, "The lady who warmed up the Cold War," *Daily Beast* (10 March 2009).

102 C. Lydon, "Suzanne Massie: Reagan and Russia," *Open Source* (20 March 2014).

103 See J. Lifflander, "'Russian lessons for Reagan' launch at Gorbachev Foundation reunites old friends," *The Moscow Times* (13 December 2017).

104 Massie, *Trust but Verify*, 369.

105 D. Reynolds, "Summitry as intercultural communication," *International Affairs*, 85:1 (2009), 125; Ivany, "Empathy," 27.

106 M. Schaller, "The ongoing mystery of Ronald Reagan," *Diplomatic History*, 34:2 (2010), 457.

107 Mann, "The lady."

108 Daniloff, "Trust but verify," 225–228.

109 Massie, *Trust but Verify*, 19.

110 One exception was Assistant Secretary of State for European and Canadian Affairs Rozanne Ridgway.

111 Massie, *Trust but Verify*, 290, 298.

112 Massie, *Trust but Verify*, 47, 296–297.

113 Massie, *Trust but Verify*, 312; Interview with Suzanne Massie.

114 Massie, *Trust but Verify*, 361.

115 "A Russian expert"; RRPL, PHF 14/224, Massie to Reagan, 1 February 1986; RRPL, PHF 19/304, Massie to Reagan, 6 February 1987; Massie to Reagan, 28 July 1985; Reagan to Massie, 12 August 1987.

116 Massie, *Trust but Verify*, 369.

117 In 2017 the Gorbachev Foundation hosted a book launch for the Russian edition of *Trust but Verify*, and both Gorbachev and Massie attended the event. See Lifflander, "Russian lessons."

118 Interview with Suzanne Massie.

119 Lydon, "Agent of influence," 28.

120 Daniloff, "Trust but verify," 226.

121 Reagan to Massie, 10 February 1986.

122 Massie, *Trust but Verify*, 61.

123 Massie, *Trust but Verify*, 368–369.

124 Massie, *Trust but Verify*, 298–300.

125 Massie, *Trust but Verify*, 112.

126 Jones, *Able Archer 83*, 58.

127 Wilson, *The Triumph*, 105–111.

128 On the strategy change, see Miller and Rubinovitz, *Grand Strategy*, 160–161.

129  Mann, *The Rebellion*, 39–43.

130  Wilson, *The Triumph*, 126–128.

131  Oberdorfer, *The Turn*, 79–105.

132  J. G. Stein, "Political learning by doing: Gorbachev as uncommitted thinker and motivated learner," *International Organization*, (1994), 155–183; Wilson, *The Triumph*, 93, 95–96, 101–103, 125–126.

133  Matlock, *Reagan and Gorbachev*, 93; Mann, *The Rebellion*, 83.

134  See Massie, *Trust but Verify*, 298.

135  Massie, *Trust but Verify*, 51–52.

# 4

# Brendan Duddy and the negotiations between the Provisional IRA and the British government during the conflict in Northern Ireland, 1973–1993

> Duddy worked selflessly and at great risk to himself over many years to bring about a peaceful settlement in Northern Ireland and credit for his achievements is long overdue. ... Neither the British government nor the IRA leaders felt able to take the next step and it was Duddy who pushed them into it.
>
> Jonathan Powell[1]

## Introduction

In the late 1960s, the dispute in Northern Ireland turned into a violent conflict, one that has claimed many victims over the years. Numerous efforts were made to end the conflict, all of which ended in failure, until April 1998, when the Good Friday Agreement was reached. Although it involved various zones of confrontation and diverse actors, at heart the conflict centered on the struggle of the Provisional Irish Republican Army against British rule in Northern Ireland. Against this background, in the 1970s Brendan Duddy – a Catholic businessman from the city of Derry/Londonderry in Northern Ireland – started to promote mediation efforts between the two opposing parties. This chapter addresses the PPE activity of Duddy, focusing on three stages in his peace efforts: the backchannel that he established and led during the PIRA truce (1975); Duddy's mediation initiatives during the first (1980) and the second (1981) Republican prisoners' hunger strikes; and the revival of Duddy's channel in 1990–1993 for clandestine negotiations on conditions for direct official negotiations between the British government and the Republican leadership.

This chapter is based, among other sources, on archival material that relates to various periods and actors: documents from Brendan Duddy's private archive at the National University of Ireland in Galway (NUI), documents from the archive of Republican leader Ruairí Ó Brádaigh at

NUI, documents from the British National Archives, and reports by both parties on the 1990–1993 communication channel.

In addition, the chapter draws on testimonials by various actors who have related their own versions of events, including Duddy and Republican and British representatives; memoirs written by some of the actors who were involved; interviews I conducted with Professor Niall Ó Dochartaigh of NUI and Eamonn Downey, Duddy's son-in-law, both of whom assisted Duddy in organizing his archive; interviews with Peter Taylor, a British journalist who produced a movie on Duddy, and Pat Sheehan, a former PIRA member and current member of the Northern Ireland Assembly, as well as a former British official and members of Duddy's family; and historical studies and media reports.

Ten years after the peace agreement was reached, Duddy agreed to reveal his story. In 2008 a BBC movie about him – *The Secret Peacemaker* – was released, and in 2009 Duddy transferred his private archive to NUI. Around the same time, the British National Archives declassified additional documents that shed more light on his PPE activities. These developments affected the historiography of the conflict and the peace efforts in Northern Ireland and led to more historical studies that referenced and analyzed Duddy's role.[2]

## Historical background

The Anglo-Irish Treaty of 1921 led to the establishment of an independent republic of Ireland, comprising twenty-six counties, while six counties in the north – where a majority of the population was Protestant – came under the control of the Stormont government, which continued to be part of the UK. In the 1960s, the Northern Ireland Civil Rights Association emerged, demanding equal rights for the Catholic minority and protesting against discrimination in various aspects of life.[3] In 1968–1969 matters spiraled out of control, escalating into a violent conflict that included clashes between protesters and security forces as well as military actions by "Republican" Catholic paramilitary organizations – which supported unification with the Republic of Ireland – and "Loyalist" Protestant paramilitary organizations – which supported the union with the UK. In light of the escalation, in 1969 the British government ordered the reinforcement of British forces in Northern Ireland.[4]

The Provisional Irish Republican Army was established in 1969. It claimed to be the successor of the original Irish Republican Army, which had fought for the independence of Ireland half a century earlier. The PIRA, also known as "the Provos," became the dominant factor in the republican movement. The organization supported armed struggle aimed at compelling the British to withdraw from Northern Ireland and uniting the six northern counties with Ireland to form one independent and socialist state.[5] It also proclaimed itself protector of the Catholic community in Northern Ireland from British and Loyalist aggression. The organization focused its military efforts against the British army: during 1971 PIRA members killed forty-two British soldiers and in 1972 they killed sixty-four soldiers. In 1972 the PIRA also began launching attacks in England. Against this background the British adopted stricter measures in Northern Ireland. In August 1971 the UK started to use internment – imprisonment without trial – and arrested hundreds of suspects. London also created a special legal framework that would facilitate its struggle against the PIRA.[6]

In January 1972, fourteen protesters were shot and killed by British soldiers during a rally in Derry, at an event that became known as "Bloody Sunday." In March 1972 London decided to dissolve the Stormont government in Northern Ireland and replace it with direct rule. In July 1972 the British army launched Operation Motorman, with the aim of increasing its control in the Republican areas of Belfast and Derry. The year 1972, during which 479 people were killed, was one of the bloodiest in the history of the conflict.[7]

In parallel to their military activity, the British also made efforts to promote dialogue with various actors in Northern Ireland. At the center of this activity was a British office established in Northern Ireland in 1969. Initially designated the UK Representative in Northern Ireland (UKREP), after the transition to direct rule in 1972 it was renamed as the Northern Ireland Office (NIO) and subordinated to Secretary of State for Northern Ireland William Whitelaw. The NIO offices were located at Laneside, on the shores of Lake Belfast, which allowed clandestine activities and meetings to take place without public or media scrutiny.[8]

In October 1971, Frank Steele, an officer of the British intelligence agency MI6, joined UKREP. Steele established contacts among the various communities of Northern Ireland. He also reached out to diverse actors in the Catholic community and even to Republicans.[9] During these years, several figures in Northern Ireland provided assistance in exchanging messages between the parties. Prominent examples include John O'Connell, an Irish politician, and John Hume, leader of the Social Democratic and Labour Party (SDLP). During this period, these figures conveyed to British officials messages from the Republicans about readiness for dialogue and discussion of a ceasefire and future settlement.[10]

In March 1972, the British opposition leader, Harold Wilson, met with PIRA leaders.[11] In June 1972, PIRA representatives met for the first time with Steele. This meeting led to a ceasefire declaration and to a meeting with Secretary of State for Northern Ireland Whitelaw, but the meeting failed and news of it leaked to the media. Two days after the meeting, the

PIRA announced a cessation of the ceasefire and the violence resumed: twenty-two bombings took place in Belfast on 21 July, and on 31 July three car bombs were activated in Derry. Whitelaw was outraged over the media leak, which had caused him much embarrassment, and over the resumption of violence. Feeling that he had been deceived, he ordered a ban on contacts with PIRA officials. He remained firmly opposed to dialogue with the PIRA, rejecting inquiries and offers on the matter.[12]

## Brendan Duddy: life story and worldview

Brendan Duddy was born in the city of Derry on 10 June 1936. Duddy, a faithful Catholic, grew up in Glen, a poor, mixed neighborhood where Catholics and Protestants lived side by side. He was exposed to the life of the Protestant community and came to know its events and holidays.[13] "Much of my early life," Duddy testified, "was associated with the Protestant population, many of my friends and associates were, and still are, Protestants and I realised that there were two communities and that the only way forward was to bridge the divide between them."[14] In 1966 Duddy opened a fish and chip restaurant on a street next to the Catholic neighborhood of Caragen. As the city began to see growing protest activities, during the mid-1960s, the restaurant became a meeting place for various political groups. These discussions exposed him to the ongoing political developments and introduced him to many of the city's political actors. In 1968, Duddy opened a restaurant in central Derry on William Street, a main artery of protest activities during the "troubles" (starting in 1969) and a conduit to the city center that also happened to be located near a British army barricade.[15]

Duddy had always taken a keen interest in politics and followed political developments: "I have been a political analyst all my life, reading about politics and listening to political broadcasts and programmes."[16] He supported the struggle for equal rights in Northern Ireland and in light of his life in a poor and mixed neighborhood, he believed that it should be a joint struggle for social equality rather than an inter-community struggle. At the same time, Duddy did not belong to any particular organization or movement, and he avoided public activity. The only time he made an exception to this rule involved a failed attempt in the early 1960s to run for city council as an independent candidate.[17]

Building on the networks he had developed, Duddy began promoting efforts aimed at peace and dialogue. In his words, he had been a "pacifist, anti-war and anti-violence" throughout his life.[18] He explained that exposure to incidents of violence and unnecessary killing in the area near his restaurant had driven him to take action and intervene: "I couldn't stand the killing.

Every citizen has his duty. It comes naturally to me."[19] Duddy considered himself a proud Irish national but at the same time he opposed armed struggle and violence, and claimed that his mission was to replace violence with dialogue.[20] According to his granddaughter, he could not bear to see an ant being hurt.[21]

Duddy stated in an interview that he was "national with a small R" ("R" referring to "Republican") and made it clear that he was not necessarily committed to a solution based on a united Ireland.[22] He believed that the only way to resolve the conflict was through dialogue and an agreement that would engage the Republicans, and he believed that those peace efforts that excluded them from the process were hopeless.[23]

In parallel to his PPE activity, Duddy demonstrated an interest over the years in the model of "group relations" developed by the Tavistock Institute in London. He participated in conferences on the topic around the world and had a special friendship with Gordon Lawrence, a leading expert in the field. The model, which is used to analyze unconscious processes in group or organizational dynamics, integrates organizational consulting with a psychoanalytical perspective. Over the years, Duddy became a facilitator of workshops using this model, even though he had no professional training in the field. This approach affected his worldview and gave him tools and resources that helped him in his PPE activity.[24]

### The beginning of Duddy's PPE activity

In the early 1970s, Duddy developed a wide network of contacts among various political circles, including British and Republican. The main Republican actor with whom Duddy established close relations was Ruairí Ó Brádaigh, leader of Sinn Féin (the political wing of the PIRA), and a member of the PIRA Army Council (PAC). According to Duddy, he met Ó Brádaigh for the first time while taking part in a discussion forum of Republican groups in county Monaghan, Ireland, in which Ó Brádaigh also participated. The two also met in 1972 at an event in the US.[25]

Duddy also established contact with Dáithí Ó Conaill, one of the founders of the PIRA and a member of the PAC. Initially Ó Brádaigh would coordinate their meetings: whenever Duddy wanted to meet with Ó Conaill he would inform Ó Brádaigh and soon thereafter would receive a message about the place and time of the meeting. Duddy also knew Martin McGuinness, a representative of the Republican movement's young generation and a resident of Derry. McGuinness worked as a young man in a company that delivered hamburgers to Duddy's restaurant, and Duddy's relationship with the McGuinness family lasted many years. McGuinness's daughters worked in Duddy's businesses and he was invited to their weddings. In addition, Duddy developed contacts with other political actors in Northern Ireland, including SDLP leader John Hume. Duddy and Hume were born within a few months of each other, grew up in the same neighborhood, and studied at the same school.[26]

After opening a restaurant in the city center, Duddy became the head of the center's Merchants Association, and from 1971 he served as a member of the City Centre Liaison Committee. This body, tasked with coordinating between the City Centre's businesses and the police in order to de-escalate the situation, was established by Frank Lagan, a Catholic Lieutenant in the Royal Ulster Constabulary (RUC), the police force in Northern Ireland, who was in charge of the city center. Working cooperatively within the committee, Duddy and Lagan developed a special friendship. The two were in daily contact and regularly visited each other's homes. Later Duddy described Lagan as "the most honourable man that I have ever met ... utterly devoted to his job and to peace. ... [He] always achieved the right balance between doing his duties as an officer and moving the community away from conflict."[27]

Lagan introduced Duddy to Frank Steele of the NIO.[28] Documents from the British National Archive reveal that the first reports on Duddy and his mediation efforts appeared in 1972. On 22 September 1972, for example, Steele reported in a telegram that Duddy – whom he described as "a northern Irish Catholic resident in Londonderry" and friend of Ruairí Ó Brádaigh – had asked to schedule a meeting in order to deliver a message from the PIRA. Steele explained that although Duddy had Republican views, he expressed them "in a sensible and moderate way" and did not believe in violence.[29] Over time, Duddy provided Steele with messages indicating Republican willingness to discuss ending the violence.[30]

One of the first instances in which Steele used Duddy was in July 1972, when he conveyed a message requesting that PIRA members clear out the weapons from Republican areas in Derry before Operation Motorman in order to avoid confrontation.[31] In January 1973 Steele sent a detailed report to London about a meeting with Duddy in which he had received an update on the latter's conversations with Ó Brádaigh (who was in prison at the time), Ó Conaill, and other Republican leaders. Duddy told Steele that his objective in meeting with the PIRA and with Steele himself was to "try and get violence ended." He stated that he sensed genuine willingness among Republicans to end the violence, but that he had not received information from the British that could help him promote such a move. Steele replied that they were not willing to negotiate with the PIRA, not even "through third parties such as himself," but that if a ceasefire were declared, they would respond accordingly.[32]

In 1973 Steele left Northern Ireland and two new officials assumed positions in the NIO: Michael Oatley, an MI6 officer, and James Allan, a Foreign Office member. Oatley continued the efforts that Steele had initiated and used the infrastructure that his predecessor had created.[33] Shortly after his arrival in Northern Ireland, he and Duddy formed a relationship that would in time serve as the core of the communication channel Duddy maintained between the British and the Republicans. Oatley entered his new post without prior knowledge about Northern Ireland, but after having been exposed to the situation, he reached the conclusion that the UK should engage with the Republicans and try to influence them. He did not believe in a military solution. In his view, a ceasefire by the PIRA would lead to a ceasefire by the Loyalist organizations, and he believed that such a ceasefire could only be achieved through negotiations. Although contact with the PIRA was prohibited, Oatley, who was known for his unconventional approach, had significant maneuverability within the NIO and no clear definition of his powers. He also felt that he had the backing of Frank Cooper, permanent under-secretary of state of the NIO, an independent thinker who was willing to take unusual and risky steps.[34]

During 1974 there were two developments that contributed to the emergence of the Duddy channel. The first was the collapse of the Sunningdale Agreement, a proposed outline for a power-sharing framework, as a result of a general strike declared in May 1974 by the Ulster Workers' Council, a Unionist organization.[35] The second event was a political change that took place in the UK with the rise of a new government, headed by Harold Wilson of the Labour Party. In the past, Wilson had demonstrated a willingness to talk with the PIRA, but he now had a weak minority government and was afraid that controversial steps in Northern Ireland would endanger the coalition.[36]

Oatley had heard about Duddy through his work with Steele.[37] Shortly after taking office, Oatley began using Duddy to send messages to the PIRA via Ó Brádaigh and Ó Conaill, who still worked the Republican side of the channel. Initially the channel was focused on ad-hoc efforts to deal with crises, such as hostage cases. Duddy was involved, for example, in an effort to release the German industrialist Thomas Niedermayer, kidnapped by the PIRA in December 1973, and in a similar effort to release Lord and Lady Donoughmore, who were kidnapped in June 1974.[38] During 1974, Duddy's channel gained credibility: the British side was impressed by the Republicans' ability to maintain secrecy, keep their promises, and deliver. This strengthened Duddy's status as a credible broker, and his channel eventually became the exclusive channel between the parties. Initially Oatley also used other channels, but towards the summer of 1974 these closed and Duddy's became "the only game in town." At that point the British asked the Republicans not to use channels other than Duddy's. The channel became very active. According to Duddy, he practically "lived in Laneside" during that period, and a strong friendship formed between himself and Oatley, a friendship that would last for decades. Both sides trusted him and valued the fact that the channel remained confidential, without any leaks. Duddy's activity over the years was fraught with risk. Even after he gained the parties' trust, there was still a danger that someone at a lower level – on either side – who did not know about the channel could become suspicious and take action against him.[39]

According to Oatley, in the early days of the channel he told his supervisor Frank Cooper that he had built a "hollow bamboo pipe," adding that "I haven't said anything yet since we are not allowed to talk to the IRA but if I go puff puff at one end then he can feel me going puff puff and if he goes puff puff back I can feel him. ... [N]ow we have this pipe, can we start putting bits of information down it to turn it into a relationship or a dialogue?"[40] Cooper gave Oatley a green light. Prime Minister Wilson, too, was informed and approved the contacts.[41] Britain's Secretary of State for Northern Ireland, Merlyn Rees, in an interview, stated that he knew Oatley had initiated a contact with the PIRA, adding that it was his (Oatley's) job to talk with everybody. Rees explained that there was no need for his approval because that was the purpose of Oatley's position.[42]

**Figure 4.1** Brendan Duddy with former MI6 officer Michael Oatley, April 1998; Duddy is on the right

## Duddy's efforts during the 1975 ceasefire

Christmas 1974 marked a dramatic milestone in Duddy's mediation activities. It occurred against the backdrop of an announcement by the PAC that it would be suspending military activities during Christmas, from 22 December 1974, to 2 January 1975. The announcement came after an attack in late November that included bombings at two pubs in Birmingham, England, in which 21 people were killed and 182 wounded. The attack prompted a firm British response and generated harsh criticism within the Catholic community.[43]

Shortly after the attack – on 10 December 1974 – Protestant clergy and PIRA representatives held a meeting in the town of Feakle at which the clergy proposed a ceasefire. In light of the secret contacts held earlier between the Republicans and the British, and criticism of the November attack in the Catholic community, the meeting gave the Republican leadership an opportunity to declare a "Christmas ceasefire" on 20 December. The public regarded this announcement as an outcome of the Feakle meeting, but it later became known that this was a cover story to help Republicans justify the ceasefire.[44] Powell claims that both sides needed a cover story to explain why the violence stopped at that point. Towards this end they chose the Feakle meeting, and two decades passed before they revealed the true story.[45] Cowper-Coles claims that the meeting was intended to protect the "bamboo channel" and that the clerics did not know of the secret channel.[46]

The PIRA announcement compelled Duddy to act. He called Oatley on Christmas Eve, urging him to take the initiative as soon as possible. At this point Duddy felt that unless efforts were made to promote contact between the parties, the indirect channel might collapse.[47] Oatley looked into the issue and informed Duddy that he had been granted permission to send a message to Republicans indicating the possibility of direct talks between the parties. Duddy took notes on their conversation and used them to prepare a written message for the Republican leadership. On Christmas morning, Duddy arrived at Ó Brádaigh's home to deliver the message from the British government seeking to arrange a meeting between the parties. Ó Brádaigh immediately informed the PAC members and they decided to hold a meeting to discuss the British message. The PAC meeting, to which Duddy was invited, took place in Dublin on 31 December 1974. Ó Brádaigh, in introducing Duddy to the council members, stated that he trusted him and guaranteed his credibility. Among the members was Billy McKee, the PIRA commander in Belfast and a highly influential figure in the organization's military arm. McKee, who had recently been released from prison and did not know Duddy, voiced suspicion about him and warned of a trap, but those members who knew Duddy confirmed that he was trustworthy and was only a "message boy."[48]

McKee later testified that he was surprised that Duddy had joined the meeting because the council's meetings had always been closed to non-members. This meeting was an important landmark in Duddy's PPE activity. He had been invited to a secret meeting of the PIRA's most important forum and received legitimacy and backing from Ó Brádaigh. Duddy said that he was asked to arrange a meeting between Oatley, from the NIO, and Billy McKee. McKee said he was ready to meet with Oatley but demanded that another representative join him as a witness: "I am not going to meet any British agent on my own."[49] The PAC members decided to accept the British proposal to arrange a meeting. In addition, they decided to extend the ceasefire by two weeks, and on 2 January 1975, they publicly announced this extension.[50]

The secret meeting between the parties took place on 7 January 1975, with the participation of Oatley and two Republican representatives: Billy McKee and another PIRA representative from Derry. When Oatley saw that another representative had joined McKee, he threatened to cancel the meeting, but Duddy managed to persuade him to stay. The meeting did not produce any meaningful outcomes, and the unilateral ceasefire declared by the PIRA ended on 16 January 1975.[51] But during the night between 16 and 17 January, Duddy delivered another message to Ó Brádaigh, stating that the British were interested in continuing the dialogue. Duddy reported that the British wanted Ó Brádaigh to join the next meeting. Ó Brádaigh informed the organization's leadership and the Republicans replied that they were willing to send two representatives to a meeting with two British representatives in order to discuss conditions for a "bilateral ceasefire" and the implementation of their main requests: a British statement of intent on withdrawal of forces; recognition of the right of the Irish people to determine their future; and the release of prisoners and cessation of arrests without trial.[52]

These developments paved the way to a meetings channel at Duddy's home in Derry. It started with a first meeting on 18 January and continued throughout 1975, with the aim of preserving and strengthening the ceasefire and discussing a long-term agreement. In terms of location, Derry had the advantage of being close to the border with Ireland, which provided convenient access for the Republican representatives who came from there.[53]

The meetings channel included strict rules aimed at keeping it confidential and protecting the participants. Duddy insisted on controlling these arrangements and demanded that only people he had selected drive the Republicans to the meetings. The Republicans never left the house during daytime hours, and even PIRA activists in Derry did not always know that their leaders had visited the city. The parties would arrive at the meetings in disguise, and Duddy's house, situated away from the road, was surrounded by a high fence that hid his guests. Knowing that his phone was bugged, Duddy consistently used codenames in his conversations. His family members, too, had to follow strict rules; his children were not allowed to invite friends over, nor were they permitted to open the door when someone arrived. On the Republican side, the main contact for coordinating meetings was Ó Brádaigh. Duddy also informed Lagan about scheduled meetings so that he could prepare accordingly.[54]

At this point Duddy's channel was based on three legs. The meetings at his house constituted the first leg. Duddy hosted the talks and was responsible for ensuring secrecy, but he was not involved in the talks themselves.[55] The second leg was the contact between Duddy and the British. Their talks were conducted by phone or in person, with meetings usually taking place in Laneside. The third leg was Duddy's dialogue with Republican leaders, over the phone and through in-person meetings. Duddy had two partners who were involved in his channel with the Republicans. The first was Denis Bradley, a pastor in Derry who later left the clergy and became a community worker. The second was Noel Gallagher, a businessman from Derry. Both were held in esteem and had influence among the Republican leadership, and Duddy consulted with them at various stages in his activities. At the same time, neither was involved in the communications between Duddy and the British.[56] The separate contacts that Duddy managed with both sides – the second and third legs – were very intense. They essentially formed the infrastructure of the channel and strengthened the process. Through these communications, Duddy not only conveyed messages between the parties, but he also presented his own analysis, explained each party's position to the other side, and described the other side's constraints and considerations.

## The 1975 meetings channel at Duddy's house

The first meeting within the framework of Duddy's channel (on 18 January 1975) was attended by Oatley and James Allan, from the British side, and Ó Brádaigh and McKee, from the Republican side. The composition of the participants remained relatively consistent except for a few replacements on the British side during the process. The Republican leaders, Ó Conaill and Seamus Twomey, did not participate in the meetings but did often wait nearby to be accessible for updates and consultations.[57]

The channel had quick, direct access to the main decision makers on both sides. On the British side, the channel worked in cooperation with Rees and the negotiators reported to his deputy, Frank Cooper.[58] Two examples illustrate this point. At one meeting the British representatives arrived for the second day of talks with a letter from Cooper in response to a Republican message conveyed on the previous day, and they explained that they had

**Figure 4.2** The guest room at Duddy's home where the meetings took place during the 1975 talks

received a personal guarantee from Cooper that both the message and the letter had been discussed at the highest levels.[59] In another instance, the British participants presented a document that they described as an outcome of talks among the highest ranks, including the prime minister and the state prosecutor.[60] They also used the channel to show the Republicans drafts of planned public speeches by Rees or other British leaders. This practice served as a confidence-building measure as well as a means of gathering feedback and gauging reactions.[61] Wilson had direct involvement in the talks but hid their existence from his Cabinet members and issued instructions not to report on the talks to Home Secretary Roy Jenkins.[62]

On the Republican side, the negotiators were senior leaders. In parallel to the talks, the PAC held meetings at which council members received reports and delivered instructions. Duddy received updates after the PAC meetings and sometimes provided tips and suggestions in advance of these meetings.[63]

At the first meetings discussions focused on terms for an agreed truce regime and were based on a twelve-point document that the PAC had formulated and a sixteen-point document that the British had presented in response: "The solution," the British said, "may lie between the two docu-ments."[64] In parallel to the meetings, Duddy separately maintained contact with each of the parties and used these communications to explain one side to the other or influence its position. In a meeting with Oatley and Allan, for example, he stressed that the PAC would not accept an agreement that allowed the RUC to continue arresting Republicans. Likewise, he held meetings with the Republican leaders (sometimes together with Denis Bradley) where he would urge them, for example, to suspend military activity against the British during the talks.[65] Occasionally Duddy formulated and promoted his own ideas and proposals. For example, he presented the British representa-tives with a paper that included proposals for policing.[66] On 7 February 1975, a dramatic meeting took place at which the parties achieved a breakthrough and resolved their final point of disagreement (the issuing of special permits for twenty-four Republicans to move about freely with weapons). This paved the way for a Republican declaration on renewal of the truce as of 10 February. Towards this end, the parties established "incident centres" for ongoing coordination, to ensure that the truce did not collapse, and the permits to carry weapons were issued and passed to Duddy.[67]

In March 1975 the channel's participants held a farewell party for Oatley, who was leaving Northern Ireland for a new position in Hong Kong. On the brink of tears, Oatley made emotional farewells to his associates. His replacement, codenamed "Rob," was in turn replaced in July 1975 by Donald Middleton. Allan, too, left in July, and was replaced by John Walker.[68]

At the meetings of March 1975 Republicans expressed disappointment over the lack of progress, and on one occasion delivered a PAC statement charging that the British were violating the agreed understandings and failing to keep their promise regarding prisoners. The British representatives took this charge seriously, arguing that the government was genuinely interested in preserving the dialogue but that it was necessary to be patient, and pointing to important measures that had emerged from the meetings.[69] Duddy intensified his pressure on the British to fulfill their promises, and demanded that they deliver a formal response to the PAC letter. The British acquiesced, offering an official response and informing Duddy that the Cabinet had approved the release of forty Republican prisoners from Long Kesh prison and the transport of other prisoners from England to Northern Ireland.[70] Duddy also made an effort to explain the constraints that the NIO was facing, and the internal struggles in the British system, to the Republicans.[71]

In an unusual move, Duddy drafted a letter from the Republican leadership to Prime Minister Wilson, calling on him to seize the opportunity and advance an initiative that would lead to a temporary and honorable end to hostilities between the parties.[72] Duddy delivered the letter to Rob, the

British representative, who subsequently informed him that Cooper had received it and it was on its way to the prime minister. This was a risky move because Duddy had drafted the letter without the Republicans' approval, but he felt that the letter represented their thoughts and that it was "the last chance to save the peace."[73]

Ó Brádaigh's papers reveal that this initiative angered the Republicans and that they reprimanded Duddy. The PAC instructed Ó Brádaigh to make clear to Duddy that he was not authorized to write to the prime minister on their behalf, and that in sending the letter he had exceeded his authority. Duddy acknowledged that the rebuke was justified and that he accepted the criticism. Ó Brádaigh also informed the British that the letter had not come from them.[74] Duddy explained his decision in retrospect, saying that if you are sincere about your task, you have to take risks.[75]

Events on the ground, however, pointed to a risk of escalation. On 2 April 1975, the PIRA planted a bomb in a travel agency in Belfast, claiming that it was their response to the British violations. Duddy immediately traveled to Belfast to meet with Rob in order to save the process. The parties' representatives met that very day at Duddy's home. The British, though outraged by the bombings, tried to convince the Republicans not to abandon the process, arguing that reverting to war was against their interest.[76] Throughout this period, sectarian killings (of Catholics by Protestants and vice versa) intensified.[77]

In spite of the events that threatened to undermine the ceasefire, the meetings continued. The discussions focused on four main topics. The first centered on implementation of the truce agreement and the handling of complaints of violations. The second involved discussions on a long-term agreement. While the Republicans demanded a British declaration of intent to leave Northern Ireland, the British demanded that the Republicans participate in the political process. The third topic of discussions comprised Republican requests for release of prisoners and detainees, and the transport of prisoners from England to Northern Ireland. Fourth, the parties also discussed the sectarian killings and, in this context, the Republicans asked the British to take harsher measures against Loyalist violence.[78]

In mid-1975 Duddy came to the conclusion that the British were not serious about making progress. He therefore sought to increase pressure on them and, towards that end, employed various tools. For example, he repeatedly warned of the consequences if the channel and the ceasefire collapsed. He said that it could lead to "war, bombs in all the major English cities, many English dead." But over time this threat lost its power. The British pointed out that Duddy had been repeating this dire prediction over several months, yet so far it had not materialized. On a few occasions Duddy also threatened to abandon his role as mediator, which would put an end to the channel. In one instance he warned that he would close the meetings channel and "begin to enjoy life with my children."[79]

Duddy faced a dilemma in his efforts and had to decide what to do next. He felt that the parties had reached a deadlock and that he could not facilitate a breakthrough. It was time to decide whether to give up, and risk the collapse of the process and subsequent escalation of violence, or to continue with his efforts even though they appeared pointless. Referring to this dilemma, Duddy wrote to imaginary students who would read his diary in the future: "What would you do? Let it happen and see the truce go out the window? Do nothing? Threaten to resign and do it? Or try to win?"[80] Duddy's strong feelings became evident during a long meeting he had with Rob and Allan on 25 June 1975. After expressing severe disappointment over the British position, he decided to end the meeting and, after exiting, approached his car and kicked the vehicle furiously. Allan, having followed him outside, saw this and apologized to Duddy, adding, "I can see you are obviously upset. We must do our homework better." Duddy claimed that this event had a stronger impact on the British than several days of talks.[81]

Duddy also tried to convince the British to move forward by highlighting the internal division over the truce within the Republican movement. He stressed that the Republican leaders faced strong internal criticism and that London should show generosity in order to assist them and to strengthen the pro-dialogue camp in the PIRA. The British representatives told Duddy on numerous occasions that they agreed with him but that it was not their decision; it was up to the senior decision makers in London and the "British system."[82] Indeed, certain parties within the British system, particularly the army and the RUC, were critical of the truce and the dialogue with Republicans.[83]

In September 1975 the channel essentially came to a close. The last of the meetings – except for a special one in February 1976 – took place during this month. On 20 September, Rees declared that a mutual ceasefire was never agreed. On 22 September, the PIRA carried out eighteen bombings in Northern Ireland and one more in London, and a few days later Republican leaders convened a press conference announcing the "moment of truth." Nevertheless, Duddy continued his contacts with the parties. The cessation of direct meetings enhanced the importance of Duddy's efforts. The meetings were essentially replaced by an exchange of messages conveyed by Duddy during October and November, with each party attacking the other and setting conditions for further dialogue.[84]

In light of the stalemate, and the danger of the truce collapsing, Duddy sought to promote other ways of reaching a breakthrough, in parallel to the channel. One course of action was a peace proposal that he outlined, which he termed the "Dungloe plan." The plan proposed a transitional period of two to five years during which the British would continue to control Northern Ireland but declare their intention of withdrawing, the Republican prisoners would be released, policing would undergo reform, and the PIRA would announce a permanent end to violence. Duddy worked on the plan with Bradley and reported on it to both parties, but it did not help in breaking the stalemate.[85] He also promoted several dialogue efforts between Republicans and Loyalists, and between Republicans and John Hume from the SDLP.[86]

In late 1975, Duddy's sense of despair reached a peak. On 10 November an explosion took place in a building that served as an incident centre and, as a result, the British announced the closure of all incident centres. Duddy heard about it on the radio and reacted: "My centres! Which I created at 5am ... with Michael Oatley."[87] It seemed to Duddy that there was nothing he could do, that the parties were heading towards war. He described his thoughts in his diary: "What would I do when war, and no reasonable political alternative, was the only option left. In the end, my decision came clearly and flatly. My job is not to invent positions, but to report only the facts ... either from the British or the PAC no reasonable hope is present."[88]

In early 1976 the focus of Duddy's efforts shifted to an issue close to his heart: the release of Republican prisoner Frank Stagg, who had been waging a hunger strike to demand that he be transferred from his prison in England to a prison in Northern Ireland. In June 1975 the British representatives had promised Duddy that Stagg would be released in August but later backed away from this promise. He then raised the issue again, to no avail. On 5 January Duddy decided, out of solidarity with Stagg, to stop eating solid food, although he also made it clear that he would stop fasting if it posed a danger to his life. Duddy reminded the British that on various occasions he had helped save the lives of people abducted by the PIRA and asked for the release of Stagg as a reciprocal gesture. His plea went unheeded, and on 12 February Stagg died, having maintained his hunger strike for sixty-two days.[89]

In January 1976, despite the collapse of the truce, Middleton told Duddy that Cooper wished to maintain the channel. The Republicans, too, were willing to keep the channel open and, on 4 February, the PAC agreed to another meeting. On this basis, Duddy was able to organize a final meeting via the channel on 10 February. The meeting ended without a substantive outcome.[90]

On 16 March 1976, Prime Minister Wilson resigned. The British representatives maintained contact with Duddy but made clear that, given the political change, no progress was anticipated in the near future. They also felt that the PIRA was growing weak both militarily and in terms of public support, and they saw no point in continuing their contacts with it. On

17 March 1976, Duddy spoke with Middleton and effectively eulogized the entire process. He argued that lack of progress on the part of the NIO had led to a resumption of PIRA violence and wasted three years of hard work.[91]

James Callaghan, who became the new prime minister in April 1976, opposed the continuation of secret contacts with the PIRA and demanded that ties with Duddy cease.[92] In September 1976 Roy Mason was appointed as secretary of state for Northern Ireland. His policy was aimed at "squeezing the terrorists" and he prohibited any contact, direct or indirect, with the PIRA.[93] In late 1976, Mason made it clear that he intended to disengage completely from Duddy, and in early 1977 Duddy was told that his role as an intermediary "had ceased to have any relevance and should be brought to an end."[94]

The truce and the channel of 1975 marked an important milestone in the history of the conflict, and their subsequent collapse contributed to a change of leadership in the Republican movement. The young generation, headed by Gerry Adams and Martin McGuinness, saw the truce as a mistake and criticized the leadership. As a result, Ó Brádaigh and McKee lost status, and in 1983 Adams replaced Ó Brádaigh as the president of Sinn Féin.[95] The channel had, however, provided the Republican movement with experience in diplomatic processes.[96]

The meetings channel was an important historical step, but the gaps between the parties had remained insurmountable. The British side's unwillingness to make significant moves that would attest to the seriousness of their intentions,[97] alongside the intensification of Republican and Loyalist violence and the internal political processes on both sides, eventually brought the process to an end. Thus, despite his tireless efforts to save the process, Duddy was unable to facilitate a breakthrough.

### Duddy's mediation efforts during the prison hunger strikes, 1980–1981

#### Duddy's channel during the first hunger strike, 1980

Duddy renewed his efforts in 1980, against the background of a hunger strike by Republican prisoners. Hunger strikes have been an important tool in Ireland's history and after 1969, during the conflict in Northern Ireland, the tool reemerged. In June 1972 forty Republican prisoners declared a hunger strike, demanding to be granted the status of war prisoners. After a strike that lasted thirty-seven days, the British government announced the granting of "special status" to the prisoners. Likewise in 1973, 1974, and

1976, Republican prisoners declared hunger strikes, which resulted in the death of two prisoners.[98]

In November 1975, Northern Ireland Secretary of State Merlyn Rees declared the repeal of the special status granted to Republican prisoners. This was part of the UK's criminalization policy, designed to portray Republican organizations as criminals.[99] As a result, Republican prisoners at Maze Prison began to conduct protest activities in the late 1970s. Initially the prisoners refused to wear prisoners' uniforms, covering themselves instead with blankets (and consequently coming to be nicknamed "blanket men"). Later they refused to leave their cells and would smear excrement on the walls (hence this was dubbed the "dirty protest"). At the end of 1980, a total of 341 prisoners were participating in the "dirty protest" at Maze Prison. Because of these actions, the prisoners lost their eligibility for early release based on "good behavior" after serving half their prison term.[100]

The protest received a great deal of media and public attention but failed to shift British policy towards the prisoners. In March 1979, the Labour government fell and the Conservative Party, headed by Margaret Thatcher, formed a new government. Humphrey Atkins was appointed as the Northern Ireland secretary of state. During 1980 various efforts to end the crisis through negotiations took place, but all ended in failure.[101]

In October 1980, seven Republican prisoners in Maze Prison declared a hunger strike.[102] In December, another twenty-three prisoners from Maze, as well as three women held at Armagh Prison, joined the strike. At first the Republican leadership outside the prison opposed the move, but eventually the PAC approved it. The prisoners presented five demands: the right not to wear a prison uniform; the right not to participate in prison work; the right of free association with other prisoners and to organize educational and recreational pursuits; the right to one visit, one letter, and one parcel per week; and full restoration of remission lost during the protest. Thatcher announced in response that the British government would never agree to grant Republican prisoners a political status.[103]

In December 1980, the Duddy–Oatley channel was revived. Although Oatley was no longer stationed in Northern Ireland, he had kept in touch with Duddy over the years. He believed that the channel was important and worth preserving and he informed Duddy that he would remain accessible if the channel became necessary, although he neither requested nor received official permission to do so.[104]

The process began with a phone call from Duddy in which the two talked about finding a solution to end the hunger strike before it led to the death of a striker, Sean McKenna, whose life was in danger. Duddy evidently initiated the conversation after hearing from Republican leaders who were interested in a settlement.[105] After speaking with Duddy, Oatley contacted Frank Cooper, then at the Ministry of Defence, who in turn connected Oatley with Ken Stowe, head of the NIO. During a meeting with Oatley, Stowe contacted the Prime Minister's Office while at the same time Oatley contacted Duddy. The encounter resulted in Stowe drafting a British proposal to resolve the crisis. Stowe further initiated a meeting with Thatcher and Atkins in which Thatcher approved the British proposal, after which Stowe gave Oatley the green light to deliver it to the Republicans.[106]

On 18 December 1980, Oatley met Duddy and Father Brendan Meagher, who served as a contact person with the prisoners' leadership, at an airport near Belfast. Oatley handed the British proposal to Meagher and informed him that the prison authorities would allow him to enter in order to convey it to the prisoners. Father Meagher delivered the document to Republican leaders waiting for him nearby. They, in turn, were disappointed by the proposal, which they found both lengthy and vague. While discussing it, they learned that the prisoners' leadership had declared an end to the strike, evidently after hearing that a British proposal was on its way from London. The prisoners had initially decided to wait until they could examine the exact wording in the document, but in light of Sean McKenna's worsening situation, they decided to end the strike in order to save his life. This decision led to the end, after fifty-three days, of the hunger strike.[107] That night, Father Meagher arrived at the prison and handed the British proposal to the prisoners. Bobby Sands, one of the prisoners' leaders, claimed that there was nothing concrete in the proposal and that "it was so wide open" that he "could drive a bus through it." [108]

The 1980 Duddy–Oatley initiative was serious and effective. It led to indirect dialogue between the parties and to a British proposal to end the crisis. However, the strike ended before the talks could yield an agreement, and the crisis therefore remained unresolved, resulting in a sense of disappointment and distrust on the part of the Republicans. It should be noted that the Republicans did not blame Duddy for the failure, but rather attributed it to the British.[109]

### Duddy's channel during the second hunger strike, 1981

After the strike ended, the Republican prisoners pursued negotiations with the prison authorities in the hope of achieving a resolution based on the British proposal, but the talks reached a deadlock. The prisoners' protest therefore continued, while the British made clear that they would oppose any change in policy so long as the protest was underway. On 1 March 1981, another hunger strike was declared at Maze Prison. This time, in contrast to the previous strike, it was decided that the strike would build gradually, with a new prisoner joining each week, rather than launching it en masse. Brendan ("Bik") McFarlane was named "Officer Commanding" of the strike and Richard O'Rawe was appointed as press officer. The PIRA leaders outside the prison were not enthusiastic about another hunger strike, preferring instead to focus on the armed struggle, but they accepted the prisoners' decision.[110] During the strike, in April 1981, the Republicans decided to nominate Bobby Sands, one of the strikers, to run for Parliament as representative from Fermanagh and South Tyrone. Sands indeed won the seat but died a month later.[111] His victory attested to the extent of public support for the hunger strike.

Duddy's efforts were revived after the Republican prisoners published a conciliatory statement on 4 July 1981, indicating a willingness to compromise. This was a catalyst for the renewal of contact between Duddy and London and for a British–Republican dialogue intermediated by Duddy.[112] As before, the channel remained confidential, with only a small circle of individuals on each side who knew about it and even fewer who knew the identity of the mediator. Before Duddy's role became public, the mysterious mediator was known only by the nickname "mountain climber." According to Duddy, the nickname originated from the fact that he used to run in the mountains of County Donegal.[113]

In contrast to the 1980 initiative, Duddy's 1981 channel operated without Oatley, who was stationed in Zimbabwe at the time. The British representative this time was Middleton, who had participated in the 1975 channel. On the Republican side of the channel were members of the Adams Commission, which included five PIRA leaders, headed by Gerry Adams, appointed to oversee decisions regarding the hunger strike.[114] The channel's participants used codenames: Duddy was nicknamed "June" or "Soon," Adams Commission members were called "shop stewards," the prisoners' leaders were "the workers," and the British were called "the management."[115] Duddy was in direct contact with the British, but for his communication with the Republicans he used Gallagher, who helped convey the messages to Martin McGuinness, who in turn delivered them to Adams. At this point, the Republican leadership was undergoing a generational transition, which gained momentum as Adams and McGuinness began to take the place of Ó Brádaigh and McKee. For this reason Duddy needed help from Gallagher, whose close ties with McGuinness allowed him to serve as a liaison with the new leadership.[116] Duddy made it clear to the Republicans that secrecy was a fundamental principle, and that in the event of a leak the channel would be closed and the British would deny its existence.[117]

The channel operated primarily by telephone – the British would speak with Duddy, Duddy with Gallagher, and Gallagher with the Republicans – and usually late at night.[118] Duddy was respected and trusted on both sides, which facilitated resumption of the channel. Adams related that the Republicans were satisfied with "mountain climber's credentials" and that the British official participating in the channel had provided them with authoritative proof of his status. The Republicans presumed that Thatcher was aware of the channel and that the British representatives were senior officials empowered to make and implement decisions. Danny Morrison, a member of the Adams Commission, has noted that the Republican leadership viewed the "mountain climber" as a significant actor with direct contact with the British government, someone whose messages were "the Real McCoy."[119] The British side also appreciated Duddy. A classified British report on the channel stated that Duddy "performed his task as well as possible."[120]

The first phone conversation of the channel occurred on 4 July, the day on which Republican prisoners issued a statement.[121] Duddy delivered a request to send a Republican representative to visit the prison and to meet with the prisoners' leadership. The British agreed to allow Morrison to visit the prison, which he did on 5 July. This step illustrated the power of the channel, given that Morrison was otherwise prohibited from visiting the prison, and that the visit took place on Sunday, when, as a rule, visits were not allowed. According to O'Rawe, the visit showed the Republicans that the channel could slice "through the procedural morass like a hot knife through butter."[122]

The channel's renewal coincided with a mediation initiative by the Irish Commission for Justice and Peace (ICJP), a body composed of representatives of the Catholic Church and SDLP. According to Duddy's reports to the British, however, the Republicans had a negative view of the ICJP's efforts.[123] The ICJP was identified with Irish actors who opposed the Republican movement (the Irish government, the Catholic Church, and SDLP), whereas Duddy had earned the trust and support of the Republicans.[124] An internal British document by Atkins, weighing the policy options in light of two competing channels, noted that the likelihood of reaching an agreement acceptable to the prisoners would be higher if negotiations took place with the Republicans, rather than through the ICJP.[125]

The Republican leaders opposed ICJP efforts, preferring direct dialogue with the British instead, "even through such unsatisfactory channels as now exist."[126] They sought to put an end to the ICJP initiative, and, towards this end, on 6 July Adams invited ICJP members to a meeting where he informed them that there existed a parallel channel with London, and asked them to suspend their efforts. The ICJP members were surprised and contacted the British to request an explanation. The British rebuked Adams, through Duddy's channel, for revealing the secret channel to the ICJP, pointing out that many actors in the British establishment were not aware of the channel and that exposure would endanger it. Nonetheless, Adams's move did not lead to a closure of the channel.[127]

On 6 July Atkins sent a report to Thatcher with an update on the hunger strike and on the new channel, including the Republican messages they received. He emphasized they were not engaged in negotiations, but that it was "only sensible" that they not refuse to listen if the Republicans wished to communicate indirectly on such a critical problem. He added that their views were important as they were "largely in control of the strikers."[128] That evening, a critical meeting took place among senior government officials, including Thatcher, Atkins, and Home Secretary William Whitelaw. They discussed recent developments in the hunger strike and decided to draft a statement to be presented to the Republicans, which, if accepted, would serve as a basis for the end of the strike and would be made public. The anticipated death of hunger striker Joe McDonnell was an influential factor, which contributed to the participants' decision to issue the statement within twenty-four hours, or at least before McDonnell's death.[129]

After Thatcher approved the final draft of the British proposal, it was delivered to Duddy by phone and he passed it along to McGuinness, who reported to Adams.[130] The British proposed that in exchange for an immediate cessation of the hunger strike, the government would announce a number of changes. The proposal included concessions on some issues (such as clothing) but was less flexible on others (such as work and association). The British stated that if they received a positive response to the proposal by the following morning, they would deliver a full draft of the statement, to be publicly issued once the strike was over. If they did not receive a positive answer by the deadline, or if information about the proposal or the contacts leaked out, they would deny the existence of the channel.[131]

The Republican leadership rejected the British proposal, arguing that it was inadequate for the purposes of ending the hunger strike and seeking clarification on certain issues. They made it clear that they would not pursue an end to the strike until the prisoners' demands had been met.[132] At the same time Adams also informed the prisoners' leaders of the decision to reject the proposal.[133] On the British side there was internal disagreement between Atkins, who represented a firm stance calling for the closure of the channel, and Foreign Ministry officials who supported the opposing position. One of the messages conveyed via Duddy was that some sections of the British establishment were interested in pursuing a deal with the Adams Commission but that they needed support from the Republicans.[134] At a high-level consultation among Thatcher, Atkins, and other senior officials, the participants agreed, despite the negative Republican response, to make another attempt by drafting a more detailed proposal, based on the original, to be delivered to the Republicans. They decided that if this did not lead to the end of the strike, Atkins would issue a new statement clarifying the British position.[135]

A few hours after the above consultation, McDonnell died, which changed the course of events.[136] His death came as a surprise because it occurred earlier than expected. The Republicans had been operating in the belief that McDonnell's pending death served to put heavy pressure on the British and increase the likelihood of further concessions, but his death upended the dynamics and shifted the pressure to the Republicans. Adams told the prisoners' leaders that after McDonnell's death he waited all night by the phone for an updated proposal, with further concessions, but the call never came. The last British message to be conveyed via the channel was, in Duddy's words, a "very frank statement" clarifying their position and explaining that, even if they wanted to, they could not accept all of the prisoners' demands.[137]

## A final attempt to resolve the crisis

In mid-July 1981 the channel was once again revived, presumably because the British wished to end the crisis before the G7 summit scheduled to begin on 21 July in Canada. Duddy's diary entries attest to intensive communication via the channel during 18 and 19 July. During this round Thatcher remained involved and received updates. The contacts took place against the background of fears surrounding two hunger strikers who seemed close to death, and the British were concerned that their deaths would lead to riots. Duddy used this fact to apply pressure on them, warning that the death of another striker would make it difficult for the Republicans to maintain contact and would cause the situation to escalate.[138]

The parties discussed the possibility of an official British representative visiting the prison for direct negotiation with the prisoners. Thatcher agreed to another move aimed at explaining the British position to the prisoners, and approved the sending of a British representative to the prison so long as that representative adhered to the principles of the public British position and did not exceed it.[139] Two British officials did visit the prison on 20 July but the hunger strikers made it clear that they would not meet them without the participation of McFarlane (commander of the hunger strike), which was unacceptable to the British.[140]

This round of talks centered on another proposal for a British statement, to be issued if the hunger strike ended. The proposed statement, based on similar positions as the previous statement from early July, was delivered to the Republicans on 19 July. In an effort to sway the Republicans, the British argued that the proposal established a "new regime" for the prison and promised to replace the prison commander in the near future. The Republican leadership rejected the British proposal, insisting that the gaps in position regarding work and association were still too wide. Duddy thanked the Republicans for their forthrightness and sincerity, adding that the channel had apparently reached a stalemate and come to an end.[141] On 20 July, Duddy wrote in his diary that "neither side can nor will move. ... Time is running out. ... I am almost defeated. I can't move forward."[142] On the same day, Atkins issued instructions to close the channel.[143]

An internal British paper concluded that the channel had helped make it clear to the Republicans that the public British positions were genuine, and that there was no room for maneuvering. It also claimed that the channel had served as a good source of information regarding the positions of the Republicans that could not have been obtained any other way.[144] On 22 July, Adams wrote to the prisoners' leadership that the channel had collapsed and that the proposals did not provide a basis for respectable agreement. He asked them to decide whether to announce the end of the hunger strike or continue in the hope that the British would meet their demands. Eventually, on 3 October, the end of the hunger strike was announced, after ten strikers had died and even though the prisoners' demands were never met. Nevertheless, the strike did bring about certain long-term changes for the better in terms of the prisoners' conditions.[145] In conclusion, Duddy's July 1981 channel had revealed some signs of ripeness for a compromise on both sides, as reflected in the prisoners' statement and the British proposal. The fact that the channel's infrastructure already existed enabled the parties to reuse it immediately after the release of the prisoners' statement. Overall, however, the gaps regarding certain issues were too vast and the parties could not bridge them.

In 2005, the story of the secret 1981 channel emerged as the centerpiece of a public controversy in Northern Ireland, following the publication of the book *Blanketmen* by Richard O'Rawe, one of the prisoners' leaders during the strike. O'Rawe presented his version of the events during the strike, criticizing the Adams Commission for rejecting the British proposal and for excluding the prisoners' leadership from the decision-making process. The book challenged the assumption that the prisoners had managed the strike and made all the decisions, and described tension and disagreement between the Republican leadership and the prisoners' leadership with regard to the channel. It generated a public uproar in which senior Republican leaders clashed with O'Rawe and denied his claims.[146] In May 2009 Duddy agreed to participate in a conference on the issue, where he presented his version. According to O'Rawe, Duddy did not look comfortable speaking before a large audience, which was understandable given that he was "a man with no shadow, a ghost who whispered in the ears of spooks and revolutionaries."[147]

## Duddy's efforts to promote official negotiations, 1990–1993

### *The renewal of the channel*

Over the years, while holding various positions around the world, Michael Oatley stayed in touch with Duddy.[148] Likewise, Duddy stayed in touch with the Republicans, particularly with McGuinness.[149] But the channel, which remained frozen after its failure in 1981, was not revived until 1990. Its renewal was related to developments in two arenas. The first involved the channel itself: Oatley was about to retire from MI6 and decided to launch one last effort before leaving. He also wanted to ensure that someone would take his place so that the channel could continue.[150]

The second arena entailed developments and changes on both sides of the conflict. On the British side, 1989 saw the appointment of a new secretary of state for Northern Ireland – Peter Brooke – who took a moderate approach to Northern Ireland, and alongside senior NIO leaders promoted a policy that opposed continuation of the status quo and supported the inclusion of Republicans in a settlement.[151] In an interview on the occasion of his appointment, Brooke stated that the IRA could not be defeated militarily and that if "the terrorists" changed their ways, the government would have to be "imaginative." In November 1990 he delivered a dramatic speech in which he declared that Britain had no strategic or economic interest in Northern Ireland.[152] His words resonated on the Republican side.[153] In addition, Britain underwent a political change in late 1990, when John Major replaced Thatcher as prime minister. Upon taking office, Major decided to give high priority to the Northern Ireland problem in his government's agenda.[154] The shift in the British approach stemmed from various factors, including the failure of efforts to defeat the PIRA militarily, the failure of the 1985 attempt to bring the conflict to an end through an agreement with Ireland, the emergence of the Republican Sinn Féin Party as a significant political force that could not be ignored, and international pressures to advance a solution.[155]

The Republican side, too, evinced signs of new thinking. The Republicans now operated as an actor who had entered the political arena (while continuing to engage in military activity), and, as a party with electoral power, they expressed their readiness for dialogue. McGuinness publicly called on the British to start a secret dialogue, and Adams sent a letter to Major demanding a British withdrawal, but the letter was perceived in London as a sign of Republican willingness to end the violence.[156] Shortly before Christmas 1990, the PIRA declared a three-day ceasefire – the first since 1975.[157]

The global changes that took place in the early 1990s also affected Northern Ireland. These included the strengthening of regional frameworks within the European Community in preparation for its 1993 transformation into the European Union (EU), which included both the UK and Ireland, as well as the end of the Cold War and the fall of the Berlin wall.[158] Meanwhile the violence persisted as the PIRA continued to engage in military activities: in September 1989, eleven members of a military orchestra were killed in Kent, in July 1990 a bomb was planted at the London Stock Exchange, and in February 1991 a car bomb exploded near the prime minister's residence.[159]

In January 1991 Duddy facilitated a meeting between Oatley and McGuinness.[160] Adams related that when the Republicans were approached about this meeting, they were skeptical but felt that if the British government wanted to talk, then they had a duty to respond.[161] This was the first British–Republican meeting since the 1970s, when the meetings channel had collapsed. At the meeting, Oatley asserted that without political dialogue, the rounds of violence would continue, and he suggested that upon his retirement a replacement be appointed and that the channel be reactivated. McGuinness reported on this to his colleagues, and the Republicans concluded that they were "morally and tactically obliged not to reject" the offer.[162]

Oatley informed London of this development, and the British began seeking a new representative to the channel. John Deverell, the head of MI5 in Northern Ireland, met with Brooke to discuss appointing a replacement for Oatley and the resumption of the channel. Brooke, who was surprised to learn about the channel, approved its reactivation, knowing he would be "in the firing line" if the story leaked. "It was a real decision, a Rubicon that I personally was having to cross, but I was satisfied that it was a proper thing for me to do."[163] MI5 demanded that the representative come from their ranks, not from MI6, and the role was assigned to former MI5 senior officer "Fred," who also went by the names "Robert McLaren" and "Colin Ferguson."[164] Fred visited Derry in June 1991 and met with Duddy, to whom he presented a letter from Brooke stating that he was the new representative. The letter attested that he was an official appointment with full authority and confirmed Brooke's support for the channel.[165]

During this round Duddy's channel was used for exchanging oral and written messages. In contrast to the format of the 1970s, the channel was not used for direct meetings – other than in two exceptional cases (Oatley–McGuinness in 1991 and Fred–McGuinness in 1993). The contact between Duddy and the British, which was intensive, took place via phone calls and in-person meetings.[166] Duddy's diary during this period (the "narrative") indicates that at certain stages communication was almost daily.[167] The channel was active on a limited scale during 1991–1992, but in early 1993 its use intensified. In 1992, Brooke left office and his successor, Patrick Mayhew, received a briefing about the channel. The Republicans were then informed that Mayhew was fully on board and that the channel would continue to operate.[168]

On the British side, the main figure was Fred, who worked with John Deverell of MI5, Permanent Under-Secretary of State for Northern Ireland John Chilcott, and Quentin Thomas of the NIO. At the height of the channel's activity, in 1993, the circle expanded to include Prime Minister Major, Foreign Secretary Douglas Hurd, and Mayhew.[169]

On the Republican side, the two main figures were senior Sinn Féin members Martin McGuinness and Gerry Kelly. Adams has stated that he knew about the channel from 1981 but "I did not know who was involved or how it worked, and had never asked." He added that McGuinness knew the personalities who were involved in the channel. According to Adams, a "core group" was formed that was responsible for the entire system of contacts vis-à-vis various bodies (British government, Irish government, SDLP, Unionists, and the US), and it was subordinate to the Ard Chomhairle, Sinn Féin's executive council. The group was chaired by Adams and included leaders such as McGuinness, Kelly, and Pat Doherty. As activity on the channel intensified, the Republicans set up a negotiations committee with formal responsibilities such as keeping records, updating the party, and overseeing the negotiations. According to Adams, all the written messages in the channel were drafted by him, McGuinness, and another one or two members in the core group.[170]

The contacts at this stage were conducted between the British government and Sinn Féin – the political wing of the Republican movement – which operated separately from the PIRA. However, Adams and McGuinness reportedly made sure to brief the PIRA about developments in the channel. Adams has described, for example, how when they informed the PIRA about the proposal for a meeting between Oatley and McGuinness, the PIRA did not voice objection but did emphasize that McGuinness would only be representing Sinn Féin, and not the PIRA, at the meeting.[171]

Secrecy remained a crucial element of the channel, and the parties used codenames in their communications.[172] This round differed from previous rounds in its increased use of Duddy's colleagues Denis Bradley and Noel Gallagher. The two helped Duddy in contacts with the Republican leadership and as part of a team that accompanied the channel. Gallagher and Bradley were close to the leadership, and especially to McGuinness. Gallagher coordinated the meetings between Duddy and McGuinness, or met with McGuinness privately and reported to Duddy.[173]

In the 1970s Duddy had had direct access to senior Republicans, par-ticularly to Ó Brádaigh, but after the change in leadership his relationship with it was weaker. According to Adams, when the channel was renewed, in the early 1990s, they were suspicious because of past experience and their sense that it had not served Republicans in previous rounds.[174] Bradley attested that with the renewal of the channel, McGuinness approached him and expressed concern regarding Duddy, but Bradley promised him that he would increase his own involvement in order to reassure him.[175]

Both parties wanted the channel to operate, but the Republicans preferred direct dialogue while the British preferred an indirect channel, managed by intelligence officers. The latter approach allowed the British to maintain a certain distance between the channel and the politicians, and to adhere to their position that direct negotiations be conditional on a ceasefire.[176] In 1992, Republicans asked the British, through the channel, about the possibility of direct dialogue, to which Fred replied that they were aware of the difficulties of dialogue through mediators, but that the conditions for direct talks had not yet been met.[177] The channel initially operated on a small scale and the British used it, among other things, to convey reports on the multi-party talks held in Northern Ireland in 1991–1992 and to share important planned speeches by Brooke, and later by Mayhew, before public delivery of those speeches. On some occasions the Republicans used the channel to provide updates regarding the dialogue between Adams and John Hume of the SDLP on a joint Irish plan for a solution in Northern Ireland.[178]

## Upgrading the channel in 1993

During 1993 the channel served as a means for pre-negotiation dialogue on transitioning to direct official negotiations. The main British demand was a ceasefire as a pre-condition for official talks, which the Republicans opposed, in part because of their experience in 1975. The PIRA declared that there would be no ceasefire in the absence of a British withdrawal.[179] In January 1993 the British used the channel to deliver the message that suspension of violence "would start the ball rolling in a significant way."[180]

On 22 February 1993, a message was conveyed in the name of the Republicans, which was to become a dramatic milestone in the process. According to Andrew, this message "marked the beginning of the long and tortuous path leading eventually to the Good Friday Agreement of 1998."[181] The message read as follows:

> The conflict is over but we need your advice on how to bring it to a close. We wish to have an unannounced cease fire in order to hold a dialogue leading to peace. We cannot announce such a move as it will lead to confusion to the volunteers, because the press will misinterpret it as surrender. We cannot meet the Secretary of State's public renunciation of violence, but it would be given privately as long as we were sure that we were not being tricked.[182]

The message was immediately passed to Deverell and Chilcott and soon reached Mayhew and the prime minister's desk. Chilcott saw the message as a sign that the parties were close to ending the violence, closer than they had been in twenty years. In his memoirs Major described the moment when he received the message, noting that it was "dramatic" but that he immediately wondered whether the message was real. Chilcott and the NIO confirmed that this was an authentic message that had come from McGuinness via a trustworthy channel.[183]

Major convened a special discussion that was attended by Mayhew and Home Secretary Kenneth Clarke, among others. Mayhew and Chilcott expressed support for a pragmatic British response that would offer flexibility, while Clarke, who saw dialogue with the Republicans as more of a danger than an opportunity, took a hawkish stance. Major decided that the Republican message was worth examining and should not be ignored: "We were well aware of the unlikelihood of success; but we felt we had a responsibility to find out whether this was a serious message, and to see if the leadership of the Provisionals ... had the will and the ability to move away from terrorism."[184]

The British representatives told Duddy that they recognized the importance of the message and would soon deliver a detailed response. They explained that the British government was willing to engage in talks, but that a preliminary phase of two to three weeks, during which violence was suspended and the talks remained secret, was a prerequisite.[185] The British formulated "the nine-paragraph document" as a formal response to the Republican message. Its delivery was delayed in light of PIRA military activities, but on 19 March Fred invited Duddy to London and gave him the document.[186] The British document asserted that neither side had a monopoly over suffering and that there was a need for a "healing process." But it stressed that dialogue could only start after a cessation of violent activity, whether announced or unannounced, and that a ceasefire on the ground would lead to a reduction of security force activities. The document made clear that the British government would not enter into negotiations with a predetermined goal, and that it recognized that a united Ireland was a possible outcome, so long as it was "on the basis of the consent of the people of Northern Ireland."[187]

Duddy met with McGuinness and presented the British document. McGuinness said that it seemed to be a serious paper, and reported to the Republican core group.[188] At that point the parties discussed facilitating a meeting on 23 March between Fred and Deverell, from the British side, and McGuinness and Kelly, from the Republican side. But on 20 March, one day after the delivery of the British document, the PIRA carried out a bomb attack in Warrington, England, in which two children were killed and dozens were injured. This prompted London to reconsider its policy, and, according to Major, it almost brought the process to an end.[189]

The event called into question the meeting and the entire channel. In light of the crisis, Duddy delivered a message to Fred, claiming that it came from McGuinness although in fact it was without the latter's knowledge. The message stated: "It is with total sadness that we have to accept responsibility for recent action. The last thing we needed at this sensitive time was what has happened."[190] The British appreciated the message, but nevertheless Fred told Duddy that Deverell would not participate in the meeting and that he was instructed to meet only with Duddy, not with the Republicans. Duddy was furious and told Fred that if the meeting did not take place he would withdraw and the channel would come to an end. Fred initially insisted that those were the instructions he had received, but after several phone calls he announced that he would attend the meeting. When he arrived, Fred explained that he had decided to take a risk.[191] In a retrospective interview, Duddy expressed great appreciation to Fred for this decision and his courage, adding that there are many people in the world who do "the right thing" but only occasionally are there people "who cross the line."[192]

The participants in the meeting were Fred, McGuinness, and Kelly. Duddy, Bradley, and Gallagher were present but did not take part in the discussion. McGuinness asked Fred many questions and Kelly wrote down and documented the meeting. Fred said that he was acting with full authority on behalf of the British government and that his aim was to promote dialogue with the Republican leadership. He stressed that a ceasefire was a condition for talks and that they could begin the minute the Republicans made a commitment to halt the violence. He noted that the government was sincere and that any solution could be raised for discussion, but that the British would not agree to issue a statement of intent to withdraw in advance of the talks.[193] According to the Republican version, Fred had said, "The final solution is union. It is going to happen anyway. ... Unionists will have to change, this island will be as one."[194]

Fred's remarks surprised Duddy, who asked him during the break if he was not deviating from the instructions he had been given. Fred replied that he was deviating from the guidelines by attending the meeting, but that the positions he presented were backed by his superiors. Towards the end of the meeting McGuinness said that they needed time to study the British document and the positions that Fred presented, and would return with a response.[195] According to Bradley, Fred had impressed McGuinness and Kelly, and it was clear that the ball was now in their court.[196]

In late April, the Republicans informed Duddy that they would accept the British proposal, and they requested to meet with Fred and Deverell to discuss proceeding to direct talks. In parallel, Fred told Duddy about a special high-level discussion during which Major had insisted on a ceasefire before any future meeting. An exchange of messages took place in early

May, indicating an impasse. The Republicans were wondering why there was a delay in proceeding towards a meeting, while the British were insisting that so long as there was no "private assurance that organized violence has been brought to an end" there would be no progress.[197]

On 10 May, McGuinness delivered a message to Duddy in which the Republicans announced that they were willing "to make the crucial move" in order to proceed "without delay" to the delegation talks, stating that they had secured the required commitment from the PIRA and expressing hope that it would allow the parties to "explore the potential for developing a real peace process." Alongside the official written message, the Republicans informed Duddy that the PIRA had agreed to a two-week suspension of violence. The Republicans also indicated that they would establish a small secretariat to prepare for the talks, and added a number of questions about the dialogue mechanism. They stated that it would be more practical to coordinate the details directly with McGuinness, but that if this were not possible, they could use the "usual channel."[198] Adams explained that although they were skeptical about the British intentions, after meeting with Fred they thought that the process should be further investigated. He described the PIRA decision as "the biggest breakthrough so far."[199]

Duddy's archival documents reveal that he, and his colleagues Gallagher and Bradley, had decided to intervene in the content of this message. They decided to remove the original wording of a "short duration" in reference to the PIRA ceasefire because they considered this a "real obstacle." According to these documents, Duddy expressed reservations to McGuinness about the sentence but McGuinness insisted that the message was not subject to change. As a result, Duddy asked if it could be conveyed orally, and McGuinness did not object. Duddy then omitted those words when he conveyed the message to the British side.[200]

The Republican message led to another high-level discussion in London. While the NIO urged pursuing the process, Clarke remained skeptical. Major outlined a four-stage plan: a ceasefire (around three months), secret pre-negotiation talks led by Fred and Deverell, a public statement by Major, and an official and direct dialogue.[201] In parallel, the British started to work on a new document that would discuss the transition to direct negotiations.[202]

Once again, however, PIRA military activity affected the dialogue process. On 21 May a bomb exploded near the Grand Opera House in Belfast, and as a result the British decided to suspend work on the new document. Major explained that they wanted to make it clear to the Republicans that terrorism and talks were incompatible and that the British would not agree even to exploratory talks under threat of violence.[203]

The event set the process back, and for several weeks the Republicans awaited a British response that did not materialize. Duddy delivered messages, demanding a reply to the Republican message, but to no avail. The Republican outrage increased when information about the channel leaked to the media. The Republicans conveyed a message of protest, to which the British replied that they were not behind the leaks and that they were committed to the channel's secrecy.[204] Domestic developments also had an impact, as the Major government increased its dependence on the support of Unionist representatives in Parliament, which reduced its leeway regarding Northern Ireland.[205]

Fred was now in a difficult position. He apologized to Duddy over the stalemate and blamed the government, especially Clarke and Mayhew, for thwarting the process.[206] This was similar to the situation faced by the British representatives in the 1975 channel. In late May 1993 Fred asked Duddy to deliver an official Republican request demanding a reply, in order to increase pressure on the government to respond. Duddy sent such a request, apparently without the Republicans' knowledge. The message conveyed that the Republicans proposed a "total cessation" of violence, although this phrase did not actually appear in the original Republican message, in which the PIRA had only agreed to a two-week ceasefire.[207] This is one example of how Fred and Duddy deviated from their instructions and mandate in order to advance the process. Fred also delivered a personal letter to McGuinness expressing anger over the lack of a British response to the Republicans' "brave and straightforward offer."[208]

The channel reached a deadlock during the summer. Duddy maintained contact with Fred but there was no progress, and their exchange of messages centered on the disagreement over the demand for ceasefire as a pre-condition. The British argued that violence prevented progress and that a dialogue could begin only after an assurance that organized violence had been brought to an end. The Republicans claimed that they had proved their commitment by offering a two-week ceasefire but that the British rejection cast doubt on London's intentions.[209] The crisis also stemmed from the fact that the Republicans had the impression that the British would agree to a two-week ceasefire as a pre-condition for dialogue and obtained PIRA approval accordingly, but it then became clear that this did not meet British requirements.[210]

The crisis facing the channel created a dilemma for Duddy, Bradley, and Gallagher similar to that Duddy had faced in 1975. Bradley suggested that Duddy announce his resignation, in order to put pressure on the British, but Duddy refused. The three also spoke with McGuinness about the possibility of revealing the channel's details to John Hume but McGuinness objected.[211]

## The closure of the Duddy channel

In November 1993, Duddy's channel came to an end and the public learned of its existence. The chain of events began with a meeting in London between Duddy and Fred, against the backdrop of the impasse in the channel. Following this meeting, Fred sent a dramatic message from the Republicans to London ("the 2 November message") asking about opening a dialogue "in the event of a total end to the hostilities." The message stated that the nine-paragraph document and 10 May document could serve as a basis for understanding.[212] The new message was enthusiastically received by the British. Major, who saw it as "a sign that the leadership of the Provisionals was prepared to contemplate a permanent cessation of violence," again convened a high-level discussion, at which participants decided to draft a document proposing exploratory talks and setting conditions for them.[213] Thus, the 2 November message revived the channel, after it had been in a state of crisis since May and in fact frozen since September.

The British delivered a detailed response by way of Duddy on 5 November. Referring to the 2 November message as significant, the British document proposed a framework for official dialogue that included three stages: (1) a secret assurance of a permanent end to the violence and a commitment to peaceful and democratic means; (2) a public declaration by the British government regarding its entry into dialogue (if the reality on the ground indicated that the Republicans were upholding their commitment); and (3) the first meeting between the parties would take place when Parliament resumed work in January (so long as the ceasefire was being maintained).[214]

Duddy delivered the document to the Republicans, who were surprised to find a reference to a Republican message allegedly conveyed on 2 November and proposing a "total end to hostilities." They asked Duddy to inform the British that this was a bogus message and to admit that he had not been authorized to convey any message whatsoever at the 2 November meeting with Fred. They expressed anger over this development and demanded that the mistake be corrected. Two days later, Duddy sent the British a written message, explaining that the 2 November message had not come from the Republicans and, indeed, had been conveyed without their authority or knowledge.[215]

Another development that occurred at this time brought the channel to a close. Duddy, Bradley, and Gallagher met with John Hume and disclosed detailed information about the channel. Hume was stunned to learn about the channel and about the positions the parties had conveyed through it. Bradley later observed that by disclosing this information they had delivered "this very hot coal into John Hume's hands."[216] The Republican leadership was furious over the move. Adams wrote that it was a "potentially dangerous and foolhardy decision, breaking all the rules which go-betweens must adhere to." He explained that they were angry that the "Derry trio" had decided to make decisions for them, and argued that this could have damaged his relationship with Hume and undermined the peace efforts. As a result of this move, the Republican leadership decided to close the channel: "They had given good service and we were grateful to them. But the back channel had had its day."[217]

On 26 November 1993, the Republicans asked Duddy to send a message to the British stating that "as a result of difficulties" they would like to replace Duddy and were seeking suggestions on how to proceed the contacts.[218] The fact that even the act of announcing his replacement necessitated Duddy's services attests to his power and role as provider of the only communication channel between the parties. Nonetheless, this development brought Duddy's longstanding mediation activity to an end.

### The exposure of the channel

In November 1993 the journalist Eamonn Mallie began to receive information about a secret channel between the British government and the Republican movement. He published a few reports on the issue, yet when he asked the NIO and the Prime Minister's Office he received a full denial: "It belongs more properly in the fantasy of spy thrillers." A source in Sinn Féin, however, confirmed that there was a channel, and a Unionist parliamentary member shared a British message that had been delivered through the channel, which served as a "smoking gun." Mallie forwarded the document to the British newspaper *The Observer*, and it was published on 28 November alongside a detailed report on the channel.[219]

Following this revelation, the parties confirmed the channel's existence and each side published its version of the story – first the British and then the Republicans.[220] In presenting the British version, Mayhew claimed that the channel had started in February 1993 as a reaction to a dramatic message from McGuinness ("the conflict is over") to which they "had a duty to respond." The British disclosed all the messages that had been delivered via the channel, and Mayhew emphasized that the British position as conveyed through the channel was identical to its public position.[221]

Mayhew explained that the contacts had taken place through an exchange of written messages, and that therefore the British had not been dishonest in asserting that they had not spoken with the Republicans. Brooke presented a similar argument in an interview: "We could continue to say that we were not in direct contact. The conduit was a voluntary one. There was somebody in place who had been involved for quite some time, and he had the advantage of retaining the confidence of both sides. It wasn't negotiation. ... It was the opportunity to carry on conversation."[222] The British stressed that there were no direct meetings and that the two meetings that did take place had not been authorized; an NIO representative described these meetings as "spook freelancing."[223]

Adams presented the Republican version and Sinn Féin published all the messages that had been exchanged through the channel. Adams denied that the Republicans had sent a message stating that "the conflict is over." He also asserted that the channel had opened not in February 1993, but rather had been operating for two decades and was revived in 1990 through a British initiative. Notably, the British later retracted their claim in this regard, and Major and Brooke admitted that the channel had actually been renewed in 1990 with Brooke's approval.[224]

The parties' respective decisions to disclose their secret exchanges made it possible to identify similarities and differences in this *Rashomon*-style story. The conflicting versions sparked a controversy, with each side claiming to have received certain messages that the other side denied sending. There were three messages received by the British that the Republicans denied having sent. Likewise, the British side denied sending the messages that Republicans claimed to have received from Fred regarding a two-week ceasefire demand and a "united Ireland."[225]

These conflicting versions triggered a historical inquiry as to the actor behind the controversial messages, and in particular the message conveyed in February 1993. McGuinness claimed that by presenting this message publicly, the British had sought to harm him and bring about his assassination.[226] Duddy argued that the wording of the message indicated surrender in Republican parlance, and that no Republican leader would convey such a message as Republicans did not use the term "conflict" but rather "war." In a 2008 interview, Duddy stated that he had not conveyed this message, and refused to say whether he thought Fred had delivered it on his own initiative. The Republican leadership suspected that Duddy had conveyed the bogus message, and a number of senior leaders visited his home and interrogated him over the course of four hours. According to Duddy, he convinced them that he had not sent the message, but this incident made it clear that the closure of the channel was final and absolute.[227]

Bradley eventually presented his version, claiming that the message was based on a document that he, Duddy, and Gallagher had written in which they presented their interpretation of the Republican position, and that Duddy had delivered this message to Fred. Bradley said that they had drafted the document out of frustration and in order to advance the process. He asserted, however, that they had not used the phrase "the conflict is over"; their wording, though in the same spirit, was vaguer.[228] Duddy was angry at Bradley's public disclosure (made before Duddy revealed his version) and sent him a letter stating that his remarks about the message were false.[229]

There seems to be a consensus in the literature that this message was formulated not by the Republican leadership, but by the people involved in the channel – Fred, Duddy, Bradley, and Gallagher.[230] British journalist Peter Taylor posited that Fred was behind the message, noting that the text (a copy of which is in Duddy's archive) was in Fred's handwriting; Ó Dochartaigh claimed that Fred "may have over-egged the pudding to break a logjam, but he was working with the deep grain of the new policy rather than as a 'rogue' agent."[231]

If Fred was indeed behind the message, then it is one of a number of situations in which he circumvented or broke the rules, such as when he met with Republicans despite instructions to the contrary. Fred's conduct made him a *persona non grata* in the British establishment, and led to his resignation in December 1993.[232] When direct negotiations eventually began, a year after the channel collapsed, Fred was not part of the British delegation. Notably, McGuinness asked the British representatives about him.[233] Over the years Fred has refused to be exposed and has never presented his version of events. Bennett-Jones has argued that, like Duddy, who received recognition for his role in the peace process, Fred too deserves recognition: "While the British politicians and IRA leaders remained cautious and entrenched in long established positions, he found a way to tempt them into taking risks and eventually reaching agreement. Sometimes civil servants should break the rules."[234]

The 2 November message is also a focal point of controversy. Duddy admitted that it resulted from a meeting between himself and Fred in London that took place amid fears that Major was seeking to advance talks with Dublin and abandon contact with Republicans. Similarly, in delivering the message following the Warrington attack (in March 1993), Duddy evidently acted without the Republicans' knowledge. He explained that the incident had jeopardized the process, which made the message necessary: "It needed to be heard by the other side to allow things to move on. They [the British] needed it, and I gave it to them."[235] Indeed, the message did help: according to Chilcott, it showed them that it was possible to continue after the incident despite the difficulty and tragedy. O'Kane argued that the bogus messages resulted from the intermediaries' frustration with the lack of progress, the lack of clarity about their role, and the many stages each message underwent along the channel.[236]

The mediators' interference in the content of the messages stemmed from their sense of helplessness when the channel reached a dead end. It was possible because of their power as intermediaries who controlled the exclusive channel between the parties. They felt that the situation was ripe for progress, but that each side was afraid to make the first move and that only intervention by a third party could break the stalemate. According to O'Kane, the intermediaries saw themselves as "mediators rather than simply facilitators" and the frequency of contact between Duddy and Fred made it difficult to distinguish between messages and analysis.[237] Downey argued that the bogus message of February 1993, once revealed, had, on the one hand, led to the end of the channel and created a risk to Duddy's life, but, on the other hand, was the catalyst for the nine-paragraph document and the 10 May message and prompted developments that would not have taken place otherwise.[238]

Thus, after almost two decades of activity, Duddy's channel came to an end. "After risking his life for twenty years," Taylor wrote, "acting as the intermediary between the IRA and the British Government, the contact was finished."[239] McGuinness, in an interview, explained that "the British government have effectively abused the contact to destruction."[240] Pat Sheehan, a former hunger striker and later a Sinn Féin representative to Parliament, said, in reference to the channel, that it is very important to have channels of communication between the parties, but that direct dialogue is always preferable because of concerns that the third party will interfere with the messages in order to promote the process.[241] On 29 November the channel conveyed a final message from the Republicans, protesting "the way this process is being abused by the politicians." The Republicans explained that their public statement was a response to "bad faith, dishonesty and leaks" on the British side. They told Fred that despite the events of 2 November, they acknowledged his endeavors.[242] On 24 December, Fred sent a personal farewell letter to Duddy: "I have never met such a combination of courage, ingenuity and dogged determination never to give up in anyone else."[243]

In his book, Major pointed to the importance of the channel and noted that he regretted its termination: "The messages we received from the Provisionals in February, May and November 1993, and our two substantive replies of 19 March and 5 November, helped to pave the way for the cessation of violence by spelling out clearly what was, and what was not, on offer – especially by defining the terms for 'exploratory dialogue'. I regretted the loss of the back channel. It gave us some difficult moments, but it played its part. Making peace is a tricky business."[244] After the channel had been shut down, the Republicans tried to contact the British directly, and Adams sent a few letters to Major. In parallel, discussions took place between Britain and Ireland – resulting in a declaration by Major and Ireland's Taoiseach Albert Reynolds in December 1993 – and Republicans engaged in contact with Ireland and the US. In August 1994, Mayhew met with Adams and McGuinness, and the PIRA declared a ceasefire. In December 1994, the first meeting of delegations from the two sides – Sinn Féin and the British government – took place, thus launching the negotiation process that eventually concluded with the "Good Friday Agreement" (also known as the "Belfast Agreement") signed on 10 April 1998.

## Analysis and conclusions: the impact of PPE Duddy on the official sphere

### *Influence patterns*

Jonathan Powell, the British government's chief negotiator in Northern Ireland from 1997 to 2007 and one of the architects of the Good Friday Agreement, described Duddy as follows:

> He was a pacifist and a firm believer in dialogue, which he worked single-mindedly to create. … His role as a brave and ingenious intermediary unpublicised for over three decades, yet he has a claim to have been among the most persistent and effective of the unsung heroes of the peace process.[245]

Peter Taylor argued that "without Duddy, it's unlikely there would have been the historic IRA ceasefire the following year that led to the Good Friday agreement, and ultimately to the peace that Northern Ireland enjoys today."[246] Stephen Lander, a former MI5 senior official, posed a similar argument, claiming that without Duddy's channel "there would have been no peace process."[247] Irish journalist Ed Moloney claimed that Duddy became "a player on the international peace circuit,"[248] and Gerry Adams stated after Duddy's death in 2017 that "Brendan was a tireless advocate for peace over four decades. … There was always a constant in his determination and commitment to finding agreement, achieving progress, and ending conflict. … He made a significant contribution to the development of the peace process."[249]

Which influence patterns were at work in Duddy's activity as a PPE? The main element was *influence through mediation* as, over the course of two decades, Duddy operated a secret – and usually sole – channel between the British government and the Republican movement. His efforts included the role of *communicator*, exchanging written and oral messages, information, drafts of speeches, clarifications, proposals, and updates. He also served as a *facilitator* who coordinated and organized direct meetings between the parties (in 1975–1976, 1991, and 1993), using his house as a secret, neutral space and maintaining special secrecy arrangements. Duddy also facilitated meetings between Republicans and other actors. Furthermore, he provided assistance as a *formulator* by presenting ideas, plans, and proposals. He also played the role of a *psychoanalyst* in trying to "educate" the parties, change their "enemy image," and expose each side to the sensitivities, and the internal complexity, on the other side. He tried to use the tactics of a *manipulator* by threatening to abandon his role or by warning of dangerous escalation. Duddy's mediation model had an influence on other conflicts. When McGuinness visited Colombia in 2014 to assist in the peace process with the Revolutionary Armed Forces of Colombia (FARC), he was surprised to discover that the Colombian government was aware of the channel, and when it opened a secret channel with FARC, that channel became known as the "Brendan Channel."[250]

Duddy's efforts also produced *influence through gestures of conciliation*, such as the ceasefire declaration and the release of prisoners. In addition, they generated *influence through crisis management*. Examples include his efforts during the kidnapping crises of 1973 and 1974 and during the hunger strikes of 1980 and 1981. Duddy's activity also led to *changes in institutional procedures* on the Republican side, impelling them to organize accordingly, to formulate positions and proposals, and to create relevant bodies for the negotiation process. On the British side, where there was no need to establish new bodies, Duddy's channel served as a trigger for high-level discussions on negotiating with the Republicans and forced the British to appoint a representative to the channel when Oatley retired. Duddy only operated secretly and never engaged in public activities. The channel only had an influence on public opinion after news of its existence was leaked in 1993. In addition, Duddy developed ideas and proposals, but it is difficult to identify any decisive effect resulting from the transfer of his ideas to the official space.

### Variables related to the PPE

Duddy was a local businessman in the city of Derry and his restaurant became a center of social and political activity. This helped him build networks with various actors and gather information. Over time he increased his engagement in the communal and political spheres, becoming involved in a few forums and circles and playing a role as a member of the City Centre Liaison Committee. A comparison with the cases of Cousins and Massie points to questions about the relationship between the character of a conflict and the PPE's access resources. In international conflicts the PPE usually needs access to official governmental actors, whereas in internal conflicts or in conflicts with non-state actors, PPEs need a different type of network and access to a different type of actor. In the latter cases, PPEs with large, strong local networks are likely to have an advantage.

Downey has argued that over the years Duddy, as a successful business-man, developed unique negotiation skills. Vered Amitzi, a good friend of

Duddy, noted that he had a special verbal ability, strong intuition, and good listening skills, while a former British official described him as an "exceptional and influential communicator."[251] Duddy also used the skills he acquired as a workshop facilitator for the "group relations" approach based on the Tavistock model.

The main power resources in Duddy's activities were the following.

1. *Access and network system.* Duddy developed relations of trust and appreciation with key actors on both sides. The relations emerged from his business and communal activity, but they expanded and intensified as each side was exposed to his contacts on the other side, which it came to view as a power resource. Both sides knew that Duddy had valuable cumulative experience and expertise gained over the course of two decades. While all the other actors changed, he remained a stable and consistent participant who had the commitment, availability, and solid infrastructure necessary to communicate with the other side. A former British official explained that Duddy was in the position of holding the key to a box that contained a telephone to reach Oatley and from him to "Number 10," and the Republicans valued the existence of this link as something they might use one day.[252]

    On the Republican side, the two main leaders with whom Duddy developed close relations were Ó Brádaigh and Ó Conaill. These relations, as well as Duddy's role in the meetings channel in 1975, strengthened his status and expanded his networks in the Republican movement. When the 1975 channel was active, Duddy was in intense contact with Republicans and privy to internal discussions of the PAC. Following internal political changes in the Republican movement, the leaders with whom Duddy was in contact were replaced by a new generation of leaders, headed by Adams and McGuinness. His association with the 1975 channel, which Adams and McGuinness regarded as an erroneous move, complicated Duddy's relationship with the new leaders, but soon they realized the importance of the channel and used it at various stages. When Duddy's mediation efforts were revived, during the hunger strikes (1980–1981) and later in the early 1990s, McGuinness served as the main Republican contact. McGuinness lived in Derry and knew Duddy well, but their relations were not as strong as those Duddy had enjoyed with his predecessors, and he therefore needed the help of Gallagher and Bradley.

    On the British side, the first key person was Frank Lagan, a Catholic RUC lieutenant. Lagan and Duddy developed close relations and Lagan introduced Duddy to Steele, as a result of which Duddy formed a connection with the NIO and later with Oatley, who replaced Steele. Duddy's friendship with Oatley lasted for many years, and they even kept in touch after Oatley left Northern Ireland for various positions around the world. Their relations formed the basis for the channel in 1975 and for its renewal in 1980 and in 1990. Over the years, other British officials worked with Duddy in the channel. In 1981 his main British contact was Middleton and in 1991–1993 it was Fred. Duddy's networks on the British side expanded over the years, but eventually he encountered a "glass ceiling" that barred his access to senior officials in the British administration.[253] This is attributable to the British interest in maintaining deniability vis-à-vis the channel, as well as a safe "buffer zone" between the channel and London. However, over the years the British representatives to the channel did have direct access to decision makers, and at various stages even prime ministers were involved in the process.

There were a few "credibility tests" over the years, when Duddy proved his ability to deliver, which in turn reinforced his status. Examples include his ability to resolve crises in 1973–1974, his success in securing a permit for Morrison to visit Maze Prison in July 1981, and the meeting he facilitated between Republican leaders and a British official in March 1993. When asked about his role as a mediator, Duddy explained that it derived from the fact that both parties trusted him and knew that he would maintain secrecy. He argued that ultimately both sides saw his activity as useful; otherwise he could not have continued.[254]

2.  *Knowledge resources.* Duddy developed unique knowledge resources regarding the parties, based on his contacts and long and intensive discussions with them. He became an expert on the positions, sensitivities, internal dynamics, and limits of the maneuverability on both sides. Ó Dochartaigh argued that, through Duddy's channel, both parties received important and exclusive information about the opposing side.[255] Duddy developed a strong familiarity with the British system and, according to Bradley, became an expert in "reading the minds of the British."[256] At the same time, Duddy was able to gain insights into the Republican thinking and an understanding of their internal dynamics and views. A British report on the 1981 channel stressed that there was little difference between Duddy's predictions regarding Republican positions and the actual views eventually presented by Republicans via the channel.[257]

3.  *Value-based resources.* Duddy's ideology motivated him to take action, but it also helped him build trust with both parties. On the Republican side, the fact that he was Catholic and committed to Irish nationalism made it possible for Republican leaders to trust him and see him as an actor who identifies with Republican goals, notwithstanding disagreements. Thus in 1981, for example, they opted for Duddy's channel over the ICJP, which opposed the Republicans. On the British side, Duddy

proved that while he was inclined towards the Republican approach, he opposed violence and was clearly committed to a peaceful solution. According to a former British official, both sides trusted Duddy because he "was an honest broker."[258]

## Variables related to the initiative

1. *Secrecy/publicity and the action pattern*. Secrecy was a basic element in Duddy's activity. It was a condition for the existence of the channel. The channel necessitated strict secrecy arrangements. It forced Duddy's family members to abide by a rigid regime and live in the shadow of this secret. His granddaughter, Sarah Duddy, noted that the family members knew there was a secret but did not discuss it, and only in the late 1990s did Duddy tell her about it. She recalled how when she would work on her history lessons as a schoolgirl, Duddy used to tell her that the accounts in the textbooks were not important because real historical events occur secretly, beneath the surface, and no one knows about them.[259] Indeed, Duddy focused on the secret action pattern to the exclusion of other action patterns. Even after the channel closed, and after the peace agreement had been signed, Duddy chose not to reveal his story. It was only in 2008 that he consented to the production of a film about him and the disclosure of his private archive.

2. *The goal of the initiative*. The first stage of Duddy's activity (1972–1974) focused on ad-hoc mediation efforts surrounding specific crises. In the second stage (1975–1976), the aim of the channel was to promote a truce regime and confidence-building measures, as well as discussions on core issues and a long-term agreement. The third stage (1980–1981) focused on a solution to the hunger strike crisis. During the fourth stage, in the early 1990s, the channel was initially used to exchange information and updates (1991–1992), but in 1993 it turned into a pre-negotiation channel for discussions on the conditions for a transition to direct, official talks.

3. *Correlation with official policy*. Duddy's efforts were usually in line with the policy of the Republican movement. Throughout the years, Republican consent was the basis for the existence of the channel. During 1975 there were some internal differences among the Republicans with regard to the dialogue via the channel. Publicly, Duddy never presented a view contrary to the Republican position, and even after the channel had closed he avoided criticizing the Republicans. Yet there were some differences of opinion between Duddy and the Republicans, mainly with regard to the use of violence. Duddy was usually a passive mediator, providing a channel to deliver messages, but sometimes he also raised new ideas, and on a few occasions even sent messages without the approval of the Republicans in order to advance the process.

4. *Direct or indirect contact.* Duddy's channel was the sole channel between the British and the Republicans. But Duddy did not have direct access to the leaders on both sides. On the British side he was in contact with lower-level officials, not with the senior political decision makers. On the Republican side, he had direct contact with the leaders during the first stage of the channel, but after the change in leadership his access became more indirect. Although he did meet with McGuinness, their communication mainly took place through Gallagher, and he had no direct contact with Adams. Duddy's circumstances entailed some difficulties, as each message had to go through a chain comprising several steps and involvement by different actors, especially during the last stage of the channel's existence. This produced some errors and had the potential to lead to "Chinese whispers," as O'Kane argued.[260] In addition, the mandate of the British representatives to the channel was limited, which created some challenges for the process, often resulting in frustration, tension, or differences of opinion between them and the decision makers in London.[261]

## External variables

1. *Characteristics of the conflict.* Duddy's efforts took place in the context of a conflict between a state (Britain) and a non-state actor (Republican movement), which formed part of the larger intractable conflict in Northern Ireland. The conflict he was addressing emerged in the 1960s, but its roots lay in the historical conflict between England and Ireland, which had national and religious elements. The complexity of the conflict also stemmed from the multiplicity of actors involved: Britain, Ireland, nationalist Republicans, SDLP, Loyalist organizations, and Unionist parties.

2. *Ripeness.* Duddy's two main mediation efforts – in 1975 and in the early 1990s – took shape under conditions that involved a certain degree of ripeness for a conflict resolution process. In both cases the effort took place against a background that included the following elements: political change on the British side (Wilson in 1974 and Major in 1990), collapse of an attempt to formulate an agreed constitutional arrangement through dialogue with the political parties in Northern Ireland (the Sunningdale process in 1974 and the multi-party talks in 1992), and continuation, and even escalation, of the violent conflict.

   There is debate in the scholarship as to the nature of British intentions in 1975. Evidently they were willing to engage in a dialogue with Republicans in order to explore certain possibilities and attempt to persuade them to join the political game. But as the channel continued to operate, it became increasingly evident that the British were primarily interested in conflict management. The Wilson government, because it was weak, feared any controversial moves. The Republicans, who came to the channel under public pressure and after being weakened by British military operations, were interested in examining the feasibility of an agreement that would allow them to shift to political activity. Yet the Republican leadership also faced strong internal opposition. Some claimed that the channel was a British ploy, although Ó Dochartaigh has rejected such claims, asserting that both sides came to the 1975 talks with a "genuine aim of exploring the potential for a negotiated compromise that would resolve the conflict and end violence."[262] Ultimately, however, the channel revealed that the gaps between the parties were impossible to bridge.

Conditions of ripeness were more apparent in the early 1990s. Both sides evinced signs of fatigue from the "long war" and willingness to consider a different way. The British side realized that a solution required the integration of Republicans into the process, and on the Republican side signs of new thinking and readiness for strategic change emerged. But neither side wanted to take the first step as both were cautious and suspicious. Major knew that any attempts by his predecessors to make progress on Northern Ireland had backfired. In his memoirs he noted that this was seen as an unsolvable issue that prime ministers should avoid.[263] On the Republican side, the trauma of the 1975 talks had left a heavy mark, and they pledged not to repeat this mistake. The fact that both sides responded seriously and positively to the 1990s initiative indicates that there was a certain degree of ripeness at that point, but the continuing violence posed a barrier that undermined British willingness to move forward.

Duddy's efforts during the hunger strikes took place after the emergence of triggers that catalyzed the revival of his channel. In December 1980 the trigger stemmed from concerns over the possible death of hunger striker Sean McKenna, and in July 1981 it was driven by the prisoners' statement, international pressure, and fears surrounding the pending death of hunger striker Joe McDonnell. In both cases, the parties were willing to renew the channel and discuss a solution to the crisis, but each party feared an arrangement that would depict it as having surrendered or retreated from its position.

3.  *The leaders' positions and the domestic conditions.* Duddy's mediation efforts were possible because he had the consent of leaders on both sides. On the British side, Harold Wilson approved the channel at the end of 1974, effectively repealing the ban imposed by his predecessor on contacts with the PIRA,[264] but in 1976 James Callaghan ordered that the contacts cease. Margaret Thatcher publicly held a firm stance against dialogue with the Republican movement. During the hunger

strikes, however, she was willing to examine the possibility of resolving the crisis through Duddy's channel with the Republicans. Charles Moore, Thatcher's biographer, wrote that in doing so she went against her public statements, which if discovered would have caused severe damage to her reputation.[265] British archival papers indicate that in internal discussions conducted while the channel was operating, Thatcher actually demonstrated a more moderate stance than Atkins.[266] John Major claimed that he knew very little about Northern Ireland when entering office, but that he decided to make it a high priority.[267] His quick response to the "conflict is over" message in 1993 reflected his sincere willingness to examine ways of achieving a breakthrough. He also became strongly involved in the process, initiating several high-level discussions.

On the Republican side, Ó Brádaigh and Ó Conaill supported a ceasefire and dialogue with the British. They were sending messages in this spirit from 1972, and even after the channel collapsed, in 1976, Ó Brádaigh maintained this position and publicly expressed a desire for peace talks with the British. Various sources at the time attested that Ó Brádaigh and Ó Conaill were interested in entering the political game and having Sinn Féin compete in the election as a rival to the SDLP.[268] By the time of the hunger strikes, Adams and McGuinness had become the leading actors in the Republican movement. In both cases (1980 and 1981) they supported negotiations on a respectable resolution of the crisis, but there is debate regarding their willingness to show flexibility and apparently there were differences of opinion between them and the prisoners' leaders.

In the early 1990s, Adams and McGuinness called for an "inclusive dialogue" while also promising to show "courage and flexibility" in the talks. This approach was reflected in their public statements, in the dialogue with Hume and Ireland, and in the peace program they released in February 1992.[269]

4.  *Parallel channels of communication.* The fact that for many years Duddy's channel was the only channel between the parties – "the only show in town," as Downey described it[270] – gave him significant power. Unlike Cousins and Massie, who worked in parallel to official channels, Duddy acted in a diplomatic vacuum that lacked official channels. At the start of his activity, in the early 1970s, there were other intermediaries who offered their help, but by 1975 his had become the sole channel. Duddy noted in his diary that in April 1976, when he was invited to a meeting in London, he asked his British counterpart how he would be introduced and was told that he would be described as "our sole intermediary with the Provisional Republican movement."[271] During the second hunger strike (1981), Duddy's activities were influenced by a parallel effort by the ICJP. Yet the Republicans preferred Duddy's channel and asked the

ICJP members to stop their efforts. Likewise, the British reached the conclusion that they should focus on dialogue through Duddy's channel. In the early 1990s Duddy's channel again operated without any parallel option. The fact that the Republican message of November 1993, announcing the termination of Duddy's role, was conveyed through Duddy himself, illustrated his monopoly over the communication between the parties. His exclusivity gave him the leverage to threaten that he would withdraw, as it would mean closure of the communication channel.

Over the years there have been additional channels between other actors in the conflict, such as the multi-party talks, dialogue between the British government and the Irish government, and the Adams–Hume talks. There were also important peace efforts by two other PPEs, who focused on other aspects of the conflict: Father Alec Reid, who served as a mediator between Adams and Hume; and Reverend Roy Magee, who had contacts with Loyalist organizations and played a role in brokering the 1994 Loyalist ceasefire.

5. *Internal governmental agents.* Michael Oatley's role in Northern Ireland was a crucial factor in promoting Duddy's activity and the creation of the channel. Oatley, as an official agent within the British system, gave priority to Duddy's peace activities and put all his weight into promoting them. He personally served as the key link between the official and unofficial diplomatic spheres. Oatley transformed the "bamboo" channel into a meetings channel in 1975, and renewed the channel in 1980 and again in 1990, before retiring.

The officials who succeeded Oatley also played an important role as Duddy's allies within the system – especially Fred, who occasionally deviated from his official instructions in order to promote the channel. At certain times the intelligence officers seemed to be far more active than the politicians in pushing for progress. Referring to the channel of the 1990s, for example, Bradley observed that "the intelligence people move within the British establishment before the politicians move."[272] Frank Lagan also deserves mention, as a governmental agent who helped Duddy at the beginning of the process, facilitating his first contacts with the British establishment. On the Republican side, Ó Brádaigh and Ó Conaill served as internal agents, who promoted dialogue and encouraged Duddy from within the Republican network.

## Notes

1  J. Powell, *Great Hatred, Little Room* (London: Vintage, 2008), 68.
2  See for example N. Ó Dochartaigh, "The role of an intermediary in back-channel negotiation: Evidence from the Brendan Duddy Papers," *Dynamics*

*of Asymmetric Conflict*, 4:3 (2011), 214–225; F. Cowper-Coles, "'Anxious for peace': The provisional IRA in dialogue with the British government, 1972–75," *Irish Studies Review*, 20:3 (2012), 223–242; T. Hennessey, *Hunger Strike* (Dublin: Irish Academic Press, 2013); Powell, *Great Hatred*; E. O'Kane, "Talking to the enemy? The role of the back-channel in the development of the Northern Ireland peace process," *Contemporary British History*, 29:3 (2015), 401–420.

3  See I. V. Johansen, "The rise and the fall of the Northern Ireland civil rights movement," in A. F. Parkinson and É. Phoenix (eds), *Conflicts in the North of Ireland, 1900–2000* (Dublin: Four Courts, 2010), 223–237.

4  J. Tonge, *Northern Ireland* (Cambridge: Polity, 2006); P. Neumann, *Britain's Long War* (New York: Palgrave Macmillan, 2003), 43–69.

5  See Peter Taylor, *Provos: The IRA and Sinn Féin* (London: Bloomsbury, 1998); R. English, *Armed Struggle: The History of the IRA* (London: Pan Books, 2004); T. P. Coogan, *The IRA* (New York: Palgrave for St. Martin's Press, 2002); E. Moloney, *A Secret History of the IRA* (New York: W. W. Norton, 2003).

6  Taylor, *Provos*, 109, 172–174; English, *Armed Struggle*, 167–170; J. Bew, M. Frampton, and I. Gurruchaga, *Talking to Terrorists* (New York: Columbia University Press, 2009), 54, 64.

7  T. Craig, "From backdoors and back lanes to backchannels: Reappraising British talks with the Provisional IRA, 1970–1974," *Contemporary British History*, 26:1 (2012), 104. On the British policy in Northern Ireland see P. Taylor, *Brits* (London: Bloomsbury, 2001).

8  Taylor, *Provos*, 128; Craig, "From backdoors," 101–102; T. Craig "Laneside, then left a bit? Britain's secret political talks with Loyalist paramilitaries in Northern Ireland, 1973–1976," *Irish Political Studies*, 29:2 (2014), 301; Moloney, *A Secret History*, 257; Taylor, *Brits*, 163.

9  Powell, *Great Hatred*, 66; Craig, "From backdoors," 102; Taylor, *Brits*, 196.

10  Craig, "From backdoors," 108; A. Mumford, "Covert peacemaking: Clandestine negotiations and backchannels with the Provisional IRA during the early 'Troubles', 1972–76," *Journal of Imperial and Commonwealth History*, 39:4 (2011), 638; Bew, Frampton, and Gurruchaga, *Talking to Terrorists*, 50.

11  Bew, Frampton and Gurruchaga, *Talking to Terrorists*, 39, 49.

12  Craig, "From backdoors," 104–108; Mumford, "Covert peacemaking," 636–639; Bew, Frampton, and Gurruchaga, *Talking to Terrorists*, 39–42; R. W. White, *Ruairí Ó Brádaigh* (Bloomington: Indiana University Press, 2006), 190; N. Ó Dochartaigh, "The contact: Understanding a communication channel between the British Government and the IRA," in J. J. Popiolkowski and N. J. Cull (eds), *Public Diplomacy, Cultural Interventions and the Peace Process in Northern Ireland* (Los Angeles: Figueroa Press, 2009), 62.

13  Interview with Eamonn Downey, 3 June 2013.

14  Brendan Duddy Papers (hereafter BDP), POL 35/45, Brendan Duddy's Statement: Bloody Sunday Enquiry; BDP, POL 35, Biographical history.

15  Brendan Duddy's Statement; Interview with Eamonn Downey.

16  Brendan Duddy's Statement.

17  Interview with Eamonn Downey; Brendan Duddy's Statement.
18  Powell, *Great Hatred*, 67; Brendan Duddy's Statement.
19  Interview with Vered Amitzi, 25 May 2015; H. Iserovich, "From Northern Ireland to Israel: The story of a peace fighter," *NRG*, 21 February 2010.
20  B. Rowan, "Derry man breaks silence on McGuinness plea," *Belfast Telegraph* (21 June 2007).
21  Interview with Sarah Duddy, 3 June 2013.
22  BDP, POL 35/666, DVD 1.2 Ó Bradaigh; DVD 1.3 Ó Conaill.
23  Interview with Eamonn Downey.
24  Interview with Vered Amitzi.
25  Brendan Duddy's Statement; DVD 1.2 Ó Bradaigh; Ó Dochartaigh, "The role," 218; Interview with Niall Ó Dochartaigh, 6 June 2013.
26  Interview with Eamonn Downey; DVD 1.3 Ó Conaill; Ó Dochartaigh, "The role," 217; Biographical history.
27  Brendan Duddy's Statement; BDP, POL 35/667, DVD 2.4 Frank Lagan.
28  Interview with Eamonn Downey.
29  Cowper-Coles, "'Anxious for peace,'" 227, 238n35.
30  Cowper-Coles, "'Anxious for peace,'" 227.
31  Ó Dochartaigh, "'The contact," 62; Taylor, *Brits*, 169; Powell, *Great Hatred*, 67.
32  Eamonn Downey private archive, Steele to Woodfield, 26 January 1973.
33  Craig "Laneside," 31; Powell, *Great Hatred*, 67.
34  Taylor, *Brits*, 164–166.
35  P. Taylor, *Behind the Mask* (New York: TV Books, 1997), 194–195; D. Bloomfield, *Peacemaking Strategies in Northern Ireland* (New York: St. Martin's Press, 1997), 30–31. The term "Unionists" refers to residents of Northern Ireland who wish to remain under British rule.
36  Taylor, *Behind the Mask*, 202.
37  Taylor, *Brits*, 169; Cowper-Coles, "'Anxious for peace,'" 228; Ó Dochartaigh, "The contact," 59–60; BDP, POL 35/666, DVD 1.4 Michael Oatley; Unattributable interview with former British official.
38  Taylor, *Behind the Mask*, 199–201; Cowper-Coles, "'Anxious for peace,'" 228; Moloney, *A Secret History*, 405; DVD 1.3 Ó Conaill; Powell, *Great Hatred*, 68.
39  Ó Dochartaigh, "The role," 217–218; Ó Dochartaigh, "The contact," 64–65; Taylor, *Brits*, 169–170; Taylor, *Behind the Mask*, 197–200; Mumford, "Covert peacemaking," 641–642; Craig, "From backdoors," 109; Cowper-Coles, "'Anxious for peace,'" 228; N. Ó Dochartaigh, "Together in the middle: Backchannel negotiation in the Irish Peace Process," *Journal of Peace Research*, 48:6 (2011), 772, 774.
40  J. Powell, *Talking to Terrorists* (London: Bodley Head, 2014), 81.
41  Taylor, *Brits*, 170; N. Ó Dochartaigh, "'Everyone trying' – the IRA ceasefire, 1975: A missed opportunity for peace?" *Field Day Review*, 7 (2011), 60; Cwper-Cole, "'Anxious for peace,'" 228; Unattributable interview with former British official.
42  Ó Dochartaigh, "'Everyone trying,'" 60; Taylor, *Behind the Mask*, 201–202.

43 R. W. White, "The 1975 British–Provisional IRA truce in perspective," *Éire-Ireland*, 45:3 (2010), 215; Taylor, *Brits*, 175, 207; White, *Ruairí Ó Brádaigh*, 221–224; Bew, Frampton, and Gurruchaga, *Talking to Terrorists*, 64.
44 White, *Ruairí Ó Brádaigh*, 221–224; Taylor, *Brits*, 176–177; Cowper-Coles, "'Anxious for peace,'" 228, 239; Taylor, *Behind the Mask*, 204–207; Unattributable interview with former British official.
45 Powell, *Great Hatred*, 69.
46 Cowper-Coles, "'Anxious for peace,'" 235, 237.
47 Powell, *Great Hatred*, 68–69.
48 Taylor, *Brits*, 178; Taylor, *Behind the Mask*, 208–209, 215; White, *Ruairí Ó Brádaigh*, 224–225; Cowper-Coles, "'Anxious for peace,'" 229.
49 Taylor, *Brits*, 179; White, *Ruairí Ó Brádaigh*, 225.
50 White, *Ruairí Ó Brádaigh*, 225.
51 Cowper-Coles, "'Anxious for peace,'" 229; White, "The 1975," 216; White, *Ruairí Ó Brádaigh*, 225; Taylor, *Brits*, 179–180; Taylor, *Behind the Mask*, 209–210.
52 Ruairí Ó Brádaigh Papers (hereafter ROP), POL 28/68, "Background to renewal of truce & subsequent negotiations"; Taylor, *Behind the Mask*, 214; White, *Ruairí Ó Brádaigh*, 226.
53 Taylor, *Behind the Mask*, 210; White, *Ruairí Ó Brádaigh*, 227; Cowper-Coles, "'Anxious for peace,'" 230.
54 Taylor, *Behind the Mask*, 210, 214; Interview with Eamonn Downey; Interview with Sarah Duddy; Cowper-Coles, "'Anxious for peace,'" 230; BDP, POL35/668, DVD 3.4 1975 talks.
55 Cowper-Coles, "'Anxious for Peace,'" 230; Ó Dochartaigh, "The role," 222; DVD 3.4 1975 talks; Interview with Niall Ó Dochartaigh.
56 Bew, Frampton, and Gurruchaga, *Talking to Terrorists*, 50; Moloney, *A Secret History*, 405–406; Interview with Eamonn Downey.
57 Cowper-Coles, "'Anxious for Peace,'" 230; White, *Ruairí Ó Brádaigh*, 226–227; Taylor, *Behind the Mask*, 214; Powell, *Great Hatred*, 69.
58 Bew, Frampton, and Gurruchaga, *Talking to Terrorists*, 54; White, *Ruairí Ó Brádaigh*, 227.
59 Taylor, *Behind the Mask*, 214–216; ROP, POL 28/68, "Formal meeting 19 January 1975 continued."
60 ROP, POL 28/68, "Formal meeting 7 February 1975"; Ó Dochartaigh, "'Everyone trying,'" 60.
61 ROP, POL 28/68, "Formal meeting, 22 January 1975; ROP, POL 28/68, "Statement by the Secretary of State for Northern Ireland, 22 January 1975."
62 Ó Dochartaigh, "'Everyone trying,'" 59–60; C. Andrew, *The Defence of the Realm* (London: Allen Lane, 2010), 625–626.
63 BDP, POL 35/63, Brendan Duddy 1975 Diary.
64 ROP, POL 28/29, "Terms for bilateral truce"; ROP, POL 28/68, "Formal meeting, 3 February 1975."
65 Brendan Duddy 1975 Diary; "Statement by the Secretary"; Taylor, *Behind the Mask*, 216.

66 Brendan Duddy 1975 Diary.

67 ROP, POL 28/68, "Formal meeting 7 February 75"; Taylor, *Behind the Mask*, 218; White, *Ruairí Ó Brádaigh*, 229, 231; Cowper-Coles, "'Anxious for peace,'" 230, 234.

68 Brendan Duddy 1975 Diary; Taylor, *Brits*, 185; Interview with Eamonn Downey; Cowper-Coles, "'Anxious for Peace,'" 230.

69 ROP, POL 28/69, "Formal meeting, 11 March 1975," "Per Sinn Fein, 10 March 1975," "Formal meeting, 13 March 1975," "Formal meeting, 16 March 1975"; BDP, POL 35/64, "Formal meeting, 15 March 1975"; Taylor, *Brits*, 181.

70 Brendan Duddy 1975 Diary; Taylor, *Behind the Mask*, 221; White, *Ruairí Ó Brádaigh*, 234.

71 Brendan Duddy 1975 Diary; DVD 1.4 Michael Oatley.

72 BDP, POL 35/64, Letter to Wilson, 29 March 1975; Taylor, *Behind the Mask*, 221–222.

73 Brendan Duddy 1975 Diary, 16.

74 BDP, POL 35/64, "Instructions, 1 April 1975."

75 DVD 1.3 Ó Conaill.

76 ROP, POL 28/69, "Formal meeting, 2 April 1975"; Brendan Duddy 1975 Diary; Taylor, *Behind the Mask*, 223.

77 Taylor, *Brits*, 180, 182; Taylor, *Behind the Mask*, 219; White, "The 1975," 218.

78 See BDP, POL 35/64, "Instructions 1 April 1975," "Formal meeting, 2 April 1975," "Formal Meeting, 9 April 1975," "Formal meeting, 17 April 1975," "Instructions, 18 April 1975," "Formal meeting, 23 April 1975," "Instructions, 6 May 1975," "Formal meeting, 7 May 1975," "Formal meeting, 14 May 1975," "Instructions, 26 May 1975," "Instructions, 5 June 1975," "Formal meeting, 4 June 1975," "Formal meeting, 11 June 1975"; ROP, POL 28/64, "Formal meeting, 28 May 1975," POL 28/70, "Formal meeting, 22 July 1975," POL 28/71, "Formal meeting, 31 July 1975; Brendan Duddy 1975 Diary; Taylor, *Behind the Mask*, 220–228; White, *Ruairí Ó Brádaigh*, 233–241.

79 Brendan Duddy 1975 Diary, 40, 46.

80 Brendan Duddy 1975 Diary, 49.

81 ROP, POL 28/69, "Report, 1 July 1975."

82 "Report, 1 July 1975"; Brendan Duddy 1975 Diary; Ó Dochartaigh, "Together in the middle," 776.

83 Ó Dochartaigh, "The contact," 66, 69; Ó Dochartaigh, "'Everyone trying,'" 54; Bew, Frampton, and Gurruchaga, *Talking to Terrorists*, 55–56, 70.

84 White, *Ruairí Ó Brádaigh*, 241–244; Cowper-Coles, "'Anxious for peace,'" 231; BDP, POL 35/64, "Assessment, 31 May 1975"; Brendan Duddy 1975 Diary; POL 35/144, Message, 10 November 1975; ROP, POL 28/78, Message, 25 September 1975.

85 Brendan Duddy 1975 Diary, 52–54.

86 L. Longford and A. McHardy, *Ulster, Past, Present and Future* (London: Weidenfeld & Nicolson, 1981), 166; Brendan Duddy 1975 Diary; ROP, POL 28/81, Message from the Brits, 22 October 1975.

87 Brendan Duddy 1975 Diary, 80; ROP, POL 28/82, "Statement Issued from NIO, 12 November 1975"; Taylor, *Behind the Mask*, 230.
88 Brendan Duddy 1975 Diary, 79.
89 Brendan Duddy 1975 Diary; BDP, POL 35/132, Brendan Duddy 1976 Diary; Ó Dochartaigh, "The contact," 67; BDP, POL 35/666, DVD 2.5 Frank Stagg; White, *Ruairí Ó Brádaigh*, 246–247.
90 Brendan Duddy 1976 Diary; Bew, Frampton, and Gurruchaga, *Talking to Terrorists*, 70; ROP, POL 28/85, "Formal meeting 10/11 February 1976"; White, *Ruairí Ó Brádaigh*, 245.
91 Brendan Duddy 1976 Diary, 13, 18–25.
92 Andrew, *The Defence*, 646.
93 Bew, Frampton, and Gurruchaga, *Talking to Terrorists*, 68–69, 71; Powell, *Great Hatred*, 70; Cowper-Coles, "'Anxious for Peace,'" 231; Unattributable interview with former British official.
94 Bew, Frampton, and Gurruchaga, *Talking to Terrorists*, 70–71.
95 Taylor, *Behind the Mask*, 230–231; White, "The 1975," 213, 218–220, 228, 236–243.
96 Cowper-Coles, "'Anxious for Peace,'" 234–235.
97 Scholars disagree about the British intentions, see White, "The 1975," 212–213, 221–224, 228–229, 243; Ó Dochartaigh, "'Everyone trying,'" 52, 55, 83; Neumann, *Britain's Long War*, 85, 92.
98 D. Beresford, *Ten Men Dead: The Story of the 1981 Irish Hunger Strike* (London: Harper Collins Publishers, 1987), 9–11, .13–14
99 Hennessey, *Hunger Strike*, 14; Taylor, *Behind the Mask*, 230.
100 Bew, Frampton, and Gurruchaga, *Talking to Terrorists*, 87; Beresford, *Ten Men*, 16–20.
101 Beresford, *Ten Men*, 22; R. O'Rawe, *Blanketmen* (Dublin: New Island, 2005), 90.
102 Six of these prisoners belonged to the PIRA and one was a member of the Irish National Liberation Army.
103 Bew, Frampton, and Gurruchaga, *Talking to Terrorists*, 87; Beresford, *Ten Men*, 23–27; O'Rawe, *Blanketmen*, 103.
104 Powell, *Great Hatred*, 70.
105 Powell, *Great Hatred*, 70; Taylor, *Provos*, 234; Interview with Eamonn Downey.
106 Powell, *Great Hatred*, 70; Hennessey, *Hunger Strike*, 117.
107 R. O'Rawe, *Afterlives* (Dublin: Lilliput Pr Ltd, 2012), 106–107; Taylor, *Provos*, 234–235; Bew, Frampton, and Gurruchaga, *Talking to Terrorists*, 88; Beresford, *Ten Men*, 3–5, 26, 28–29; Hennessey, *Hunger Strike*, 117–118; O'Rawe, *Blanketmen*, 108–109; P. O'Malley, *Biting at the Grave* (Boston: Beacon Press, 1990), 31.
108 Taylor, *Provos*, 235; Beresford, *Ten Men*, 30; O'Rawe, *Blanketmen*, 109.
109 Taylor, *Provos*, 246.
110 Taylor, *Provos*, 235–238; Beresford, *Ten Men*, 28, 37–46, 62; O'Rawe, *Blanketmen*, 119; Bew, Frampton, and Gurruchaga, *Talking to Terrorists*, 89.

111  Bew, Frampton, and Gurruchaga, *Talking to Terrorists*, 89–90; Beresford, *Ten Men*, 76, 84, 98–104.

112  Beresford, *Ten Men*, 224; O'Rawe, *Blanketmen*, 166–171; P. Bishop and E. Mallie, *The Provisional IRA* (London: Heinemann, 1987), 372; Hennessey, *Hunger Strike*, 302–303; Taylor, *Provos*, 246; Beresford, *Ten Men*, 225.

113  Beresford, *Ten Men*, 26; O'Malley, *Biting at the Grave*, 81; Hennessey, *Hunger Strike*, 309; Interview with Pat Sheehan, 28 May 2013; O'Rawe, *Afterlives*, 106; Hennessey, *Hunger Strike*, 314; *The Secret Peacemaker* (BBC, 2008).

114  Interview with Eamonn Downey.

115  R. Nail, "The smoking gun," *Slugger O'Toole* (23 November 2011); Beresford, *Ten Men*, 250, 325; Hennessey, *Hunger Strike*, 309; The National Archives (UK); PREM 19/506 f298, Northern Ireland Office Letter to No. 10, 6 July 1981; E. Phoenix, "Northern Ireland 1981 archives released," *BBC* (30 December 2011).

116  O'Rawe, *Blanketmen*, 32; O'Rawe, *Afterlives*, 100; BDP, POL 35/167, The Red Book (Duddy's handwritten account of the negotiations during the 1981 hunger strike), 5–6; Interview with Niall Ó Dochartaigh; Interview with Eamonn Downey; Unattributable interview with former British official.

117  Beresford, *Ten Men*, 227; O'Rawe, *Blanketmen*, 173.

118  O'Rawe, *Blanketmen*, 173–174; Beresford, *Ten Menad*, 26; Interview with Eamonn Downey.

119  O'Malley, *Biting at the Grave*, 81; O'Rawe, *Afterlives*, 37.

120  Northern Ireland Office Letter to No. 10, 13–14.

121  Northern Ireland Office Letter to No. 10, 1.

122  Beresford, *Ten Men*, 226; O'Rawe, *Blanketmen*, 172–173.

123  O'Malley, *Biting at the Grave*, 87–99; O'Rawe, *Blanketmen*, 156; Northern Ireland Office Letter to No. 10, 6.

124  Beresford, *Ten Men*, 225.

125  The National Archives (UK), PREM 19/506 f291, Atkins Minute to MT, 6 July 1981.

126  The Red Book, 3.

127  Beresford, *Ten Men*, 228–229; O'Malley, *Biting at the Grave*, 95–96; O'Rawe, *Blanketmen*, 181–182; O'Rawe, *Afterlives*, 91–94.

128  Atkins Minute to MT.

129  The National Archives (UK), PREM 19/506 f279, No. 10 record of conversation, 7 July 1981.

130  O'Rawe, *Afterlives*, 64, 165.

131  Beresford, *Ten Men*, 225–226; The National Archives (UK), PREM 19/506 f313, No. 10 Minute, 6 July 1981; The Red Book, 1.

132  The Red Book, 1, 3; O'Rawe, *Afterlives*, 122; Atkins Minute to MT.

133  O'Rawe, *Afterlives*, 2; Hennessey, *Hunger Strike*, 328.

134  The Red Book, 4–5.

135  The National Archives (UK), NIO AP/07/50, MT meeting with Northern Ireland Secretary, 8 July 1981.

136 Beresford, *Ten Men*, 231; O'Malley, *Biting at the Grave*, 98.

137 O'Rawe, *Blanketmen*, 188–189, 201.

138 The National Archives (UK), PREM 19/506 f196, No. 10 record of conversation, 18 July 1981; The National Archives (UK), PREM 19/506 f190, Northern Ireland Office Letter to No. 10, 21 July 1981; The Red Book, 4–9.

139 No. 10 record of conversation, 18 July 1981.

140 Northern Ireland Office Letter to No. 10, 21 July 1981.

141 Beresford, *Ten Men*, 250–252; Taylor, *Provos*, 247; Northern Ireland Office Letter to No. 10, 21 July 1981; The Red Book, 6–8.

142 The Red Book, 9.

143 Northern Ireland Office Letter to No. 10, 21 July 1981.

144 Northern Ireland Office Letter to No. 10, 21 July 1981.

145 O'Rawe, *Blanketmen*, 200, 236, 238; Hennessey, *Hunger Strike*, 382–383.

146 O'Rawe, *Afterlives*, 2, 16, 119; O'Rawe, *Blanketmen*, 172–181, 204–205; Hennessey, *Hunger Strike*, 6–8.

147 O'Rawe, *Afterlives*, 135–136.

148 Powell, *Great Hatred*, 70; O'Kane, "Talking to," 403; O. Bennett-Jones, "What Fred did," *London Review of Books*, 37:2 (2015), www.lrb.co.uk/the-paper/v37/n02/owen-bennett-jones/what-fred-did (accessed 19 April 2022); Interview with Eamonn Downey.

149 Taylor, *Provos*, 319; Sinn Féin, *Setting the Record* (Dublin: Sinn Féin, 1994), 8.

150 O'Kane, "Talking to," 403; E. Mallie and D. McKittrick, *The Fight for Peace* (London: Heinemann, 1996), 246.

151 J. Major, *John Major* (New York: Harper Collins Publishers, 1999), 435; N. Ó Dochartaigh, "The longest negotiation: British policy, IRA strategy and the making of the Northern Ireland peace settlement," *Political Studies*, 63:1 (2015), 209–210.

152 G. Adams, *Hope and History* (Dingle: Brandon, 2003), 92; Powell, *Great Hatred*, 64; Bew, Frampton, and Gurruchaga, *Talking to Terrorists*, 115; E. Mallie and D. McKittrick, *Endgame in Ireland* (London: Hodder & Stoughton, 2001), 87.

153 Adams, *Hope and History*, 92, 97, 98.

154 Major, *John Major*, 433.

155 Bennett-Jones, "What Fred did"; Ó Dochartaigh, "The longest negotiation," 211–214.

156 Ó Dochartaigh, "Together in the middle," 773; Mallie and McKittrick, *Endgame*, 84; Adams, *Hope and History*, 99.

157 Taylor, *Provos*, 320; Adams, *Hope and History*, 100.

158 Adams, *Hope and History*, 97–98.

159 See CAIN Web Service, "A Chronology of the Conflict – 1968 to the Present": http://cain.ulst.ac.uk/othelem/chron.htm (accessed 25 March 2021).

160 Powell, *Great Hatred*, 68, 70; Bew, Frampton, and Gurruchaga, *Talking to Terrorists*, 117; Taylor, *Provos*, 320.

161  Adams, *Hope and History*, 95.

162  Sinn Féin, *Setting the Record*, 8; Taylor, *Provos*, 320–321; Adams, *Hope and History*, 97.

163  Mallie and McKittrick, *Endgame*, 88; Adams, *Hope and History*, 93–94; Major, *John Major*, 437; Unattributable interview with former British official.

164  O'Kane, "Talking to," 404; Powell, *Great Hatred*, 71; Bennett-Jones "What Fred did"; Adams, *Hope and History*, 98; Interview with Eamonn Downey.

165  BDP, POL 35/590, "Notes regarding the earliest contact with Fred"; Sinn Féin, *Setting the Record*, 9, 12; Major, *John Major*, 436; Mallie and McKittrick, *The Fight*, 244; *The Secret Peacemaker*.

166  Sinn Féin, *Setting the Record*, 9; Adams, *Hope and History*, 104; Taylor, *Provos*, 329.

167  BDP, POL 35/266, The Narrative.

168  Sinn Féin, *Setting the Record*, 9.

169  O'Kane, "Talking to," 404; Adams, *Hope and History*, 117.

170  Adams, *Hope and History*, 94, 117–118, 142.

171  Adams, *Hope and History*, 95–97; Sinn Féin, *Setting the Record*, 11, 117.

172  BDP, POL 35/291, Message from Mr. Brown, 4 June 1993; BDP, POL 35/294, Message from Mr. Brown, 10 June 1993.

173  The Narrative, 2, 6, 41; O'Kane, "Talking to," 403–404; Bennett-Jones, "What Fred did"; Interview with Eamonn Downey; Mallie and McKittrick, *Endgame*, 99–100. Given the involvement of Bradley and Gallagher, some saw it as a channel of three at this stage. Adams, for example, described it as a "Derry Trio" channel. But the communication with the British went only through Duddy. Bradley revealed his part in the channel before Duddy did, whereas Gallagher chose not to disclose his role (Adams, *Hope and History*, 93. N. Ó Dochartaigh, "Letters," *London Review of Books* 37:3 (5 February 2015); Interview with Niall Ó Dochartaigh; Ó Dochartaigh, "The contact," 64; Interview with Eamonn Downey; Interview with Peter Taylor, 8 June 2013).

174  Adams, *Hope and History*, 94–95; Interview with Niall Ó Dochartaigh.

175  Mallie and McKittrick, *Endgame*, 99,104.

176  O'Kane, "Talking to," 410; Adams, *Hope and History*, 94.

177  BDP, POL 35/591, Communiqué from CF to JT, 18 February 1992.

178  Sinn Féin, *Setting the Record*; Powell, *Great Hatred*, 71; Adams, *Hope and History*, 98, 102, 107, 109, 115, 144; BDP, POL 35/251, Report, 26 October 1992; Major, *John Major*, 436–442; Bew, Frampton, and Gurruchaga, *Talking to Terrorists*, 118; Mallie and McKittrick, *Endgame*, 102; The Narrative, 8, 33; Mallie and McKittrick, *The Fight*, 247.

179  Adams, *Hope and History*, 95, 120; Bew, Frampton, and Gurruchaga, *Talking to Terrorists*, 118.

180  Sinn Féin, *Setting the Record*, 16.

181  Andrew, *The Defence*, 782.

182  Major, *John Major*, 431; Taylor, *Provos*, 330; BDP, POL 35/262, Message: The conflict is over, 22 February 1993; Powell, *Great Hatred*, 71–72; O'Kane, "Talking to," 405; Bew, Frampton, and Gurruchaga, *Talking to Terrorists*, 118.

183  Major, *John Major*, 431–432; O'Kane, "Talking to," 405; Bew, Frampton, and Gurruchaga, *Talking to Terrorists*, 119; Mallie and McKittrick, *Endgame*, 89; Bennett-Jones "What Fred did."

184  Major, *John Major*, 433; Mallie and McKittrick, *Endgame*, 91.

185  Sinn Féin, *Setting the Record*, 18; M. Brennock, "Seeking a dialogue leading to peace," *Irish Times* (30 November 1993); Adams, *Hope and History*, 116.

186  The Narrative 1–3, 6; BDP, POL 35/268, Messages from Robert, March 1993; Sinn Féin, *Setting the Record*, 19; BDP, POL 35/269, "Notes by Éamonn Downey, March 1993."

187  BDP, POL 35/270, "The nine-paragraph document, 19 March 1993"; Taylor, *Provos*, 332; Bew, Frampton, and Gurruchaga, *Talking to Terrorists*, 119; Adams, *Hope and History*, 117; Major, *John Major*, 442–443.

188  The Narrative, 7; Adams, *Hope and History*, 117.

189  The Narrative, 2, 7; BDP, POL 35/271, "Notes by Éamonn Downey, March–April 1993"; Sinn Féin, *Setting the Record*, 18–19; Taylor, *Provos*, 333; Mallie and McKittrick, *Endgame*, 92, 107; Major, *John Major*, 443.

190  O'Kane, "Talking to," 409.

191  The Narrative, 7–10; "Notes by Éamonn Downey, March–April 1993," 3–8; Brennock, "Seeking a dialogue"; Taylor, *Provos*, 333; Bennett-Jones "What Fred did"; Mallie and McKittrick, *Endgame*, 109; Major, *John Major*, 446.

192  *The Secret Peacemaker*.

193  The Narrative, 13–15; Notes by Éamonn Downey, March–April 1993," 10; Sinn Féin, *Setting the Record*, 20; Mallie and McKittrick, *Endgame*, 111–115; Adams, *Hope and History*, 117.

194  Sinn Féin, *Setting the Record*, 20–21; Taylor, *Provos*, 333; Bennett-Jones "What Fred did"; Adams, *Hope and History*, 118–119.

195  The Narrative, 15; Bennett-Jones "What Fred did"; Mallie and McKittrick, *Endgame*, 114.

196  Mallie and McKittrick, *Endgame*, 115.

197  Sinn Féin, *Setting the Record*, 22–23; The Narrative, 35–38; Brennock, "Seeking a dialogue"; BDP, POL 35/281, Message from R., 6 May 1993.

198  BDP, POL 35/283, Message from Sinn Féin, 10 May 1993; Mallie and McKittrick, *Endgame*, 95; Adams, *Hope and History*, 121; Sinn Féin, *Setting the Record*, 23.

199  Adams, *Hope and History*, 121.

200  The Narrative, 41–42; Message from Sinn Féin, 10 May 1993; Bennett-Jones, "What Fred did"; BDP, POL 35/597, "Notes about setting the record."

201  The Narrative, 43–45, 53–54; Sinn Féin, *Setting the Record*, 10, 25–26; Adams, *Hope and History*, 122; Mallie and McKittrick, *Endgame*, 96.

202  Major, *John Major*, 444.

203  Mallie and McKittrick, *Endgame*, 96–97; Major, *John Major*, 444.

204  Sinn Féin, *Setting the Record*, 27–30; Adams, *Hope and History*, 122, 124, 127–128, 141; Message from Mr. Brown, 4 June 1993; Message from Mr. Brown, 10 June 1993; The Narrative, 54; BDP, POL 35/308, Message from Sinn Féin, 30 August 1993; BDP, POL 35/310, Message from the British government, 3 September 1993; Mallie and McKittrick, *Endgame*, 97.

205  Sinn Féin, *Setting the Record*, 10; Adams, *Hope and History*, 127; Taylor, *Provos*, 337.

206  The Narrative, 62; Mallie and McKittrick, *Endgame*, 119.

207  Sinn Féin, *Setting the Record*, 26; BDP, POL 35/287, Message from Mr. Campbell, 1 June 1993; Brennock, "Seeking a dialogue"; The Narrative, 54; O'Kane, "Talking to," 407.

208  Sinn Féin, *Setting the Record*, 26; BDP, POL 35/289, Message from R., 3 June 1993.

209  Sinn Féin, *Setting the Record*, 28–31; Major, *John Major*, 444; BDP, POL 35/309, Message from the British government, 14 August 1993; BDP, POL 35/312, Response to 1 September communication; Adams, *Hope and History*, 133; Mallie and McKittrick, *The Fight*, 252.

210  Adams, *Hope and History*, 132–133, 144.

211  The Narrative, 62–63; Mallie and McKittrick, *Endgame*, 119; O'Kane, "Talking to," 415.

212  Taylor, *Provos*, 341; BDP, POL 35/318, Message, 2 November 1993; Major, *John Major*, 444.

213  Major, *John Major*, 444–445.

214  Sinn Féin, *Setting the Record*, 4, 31–33; BDP, POL 35/319, "Substantive response, 5 November 1993"; Taylor, *Provos*, 341; Powell, *Great Hatred*, 71; Major, *John Major*, 445.

215  Sinn Féin, *Setting the Record*, 4, 31–33; BDP, POL 35/320, Message, 8 November 1993, POL 35/321, Message, 10 November 1993; Taylor, *Provos*, 341.

216  Mallie and McKittrick, *Endgame*, 121.

217  Adams, *Hope and History*, 145.

218  BDP, POL 35/327, Message from Sinn Féin, 26 November 1993; O'Kane, "Talking to," 415.

219  Mallie and McKittrick, *The Fight*, 233–234, 238; Sinn Féin, *Setting the Record*, 1–2; Powell, *Great Hatred*, 73.

220  Sinn Féin, *Setting the Record*, 5; Adams, *Hope and History*, 144.

221  See Mayhew's speech, 2 December 1993: http://www.publications.parliament.uk/pa/cm199394/cmhansrd/1993-11-29/Debate-1.html (accessed 25 March 2021). A few days after publishing the British version, Mayhew announced that there were some "errors" and a revised version was published (Major, *John Major*, 446; Mallie and McKittrick, *The Fight*, 241–242).

222  Mallie and McKittrick, *The Fight*, 240, 244.

223  Mallie and McKittrick, *The Fight*, 240.

224  Mallie and McKittrick, *The Fight*, 244; Major, *John Major*, 442.

225  Sinn Féin, *Setting the Record*, 18, 21, 32; Major, *John Major*, 446. The Republicans refer to the "The conflict is over" message (February 1993), message on Warrington attack (March 1993), and on "total end to hostilities" (November 1993).

226  Powell, *Great Hatred*, 72.

227  *The Secret Peacemaker*; O'Kane, "Talking to," 406; P. Taylor, "Disobeyed orders and a dangerous message," *The Guardian* (18 March 2008); Interview with Eamonn Downey.

228 Mallie and McKittrick, *Endgame*, 106–107; Bennett-Jones, "What Fred did."

229 BDP, POL 35/610, Duddy to Bradley, 15 June 2001; O'Kane, "Talking to," 406.

230 Bennett-Jones, "What Fred did"; Powell, *Talking to Terrorists*, 119.

231 O'Kane, "Talking to," 406; Taylor, *Provos*, 330; Interview with Eamonn Downey; Message: The conflict is over; Ó Dochartaigh, "Letters."

232 Interview with Eamonn Downey; Bennett-Jones, "What Fred did."

233 Adams, *Hope and History*, 200.

234 Bennett-Jones, "What Fred did."

235 O'Kane, "Talking to," 409–410.

236 O'Kane, "Talking to," 409–410; Sinn Féin, *Setting the Record*, 21.

237 O'Kane, "Talking to," 416.

238 Interview with Eamonn Downey.

239 Taylor, *Provos*, 342.

240 Taylor, *Provos*, 341; Interview with Peter Taylor.

241 Interview with Pat Sheehan.

242 BDP, POL 35/329, Message from Sinn Féin, 29 November 1993.

243 Bennett-Jones, "What Fred did"; BDP, POL 35/334, Letter from Robert to Brendan, 24 December 1993.

244 Major, *John Major*, 447.

245 Powell, *Great Hatred*, 67.

246 Taylor, "Disobeyed orders."

247 Andrew, *The Defence*, 783.

248 Moloney, *A Secret History*, 405.

249 The Newsroom, "Gerry Adams says the late Brendan Duddy was a 'tireless advocate for peace,'" *Derry Journal* (13 May 2017).

250 "Brendan Duddy and the Colombians," *Derry Journal* (8 April 2014).

251 Interview with Eamonn Downey; Interview with Vered Amitzi; Unattributable interview with former British official.

252 Unattributable interview with former British official.

253 Interview with Eamonn Downey.

254 BDP, POL 35/366 DVD 1.5 Role of intermediary.

255 Interview with Niall Ó Dochartaigh.

256 "Priest worded IRA message to PM," *Irish News* (15 June 2001).

257 Northern Ireland Office Letter to No. 10, 6 July 1981.

258 Unattributable interview with former British official.

259 Interview with Sarah Duddy.

260 O'Kane, "Talking to," 416.

261 Cowper-Coles, "'Anxious for Peace,'" 234.

262 Ó Dochartaigh, "'Everyone trying,'" 55; White, "The 1975," 227; Taylor, *Provos*, 169; Taylor, *Brits*, 170–172.

263 Major, *John Major*, 433.

264 Ó Dochartaigh, "'Everyone trying,'" 59–60; Cowper-Coles, "'Anxious for peace,'" 228.

265 O'Kane, "Talking to," 410–411.

266 No. 10 record of conversation, 7 July 1981.

267 Major, *John Major*, 433–434; Powell, *Great Hatred*, 65.

268 Cowper-Coles, "'Anxious for peace,'" 227, 232–233.

269 Sinn Féin, *Setting the Record*, 17; Sinn Féin, *Towards a Lasting Peace in Ireland* (Dublin: Sinn Féin, 1994); Andrew, *The Defence*, 783.

270 Interview with Eamonn Downey.

271 Brendan Duddy 1976 Diary, 16.

272 Mallie and McKittrick, *Endgame*, 103–104.

# 5

# Uri Avnery and his dialogue with the PLO in the context of the Israeli–Palestinian conflict, 1975–1985

This country has seen unusual moves initiated by individuals who sought to break the cycle of hatred and suspicion in which Jewish–Arab relations are trapped. Some were viewed at the time as adventurers, and often as eccentric; in hindsight, it might be more accurate to describe them as pioneers. Such is Uri Avnery, given his early contacts with PLO leaders.

Uzi Benziman, 2003[1]

## Introduction

The Israeli–Arab conflict, and in particular the Israeli–Palestinian conflict, has been one of the main conflict arenas in the history of the twentieth century. Since 1948, with the establishment of the State of Israel, the conflict has included numerous rounds of war and violence, and for many years it was characterized by the absence of official communication channels between the parties. Against this background, Uri Avnery, editor of the weekly *Haolam Hazeh*, worked to build dialogue channels with Palestinian and Arab actors and to promote his ideas for peace in the Middle East.

This chapter deals with the activity of Avnery as a PPE, and with the dialogue channels he established. His unofficial diplomatic activity started in the 1950s, but the focus of the chapter touches on Avnery's contacts with the Palestine Liberation Organization, beginning with his meetings with PLO official Said Hammami in 1975, through the establishment of a channel between ICIPP members and Issam Sartawi and other PLO members, to Avnery's direct dialogue with PLO chairman Yasser Arafat in the early 1980s. The chapter also discusses how Avnery used his news magazine as a tool in his peace efforts.

The chapter is based on archival resources, including the private archive of Uri Avnery, the archive of Mattityahu Peled, and the archive of Austria's chancellor Bruno Kreisky; memoires of relevant actors, such as Avnery, Arie Lova Eliav, David Shaham, and Mahmoud Abbas (Abu Mazen); my interviews with Uri Avnery, Yossi Amitai, and Sabri Jiryis; historical studies on the Israeli–Palestinian conflict, the PLO, and the Israeli peace movement; and media reports, including articles by Avnery in his weekly *Haolam Hazeh*.

The existing literature does not provide comprehensive, dedicated studies that tell the story of the dialogue that Avnery and the ICIPP conducted with the PLO, although the topic has been discussed in scholarship on specific figures who participated in the process (e.g., studies on Yaakov Arnon, Matti Peled, and Issam Sartawi),[2] on the Israeli peace movement,[3] and on the PLO.[4] In 1989 Avnery published a book on his talks with the PLO.[5] The present study aims to contribute to this body of work and to offer an in-depth analysis of Avnery's unofficial diplomacy and its implications as a case study of private peace entrepreneurship.

## Historical background

The Israeli–Palestinian conflict emerged towards the end of the nineteenth century and, until the establishment of Israel in 1948, took the form of an intercommunity conflict. During the period of British rule in Eretz Israel/Palestine (1917–1948), numerous rounds of violence took place between the two communities: in 1920, 1921, 1929, and 1936–1939. After the 1948 war, the conflict came to be characterized as an inter-state Israeli–Arab conflict, and the Palestinian question vanished from the international agenda, with the issue now presented mainly as a refugee problem.[6] In the late 1950s a group of Palestinian activists in Kuwait founded the organization Fatah – the Palestinian National Liberation Movement – which called for armed struggle against Israel and based itself on the principle of the independence of Palestinian decision making, demanding freedom of action without dependence on Arab regimes. The main founders of Fatah were Yasser Arafat, Khalil al-Wazir, and Salah Khalaf, and on 31 December 1964, the organization carried out its first attack against Israel. In parallel, also in 1964, the PLO was founded, following a decision of the Arab League summit in Cairo, in January 1964, regarding efforts to establish a political organization that would represent the Palestinians. Ahmad Shukeiri, the Palestinian representative in the Arab League, became the head of the PLO, acting under the sponsorship of Egypt and in coordination with Jordan.[7]

During the 1967 war, the Arab countries suffered a military defeat and Israel occupied the West Bank and Gaza Strip (WBGS). After the war, there emerged new Palestinian organizations that supported the armed struggle, such as the Popular Front for the Liberation of Palestine and the Democratic

Front for the Liberation of Palestine. Shukeiri was compelled at this stage
to step down from his post and the armed Palestinian organizations, led by
Fatah, took over the PLO. In 1969 Arafat became the PLO chairman. The
PLO Executive Committee served as the government and the Palestinian
National Council (PNC) as the parliament. During these years the PLO
organizations were based in Jordan, but in 1970 the presence of armed
Palestinian organizations in the country became a genuine threat to the
existence of the Hashemite regime, which decided to use its power to destroy
the PLO stronghold in Jordan.[8] The PLO headquarters moved to Lebanon
and launched attacks against Israel and Israeli targets around the world.

The Arab–Israeli War of 1973 was a crucial landmark in the history of
the PLO. In light of the war, and a decision by the Arab countries – headed
by Egypt – to adopt a diplomatic strategy in the conflict with Israel, two
trends emerged. First, the PLO's international status improved. It was
recognized by the Arab League (at the October 1974 summit) as the sole
representative of the Palestinian people, and it was granted observer status
at the United Nations.[9] Second, the political strategy of the PLO started to
change. The PLO's "Ten Point Plan," adopted by the PNC at its June 1974
session, expressed support for the establishment of national authority in
every part of Palestinian territory that would be liberated. This decision
implied a willingness to establish a Palestinian state alongside Israel and
reflected a change from the position expressed in the PLO Charter, which
called for the liberation of the whole of Palestine, and from the vision of a
"secular democratic state" in Mandatory Palestine, which the PLO had
embraced in 1969.[10] The change in the organization's position led to an
internal dispute within the PLO and to the creation of a "rejectionist front."

Despite the opposition, the PLO showed signs of change and expressed
support for the Joint US–Soviet Statement (1977), the Brezhnev plan (1981),
and the "Fez plan" (1982). This process took place against a background
of struggle between the pragmatic camp in the PLO, led by Fatah figures,
and the radical organizations, as well as intervention by and pressure from
various Arab countries. Arafat ascribed supreme importance to maintaining
national unity and tried to balance between the camps. As a result, the
PLO's statements were often characterized by ambiguous wording and
contradictory messages.[11]

These changes in the PLO's position resulted from an interest on the part
of certain key PLO figures in integrating into the diplomatic process that
emerged in the Middle East after 1973. Israel strongly opposed such integration, as it considered the PLO a terrorist organization that could not be a
negotiating partner, and this position was backed by a wide consensus in
Israel. Numerous attacks by the PLO during these years, in Israel and around
the world, reinforced this view in Israel. At that time Israeli governments

did not see the Palestinians as an independent actor, and even the more dovish political forces, including the Labor Party, believed that an agreement on the future of the WBGS should be discussed with Jordan. The US did not support inclusion of the PLO in the Geneva conference of December 1973, and in September 1975 it promised Israel that it would not recognize the PLO or engage in dialogue with it so long as the organization did not recognize Israel's right to exist and accept UN Security Council resolutions 242 and 338, which outlined the principle of land for peace.[12]

## Uri Avnery: life story and worldview

Uri Avnery was born in Germany on 10 September 1923, as Helmut Ostermann. At age ten, he immigrated with his family to Palestine, following the Nazi Party's rise to power. In 1938 he joined the *Irgun*, a Zionist para-military organization, but became increasingly critical of the organization's policy and left after three years. He later claimed that this period helped him better understand Palestinians who joined armed organizations.[13] In 1946 Avnery started to engage in the two fields in which he worked all his life: political activity and journalism. He was among the founders of a group named "Young Land of Israel," which published a journal titled *The Struggle* and supported a joint front of the Hebrew nation and the national Arab movement. A year after that, Avnery published a pamphlet titled *War and Peace in the Semitic Space*, in which he presented the idea of a "Semitic Union" – a federation of the Fertile Crescent states – an idea that would remain at the center of his political philosophy for many years.[14]

In the 1948 war Avnery served in the Israeli commando unit "Samson's Foxes" and was injured in a battle in the Negev. During the war he wrote columns that he published as a collection after the war, under the title *In the Fields of the Philistines – 1948: A War Diary*. It became a bestseller and brought Avnery much publicity.[15] The 1948 war affected his political worldview and reinforced his acknowledgement of the existence of two peoples sharing the land. Avnery claimed that the war made him see the Palestinian problem "as a reality, not as an abstract problem."[16] A year after the war, he decided to publish another book, *The Other Side of the Coin*, in which he exposed the dark sides of the war and described atrocities, looting, and the deportation of refugees. Because of the book, Avnery faced public criticism and attacks and turned from a "hero" to a "defeatist."[17]

In 1950 Avnery bought the weekly *Haolam Hazeh* ("This World") and for forty years he served as the editor-in-chief, expressing his own views every week in his regular column. The magazine promoted an anti-government and anti-establishment position and became very popular and influential in the public discourse. The state authorities boycotted it, hoping to shut it down. It was also a target of violence: bombs were placed in its offices and the print shop, as well as Avnery and his deputy being physically attacked.[18]

As an editor, Avnery developed a large network system in the political, social, and cultural arenas in Israel, and he became a well-known public figure with a wide and loyal readership. Despite the antagonistic approach of the establishment towards the paper, Avnery managed to achieve good access to key actors in the governmental and political system.

Avnery combined his journalistic work with political activism and worked vigorously to spread and promote his ideas. He used his magazine, and especially his column, towards this end but was also involved in various political forums and organizations. After the 1956 Sinai war, Avnery participated in founding a new political movement called the Semitic Action. Its manifest declared that "the Land of Israel is the homeland of two nations: the Hebrew, which achieved its independence in the framework of the State of Israel, and the Arab-Palestinian, which has not yet gained independence." The document proposed that a federative union be established based on partnership between the Arab nation and the Hebrew nation, called for the integration of Israel in the region, and attacked government policy for turning Israel into a "separatist, isolated state in the area."[19] In 1965 Avnery decided to enter the political arena and, with his associate editor Shalom Cohen, founded the party Haolam Hazeh: Koach Hadash ("This World: New Power"). He served as a Knesset member (MK) for two consecutive terms, from 1965 to 1973. During the first term the party had one seat and during the second, two seats.[20]

When the 1967 Arab–Israeli war broke out, Avnery declared it a war of self-defense and took part in the euphoria of victory that washed over the country. However, he regarded the outcome of the war as a great opportunity to advance an Israeli–Palestinian peace, and in its aftermath he promoted the idea of establishing a Palestinian state alongside Israel. He called on Prime Minsister Levy Eshkol to conduct a referendum in the WBGS on an independent state as part of a federative arrangement with Israel.[21] After the war he published a book, *War of the Seventh Day*, in which he presented his political plan and proposed a two-state solution.[22] Avnery saw the Palestine problem as the heart of the Israeli–Arab conflict. He called for diplomatic efforts to be focused on this issue and rejected the "Jordanian option."[23] The Israeli public began to identify Avnery with his political struggle on behalf of the Palestinian issue, and many saw him as the pioneer of the two-state solution. Israeli writer Amos Kenan claimed that Avnery "discovered" Palestine for the Israeli public, just as Amerigo Vespucci had discovered America, at a time when the public refused to recognize the existence of a Palestinian people.[24]

## The beginning of Avnery's PPE activities

In the late 1950s, after establishing the Semitic Action, Avnery initiated meetings with international journalists, diplomats, and intellectuals, including representatives from the Arab world, in order to spread the ideas of the new movement. He acted as a "journalist PPE" and reported on some of the meetings in his magazine. In February 1959, he published a report titled "The Ambassador of Craziness," on meetings with "more than one hundred people in seven countries" during the course of one journey.[25] A significant part of this initiative was his efforts to reach out to Arab representatives. In his articles on these meetings, Avnery (sometimes without revealing the names of his counterparts) emphasized that he was the only Israeli who had met with them, stressing his unique status and the diplomatic vacuum in the Israeli–Arab arena. Avnery stressed that he participated in these meetings as a private citizen who did not represent the official governmental position: "I am an Israeli journalist, I do not represent the government of Israel or any other Israeli institute. I represent an idea which is still, I believe, that of a minority in my homeland."[26]

During these years, Avnery took his first steps as a PPE and met, among others, with Hisham Joad, Iraq's ambassador to the UN, Abd al-Qadir Shanderli, FLN representative at the UN, Mongi Slim, Tunisia's ambassador to the UN, and Izzat Tannous, representative of the Palestine Arab Higher Committee at the UN.[27]

During the 1960s Avnery participated in the "Florence Conferences" – Mediterranean conferences that were aimed at informally bringing together Arab and Israeli public figures. They were organized by Giorgio La Pira, the mayor of Florence, and Joe Golan, the advisor on Arab affairs to the president of the World Jewish Congress, Nahum Goldmann. These events were a good opportunity for Avnery to meet Arab representatives, and he reported on the meetings in his magazine.[28] Avnery also participated in a "Conference for Peace and Justice" that took place in Bologna in May 1973, attended by various Israeli and Arab public figures, including Khaled Mohieddin, one of the leaders of the Egyptian revolution of 1952.[29]

In March 1965 Tunisia's president Habib Bourguiba expressed unprecedented ideas and suggested that the Arab world recognize Israel on the condition that it accepted UN General Assembly resolutions 181 (the Partition Plan, 1947) and 194 (on the Palestinian refugee problem, 1948).[30] Avnery saw this as a dramatic step and devoted numerous reports to Bourguiba's initiative, criticizing Israel for its lack of response.[31] Against this background, in April 1965 Avnery took a diplomatic journey, the highlight of which was a meeting with Mohammed Masmoudi, Tunisia's ambassador to France. Avnery reported on the meeting but concealed the identity of the ambassador, identifying him as "a senior leader in the Arab world." He used his stage to spread word of Bourguiba's declaration and call on Israel to respond with its own peace gesture.[32]

Besides Avnery's action pattern vis-à-vis public opinion, he used this meeting as a basis for the action pattern of secret activity vis-à-vis decision makers. According to Avnery, Masmoudi told him about a crisis with France and proposed that Israel use its influence with the French president, Charles de Gaulle, in order to improve relations between France and Tunisia. In exchange Bourguiba would renew his peace initiative. Avnery was excited about "the mission that I was tasked to fulfil" and upon his return to Israel, he requested a meeting with the foreign minister, Abba Eban. Avnery informed Eban about Masmoudi's proposal, but Eban doubted Israel's ability to act on the matter and described the idea as a "tall order."[33]

We can identify two important tools that assisted Avnery in his PPE efforts at this stage. The first consists of the international networks he established, which provided him with access to actors in the Arab world at a time when Israeli–Arab meetings were an impossible mission. Avnery wrote that he became a member in an international club "of good-willed people" with an "excellent network system." "They do not have an organization or password," he explained, but "they know each other instinctively and engage in [making] contacts that disregard borders."[34] Avnery had contacts with diplomats, journalists, intellectuals, religious persons, and peace activists from all over the world. Some of them were key actors in his peace activity. Eric Rouleau, for example, the chief Middle East correspondent for *Le Monde*, facilitated contact between Avnery and Arab figures such as Ambassador Masmoudi and the Egyptian writer Lotfi al-Kholi. Another example is Henri Curiel, a Jewish-Egyptian leftist activist who moved to France and worked to promote Jewish–Arab dialogue. He mediated between Avnery and the FLN, and later assisted in establishing contact between Avnery and the PLO.[35]

The second tool was the distinguishability of Avnery's views from the Israeli government's official positions. This element contributed to the readiness of various actors to meet with Avnery. For example, the Iraqi diplomat Joad knew that Avnery belonged to a movement that supported the Iraqi revolution and he had heard about the movement's ideas, which helped secure his consent to meet with Avnery. In his meetings with FLN representatives, Avnery emphasized his support for the Algerian struggle and they expressed gratitude.[36] During these meetings Avnery stressed that there were differences between his approach and that of his government, but at the same time he noted that he was a "national Hebrew" who hoped for a "strong and solid Hebrew nation" and his opposition to government policy did not mean opposition to the existence of Israel.[37]

Avnery was concerned about the reaction of the security establishment to his meetings with Arab representatives. After he attended a reception for the FLN in New York hosted by the Moroccan and Tunisian governments, he wondered how Israel's security agencies might react, but to his surprise there was no reaction. He insisted that a meeting with an Egyptian figure be in a public place in order to preclude any claim that it was an underground meeting with the enemy.[38] In some cases, he informed Israeli officials about his meetings. For example, during his meeting with Joad he noticed that an Israeli diplomat was observing their conversation, and to ensure he would not be prosecuted for that meeting, on his way home he met with Eliyahu Sasson, Israel's ambassador in Italy, and informed him about the meeting.[39]

## Avnery's dialogue with PLO representative Said Hammami, 1975–1976

On 16 November 1973, shortly after the war, the British daily *Times* published an article by the PLO representative in London, Said Hammami, who presented a surprising approach that departed from the organization's official stance. Hammami wrote that "many Palestinians" believe that a Palestinian state in the WBGS "is a necessary part of any peace package" and would lead to "the emptying and closing down of the refugee camps, thereby drawing out the poison at the heart of Arab–Israeli enmity."[40] The editor mentioned that Hammami was presenting his own personal view but noted that he was known to be "very close" to Arafat. On 17 December 1973, Hammami published another article in which he argued that "the Palestinian-Arabs and the Israeli Jews were and still are the principal parties to the conflict" and that the first step should be mutual recognition in which the two parties "should recognize one another as peoples, with all the rights to which a people is entitled."[41]

Hammami was born in Jaffa in 1941 and at age seven, during the 1948 war, left with his family. In 1963 he joined Fatah and in 1972 he was nominated as the first PLO representative to London.[42] His articles were unprecedented but they did not receive special attention in Israel. Avnery, on the other hand, enthusiastically seized on them as the sign he had longed for over the years: "I felt like a skipper catching the first glimpse of a submarine with which he had had sonar contact for some time."[43] Avnery estimated that it would not have been published without Arafat's approval and this assumption turned out to be right, as some time later Hammami showed him the article with Arafat's comments in his own handwriting. Hammami's articles were a trigger for Avnery's efforts to start a dialogue with the PLO. Avnery met Edward Mortimer, the Middle East correspondent for the *Times*, while covering the Geneva conference (in December 1973) and asked him to see whether Hammami would agree to meet him secretly. Mortimer delivered the message to Hammami and only a year later, towards the end of 1974, did he return with an affirmative response.[44]

At this stage, the PLO leaders were aware of Avnery and his views. This is evidenced, for example, by a book that the PLO Research Center published in 1971, titled *Uri Avnery and Neo-Zionism*, in which the author, Camille Mansour, analyzed and criticized Avnery's ideas on the Palestinian issue.[45] The PLO leadership was also exposed to Avnery's articles in *Haolam Hazeh*, and in time Arafat told Avnery that he had followed his writings. For some years the magazine published an edition in Arabic, which Arafat read. After it stopped issuing an Arabic edition, Arafat's aide Imad Shaqour (originally an Israeli citizen from the Arab town of Sakhnin) would translate it for him.[46]

Avnery's message to Hammami arrived precisely at a time when the PLO was beginning to undergo a process of change. Arafat told the British journalist Alan Hart that at that stage they were not ready to publicly reveal their position on a possible compromise, as they still had to prepare their public. He said that during 1974 "certain of our people were officially authorized to maintain secret contacts with Israelis and with important people in the West. Their responsibility was to say in secret what at the time we could not say in public."[47] In his book, PLO leader Mahmoud Abbas (Abu Mazen), who played an important role in this process, described the background for this step. He argued that in the early 1970s he was surprised at the level of ignorance in the Arab world regarding Israel, and within the PLO, as well. As a result, Abbas decided to promote research on Israel and called for a dialogue with Jewish and Israeli forces. PLO representatives serving in Europe supported the idea, but it met with opposition from various actors in the Palestinian and Arab arenas.[48] Sabri Jiryis has described Abbas as the "driving force" and "bulldozer" within the PLO behind the idea of dialogue with Israelis – an idea he consistently supported and actively promoted.[49] According to Szyszkowitz, Abbas began to consider contact with Israelis in the very early 1970s, when it was regarded as taboo, and the first person he approached was Issam Sartawi, who immediately supported the idea.[50]

Issam Sartawi was born in the city of Acre in 1936 and left with his family for Iraq during the 1948 war. He studied medicine in Iraq and the US and became a cardiologist. But after the 1967 war, he returned to the Middle East and joined Fatah. Shortly thereafter, he founded the Action Organization for the Liberation of Palestine, which was involved in various attacks, including the attack on Israeli passengers at Munich Airport in 1970. In 1971 Sartawi and his organization's members returned to Fatah and he was nominated as a member of Fatah's Revolutionary Council.[51]

Abbas and Sartawi started to work on a dialogue with Israelis and they received Arafat's support: "We knew that we were going against the tide," Abbas explained, "but we were standing completely behind the idea."[52]

In 1973, Fatah's central committee established a special team to monitor developments in Israel and examine the possibility of a dialogue with Israelis. The team members were Abbas, Sartawi, and PLO leader Khalil al-Wazir (Abu Jihad), as well as Sabri Jiryis and Habib Qahwaji, Israeli citizens who had left Israel and joined the Fatah.[53] Afif Safieh, a senior PLO diplomat, claimed that in the mid-1970s the Palestinian leadership instructed Hammami and Sartawi to "engage in dialogue with dovish personalities in the Israeli political spectrum."[54] By the late 1960s and early 1970s, the PLO had developed contacts with anti-Zionist forces in Israel, including the Israeli Communist Party and *Matzpen* organization, as well as Jewish figures in Arab countries. But it was only after 1973 that these efforts evolved into a willingness to meet with Israeli Zionist forces.[55] According to Agha et al., the PLO's readiness to pursue a dialogue with Israelis during these years resulted, among other factors, from its desire to integrate into the political process that had begun in the Middle East after the 1973 war and to be recognized as a legitimate negotiating partner.[56]

Avnery's first meeting with Hammami was scheduled for 27 January 1975, in London. He decided to inform only his attorney. He knew that keeping it a secret could put him at risk of criminal charges, but he worried that involvement of officials would sabotage the initiative. Both Avnery and Hammami were taking a huge risk by holding this meeting: it could turn out to be a trap; moreover, there were many, on both sides, who would consider the meeting a treason, and they could have been attacked. In the meeting Hammami presented the positions he had outlined in his articles, stressed that he regarded Zionism as invalid but recognized the existence of the Israeli nation and its right of self-determination, and expressed support for the two-state solution.[57]

Two central issues were raised in the meeting. The first concerned the question of deliverability: Whom does Hammami represent? Do his positions represent the PLO and Arafat, and is he speaking in the name of the PLO leadership? When Avnery raised this issue, Hammami replied that he had come to the meeting as a PLO representative. He indicated that Arafat knew his views, had approved his articles, and, despite the criticism leveled against him, he remained the PLO representative in London.[58] Hart argued that those analysts who assumed that Hammami was a "lone wolf," who sought to urge the leadership to follow him, were wrong, and that he was actually working as Arafat's emissary.[59]

The second issue to arise was the idea of a conciliatory Palestinian gesture. Avnery told Hammami, and repeated the message in his talks with the PLO over the years, that the way to change government policy in Israel was to change public opinion, which could only happen as a result of dramatic events that would change Israeli mindsets. Avnery raised a few proposals, such as a public meeting with Arafat, a public response by Arafat to Avnery's questions, or a public meeting between Israelis and PLO officials in Europe. Hammami explained that patience was needed and such steps required ripeness because of internal disagreement within the PLO. The conversation demonstrated that Avnery was willing to take risks and pay a price for his PPE activity. When Hammami asked him if a meeting with Arafat might lead to his prosecution, Avnery replied that it probably would, but that a trial on this issue could be a "powerful tool" to influence public opinion in both Israel and the Arab world. At the end of the meeting, Avnery and Hammami outlined a framework for future contact, which would include meetings in London and phone calls. They agreed to keep their talks a secret, although Hammami would report to Arafat and Avnery would be entitled to report to Israeli leaders that he trusted.[60] Avnery contacted two ministers after the meeting – Foreign Minister Yigal Alon and Justice Minister Haim Tzadok. The former was not interested in meeting with Avnery, while the latter met with Avnery and showed interest in his report.[61]

After the meeting, Hammami continued to disseminate his ideas publicly. In March 1975 he drafted a plan titled "A Palestinian Strategy for Peaceful Coexistence," which he presented during a public speech in London and published as a paper. It was a dramatic move, and according to Agha et al., the talks with Avnery had encouraged Hammami to continue his public campaign and had led to the speech in London.[62] The plan proposed a Palestinian state beside Israel along 1967 lines, with an open border and economic and cultural cooperation, and suggested a dialogue with everyone in Israel who was ready to talk with Palestinians about agreed coexistence arrangements. The plan questioned and challenged the efficacy of continuing the armed struggle. However, Hammami's plan also included a condemnation of Zionism and of Israel, and claimed that in the distant future there could be a solution involving special arrangements between the two peoples for living jointly in one state – a "state in partnership."[63] The plan was published with Arafat's approval. Hammami's statements had no resonance in Israel: they received almost no mention in the media, and there was no response from the government. This surprised Hammami, who told Avnery that the lack of an Israeli reaction could weaken the moderate forces in the PLO.[64]

The second meeting between Avnery and Hammami was held in London on 14 October 1975, and once again Avnery pushed for a dramatic step that would show the Israelis that the PLO had changed. Avnery suggested, for example, an interview with Hammami for *Haolam Hazeh* or Israeli television, or a joint interview with both of them on the BBC. Hammami, again, had doubts and emphasized that the time was not yet ripe for these moves. Two other ideas were raised, which Avnery promised to convey to Prime Minister Yitzhak Rabin: the possibility of a secret Rabin–Arafat meeting, and a visit by Hammami to Jaffa.[65]

After returning home, Avnery wrote a letter to Rabin, explaining that he had held long talks with the PLO representative in London and suggesting a meeting in order to report on them "on a personal and unofficial basis, and of course without publicity."[66] The very next day Rabin's bureau chief informed Avnery that Rabin was willing to meet with him. Rabin and Avnery had already met in 1969, when Rabin was the ambassador to the US, and discussed the Palestinian issue. After that meeting, Avnery wrote to Rabin that a peace agreement that did not involve the Palestinians "will be of dubious value in the long run."[67] Avnery had also asked Justice Minister Tzadok, in early 1975, to inform Rabin of his meeting with Hammami. In July 1975 Avnery wrote to Rabin about a conversation he had had with a Soviet official, during a conference in Rome, and Rabin thanked him for the update.[68]

Rabin's approach to Avnery's PPE efforts with the PLO, as reflected in their meeting, can be characterized as a response pattern of indifference. Rabin did not ask Avnery to stop meeting, but neither did he indicate any support or interest in using the process or its outcomes. Rabin stressed his firm position against negotiations with the PLO, but he was willing to hear Avnery's report on his meetings. According to Avnery, at the beginning of the meeting Rabin clarified that Avnery did not "report" to him, because that would mean that his mission was official or semi-official, whereas in fact he was only acting as a private citizen. However, Rabin added that if Avnery met with interesting people, and he thought that the prime minister should hear about such meetings, then it would be appropriate to share the information with the prime minister. Rabin further asserted that he was always willing to listen. Rabin told Avnery that his opposition to dialogue with the PLO stemmed from his opposition to the idea of a Palestinian state, and, in his view, if one was not interested in achieving this solution then there was no reason to take a step towards it. Rabin argued that the Palestinians would never sign a peace agreement with Israel, and he told Avnery that by publicly calling for talks with the PLO he was helping the organization gain international legitimacy. Avnery tried to convince Rabin and debated the "Jordanian option" with him, but Rabin was firm in his position. The prime minister rejected all of Avnery's proposals for gestures towards the PLO: he refused to meet with Arafat, let Hammami visit Jaffa, or allow Palestinian leaders in exile to return.[69] After the meeting, Avnery wrote to Hammami that Rabin was "friendly" and that the discussion was "logical" and further updated him on a meeting he had held with Foreign Minister Eban.[70]

Avnery regarded his meeting with Rabin as official state approval for his meetings with Palestinians, allowing him to continue without fearing the security system.[71] Rabin asked him to meet with Avraham Ahituv, head of the Israel Security Agency (Shabak, or Shin Bet), in order to confirm the legal aspects of the meetings. Ahituv explained to Avnery that under the law, there were three conditions that justified these types of meetings: that they had a reasonable goal, that they were not intended to jeopardize national security, and that they were not conducted clandestinely. He told Avnery that there was no suspicion that his talks were intended to threaten national security, and they had a reasonable purpose, but he recommended that future meetings be held in public places, and Avnery followed this advice.[72]

In his meetings with Rabin and with other officials, Avnery used the secret action pattern towards decision makers, a pattern he also used on other occasions over the years, but his main focus was the public action pattern towards public opinion. That is why in parallel with his contact with Hammami, Avnery strove to establish a new public movement that would respond to the change in the PLO, grant legitimacy to the talks, and promote Israeli–Palestinian peace. He was also influenced by a proposal Hammami raised in one of their meetings: if an Israeli peace organization were established, the PLO would agree to maintain continuous dialogue with it. Avnery felt that his activity was subject to a vicious cycle, whereby the moderate forces in Israel need gestures from the PLO in order to gain power and support, while at the same time the moderate forces in the PLO needed proof that there was a powerful Israeli moderate camp in order to promote change and overcome the opposition of extremists in the PLO.[73]

In June 1975, Avnery, with Dr. Yossi Amitai and the writer Amos Kenan, published a manifesto for the establishment of the Israeli Council for Israeli–Palestinian Peace. It expressed support for the idea of a two-state solution, based on 1967 lines, and talks with any Palestinian actor who was ready for a dialogue between the peoples.[74] On this basis, they worked to recruit additional public figures to join the movement. Avnery was especially interested in figures who came from the establishment or the military and had a respectable public status that would provide the council with a centrist – rather than "radical" – image, in order to have more impact. Against this background, the following figures joined the new movement: Mattityahu Peled, former major-general in the Israel Defense Forces (IDF); Arie Lova Eliav, former secretary-general of the Labor Party and a former deputy minister; Yaakov Arnon, former director-general of the Finance Ministry; Meir Pa'il, former IDF colonel; and David Shaham, former editor of the Labor journal *Ot*.[75]

In December 1975, the ICIPP was officially inaugurated in a public event that drew much attention in Israel and around the world.[76] There were some disagreements among the council's Executive Committee members, between the more leftist camp (Avnery, Peled, Amitai) and the more centrist camp (Eliav and Pa'il), but eventually they agreed on a joint platform, which was published in February 1976. The new document was more cautious than the original platform but maintained its spirit. More than one hundred public figures, including writers, journalists, and academics, signed the platform.[77] It was important for the council to stress that this was a Zionist movement. After the Sephardi Community Committee published a statement against the new movement, adding that it included "anti-Zionist figures," the council filed a libel suit against the committee, prevailed in court, and received compensation.[78]

Avnery used the fact that he had contacts among PLO officials as a power resource in recruiting members to the new movement. This helped him persuade them that significant changes were taking place in the PLO.[79] David Shaham claimed that when Avnery invited him and Peled to join the council, he played them an audio recording from a phone conversation with Hammami in order to prove his argument.[80] In the press conference of June 1975, Avnery said that he had met with a PLO representative in Europe but did not mention the name.[81]

In addition to the new movement, Avnery promoted other measures that made use of his contact with the PLO to influence public opinion. He met, for example, with newspaper editors in Israel and briefed them on the changes in the PLO, especially with regard to Hammami. As a result the media paid more attention to Hammami's statements.[82] Avnery also used his own magazine to publish a detailed article on Hammami's biography.[83]

In November 1975, Hammami told Avnery that Arafat was planning to deliver a moderate statement on Israel during a visit to Moscow. In response, Avnery led a media campaign to highlight this statement. He was interviewed on television and convened a press conference to explain how Arafat's statement indicated a change in the PLO's policy. His analysis was based on a long conversation he had had with Hammami, who explained the messages that were encoded in the statement. For example, the wording "according to the UN resolutions" in the statement referred to UN Security Council Resolution 242. Hammami also asked Avnery to announce that the PLO was willing to recognize Israel *de facto*, in exchange for an invitation to the Geneva conference, and Avnery delivered this message to Rabin. Avnery did not mention Hammami in the press conference, but rather attributed the information to "PLO sources in Europe." The report received wide media coverage, and the question of future recognition by the PLO was raised in a press conference with Prime Minister Rabin. Avnery wrote to Hammami that "things here are moving faster than I dared to hope. ... I feel that we are closer to peace than we can imagine. For people like you and me there is a role to play in that – a small but crucial role."[84]

Avnery and Hammami developed very warm and friendly relations, maintaining frequent and regular contact. Avnery described their relationship as a "brotherhood of warriors" in a joint battle, and Hammami told Avnery that he had described their meeting to his supervisors in Beirut as a "meeting between friends."[85] They spoke by phone on a regular basis, and when they met in London they had conversations on a wide range of issues. Avnery tried to track down the Hammami family's former home in Jaffa and sent him pictures from the area. Hammami helped Avnery to develop a deeper understanding of the changes and struggles within the PLO. In their talks, each side raised questions and asked for clarifications about events, statements, and developments on the other side. Avnery also updated Hammami on the process of establishing the council.[86] After an assassination attempt against Avnery in December 1975, Hammami called Avnery at the hospital and conveyed wishes for his recovery on behalf of himself and Arafat.[87] On 31 December 1975, Avnery sent Hammami a postcard with a picture of the Dome of the Rock in Jerusalem for the New Year and wrote that "one day we will meet here – in peace."[88]

In their meetings, Avnery kept pushing Hammami for public gestures. He suggested that Hammami reply publicly to questions from the council and requested that Hammami send a greetings card for the event launching the new movement, but neither idea materialized. Hammami explained to Avnery that patience was required and that internal PLO disagreement as well as internal Arab rivalry hampered their ability to make such moves. Goldstein and Dayan claimed that the PLO wanted to reserve such gestures for official negotiations with the Israeli government rather than squander them on a small group.[89]

On 30 March 1976, Avnery left for another meeting with Hammami in London. After returning to Israel, he sent Rabin a written report on the talks with Hammami and on a meeting he had held with Austrian chancellor Bruno Kreisky. Avnery told Rabin that according to Hammami, Arafat was willing to accept a Palestinian state in the WBGS and supported a federation of Israel, Palestine, and Jordan in the long term.[90]

At that point, Avnery felt that the intensity of his contact with Hammami was decreasing. It turned out that the PLO had decided that Hammami would no longer have responsibility for the dialogue with the Israelis. This decision was taken in light of an internal debate: Arafat, Abbas, and Sartawi thought that the PLO should talk with Zionist Israeli forces, in order to get closer to the Israeli mainstream, and saw no point in contacts with anti-Zionist forces, whereas Hammami refused to suspend the contact with these forces, arguing that they were loyal to the PLO. As a result, Hammami was replaced with Sartawi, who was given the responsibility for contact with the Israelis.[91]

Avnery and Hammami met for the last time in the margins of a conference in London in September 1977. Avnery felt that Hammami had been avoiding him during the conference, and on the last day they talked in a side room. Avnery noticed that Hammami looked glum and appeared to be under heavy pressure and in fear. On 4 January 1978, Said Hammami was assassinated in his office in London. The attack was allegedly carried out by the Abu Nidal Organization, a Palestinian group headed by Sabri Khalil al-Banna and supported by Iraq, which promoted a militant stance against the moderate forces in the PLO. The fear of assassination had surfaced often in talks between Avnery and Hammami, usually as jokes, but Avnery had not realized that the threat was so imminent.[92]

## The beginning of contact with PLO representative Issam Sartawi, 1976–1977

At the end of June 1976 Avnery and his colleagues at the council received a first signal from Sartawi. The contact was facilitated through Henri Curiel, who had mediated in the past between Avnery and the FLN and worked, together with a group of communists exiled from Egypt and based in Paris (the "Curiel group"), on promoting channels of dialogue between Israelis and Arabs. Sartawi had moved to France for his new position and there he had met Curiel, who organized a meeting between Sartawi and a leftist Israeli activist, Professor Daniel Amit. In the meeting Sartawi said that the PLO had tasked him with the mission of conducting a dialogue with the Israelis, and he expressed his willingness to meet with ICIPP members. Amit delivered the message to the council, which led to an internal discussion on how to respond. On the one hand, it was exactly the sign they had been waiting for and the reason they had established the movement. On the other hand, the council members wondered who Sartawi was and why the message was conveyed via Curiel rather than the Avnery–Hammami channel. Eventually they decided to accept the proposal and send Peled to an exploratory meeting with Sartawi.[93]

The Peled–Sartawi meeting took place on 21 July in Paris. The two main issues that had been raised in the first Avnery–Hammami meeting were discussed: the representation question and the request for a Palestinian gesture. On the first issue, Sartawi clarified that "I am coming on behalf of my leaders, in their name and on their mission." Regarding the second issue, Peled suggested that the PLO publicly declare that it did not seek to destroy Israel and wished to establish a state in the WBGS that would live in peace beside Israel.[94] Peled gave the council leadership a positive report on the meeting, and Sartawi was impressed with Peled. This paved the way for the creation of a dialogue channel between the council and the PLO. They agreed that their meetings would be clandestine, and accordingly the council members decided not to inform any official or governmental figures before the first meeting.[95]

The new channel included two meetings in a large forum (in September and October of 1976) and meetings of a smaller scope (usually Avnery–Sartawi or Peled–Sartawi). The Curiel group assisted in facilitating the meetings, which were usually held in a villa of one of the group members in the village of Rambouillet in France. The group worked to make sure that the meeting remained a secret, and their experience in underground activism in Egypt helped them in this regard.[96] They continued to serve as facilitators after Curiel was assassinated in May 1978.

On the Israeli side, the participants were Avnery, Peled, Eliav, Arnon, Amitai, and Pa'il, while on the PLO side the participants were Sartawi, his assistant Razi Khouri, and Sabri Jiryis.[97] Jiryis worked at the Palestine Research Center in Beirut and became the director of the center in 1978. In May 1975 he published a series of articles in the Lebanese newspaper *Al-Nahar* in which he expressed support for a political solution with Israel. After Sartawi was appointed to his new position, he approached Jiryis and asked him to join him.[98]

Sartawi told the council members that he had received his mandate from Arafat and that he represented Fatah. The council members explained that they represented their movement but did not have a mandate from the government. Peled pointed out that the meetings were characterized by a lack of correlation in rank between the representatives: PLO officials alongside private Israeli citizens without official authority.[99] The participants discussed the principles for a future settlement (including the questions of borders, Jerusalem, and the refugees) and possible steps to promote the goal of an Israeli–Palestinian agreement and raise support on both sides. The parties agreed not to discuss historical issues and not to argue about "who is right" and "who started." The Israelis suggested publishing a statement on the meetings in order to make the Israeli public aware of the dialogue and the changes in the PLO, but Sartawi strongly opposed this, explaining that secrecy was a condition for the talks. He expressed concern that forces in the "rejectionist front" would target him if they found out.[100]

Another idea was to incorporate international actors in the initiative, so as to make them aware of the meetings and the understandings reached therein, in the hope that this would promote the peace process. The Israelis saw this option as compensation for the lack of publicity. This is an example of the third action pattern towards an external actor. Eliav suggested meeting with former French prime minister Pierre Mendès France, Sartawi supported the idea, and Curiel immediately organized a meeting with Mendès France, who praised the initiative and promised to help. The parties told him they would support an agreement based on 1967 lines that would put an end to the conflict. Mendès France described the meeting as the beginning of a "historical turning point" and expressed appreciation for the participants' courage: "you know better than I the political risks and physical threats you are putting yourself in by taking this dramatic step."[101]

Avnery also brought Bruno Kreisky into the process. Avnery and Kreisky had met for the first time in the 1950s, and in the mid-1970s – after Avnery interviewed Kreisky – a special, friendly relationship had developed between them. Since then they had kept in contact and used to meet and exchange letters. In December 1976 Avnery met with Kreisky and told him about the channel and Sartawi. Kreisky showed interest in Sartawi, and Avnery facilitated a meeting between them.[102] This meeting led to a friendship between the two and the relations in this triangle served as an infrastructure for diplomatic efforts by Kreisky in the Israeli–Palestinian context. The three met, for example, in June 1977 and discussed the idea of organizing an international conference with Israelis, Palestinians, and Arabs under the sponsorship of Kreisky and other international leaders.[103] The contact between Kreisky and Sartawi served as a basis for the exchange of ideas on the PLO's position and possible steps to include the PLO in the peace process.[104]

The channel members also met other international actors, such as Senegalese president Léopold Sédar Senghor, Ivory Coast president Félix Houphouët-Boigny, and Swedish prime minister Olof Palme. The goal was to use these international figures, and their status and networks, to promote the dialogue channel. In some cases, these leaders brought up the issue in their talks with Israeli officials. Houphouët-Boigny, for example, met with Prime Minister Rabin a few days after meeting with Sartawi and Eliav, and he mentioned his positive impression of the channel, but Rabin responded derisively, arguing that Eliav represented the "margins of the margins" of the Israeli public and Sartawi is a "terrorist."[105]

The council members reported to various state officials. Peled reported to Rabin, with whom he had very friendly relations because of their shared history in the Palmach (Jewish paramilitary organization in Mandatory Palestine) and the IDF.[106] Rabin wrote that Peled was "an old personal friend of mine, a partner in service in the Palmach from 1943, and a man I truly respected, despite political disagreements."[107] Peled relayed to his colleagues in the council that after he told Rabin about the meeting, the latter remained "cold and almost indifferent." Rabin told Peled that he was interested in hearing about the meetings but refused to commit to the gestures Peled suggested.[108] In his book, *Service Notebook*, Rabin referred to the meetings Peled and his colleagues had held with the PLO and explained his position:

> I believed Matti when he told me that he and his friends saw themselves as Zionists who believed that Israel could talk with the PLO on the basis of a Palestinian state that would live in peace and good neighborliness with Israel. I did not see a point in arguing that Matti and his friends had met with the representatives of the enemy – as others in Israel tended to blame them. Formality in this case did not seem the most important issue to me. ... I had no doubt that Peled and his group's members were being fooled. I was not gloating. I felt sorry for these good and naïve Israelis, who had good intentions but their political perception was wrong. ... Even though I did not believe in the chances of Peled and his friends to make a change in the attitude of the PLO, and a transformation in its position – I did not get in their way.[109]

Avnery maintained contact with Rabin. He met with Rabin in November 1976, and in December 1976 sent him a letter reporting on another meeting with a PLO official in Europe. Rabin had previously told Avnery that he believed in open borders in a future peace agreement, and Avnery, after raising the issue in his talks, reported to Rabin that the PLO leaders considered open borders a pre-condition for any agreement, and that Hammami had also mentioned this in his plan.[110]

Peled reported to Foreign Minister Yigal Alon. Alon threatened Peled that he would "rat him out" to Rabin, but Peled replied that he was planning to report to Rabin anyway.[111] Eliav informed ministers and MKs who belonged to the dovish section in the Labor Party. The fact that he was the secretary-general of the party facilitated his access to these figures. He reported, among others, to Minister of Justice Haim Zadok, Minister of Health Victor Shem-Tov, Minister of Housing Avraham Ofer, and the MKs Yitzhak Navon, Haika Grossman, and Yossi Sarid. Eliav also updated President Ephraim Katzir and informed his good friend Shlomo Gazit, who at the time was head of Military Intelligence.[112] According to Eliav, Shem-Tov was warm and attentive, and Ofer and others showed great openness.[113] Zadok claimed that he did not ascribe importance to these meetings and thought that Israeli political forces were being used for PLO goals.[114]

According to Hermann, the fact that senior decision makers, including Rabin, agreed to hear reports on the meetings and did not try to stop them attested to their de-facto recognition of the value of communication between the parties.[115] At the same time, Sartawi delivered his reports to Arafat, and other PLO leaders, and he told the council members that despite the opposition in the PLO, Arafat had given him backing and instructed him to continue the dialogue.[116]

Even though it was agreed that the meetings would be kept a secret, in September and October 1976 a few media reports about them appeared,[117] but these reports did not prevent the meetings from continuing. Avnery had a special meeting with Khouri, Sartawi's assistant, and apologized for the leaks. In light of this meeting Sartawi called Avnery and told him that the meetings would continue but secrecy arrangements would have to be strengthened. Many suspected that Pa'il had leaked the information, and in time he admitted as much, explaining that he thought it would promote the goal of the council. "The rationale was twofold," he explained. "First – I am in politics in order to convince Jews. I wanted to publicize our meetings and the constructive value they had begun to generate, hoping this would raise awareness of peace among the Israelis; second – only when we see whether the Palestinians deny it or not, will we know where we stand on this issue."[118] It can also be assumed that Pa'il, a politician who served at that time as a Knesset member, wanted to reveal his role in the initiative. This points to one of the risks that characterize the activity of a politician PPE.

The media reports generated a stormy debate in the Israeli government and parliament. The debate focused on the legal question: is it legal to meet with the PLO? Minister of Justice Zadok presented the government position and differentiated between the political aspect and the legal aspect. In terms of the political aspect, he argued, the government position against negotiation with the PLO still applied, and the government also opposed meetings between private citizens and the PLO. In terms of the legal aspect, Zadok explained that conviction for contact with a foreign agent required proof that the meetings were conducted without a reasonable explanation and that the participants intended to jeopardize national security, and he stressed that no proof had been presented to the attorney-general that could justify indictment on this matter. Zadok argued that a distinction should be drawn between government policy, which opposed negotiation with the PLO, and "the right of citizens to meet with whomever they want as long as they are not breaking the state's laws."[119] Right-wing politicians criticized Rabin for being willing to receive reports on these meetings. MK Amnon Lin (Likud) warned that this fact could be interpreted by the international community as a change in Israel's position and lead to international pressure.[120] The council had an advantage in the Knesset debate because two of its leaders – Eliav and Pa'il – were MKs (politician PPEs), which gave them the ability to reply. But they were compelled to speak about the meetings in vague terms, as they were committed to the secrecy of the initiative.

The media leaks threatened to undermine trust with the PLO and led to political criticism, but they also had positive repercussions: they led to wide coverage in the Israeli, Arab, and world media, and to a public discourse on the topic. On the Israeli side, they granted the meetings an official stamp of legality, and on the Palestinian side, aside from a few critical statements by the PLO's radical forces, the story was well received, without special incident.[121] In the following months additional reports on the meetings appeared in the Israeli, Arab, and international media.[122]

On 1 January 1977 an event that initially seemed like a breakthrough in the talks turned out to be a disappointment. Peled and Sartawi met in Paris, where Sartawi agreed for the first time to issue a joint statement on the meeting, without mentioning his name. The statement declared that a meeting had taken place between "a member in the PLO leadership" and Peled, and that the PLO regarded the principles implicit in the council's platform as a basis for resolution of the conflict. It also stated that the PLO was maintaining close relations with the council and that the meetings would continue.[123] Sartawi took a significant step in agreeing to this, probably without approval from the PLO leadership.[124]

Avnery distributed the statement to all the media outlets, and the next day (2 January 1977) the council leaders convened a press conference in which they reported on the move to Israeli and international journalists.[125] The council members said that they were expecting confirmation from the PLO in the following days, but that same evening Farouk Kaddoumi, the head of the PLO's political department and one of the opponents of the dialogue with the Israelis, issued a statement saying that "there is no truth to the claim that two days ago in Paris a PLO representative signed a document with Dr. Peled concerning Palestine."[126] The statement was true – the PLO representative had not signed a document, but this statement was interpreted as a denial of the meetings, which was a hard blow for the council and its supporters. Kaddoumi's statement stemmed in part from the tension between him and Sartawi, against a background of political disagreement and power struggles. It was also influenced by the fact that Peled had implied that the PLO's approval of the council's platform meant that it recognized the Zionist principles in the document. Avnery argued that the statement of denial caused heavy damage to the council.[127]

A few months after the Israeli parliament discussed the issue (in November 1976), it was addressed in a March 1977 meeting of the Palestinian National Council in Cairo. Sartawi faced criticism from various organizations' representatives in the PLO, including Fatah representatives, for his meetings with Israelis. Against this background, Abbas supported Sartawi and gave a long speech, presenting the logic behind the dialogue channel. Abbas explained that in defending Sartawi, he was actually defending the ideas he had been expressing for years. He claimed that the criticism should be aimed directly at him because Sartawi was not acting on his own behalf, but according to instructions Abbas had given him, and the decision had been made by some of the Fatah leaders.[128]

Arafat also defended Sartawi and described him as a great Palestinian patriot, but during the discussion on formulating the concluding decision he tried to reach a consensus that would please the various factions. The final result was a statement that, on the one hand, recognized "the importance of relations and coordination with Jewish democratic and progressive forces" for the first time, but on the other hand, asserted that they should be opposed to Zionism. This decision contradicted the spirit of the channel with council members, who stressed at every opportunity, both to the Israeli public and to the PLO officials they met, that their organization was Zionist. But Arafat, Abbas, and Sartawi presented this decision as official backing from the PNC for the continuation of meetings with the Israelis, and in their statements they referred only to the article that used the term "Jewish democratic and progressive forces," avoiding reference to the condition of being anti-Zionist.[129]

In May 1977 the right-wing Likud party won the Israeli elections and Menachem Begin became the prime minister. The left-wing party Sheli, which included council members Avnery, Eliav, and Pa'il, received only two seats. The party leaders felt that Kaddoumi's statement and the PNC decision had damaged their image. They blamed the Palestinians for not declaring publicly that they were ready to recognize Israel. Sartawi, too, argued that Kaddoumi had helped Begin.[130]

It was a moment of crisis. On the Israeli side, Eliav and Pa'il were disappointed and abandoned the dialogue channel, while Avnery, Peled, and Arnon – known as "the three Musketeers" – continued the talks. On the Palestinian side, Sartawi faced internal criticism and the council's political weakness had become apparent following the Israeli election results. In addition, Abdallah Frangi, the PLO representative in Bonn, Germany, declared that in light of the election results, the PLO had decided to stop meeting with the Israelis.[131] His declaration coincided with a meeting between Avnery and Sartawi in Paris. Sartawi was surprised by this decision, which had been made without his knowledge, and was outraged.[132] Arafat, as the PLO leader, tried to maneuver between the factions, sometimes playing both sides. While he gave Sartawi a mandate and leeway at the talks, he also adopted a cautious approach, aiming to please those who opposed the meetings as well.[133]

In light of the crisis, Sartawi suggested that Avnery write a letter to Arafat, to be published in *Haolam Hazeh* as an open letter. Sartawi knew that Arafat was following Avnery's articles. Avnery agreed and published the letter after returning to Israel. "A senior figure in the PLO," he wrote, "actually dictated a letter to his superior, and an Israeli journalist put it in writing in order to publish it in an Israeli newspaper, signed by an Israeli."[134] Avnery praised Arafat's courage in deciding to initiate a dialogue with the council and argued that these meetings proved that it was possible to achieve peace between the people, and that there were forces on both sides who worked for peace. But at the same time, he warned that an opportunity was being missed and blamed both parties – the Israeli government was refusing to change its position and the PLO was publicly denying the meetings. Avnery called on Arafat to reconsider the decision to halt the meetings – a decision that gave Begin "the biggest present the PLO could give" – and to stand strong against the pressure he was facing on this issue.[135]

## The meetings channel after Begin's rise to power, 1977–1982

After Likud's victory in the 1977 election, the PLO declared that it was suspending the talks, but the contacts still continued.[136] An analysis of the dialogue during the Begin period reveals that during the early years, between 1977 and 1980, the intensity of the council's activity and meetings with the PLO declined. During this period, Egyptian president Anwar Sadat's visit to Jerusalem (1977) and Israeli–Egyptian peace negotiations (1977–1979) were the focus of the Middle East diplomatic discourse. The PLO attacked the Israel–Egypt Camp Davis agreement (1978), and the rejectionist front in the PLO grew stronger while the moderate forces became weaker.[137] After Camp David, Avnery used Sartawi to deliver a personal letter to Arafat, asking him to learn from the success of Sadat's visit and take the initiative of making a public gesture towards the Israeli public.[138]

During this period, Avnery also worked to establish contacts with Egypt. In May 1976 he wrote a letter to Sadat and offered to interview him as a public gesture, but without success. In December 1977, after Sadat visited Israel, Avnery visited Egypt with the help of Kreisky and Austria's embassy in Cairo. He visited Egypt again in 1978 and 1979, and met with Boutros Boutros-Ghali, Egypt's foreign minister, and the Egyptian diplomat Tahseen Bashir.[139]

In the early 1980s, a positive change took place in the dialogue between the council and the PLO, and it reached its peak in the 1982 Lebanon war. Avnery and Sartawi developed a special relationship during these years and maintained continuous contact through frequent phone calls, letters, and meetings in Europe. They had long conversations on a wide variety of topics and sent each other newspaper clippings. According to Avnery, they were very similar in many aspects and both had a sense of adventure. An American journalist who knew both of them told Avnery that they were "two versions of the same person."[140] Peled and Sartawi developed a good relationship as well. Sartawi and other Palestinian leaders were impressed by Peled's military rank, referring to him as "General Peled," and admired his control of the Arabic language and familiarity with pre-modern Arabic poetry.[141]

The 1977 Likud victory dramatically reduced the accessibility-related resources of the Israeli PPEs to decision makers, as well as the PPEs' expectation of influencing the leadership. But on one issue there were instances of cooperation with the establishment: the efforts to release prisoners of war (POWs) and to obtain information on missing soldiers. After the Litani operation in 1978, Shin Bet officials approached Avnery, with the knowledge of Minister of Defense Ezer Weizman, and asked for his help in efforts to secure the release of Avraham Amram, a soldier captured during the operation. Avnery met with Sartawi and proposed that the PLO release the soldier to the council as a gesture of good will, drawing a comparison to similar efforts by peace activists who were able to secure the release of American POWs during the Vietnam war. Sartawi traveled to Beirut and spoke with Arafat but returned empty-handed. Shortly thereafter Begin saw Avnery and told him, "I heard you are working for the release of our hostage, well done!"[142]

Another instance in which officials asked to use the dialogue channel occurred in the autumn of 1982, this time with the goal of releasing POWs from the Lebanon war. Begin asked Eliav to use his connections with Kreisky and Sartawi for this purpose. Eliav agreed and met with Kreisky, who was willing to help and invited Sartawi to Vienna. Eliav explained that he was working with the support of the Israeli government and on behalf of the soldiers' families. Eliav, Sartawi, and Kreisky met and started to promote the initiative. Sartawi served as the contact with Arafat, Eliav worked with the Israeli government and the soldiers' families, and Kreisky appointed Herbert Amry, former Austrian ambassador to Beirut, to lead mediation efforts with Syria and with the Popular Front for the Liberation of Palestine – General Command (PFLP-GC, a Palestinian organization). As a result of the Eliav–Sartawi initiative, a short video was delivered to Jerusalem as proof of life of the six soldiers captured by Fatah, and a video with the PLO prisoner Salah Tamari was delivered to the PLO. This provided a starting point for negotiations, facilitated by Austrian mediation, which led to prisoner exchange deals between Israel and Fatah (1983), Syria (1984), and PFLP-GC (1985).[143] Prime Minister Shimon Peres also used Eliav's assistance during the time of the unity government (1984–1986) to work with Kreisky on locating missing IDF soldiers.[144]

At the time Sartawi seemed willing to engage in public activity that went beyond the official stance of the PLO and to confront his opponents in the PLO. In October 1979, for example, Sartawi was invited to receive the Bruno Kreisky Prize in Vienna, together with Eliav, and he decided to participate in the ceremony even though the PLO leadership instructed him not to go. Sartawi's presence at the ceremony, sitting near a "Zionist leader," generated strong criticism in the PLO. Following the event, the PFLP-GC called for his expulsion from the PNC and other PLO bodies. "They are asking for my head," he told Avnery. "I am being attacked from all sides." Sartawi was summoned back to Beirut to face justice, but Arafat backed him and he returned to normal activity. Kreisky came to Sartawi's aid, and after receiving a message from Avnery, he wrote to Arafat that he would consider this a test case for future relations between the PLO and Europe.[145]

In September 1980 Sartawi invited Avnery, Peled, and Arnon to a special meeting in Rambouillet. In the meeting he presented an ambitious plan that would include a series of dramatic events, such as public meetings between Israeli peace activists and PLO officials, with the aim of strengthening the Israeli peace camp in advance of the 1981 general election. The plan accorded with the strategy that Avnery had been urging in his meetings with Hammami and Sartawi over the years. Sartawi explained that developments in the Arab world, in light of the Iran–Iraq war, had weakened Syria and Libya and provided the PLO with greater maneuverability. One such sign was that a few days earlier, at a conference in Bulgaria, Arafat had publicly met with a delegation of the Israeli Communist Party that included two Knesset members. Even though the Israelis who attended this meeting were non-Zionist, it seemed like a first step that could pave the way to public meetings with Zionist Israeli PPEs. Another idea floated at the meeting was to contact Arab or European leaders who would provide a "supportive international atmosphere" for their dialogue.[146]

The first step in this direction took place shortly thereafter. In December 1980 Sartawi convened a meeting between the three PPEs and King Hassan II of Morocco. Morocco's embassy in Paris handled the travel arrangements and provided the three Israelis travel documents with fake Arab names. In Morocco, the council members met first with Ahmad Iben Suda, the king's bureau chief, Ahmed Alkhadra, the king's advisor, and two PLO officials: Khaled al-Hassan, one of Fatah's founders, and Abu Marwan, the PLO representative in Rabat. The meeting marked another step in expanding the circle of PLO officials who met with the council. Sartawi told al-Hassan that he was glad he had joined the meeting because "these people started to suspect that I am all alone and that I am a fraud by claiming to represent the PLO." Indeed, Arafat had personally approved the visit to Morocco. At this first meeting the participants discussed a few suggestions for gestures that could be proposed to the king, such as a special speech on peace with Israel or an invitation to a delegation of Israeli peace activists to Morocco. Towards the end of their visit, the council leaders met with the king, whose view of the various proposals was positive.[147] This was an attempt to use the action pattern that involves a third party, and because it was a confidential meeting it had no influence on public opinion. Soon thereafter Sartawi met with Avnery, and informed him that it seemed the ideas raised at the meeting were not going to be implemented.[148]

During 1980–1981, there were a few indications that Avnery's efforts to convince the PLO to publicize the dialogue had borne fruit, as PLO officials began to speak about it publicly:

1. Sartawi said in an interview that there was a Zionist peace camp that acknowledged the Palestinians' rights and agreed to a Palestinian state beside Israel (December 1980).
2. Arafat confirmed in an interview that the PLO was in contact with "the Israeli peace party Sheli" and added that "anyone who is willing to join the dialogue with us should also join" (December 1980).
3. Sartawi sent an open letter to a conference being held in Jerusalem to mark the fifth anniversary of the council's establishment (January 1981). In the past, Sartawi had refused to do so. Avnery had asked Sartawi to mention Israel in the letter, and Sartawi agreed, writing that "sooner than our enemies think, peace between the Palestinian state and the state of Israel, and their people, will rise and will prevail."[149]

In parallel, Avnery initiated a gesture by presenting the Palestinian flag alongside the Israeli flag. At the conference the council presented a poster with both flags, and during his last speech in the Knesset (in February 1981) Avnery raised a sign with the two flags. The legal authorities in Israel examined the legality of this move, given that the flag was identified with an organization that sought to destroy Israel, and the police summoned Avnery and Peled for interrogation. Avnery claimed that if the Palestinian flag was combined with the Israeli flag, it was clear that the destruction of Israel was not the intention, and the attorney-general accepted this argument. This move attracted attention in the world media and on the Palestinian side. The PLO spokesperson indicated that the display of the flag at the council's conference was "a very interesting and important development" and the Palestinian paper *Filastin at-Thawra* reported on the display of the flag at the Knesset on its first page.[150]

In March 1981, on the eve of the Israeli election, Sartawi raised a new idea with Avnery. He suggested that the PLO invite an Israeli peace delegation to the next PNC meeting in Damascus. Avnery agreed and thought that Arnon and Peled would also agree, even though this would probably lead to criminal charges for contact with the enemy and travel to an enemy state. Avnery and Sartawi drafted a letter in which Avnery proposed the idea to Arafat.[151] Avnery also sent similar letters to other PLO officials.[152] Yet despite Avnery and Sartawi's efforts, the idea was not implemented.

The PNC meeting in April 1981 served as another arena for a rift between Sartawi and his opponents. Many criticized Sartawi, and when he asked to speak his request was rejected. He then convened a press conference at which he announced his resignation from the PNC. His announcement exposed the world to the internal dispute within the PLO. He claimed that he had wanted to report to the PNC on his dialogue with the Israelis and request a decision on its continuation, but after not being allowed to speak he decided to resign and suspend the dialogue.[153] Arafat, as in other cases, tried to navigate both sides. On the one hand, he did not support Sartawi during the PNC meeting or demand that he be allowed to speak. But on the other hand, he said he would not accept Sartawi's resignation.[154] Sartawi's move symbolized his willingness at this stage to lead a struggle in the public sphere, and it resulted from his anger over the double standard in the policy of the PLO leadership, which sent him to the talks but at the same time left him exposed to attacks without full backing. Sartawi's statement in Damascus had a resounding echo in the Israeli media, which covered it in detail and in a positive light.[155]

In June 1981 the Likud party won the Israeli election and Sheli failed to pass the threshold for a seat in parliament. This indicates that the PPEs had failed to raise public support and change the policy. Sartawi maintained contact with the Israeli PPEs, with Arafat's backing, and continued to meet with Avnery.[156] Sartawi also continued his public struggle. In a January 1982 interview, he blamed the PLO for Likud's victory and held it responsible for sabotaging the Israeli peace camp. "We should have publicized my secret talks with progressive Israelis beginning in the fall of 1976," he said.[157]

## Unofficial contacts in light of the Lebanon war, 1982–1983

In July 1981 the Israel–Lebanon border became an arena of confrontation between Israel and the Palestinian forces in Southern Lebanon, with exchanges of artillery fire and Israeli air attacks. Mediation efforts by the US envoy Philip Habib led to a ceasefire agreement between Israel and the PLO. On 3 June 1982, Shlomo Argov, the Israeli ambassador to London, was shot in an assassination attempt by the Abu Nidal Organization. This incident led to another Israeli operation, aimed at destroying the Palestinian military presence in Lebanon, which marked the beginning of the first Lebanon war.[158] Paradoxically, the military escalation led to a breakthrough in the unofficial diplomatic efforts of Avnery and his colleagues to cultivate contact with the PLO. A month after the war started, an event that eventually became the most famous symbol of Avnery's PPE activity, and a turning point for unofficial contact with the PLO, took place: a meeting between Avnery and Arafat, in Beirut on 3 July 1982. It was a dramatic event: a meeting with the person who was perceived in Israel as its worst and most ruthless enemy, and the head of a terrorist organization, in the midst of a war and in the heart of the war zone, during a siege on Beirut, accompanied by bombings on PLO bases. The meeting was recorded, documented, and covered at length by the media in Israel and around the world. It can be seen as an example of a "transformative media event," as termed by Dayan and Katz.[159]

Avnery arrived in Lebanon with Anat Saragosty and Sarit Yishay, journalists from *Haolam Hazeh*, using a formal invitation issued by the IDF Spokesperson's Unit to all the newspaper editors to visit Lebanon. During the visit in East Beirut, Avnery was able to contact Arafat's office in West Beirut, with Sartawi's assistance, and a meeting with Arafat was set up. Avnery was instructed to get to one of the checkpoints, where the PLO picked him up, together with Saragosty, Yishay, and a German TV crew that joined them, and helped them cross the lines of four different forces (the Lebanese Phalanges, the Lebanon army, the PLO, and the Syrian army) and arrive at the house in which the meeting took place.[160]

Three main resources were especially helpful in making Avnery's meeting with Arafat possible. The first was the contacts with various PLO officials. Sartawi helped facilitate the meeting and gave Avnery the phone number of Arafat's office. Razi Khouri, whom Avnery knew through the channel, helped Avnery cross from East to West Beirut. The second resource was the fact that Avnery was an editor. This role enabled him to enter Lebanon using an invitation from the IDF. Avnery also used his network with international journalists, including the German journalist Gerhult Ahrenz, who covered the Lebanon war and knew Beirut very well. The third resource was the fact that Arafat was aware of Avnery and his activity. Arafat had received reports on the meetings between Avnery and the PLO and was aware of his writing. At the beginning of the meeting, Arafat mentioned that he had read Avnery's articles and that he was following his – and his colleagues' – activities, for which he was grateful.[161]

The meeting with Arafat was also a journalistic accomplishment, but Avnery considered it a peak moment in his PPE activity and a crucial step that could promote his main goal: changing public opinion in Israel. "I did not come for a polite conversation," he explained, "nor for the adventure or even for the scoop. I wanted to deliver a message."[162]

At the meeting, Avnery focused on questions that would provide him with "ammunition" to help shift public opinion, discredit the common perception of the PLO, and transform the "enemy image." Avnery asked Arafat, for example, how the Israeli public might be convinced that the PLO wanted peace and that a Palestinian state would lead to a comprehensive solution. Avnery and Yishai also confronted Arafat with the main Israeli arguments against the PLO, including for example the approach in the PLO

Charter to the Jewish people and the Israeli belief that the Palestinians wished to drive all the Jews into the sea. Arafat replied that the PLO accepted a few peace plans, including the US–Soviet Statement (1977), the Brezhnev plan (1981), and Fahed's plan (1981), as a basis for an agreement and claimed that no Palestinian wished to drive the Jews into the sea. After being pushed to address questions about the solution, Arafat explained that the PLO offered two solutions: one secular democratic state or two states.[163]

Avnery also stated his position during the meeting, in addition to asking questions. He told Arafat that in Israel there was a minority that supported Begin and a minority that supported peace and opposed the war, and that most of the public was in the middle and should be encouraged to go in the direction of peace.[164] At the end of the meeting, Arafat allowed Avnery to meet with the Israeli pilot Aharon Ahiaz, who had been captured by the PLO, and Avnery delivered a letter from the captured pilot to his family in Israel.[165]

Shortly after the meeting, even before Avnery had returned to Israel, the PLO issued a statement on the meeting, which created a political storm in Israel. Ministers and MKs asked the attorney-general to consider prosecuting Avnery. Minister Yizhak Modei (Likud) said that "Avnery, who met with Arafat during a war, has in so doing joined the enemies of Israel." The Labor Party also denounced the meeting.[166] It is evident that in this case, as in other similar cases at later stages, the publicity surrounding the meeting, which Avnery had sought in order to enlist public support, also exacerbated the opposition and provoked objections to the meetings.

Prime Minister Begin prevented a discussion on the subject in government, arguing it was a legal issue to be decided by the attorney-general. Begin commented that it was ironic that Avnery had wanted to meet with Arafat for fifteen years but was not granted consent, and was finally able to meet him thanks only to the IDF and the war.[167] A police investigation was launched against Avnery but ultimately the attorney-general, Yizhak Zamir, announced that Avnery would not be prosecuted and that there was no evidence that he had committed a criminal offense.[168] Facing calls for his prosecution, Avnery used his journalist's hat and argued in his defense that "I came to Arafat as a journalist, carrying a journalist's card of the Israeli government, and I traveled to Beirut using the travel arrangements that were provided to journalists by the IDF."[169] His lawyer claimed that in the past Avnery had updated state officials on his meetings, and the minister of defense had asked for his help in efforts to secure the release of a captured soldier.[170]

Avnery published the full transcript of the interview in his magazine and gave his report the heading "We Want Peace."[171] We can see some similarities to Cousins's interview with the Soviet leader Khrushchev, which attempted to reveal a different side of the Soviet leader. In both cases the journalist PPEs used pictures as a way to change the "enemy image." In Cousins's article it was a picture of Khrushchev playing with Cousins's daughters and in Avnery's article it was a picture of Arafat holding Imad Shaqour's daughter.

The Avnery–Arafat meeting in Beirut was a significant landmark in the dialogue between the PPEs and the PLO. After the meeting, it appeared that the dam had burst and the existence of the channel had come to light. Two weeks later, Avnery, Peled, and Sartawi convened a joint press conference in Paris, and a few days after that Peled and Sartawi held another press conference in London.[172]

In mid-July Avnery also met with PLO leader Khaled al-Hassan in New York, and al-Hassan agreed to Avnery reporting on the meeting. According to Avnery, once Arafat had held a public meeting with him, other PLO officials saw no point in keeping their meetings a secret. Al-Hassan asked Avnery to announce that the PLO was willing to end the hostilities if Israel and the PLO established mutual recognition. Avnery wrote in detail about the meeting in his magazine, devoting the cover to the story and emphasizing the PLO's proposal to "stop terrorism."[173] On 18 September another public meeting took place: Avnery and Imad Sahqour sat together on the stage in a conference in the Netherlands. On 21 October Avnery, Peled, and Sartawi met in Paris and Sartawi informed them that they were invited to meet with Morocco's king a few days later in New York. At that meeting, the king stressed his interest in strengthening the moderate forces in Israel but clarified that he would decide when to report on the meeting. A few months later, the king publicized the story and called for Israeli–PLO meetings in Morocco.[174] After it became public knowledge, Avnery published an article on the meeting with the king and on the earlier visit to Morocco.[175]

The peak moment in this process took place in January 1983, in a publicized meeting between the three PPE council members and Arafat in Tunis. On 18 January Avnery, Peled, and Arnon, as well as Sartawi, arrived in Tunis. First they met with Mahmoud Abbas, who had been supervising the dialogue process but was meeting with Israeli PPEs for the first time. After that, a larger meeting was held with Arafat, Abbas, Sartawi, Shaqour, and the PLO ambassador to Tunis. "It was Issam's big day," Avnery wrote; "his great personal victory that he has wished for over the years."[176] The discussion was focused, as in previous meetings, on possible steps that would influence Israeli public opinion and strengthen the peace camp. The Israelis raised two main ideas: a public declaration of the PLO's willingness to recognize Israel if Israel recognized it, and an invitation for the PPEs to attend the next PNC meeting. It was agreed that they would issue a joint statement at the end of the meeting, and a photographer was asked to document the event.[177] This was the first meeting, since the council's establishment in

1975, in which the council members met with the PLO leadership and a joint statement was issued concurrently by the Palestinian news agency Wafa and the council. The following is the text of the statement that was released to the press:

> The PLO chairman met with a delegation of the Israeli Council for Israeli–Palestinian Peace, which included Major-General (res.) Matti Peled, Uri Avnery, and Dr. Yaakov Arnon. On the Palestinian side, Dr. Abu Mazen, Dr. Issam Sartawi, and Imad Shaqour participated in the meeting. In the meeting, the situation in the Middle East was reviewed in depth, and possible courses of action for sustainable and just peace in the Middle East were examined. Chairman Arafat expressed his appreciation for the role that the Israeli peace forces are playing and their struggle for a just and stable peace.[178]

The wording in the statement reflects two important achievements for the Israeli PPEs. First, the use of the term "Israeli peace forces" implies a change to the principle of having contact only with anti-Zionist forces; second, the PLO's willingness to pursue joint "courses of action" with Israelis was unprecedented. Avnery pointed to the picture of the meeting as the main achievement: "Millions of Israelis and Palestinians saw a picture of Yasser Arafat sitting next to an IDF major-general, a former Knesset member and a former director-general of an Israeli government office. The visual impact had to change the positions of people on both sides, [whether] consciously or unconsciously."[179] In addition, the presence of Sartawi next to Arafat reinforced the claim that he was working in the name of the PLO leadership.[180]

The meeting in Tunis should be understood in the context of the changes that took place after the Lebanon war and the relocation of the PLO's headquarters and forces from Beirut to Tunisia. This granted Arafat greater maneuverability and the leeway to pursue independent moves.[181] The large demonstrations in Israel against the Lebanon war also caused the PLO to realize that there was a strong peace camp in Israel.

For both sides, the meeting in Tunisia led to a political storm and strong expressions of criticism and opposition. On the Israeli side the issue was discussed in the government and in the Knesset. Three ministers, including Foreign Minister Yitzhak Shamir, declared that if the current legal situation allowed this kind of meeting, then there was a need for legislation that would define it as a criminal offense.[182] This call was supplemented by additional demands that the Israeli PPEs be prosecuted, but none of these calls was translated into legislation. According to Bar-On, the Israeli public did not see the meeting as an important gesture by the PLO chairman, but rather as a ploy to use naive Israelis for propaganda purposes.[183] The PPEs complained that no governmental actor expressed interest in what they had

Figure 5.1 Meeting between members of the Israeli Council for Israeli–Palestinian Peace and PLO leaders in Tunisia, January 1983; left to right: Yaakov Arnon, Uri Avnery, Yasser Arafat, Matti Peled, Issam Sartawi, Mahmoud Abbas, and Imad Shaqour

heard from Arafat at the meeting.[184] In Sheli opinions were divided over the meeting, and the disagreements within the movement regarding the war and contacts with the PLO led to its dissolution.[185]

On the Palestinian side, the opposition was very vocal, asserting that Arafat had gone too far. The criticism came from the Popular Front for the Liberation of Palestine, the Democratic Front for the Liberation of Palestine, and the governments of Syria and Libya, among others. The Abu Nidal Organization declared that Arafat had "betrayed the Palestinian people."[186] Within Fatah's Revolutionary Council, speakers criticized Arafat and Sartawi and it was decided to suspend contacts with Zionist Israelis.[187] The subject of dialogue with the Israelis was raised again at the PNC meeting in February 1983 in Algeria. Sartawi repeated the tactics he had used in 1981, and after not being given the opportunity to speak, announced his resignation, but the PNC spokesperson claimed that it was rejected.[188]

After the 1983 PNC meeting, Sartawi kept pulling the rope he was given until it was close to fraying. According to Szyszkowitz, after the PNC many considered Sartawi to be a "dead man walking."[189] On 27 February 1983,

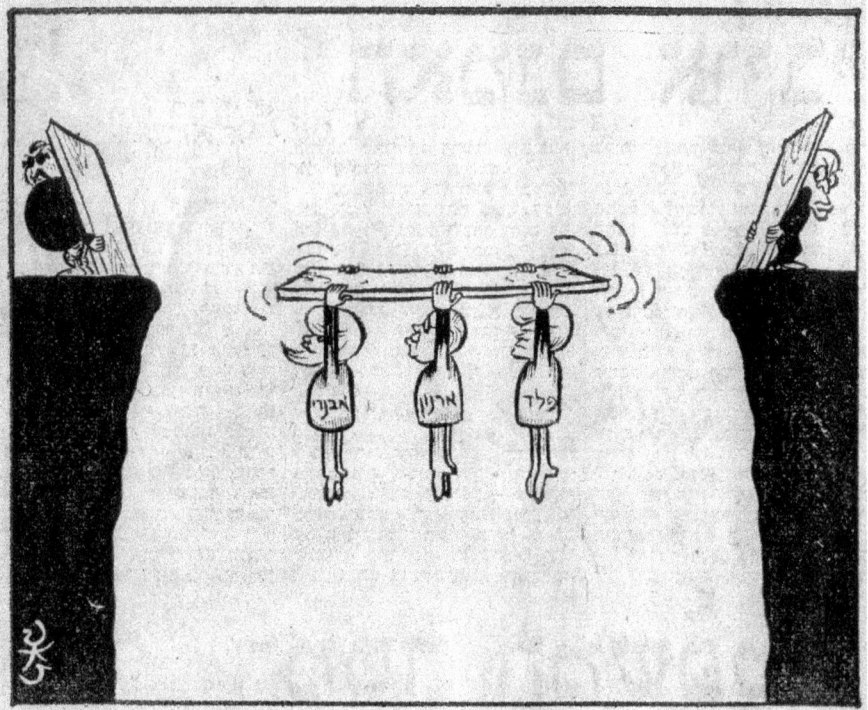

**Figure 5.2** Cartoon by Ze'ev after the meeting in Tunisia, published in *Haaretz* on 25 January 1983; the figure on the right is Israeli prime minister Menachem Begin, the figure on the left is PLO chairman Yasser Arafat, and in the middle are Uri Avnery, Matti Peled, and Yaakov Arnon

a group of Israeli and Jewish peace activists convened a conference in London, to which they invited Avnery and Sartawi. Sartawi knew that his participation would be a clear violation of Fatah's decisions. He considered canceling, but because of pressure from the organizers he decided to participate. At the event, Jewish and Palestinian groups protested against the speakers and interrupted the speeches by Avnery and Sartawi. During his speech Sartawi stated that he had had second thoughts about attending the conference, but "after I heard what I heard here, I am very glad I came. ... If someone thinks that weak people make peace – he is wrong. The peace makers are very tough people. ... You can't silence us by shouting. ... I needed this experience in order to reinforce my firm decision to struggle for peace."[190] Sartawi's speech reflected his determination, after the 1983 PNC meeting, to fight back, and he told Avnery that he was thinking of establishing a Palestinian peace party that would be part of the PNC as an independent force. He argued that there was a strong minority in the PLO that impeded any step towards peace and there was no group pushing for the other side. Sartawi, wanting to spread his ideas, gave many interviews and speeches, using the media interest that resulted from the storm in the PNC. He claimed that he represented the silent majority of Palestinians and called on the PLO to adopt a more realistic approach.[191]

On 25 March Sartawi and Avnery participated in a conference in The Hague. In his speech, Sartawi praised Avnery's meeting with Arafat in Beirut: "In contrast to standard practice during wartime," he said, "Uri Avnery risked his life and crossed the lines of fire in Beirut in order to bring a message of love to his brothers who were being slaughtered in Beirut. It was a special act, a beautiful act; I cannot describe the beauty of this act."[192] This was the last time that Avnery and Sartawi saw each other. On 10 April 1983, Issam Sartawi was assassinated during a congress of the Socialist International in Lisbon, Portugal. After his assassination, the Abu Nidal Organization announced that they had executed "the criminal traitor Sartawi" in accordance with a "death penalty" sentence.[193]

Sartawi knew that his life was at risk. When he met with Avnery in cafés, he always chose an isolated spot and sat facing the entrance. Sometimes, before they entered a car, he would ask Avnery to stand back to prevent him being hurt in case the car exploded.[194] Sartawi's assassination was a hard blow for Avnery. "He was like a brother to me," he wrote. "I have never felt such a deep friendship with any other person."[195] The council subsequently held a memorial ceremony in Tel Aviv in honor of Sartawi.[196]

After his assassination, Sartawi was portrayed in the Israeli media as a man of peace, and even figures who had opposed the dialogue with him expressed this sentiment. The journalist Yaakov Karoz (*Yedioth Ahronoth*) compared him to Jordan's King Abdullah and Egyptian president Sadat, who had been assassinated for their willingness to talk with Israel. A cartoon in *Maariv* showed Sartawi's body lying on the ground next to his briefcase, on which were written the words "There is someone to talk to!"[197] Even the head of the Labor Party, Shimon Peres, who had tried to prevent Sartawi from speaking at the Socialist International congress, said after the assassination that "the bullet that hit Sartawi was targeted to strike at the spirit of moderation and human courage."[198]

## Unofficial contacts with the PLO after Sartawi's assassination

In the spring of 1983 the dialogue channel faced a crisis. Opposing voices in the PLO and the assassination of Sartawi constituted a fatal blow to the process. Sartawi was the contact person between the PPEs and the PLO, and after his death no one was nominated to replace him. But the PLO leadership stressed that contact would continue, and this message was delivered in practice when Arafat sent Shaqour to participate, with Avnery, in a conference in Italy. Shaqour told Avnery that they were struggling internally with the challenge of how to explain the purpose of the dialogue so long as it was not yielding results and Israel's position remained unchanged.[199] Avnery tried to build a new channel through the PLO representative in Rome, Nimer Hamed, but the contact was not consistent as it had been with Sartawi.[200]

From this point forward the channel was based on direct contact with Arafat and included meetings with him and with Abbas. The council members met with Arafat at a conference in Geneva in August 1983 and in Tunisia in April 1984 and February 1985. In contrast to its policy in the past, the PLO publicly acknowledged these meetings. After a meeting in 1985, the PLO published a statement in which Arafat "expressed his gratitude to the Israeli peace forces who support the principle of self-determination of the Palestinian people and emphasized the interest of the PLO in an expanding dialogue with these forces."[201] In addition, at the PNC meeting in Jordan in November 1984, the PLO political committee suggested expanding its terminology by no longer using the old term "Jewish forces" – so as to clarify that the dialogue was aimed at all Israeli groups who recognized the Palestinian right of self-determination. The contacts with Israelis were under the supervision of Arafat and Abbas, aided by two other PLO members who had been expelled from the West Bank: Mohammed Milhem and Fahed Qawasmeh.[202]

During the meetings at this stage (1983–1985) the PPEs and the PLO leaders discussed the idea of an international peace conference under UN auspices, with the participation of the various parties, including Israel and the PLO. The PLO accepted the idea and the Israeli PPEs criticized the resistance of Israel and the US to the idea.[203] The Israeli PPEs also suggested declaring a mutual ceasefire, but Arafat replied that they could consider this only if Israel accepted the idea of a peace conference. Avnery also urged Arafat to declare that the PLO was opposed to attacks against civilians.[204] Avnery and his colleagues continued to work on behalf of POWs and missing soldiers from the Lebanon war. Families of the soldiers contacted Avnery, with Begin's approval, and asked for his help. Avnery wrote to Arafat in July 1983, requesting that the soldiers be allowed to send letters to their families and suggesting that he and Peled serve as mediators, but the initiative failed. The PPEs raised the issue again in a meeting in 1984, asking for information on the missing soldiers. Arafat promised to follow up but he never provided any information.[205]

This moment, in the mid-1980s, can be seen as a turning point at which the historical role of the Israeli Council for Israeli–Palestinian Peace came to an end and its leaders passed the torch to their successors. The idea that Avnery had been promoting since the mid-1970s began to gain increasing support and the circle of the Israelis who took part in these meetings, or supported them, expanded and drew closer to the political center. Goldstein and Dayan described this process, which started in the Lebanon war and increased during the 1980s:

> The demand for a direct dialogue with the PLO and the recognition of a need to create a Palestinian state, which was accepted by a very small minority of the Israeli public opinion when the council was established in 1975, gained more and more supporters. ... The circle of Israelis who met under various circumstances and at various events with PLO members had also become wider. ... But as the positions of the Israeli Council for Israeli–Palestinian Peace became increasingly acceptable, the council lost its power, its importance, and its relevance.[206]

At the same time, the PLO developed an interest in expanding its contacts and reaching more centrist actors. Sartawi had stated in 1980 that Sheli members deserved "gratitude for being the pioneers" but that this phase had run its course and the dialogue should be extended to wider circles.[207] In July 1982, Sartawi publicly called on "good-willed, peace-loving" Israeli figures to meet with him. He claimed that "a bad Israeli who wishes to meet with me transforms in my view into a good Israeli." Shortly thereafter, the PLO representative in Rome, Nimer Hamed, declared that the PLO was willing to enter a dialogue with the Labor Party, and Arafat announced that he was prepared to talk with any Israeli party that opposed Begin.[208] This change was also reflected in the terminology that PLO institutions started to use, and in 1987 the PNC's Political Committee used the term "Israeli democratic forces" who support the Palestinian struggle against the occupation and their right to an independent state.[209]

An analysis of the contacts between Israelis PPEs and the PLO indicates a gradual process in which more and more actors in Israel became involved and the PPEs shifted from the political margins to the center. We can identify a few stages. During the *first* stage, the actors were anti-Zionist figures from the Israeli Communist Party and the socialist organization Matzpen; during the *second* stage it was Avnery who broke the taboo, in 1975, becoming the first Zionist to meet with the PLO, and later other council members, such as Peled, Arnon, and Eliav, joined the process. During the *third* stage, figures from the more centrist Zionist left joined the process. These included, for example, members of the Peace Now movement, who were reprimanded by the movement's leadership after they met with Sartawi in September 1980.[210] During the *fourth* stage, in 1985, Knesset members from the Zionist left Ma'arach Party met with Imad Shaqour.[211] During the *fifth* stage, in the latter half of the 1980s, various groups joined and the participants became more diverse. These included Oriental Jewish peace activists, Israeli and Palestinian public figures who took part in academic workshops organized by Professor Herbert Kelman (Harvard University), and even semi-official meetings with the PLO, with the support of Prime Minister Peres.[212] The *sixth* stage began after the Intifada (1987), Jordan's disengagement from the West Bank (1988), and the PLO's acceptance of the UN Security Council Resolution 242 (1988). These conditions convinced the Israeli left of the need to negotiate with the PLO, and Peace Now officially called for talks with the PLO.[213] At that point even figures in the government, such as Minister Ezer Wiezman and Deputy Minister Yossi Beilin, met with the PLO (1989).[214]

In parallel to this process, the opposition in Israel to these meetings became stronger and more vocal. The public meetings in 1982–1985 were accompanied by demands for prosecution, but the attorney-general found that no crime had been committed. As a result, additional political figures called for the law to be amended, which in turn led to new legislation, adopted in August 1986, defining these meetings as illegal.[215]

After the new law came into effect, some PPEs, including Avnery, found creative ways to use the articles in the law that listed conditions under which such meetings were permissible, for example by having international journalists join a meeting in order to present it as a press conference.[216] Some politician PPEs also used their parliamentary immunity. Other PPEs, such as Abie Nathan, deliberately participated in public meetings with Arafat, in violation of the new law and in order to challenge it. Nathan was imprisoned twice for doing so. Other PPEs focused their dialogue efforts on the Palestinian leadership in the WBGS (the "internal PLO"), to which the law did not apply. One of the channels that were developed with these leaders was that of Yair Hirschfeld, joined by Ron Pundak, which provided the basis for their role in the Oslo channel in 1993.[217]

In January 1993 Israel's government, headed by Prime Minister Rabin, revoked the law that prohibited meetings with the PLO, and in September 1993 Israel and the PLO signed letters of mutual recognition and the Declaration of Principles on Interim Self-Government Arrangements (Oslo Accords). Rabin and Arafat met at the signing ceremony in the White House, almost twenty years after Avnery had first urged the two to meet.

The PPE Ron Pundak, one of the architects of the Oslo Accords, has pointed to the important role of Avnery and the pioneers of the meetings with the PLO: "They allowed us to act, they created the mechanism on the other side, they created the public perception that allows it."[218] Likewise, Israeli minister Shlomo Ben Ami, who participated in the peace summit with the PLO in July 2000, wrote that "the pioneers who were at the forefront, such as Arie Lova Eliav and Matti Peled, and many others, predicted and preached about the inevitable decision and its difficult price, and for that they were excluded and sidelined as helpless leftists."[219]

On 1 July 1994, the day Arafat arrived in Gaza – thanks to the Oslo Accords – Avnery came to watch the event. When Arafat heard that Avnery was there, he demanded that he be allowed in and asked Avnery to sit beside him on the stage during a press conference he was holding. Arafat reminded Avnery that at their meeting, in July 1982, Avnery had asked him where he was heading, and Arafat had replied that he was returning home: "I told you that I am going home, and here I am."[220]

### Analysis and conclusions: the impact that PPE Avnery had on the official sphere

#### *Influence patterns*

According to Agha et al., the activities of Avnery, Hammami, Peled, and Sartawi served as "an important precedent" for Israeli–Palestinian talks over the next two decades. They argued that these individuals broke the taboo, enabled a public discourse with the other side to take place, crossed psychological and political red lines, and helped create an appropriate atmosphere for track two, and eventually official, talks.[221] Curiel claimed that even though the meetings in Paris did not yield results, they still had an important impact. He argued that they influenced the Israeli public, the Palestinian leadership, and other actors in the international arena.[222] Gresh argued that the meetings forced the Palestinians to gradually acknowledge Israeli nationalism and the binational reality that exists in the land.[223]

Scholars have expressed differing views regarding the impact of the unofficial contacts. Hirschfeld wrote that, in retrospect, these talks had historical importance, but they were a "complete failure from the political perspective."[224] Bar-On argued that, on the one hand, these efforts did not lead to a significant change on either side: in Israel the government continued to oppose negotiations with the PLO and the council remained a marginal group, and on the Palestinian side, the leadership continued to prefer the military struggle over reconciliation; but on the other hand, the contacts had an important impact in the long term: they opened the door to future dialogue efforts and turned reconciliation into a plausible idea.[225] Some scholars drew a link between the council's peace efforts and the 1993 Oslo channel. Hermann, for example, wrote that the council's meetings created a precedent for the unofficial channel in Oslo.[226]

In his book, Abbas analyzed the conditions that led to Oslo and mentioned the contacts with Israeli and Jewish forces as an important element that changed Israeli public opinion by showing that peace and coexistence were possible. "As we honour our fallen heroes, we honour the heroes of peace."[227] Avnery pointed to three main achievements: a mutual learning process in which the Israelis learned about the sensitivities of the Palestinian side and how to evaluate which action courses could succeed, while realism was strengthened among the moderate forces in the PLO; mutual persuasion that narrowed the gaps between them; and exposure of the parties to the human dimension of the other side, while also shattering the perception that meeting with the enemy was treason.[228]

Which influence patterns were at work in Uri Avnery's activity as a PPE? One important element was *influence through gestures of conciliation*. Avnery and his colleagues pushed for this goal and eventually succeeded, as their efforts resulted in official gestures by the PLO. Examples include the joint statement in January 1983, Sartawi's letter of greeting in January 1981, and PLO leaders' interviews with Avnery and conciliatory messages delivered through his magazine. Initially the PLO leaders rejected the gestures proposed, and it took some time for the conditions to ripen. However, the dialogue process assisted the moderate forces in the PLO and reinforced their commitment. According to Peled, the contacts helped the peace camp on the Palestinian side, enabling the Palestinian partners to the dialogue to begin expressing their views more strongly and clearly.[229]

Second, Avnery's activity had an *influence on the public discourse*. Avnery saw this goal as the main focus of his PPE activity over the years. His activity had an impact on the "agenda setting" and led to the creation of "news slots" that dealt with moderate statements by the PLO, the internal debate within the PLO, and the possibility of a dialogue with the PLO. All of these issues were initially deviations from the existing discourse in the Israeli media. Avnery introduced Hammami and Sartawi to the public and brought their voices into the Israeli discourse. Avnery gave resonance in the media to every conciliatory sign from the PLO in order to reinforce its impact. He used various tools towards this end, including his magazine and his weekly columns, press conferences, and briefings for journalists and editors. The public meetings with the PLO received extensive media coverage and became an important issue on the political agenda and in Knesset and government discussions, thus forcing political actors to address the topic. Avnery also promoted the "doubting" strategy, seeking to change the enemy image and humanize the PLO. Peled claimed that the 1983 meeting in Tunis helped shatter the Israeli perception of Arafat as a monster.[230] The public learned about the changes in the PLO and saw a PLO official – Sartawi – who struggled and even died for peace. Avnery used "information politics," as termed by Keck and Sikkink, and became an independent source of information on the PLO.[231] The PPEs' activity also helped the Palestinians see the internal differences in Israel. Arafat and Sartawi, in their declarations to the Palestinian public, expressed their appreciation of the Israeli PPEs, and PLO official Ahmad Sidqi al-Dajani stated in 1979 that the PLO recognized the difference between peaceful Zionists, such as the council members, and "fanatics."[232] As noted, the influence on public opinion cut both ways: breaking the taboo and enlarging the base of support for dialogue with the PLO, while at the same time amplifying the opponents' voices and provoking measures against the unofficial dialogue.

Avnery's, and the council's, activity also led to *changes in institutional procedures* within the PLO. The meetings forced the PLO leadership to organize itself accordingly and establish bodies to supervise the dialogue. It also led to internal discussions and decision-making processes in the PNC and other PLO bodies regarding the organization's strategy and position on negotiations with Israelis and with Israel. Gresh, who was close to the PLO, argued that these contacts prompted the Palestinian leaders to formulate ideas and proposals.[233]

We can also identify *influence through mediation* as an element in this case study. Avnery, Peled, and Eliav were involved in delivering messages between Arab and Palestinian actors and Israeli officials. Avnery conveyed a proposal from Tunisia in 1965, for example, and messages from the PLO in 1975. Although the Israeli government refused to endorse or use the channel to start official talks, Israeli officials did choose to use this tool on various occasions involving POWs and missing soldiers. The Eliav–Sartawi–Kreisky channel that operated during the Begin administration is a good example of successful mediation efforts through an unofficial channel with official endorsement. It also provides an example of *influence through crisis management* because it facilitated efforts to find solutions to the humanitarian problem that developed in light of the Lebanon war. The Eliav–Sartawi–Kriesky channel is also one example, among others, of *influence through an external actor*. A few international leaders and figures became involved in the dialogue process, including Kreisky (Austria), Hassan II (Morocco), Mendès France (France), and Senghor (Senegal). Their inclusion in the process integrated the PPE activity into the international sphere and made use of international actors to promote the initiative. In some cases, such involvement affected the bilateral relations of the respective state with Israel or the PLO, and the issue of the PPE–PLO channel was raised in meetings between foreign leaders and Israeli or Palestinian leaders. Concerning *influence through the transmission of ideas*, it seems that no specific proposals advanced directly to the official sphere, but Avnery did play a role in promoting the core concepts of dialogue with the PLO and the two-state solution.

## Variables related to the PPE

Uri Avnery was a *journalist PPE*, an editor of the popular weekly *Haolam Hazeh*, and this was the basis for his resources and networks system. His magazine provided him an important platform for spreading his ideas and he used it as a tool in his PPE activity. He wrote about many of his meetings and initiatives over the years – from his meetings with Arab representatives in 1959 to the meeting with Arafat in Tunisia in 1983. As an editor, Avnery had control over the reports in his magazine, as well as the headlines and pictures, which was an important power resource. He also used the magazine to expose the public to conciliatory Arab and Palestinian messages and to address Arab and Palestinian leaders. Arafat was aware of the public letters Avnery wrote to him. His journalist's hat served as a cover and source of immunity in some cases, including the meeting in Beirut in 1982. His position also helped him build a wide network in Israel and around the world, thereby accumulating knowledge resources regarding the diplomatic and political arenas, establishing his public status and reputation, and gaining publicity among wide audiences of readers and supporters. As in other cases of journalist PPEs, Avnery sometimes experienced tension between his desire to publish scoops and the need to keep certain meetings secret, and he prioritized the latter. His meetings with Sartawi in the mid-1970s were kept secret, and, following the leaks to the Arab media in 1977, an editorial appeared in *Haolam Hazeh* explaining that the magazine had all the information about these meetings and had "missed" many opportunities for international scoops because it "faithfully upheld the commitment that the editor took upon himself, and in doing so, according to our beliefs, we served the best interests of the State of Israel."[234]

Avnery was also a social activist and a *politician PPE* who belonged to a few political movements and parties. He served as a Knesset member for two and a half terms. This provided him with the resources of public legitimacy, publicity, access to decision makers, and tools to influence the agenda. Avnery claimed that one of the events that contributed to his decision to run for the Knesset was an incident at the 1965 Florence conference, when he proposed a draft resolution and MK David Hacohen (Mapai) shouted that "Avnery did not represent anyone" in the Israeli public.[235] Being an MK provided proof of some public support, but also indicated that the support was limited. In 1978 Begin wrote to Avnery, arguing that he could not speak in the name of Israelis and stressing that the previous round of elections had proved as much.[236] The decision to establish the council was intended to provide public support for the dialogue with the PLO and underscore that Avnery was not acting alone but in fact was part of a large group. The addition of members such as Peled,

Eliav, and Arnon was aimed at enhancing legitimacy and creating a more "centrist" image.

The main power resources in Avnery's activities were the following:

1. *Access and network system.* On the Palestinian side, Avnery gradually developed a network system with PLO officials, which was expanded over the years. It started with Hammami and Sartawi and eventually reached Arafat and Abbas. During the first stage, the fact that the PLO leaders were aware of Avnery's writing and activities was helpful. In 1971 the PLO Research Center published a book on Avnery's political views. In addition, two PLO members who had previously been Israeli, Shaqour and Jiryis, knew Avnery personally.[237] The leadership in Beirut received reports from Hammami and Sartawi on their meetings with Avnery. The meeting with Arafat in 1982 was an important landmark, and because it was documented it conveyed a clear message of legitimacy regarding public meetings with Avnery and other Israeli PPEs. Through this meeting Avnery proved to the Palestinians that he was willing to take risks and pay a price for his PPE efforts. This had a significant meaning for the PLO leaders and was something Sartawi emphasized. The Palestinians also appreciated the symbolic move of presenting the Palestinian flag in the Knesset, alongside the Israeli flag. The personal relationships that Avnery developed with Hammami, Sartawi, and Arafat played an important role as well and served as a great power resource. The personal relationship between the three council leaders and Sartawi was deep, consistent, and based on trust. Sartawi explained that "if I say to Mati, Yaakov, and Uri 'come with me immediately, I cannot tell you to which country and for what purpose' – they will not hesitate and they will come, and if they say the same thing to me, I will come with my eyes closed."[238] Avnery and Arafat also developed relations of trust, and when Avnery asked Arafat in 1985 if he would agree to meet with Israeli journalists, Arafat replied that he was "willing to meet with everybody that you send me, without knowing his identity."[239]

   On the Israeli side, despite the hostility towards Avnery in various governmental and public circles, he had a wide network system in Israeli society with politicians, government officials, journalists, and intellectuals. This helped him in his PPE efforts. However, he was limited in his ability to influence decision makers, especially after Likud's victory in 1977. In the international field, Avnery built networks that assisted him in his activities and in some cases helped him gain access to Arab and Palestinian actors.

2. *Knowledge resources.* Avnery acquired unique knowledge resources and expertise regarding the PLO – its various factions, institutes, internal debates, and relations with Arab countries. These were based on conversations with PLO officials, updates from Sartawi, and discussions with

diplomats and journalists: "I had better information than the Mossad and the Shin Bet," Avnery claimed.[240] His knowledge resources as an editor also helped him, as illustrated by a discussion he had with Arafat regarding public gestures, in which he mentioned that he was speaking as "a professional in the field of mass communication."[241] Likewise, his knowledge of Israeli politics and public opinion, which he obtained as a journalist and a politician, assisted him in his efforts to influence the public.

3. *Value-based resources.* Avnery's political views were well known, and he expressed them through every available platform: articles, books, speeches, and interviews. He consistently emphasized the difference between his position and government policy, a fact that served as an important resource in his PPE activity and helped him gain legitimacy and credibility in the eyes of the other side. In parallel, Avnery also stressed that he was an Israeli patriot, and that his public struggle stemmed from a deep commitment to the Israeli interest. This was an important resource in addressing the Israeli public. It enabled him to recruit to the council figures who had previously been part of the official establishment, and it was also the reason that the council decided to file a libel suit after its members were called "anti-Zionist." Avnery emphasized the difference between his activity and the meetings of anti-Zionist forces with the PLO, and he refused to include them in the council. However, Avnery's political views, and his anti-establishment stance, prevented him from gaining better access to government circles.

### Variables related to the initiative

1. *Secrecy/publicity and the action pattern.* The main action pattern Avnery used was public action aimed at influencing public opinion. He sought to give publicity to the meetings, while keeping his promises regarding secrecy when it was required. During the first stage, in the mid-1970s, the meetings remained a secret; the turning point was the public meeting with Arafat in 1982. Under the first Rabin administration (1974–1977), Avnery and other council leaders, in some instances, used the action pattern of secrecy vis-à-vis decision makers. They reported on the meetings to a few decision makers. Under the Begin and Shamir administrations (1977–1984) and the unity governments (1984–1990), the use of this pattern stopped as Avnery saw no point in it. In addition, Avnery and the council leaders used action through a third party and included various international actors in their initiative.

2. *The goal of the initiative.* Avnery's early PPE efforts, in the 1950s and 1960s, were aimed at the general goal of promoting Israeli–Arab relations and the idea of a Semitic union. But once he began holding meetings with the PLO, the goal became more defined: official dialogue and

mutual recognition between Israel and the PLO. They discussed pre-negotiation issues, such as conditions for negotiation and the framework of negotiations. In order to achieve this goal, they promoted the idea of a public gesture that would pave the way for negotiation. The more ambitious goal was to promote a two-state solution, and the PPEs also discussed the details of a future agreement and issues such as Jerusalem and borders. Another subject was the goal of releasing POWs and obtaining information on missing soldiers, which represented a more specific goal.

3.  *Correlation with official policy.* Avnery's activity in the 1950 and 1960s conflicted with official policy. He supported the FLN's struggle for independence, for example, while the Israeli government supported France. He was enthusiastic about Bourguiba's declaration, whereas the government rejected it. Likewise, his dialogue with the PLO conflicted with the official policy of all the governments, right and left, which opposed negotiations with the PLO and a Palestinian state beside Israel. Avnery was a *dissident PPE* who promoted a very critical stance against the government. The discord between his stance and official policy was especially blatant during the Lebanon war, when the government was seeking to destroy the PLO while Avnery was opposing the war and calling for dialogue with the PLO. During the first Rabin administration, the prime minister was open to hearing about the meetings, even though he opposed them (pattern of indifference), but after 1977 the decision makers maintained a very firm policy against these unofficial meetings, which culminated with the new law of 1986 (pattern of resistance). Peled explained that after the Likud came to power, the practice of reporting to state officials declined dramatically, for two reasons: first, because the meetings had become fairly regular and were receiving media coverage; and second, because the PPEs felt that the government had no interest in moves that went beyond its own stated position.[242]

4.  *Direct or indirect contact.* Between 1975 and 1982, the channel was not directly with the leader of the PLO, but with a mid-level PLO official. This changed after the Lebanon war. On the Israeli side, the PPEs had direct access to Israeli leaders during the Rabin administration and almost no direct contact after that, although during the Begin administrations Eliav had access to Begin and Weizman. They used his help in efforts on behalf of Israeli POWs, and Eliav also tried to convince Begin to integrate Palestinians in the negotiations with Egypt.[243]

### External variables

1.  *Characteristics of the conflict.* The context in which these contacts took place was the conflict between Israel and the PLO – a conflict between a state and a non-state actor under conditions of no official recognition

or diplomatic relations between the parties. It is an intractable conflict with issues that relate to symbols, identity, national and religious narratives, and conflict over protected values.

2. *Ripeness.* On the Israeli side, signs of ripeness for a political process and concessions began to emerge after 1973, but mainly in relation to Egypt rather than the Palestinians. The Lebanon war raised the Palestinian issue once again, but Israeli ripeness on this front only developed at the end of the 1980s. The PLO was considered a murderous terrorist organization that could not be a partner for peace, and even the "dovish" forces in Israel, who agreed to a territorial compromise, supported the "Jordanian option." At that point, among Israelis, the Palestinians were not considered an independent actor, and the consensus was that any solution to the Palestinian problem would be with Egypt or Jordan. Likewise, in the international arena there was no consensus on integrating the PLO into the peace process, and the US was opposed to including the organization unless it accepted the following conditions: recognition of Israel, acceptance of UN Security Council resolutions 242 and 338, and renouncement of terrorism. The European stance was different, and in 1980 the European Community's "Venice Declaration" called for the inclusion of the PLO in the peace process.[244] A few important developments, including the first intifada (1987), Jordan's disengagement from the West Bank (1988), the Palestinian Declaration of Independence and acceptance of Resolutions 242 and 338 (1988), and the dialogue between the US and the PLO (1988), contributed to ripening the conditions for an Israeli move towards talks with the Palestinians. Although it is difficult to be certain, a decision by an Israeli leader to talk with the PLO, and to promote mutual recognition between the parties, might have led to this public ripeness sooner.

On the Palestinian side, the 1973 war sparked an internal discussion on the need to promote a political strategy, alongside the military strategy, and the process of change developed gradually. However, the desire to maintain unity despite internal disagreements between the various factions, as well as the pressure from various Arab countries, made it difficult for the PLO leadership to complete the process and it only proceeded in small steps, sometimes expressing contradictory positions or issuing deliberately vague statements. After the Lebanon war and the relocation of PLO headquarters to Tunisia, the PLO had greater maneuverability and the need for a political option became clearer. But the ripeness process reached its peak moment only in 1988, after the first intifada, and in light of the willingness of the US to begin a secret dialogue with the PLO.

3. *The position of leaders and the domestic conditions.* On the Israeli side, during the period of these contacts, all the governments opposed

negotiations with the PLO (while they were willing at times to negotiate, indirectly, with the PLO on POWs and missing soldiers). Rabin supported talks with Jordan but not with the PLO; Begin's position was more firmly against the PLO, and in 1982 his government launched an operation against its presence in Lebanon. The Israeli public supported this position in the 1970s: in 1974 only 7 percent supported talks with the PLO and in 1979 the figure was 20 percent. At the end of the 1980s public perception changed and by 1989 public support had risen to 40 percent.[245] On the Palestinian side, an internal debate had been taking place in the PLO since 1973. From the mid-1970s, a strong group in the Fatah supported a policy change in favor of the two-state solution, while the factions in the "rejectionist front" opposed any compromise. Arafat remained in the middle, and even though he was probably closer to the first camp, he tried to maneuver between them. He gave his approval for Hammami's and Sartawi's meetings, and later took part himself in meetings with Israeli PPEs, but at the same time he tried to appease opponents and expressed contradictory positions. After the Lebanon war and the move to Tunis, his political messages became more pragmatic and moderate, and he also increased his support for dialogue with PPEs. Arafat completed this process in 1988 when he publicly accepted the two-state solution and Resolutions 242 and 338 and renounced terrorism.

4. *Parallel channels of communication.* Avnery's contacts with the PLO were developed under conditions of a diplomatic vacuum with no direct or indirect, official or unofficial, communication channels between the parties. In the second half of the 1970s there was no external actor who wanted, or was able, to serve as a mediator. At the beginning of the 1980s, in light of the military clash in Lebanon, external actors became involved in indirect negotiations: in 1981 the American mediator Philip Habib facilitated a ceasefire between Israel and the PLO, and after the Lebanon war the Austrian mediator Herbert Amry brokered prisoner exchange deals between Israel and Fatah (1983). During the 1980s, more unofficial channels were developed between Israeli PPEs and the PLO.

5. *Internal governmental agents.* In this case study, there were no governmental agents on the Israeli side who supported and endorsed the PPE activity. There were some political actors who were willing to hear reports, but no more than that. On the Palestinian side, the PLO officials Hammami and Sartawi were official actors who promoted and pushed the PPE activity as much as possible within the official PLO framework, sometimes even going beyond official policy, and eventually they paid with their lives.

# Notes

1  O. Benziman, "Tel Aviv will be Geneva," *Haaretz* (30 November 2003).
2  Y. Goldstein and A. Dayan, *They Called Him Jaap: Yaakov Arnon between Amsterdam and Jerusalem* (Tel Aviv: Hakibutz Ha-meuhad, 2010); N. Yesod, *Matti Peled* (MA Thesis) (Haifa: Haifa Univeristy, 2004); T. Szyszkowitz, *Der Friedenskämpfer: Arafats Geheimer Gesandter Issam Sartawi* (Vienna: Picus Verlag, 2011).
3  M. Bar-On, *In Pursuit of Peace: A History of the Israeli Peace Movement* (Washington: United States Institute of Peace Press, 1996); T. Hermann, *The Israeli Peace Movement* (New York: Cambridge University Press, 2009).
4  A. Gresh, *The PLO: The Struggle Within* (London: Zed Books, 1988).
5  Avnery, *My Enemy*.
6  B. Morris, *Righteous Victims: A History of the Zionist–Arab Conflict* (London: John Murray, 2000), 37–160; Y. Sayigh, *Armed Struggle and the Search for State: The Palestinian National Movement, 1949–1993* (Oxford: Clarendon Press, 1997), 25–70.
7  See H. Cobban, *The Palestinian Liberation Organisation* (Cambridge: Cambridge University Press, 1984), 21–35; Sayigh, *Armed Struggle*, 80–92, 104–108.
8  M. Shemesh, *The Palestinian Entity 1959–1974* (London: Frank Cass, 1996), 80–94, 128–152; J. Becker, *The PLO* (New York: St. Martin's Press, 1984), 68–77.
9  A. Sela, *The Decline of the Arab–Israeli Conflict* (Albany: State University of New York Press, 1998), 165–170.
10 M. Muslih, "Towards coexistence: An analysis of the resolutions of the Palestine National Council," *Journal of Palestine Studies*, 19:4 (1990), 3–29; Shemesh, *The Palestinian*, 285–296.
11 A. Sela, "The PLO at fifty: A historical perspective," *Contemporary Review of the Middle East*, 1:3 (2014), 269–333; Gresh, *The PLO*, 136–171.
12 A. Shlaim, *The Iron Wall* (New York: Norton, 2000), 329–334; Yitzhak Rabin, *Service Notebook* (Tel Aviv: Maariv, 1979), 492–493.
13 Avnery, *My Enemy*, 39; U. Avnery, *Optimistic* (Tel Aviv: Miskal, 2014), 94–115.
14 N. Erel, *Without Fear and Prejudice: Uri Avnery and Ha'oloam Ha'ze* (Jerusalem: Magnes, 2006), 36–46; Avnery, *Optimistic*, 188–206.
15 Avnery, *Optimistic*, 216–319; U. Avnery, *In the Fields of the Philistines* (Tel Aviv: Hakibbutz Hameuchad, 1998).
16 Erel, *Without Fear*, 52; Avnery, *Optimistic*, 306–307.
17 Erel, *Without Fear*, 50–51; Avnery, *Optimistic*, 339–340.
18 Erel, *Without Fear*, 228–275; Avnery, *Optimistic*, 353–355, 403–406.
19 Semitic Action, *The Hebrew Manifesto* (Tel-Aviv: The Semitic Action Center, 1958), 8–11; Avnery, *Optimistic*, 516–525.
20 Avnery, *Optimistic*, 19–20; A. Zichroni, *1 Against 119: Uri Avnery in the Knesset* (Tel-Aviv: Daf Hadash, 1969).
21 Avnery, *My Enemy*, 46–47; Avnery, *Optimistic 2* (Tel-Aviv: Miskal, 2016), 102–103, 107–109.

22  U. Avnery, *War of the Seventh Day* (Tel-Aviv: Daf Hadash, 1969), 63–71, 193–222.
23  Avnery, *My Enemy*, 104–109; Avnery, *Optimistic 2*, 119.
24  Avnery, *Optimistic 2*, 105.
25  U. Avnery, "The ambassador of craziness," *Haolam Hazeh* (18 February 1959), 3.
26  U. Avnery, "Talks with Arabs," *Haolam Hazeh* (4 February 1959), 3.
27  Avnery, "Talks with Arabs," 3–5; U. Avnery, "Abdel Nasser invited Sharett," *Haolam Hazeh* (11 Feburary 1959), 3–5; Avnery, "The ambassador," 3–5, 18; Erel, *Without Fear*, 99–103; "U. Avnery met Arab representatives," *Davar* (3 February 1959).
28  Avnery, *Optimistic*, 561–566; U. Avnery, "A push to God," *Haolam Hazeh* (9 July 1964), 5–7, 24.
29  Gresh, *The PLO*, 195; H. Curiel, *On Peace's Altar* (Jerusalem: Mifras, 1980), 138–151.
30  Sela, *The Decline*, 80–81.
31  U. Avnery, "Meeting with the future," *Haolam Hazeh* (12 May 1965), 8–9, 27; Avnery, *Optimistic*, 487; Erel, *Without Fear*, 104–106.
32  Uri Avnery Archive (hereafter UAA), Avnery to Eban, 21 April 1965; Avnery to the Tunisian ambassadors to France, 6 May 1965; Avnery, "Meeting with the future," 8–9, 27.
33  Avnery to Eban, 21 April 1965; M. Lasker, "Between Burgibizm and Nasserism: Israeli–Tunisia relations and Israeli–Arab relations during the 1950s and 1960s," *Iyunim Bitkumat Israel*, 11 (2001), 68–69.
34  Avnery, "The ambassador," 4.
35  Erel, *Without Fear*, 101, 103, 106; Avnery, "The ambassador," 5, 18; Avnery, *Optimistic*, 541–545, 551–556; Avnery, *Optimistic 2*, 73–74.
36  Avnery, *My Enemy*, 43; Avnery, *Optimistic*, 535; Avnery, "Talks with Arabs," 4–5.
37  Avnery, "Talks with Arabs," 3, 5.
38  Avnery, *My Enemy*, 44; Avnery, *Optimistic 2*, 74.
39  Interview with Uri Avnery, 28 February 2014; Avnery, *Optimistic*, 535.
40  S. Hammami, "The Palestinian way to Middle East peace," *Times* (16 November 1973); Bar-On, *In Pursuit*, 203.
41  S. Hammami, "Making the first move towards peace in Palestine," *Times* (17 December 1973); Bar-On, *In Pursuit*, 203.
42  Avnery, *My Enemy*, 62–67; Goldstein and Dayan, *They Called Him Jaap*, 167; A. Safieh, *The Peace Process* (London: Saqi, 2010), 269.
43  Avnery, *My Enemy*, 68; Bar-On, *In Pursuit*, 203.
44  Avnery, *Optimistic 2*, 222–224; Avnery, *My Enemy*, 50, 55; Bar-On, *In Pursuit*, 203.
45  C. Mansour, *Uri Avnery and Neo-Zionism* (Beirut: The Palestine Research Center, 1971).
46  Interview with Uri Avnery; Avnery, *My Enemy*, 68, 131; Mansour, *Uri Avnery*, 127–130. Hammami told Avnery on 6 February 1976, "You must always keep

in mind a very clear fact that our people read all what you write and take it very seriously." See UAA, Conversations with Said Hammami – Transcript from Tapes.

47 A. Hart, *Arafat* (Bloomington: Indiana University Press, 1989), 343–344.

48 Abbas, *Through Secret*, 10–13.

49 Interview with Sabri Jiryis, 2 October 2016.

50 Szyszkowitz, *Der Friedenskämpfer*, 36.

51 Goldstein and Dayan, *They Called Him Jaap*, 186–187; Avnery, *My Enemy*, 158–163; Szyszkowitz, *Der Friedenskämpfer*, 14–33.

52 Szyszkowitz, *Der Friedenskämpfer*, 37, 39. Hammami told Avnery that Abbas stood behind the peace camp that was emerging in the PLO, and Arafat told Avnery that Abbas had supported peace with Israel even before Sartawi, see U. Avnery, "Uri Avnery reports on the meeting," *Haolam Hazeh* (26 January 1983), 68.

53 "The Paris talks in Arab eyes," *Haolam Hazeh* (23 February 1977).

54 Safieh, *The Peace Process*, 55.

55 Gresh, *The PLO*, 195; Szyszkowitz, *Der Friedenskämpfer*, 45; Goldstein and Dayan, *They Called Him Jaap*, 167.

56 Agha et al., *Track-II*, 10–11.

57 Avnery, *My Enemy*, 55, 58.

58 Avnery, *My Enemy*, 58; UAA, Meeting with Hammami, January 1975.

59 Hart, *Arafat*, 353.

60 Avnery, *My Enemy*, 60; Avnery, *Optimistic 2*, 229–231.

61 UAA, Avnery to Alon, 4 February 1975; Avnery, *My Enemy*, 103; Goldstein and Dayan, *They Called Him Jaap*, 172.

62 Agha et al., *Track-II*, 11; Goldstein and Dayan, *They Called Him Jaap*, 167–168; Bar-On, *In Pursuit*, 203.

63 S. Hammami, "A Palestinian strategy for peaceful coexistence: On the future of Palestine": http://aldeilis.net/english/a-palestinian-strategy-for-peaceful-coexistence/ (accessed 25 March 2021).

64 Avnery, *My Enemy*, 69, 91; Goldstein and Dayan, *They Called Him Jaap*, 167–168.

65 UAA, Meeting with Hammami, 14–16 October 1975; Avnery, *My Enemy*, 94–98; Goldstein and Dayan, *They Called Him Jaap*, 167, 171.

66 UAA, Avnery to Rabin, 19 October 1975.

67 UAA, Avnery to Rabin, 16 June 1969; Avnery, *My Enemy*, 101–102.

68 UAA, Avnery to Rabin, 18 July 1975, Rabin to Avnery, 24 July 1975; Avnery, *My Enemy*, 103.

69 Avnery, *My Enemy*, 100, 104, 109–111; Goldstein and Dayan, *They Called Him Jaap*, 172; UAA, Notes for the meeting with Rabin, 28 October 1975.

70 UAA, Avneri to Hammami, 4 November 1975.

71 Avnery, *My Enemy*, 104, 111; Goldstein and Dayan, *They Called Him Jaap*, 173.

72 Avnery, *Optimistic 2*, 239–240.

73 Avnery, *My Enemy*, 60, 91, 117; Bar-On, *In Pursuit*, 204; Interview with Yossi Amitai, 28 April 2016; Szyszkowitz, *Der Friedenskämpfer*, 46.

74  Avnery, *My Enemy*, 91–93; Bar-On, *In Pursuit*, 204; UAA, "We believe," *Jerusalem Post* (10 June 1975). The movement was initially called "the Israeli Council for Israel–Palestine Peace" but later the name was changed because members of the council objected to inclusion of the term "Palestine"; see Avnery, *Optimistic 2*, 274.

75  Avnery, *My Enemy*, 117–119; A. Eliav, *Autobiography* (Tel Aviv: Am Oved, 1984), 241; Goldstein and Dayan, *They Called Him Jaap*, 178–179; D. Shaham, *Zehav Ha-misholim: An Autobiography of Thoughts* (Tel Aviv: Zmorab Bitan, 1999), 344; UAA, Avnery to Hammami, 11 Decmber 1975.

76  Bar-On, *In Pursuit*, 205; Eliav, *Autobiography*, 239; Shaham, *Zehav Ha-misholim*, 346–347; "Israeli group urges Palestinian talks," *New York Times* (13 January 1976).

77  Eliav, *Autobiography*, 240; Goldstein and Dayan, *They Called Him Jaap*, 179–182; Shaham, *Zehav Ha-misholim*, 344–345; The Israeli Council for Israeli–Palestinian Peace, "Pamphlet," *Haolam Hazeh* (3 March 1976).

78  Goldstein and Dayan, *They Called Him Jaap*, 182–183; Eliav, *Autobiography*, 241–242; UAA, Council of Sephardi and Oriental Communities to Avnery, 19 January 1977.

79  Avnery, *My Enemy*, 116; Goldstein and Dayan, *They Called Him Jaap*, 170.

80  Shaham, *Zehav Ha-misholim*, 343.

81  "Initiating meeting with the PLO in Europe," *Davar*, 11 June 1975; Avnery, *My Enemy*, 91–93.

82  "PLO representative in London: I recognize Israel," *Yedioth Ahronoth* (12 October 1975); "PLO spokesperson in London Said Hammami in an interview," *Yedioth Ahronoth* (20 November 1975); Avnery, *My Enemy*, 113; Goldstein and Dayan, *They Called Him Jaap*, 174–175.

83  "Hammami," *Haolam Hazeh* (26 November 1975), 11–12, 32; UAA, Avnery to Hammami, 26 November 1975; Avnery made efforts to prevent an impression that he had personal contacts with Hammami and attributed the information to British friends and others.

84  UAA, Avnery to Hammami, 26 November 1975; Avnery, *My Enemy*, 114–115; Goldstein and Dayan, *They Called Him Jaap*, 175–176; "Avnery: Arafat gave up on 'A national secular state,'" *Yedioth Ahronoth* (3 Decmber 1975); "Was the information accurate?" *Haolam Hazeh* (10 December 1975).

85  Avnery, *My Enemy*, 56, 137; Szyszkowitz, *Der Friedenskämpfer*, 46.

86  Avnery, *My Enemy*, 57, 62, 73–88, 96, 121–126, 131; UAA, Conversations with Said Hammami; Phonecalls with Hammami 1975–76; Avneri to Hammami, 4 November 1975; Avnery to Hammami, 26 November 1975; Conversation with Said Hammami, 14–16 October 1975; Avnery to Hammami, 11 December 1975.

87  Avnery was stabbed by a mentally unstable man, see Avnery, *My Enemy*, 112.

88  UAA, Avnery to Hammami, 31 December 1976.

89  Avnery, *My Enemy*, 121, 126, 134; Goldstein and Dayan, *They Called Him Jaap*, 177, 185; Conversations with Said Hammami; Avnery to Hammami, 11 Decmber 1975; Avneri to Hammami, 4 November 1975; Avnery to Said

Hammami, 26 November 1975; UAA, Avnery, Amitai and Kenan to Hammami, 2 November 1975.

90 Avnery and Hammami met on 31 March and 4 April. UAA, Meeting with Hammami, 31 March 1976; Meeting with Hammami, 4 April 1976; Avnery to Rabin, 21 April 1976; Avnery, *My Enemy*, 106, 135; Goldstein and Dayan, *They Called Him Jaap*, 186.

91 Avnery, *My Enemy*, 130, 172–173; Bar-On, *In Pursuit*, 390; Szyszkowitz, *Der Friedenskämpfer*, 47.

92 Avnery, *My Enemy*, 90, 137, 143; Hart, *Arafat*, 353; Agha et al., *Track-II*, 13.

93 Goldstein and Dayan, *They Called Him Jaap*, 187–190; Szyszkowitz, *Der Friedenskämpfer*, 51–53; Bar-On, *In Pursuit*, 205–206; Eliav, *Autobiography*, 242–245; Shaham, *Zehav Ha-misholim*, 365.

94 M. Peled, "My meetings with PLO representatives," *Maariv* (7 January 1977); Goldstein and Dayan, *They Called Him Jaap*, 190; Yesod, *Matti Peled*, 21.

95 Goldstein and Dayan, *They Called Him Jaap*, 191–193; Eliav, *Autobiography*, 243; Szyszkowitz, *Der Friedenskämpfer*, 56.

96 Szyszkowitz, *Der Friedenskämpfer*, 57; Interview with Yossi Amitai.

97 Goldstein and Dayan, *They Called Him Jaap*, 191–192, 202–203; Avnery, *My Enemy*, 149–150; Bar-On, *In Pursuit*, 204; Szyszkowitz, *Der Friedenskämpfer*, 48; UAA, Meeting 17–18 October 1976. Avnery did not participate in the first meeting. In the discussion about the delegation, some argued that the council should send new members who had not previously been involved in talks with the PLO and members who were closer to the political mainstream (see Avnery, *Optimist 2*, 281).

98 Interview with Sabri Jiryis; Szyszkowitz, *Der Friedenskämpfer*, 48–49; S. Jiryis, "The Palestinian problem – the other side of the coin," *Al-Nahar* (13 May 1975). Jiryis has stated that while Sartawi believed that the dialogue could pave the way to peace, he personally was more skeptical. Although he voiced support for the effort, he did not attach much importance to it and in fact advised that not too many hopes be pinned on it.

99 M. Peled, "My meetings with PLO representatives (part 2)," *Maariv* (21 January 1977); Eliav, *Autobiography*, 248; Goldstein and Dayan, *They Called Him Jaap*, 196.

100 Eliav, *Autobiography*, 248–249; Goldstein and Dayan, *They Called Him Jaap*, 194–195, 197, 205; Peled, "My meetings"; Bar-On, *In Pursuit*, 206–207.

101 Yesod, *Matti Peled*, 21–22; Bar-On, *In Pursuit*, 207; Szyszkowitz, *Der Friedenskämpfer*, 58–59; Eliav, *Autobiography*, 249–252.

102 Szyszkowitz, *Der Friedenskämpfer*, 66–67; Avnery, *My Enemy*, 182–184; Avnery, *Optimistic*, 532. See Bruno Kreisky Archive (hereafter BKA), 23.

103 BKA, Meeting Kreisky–Kahane–Issam, 19 June 1977; Avnery, *My Enemy*, 193–194; Agha et al., *Track-II*, 12–13.

104 BKA, Sartawi to Kreisky, 12 July 1978; Yesod, *Matti Peled*, 25–26.

105 Bar-On, *In Pursuit*, 390; D. Rubinstein, "The foreign policy of Lova Eliav," *Davar* (4 March 1977); Gresh, *The PLO*, 197; S. Nakdimon, "Meetings with PLO," *Yedioth Ahronoth* (3 October 1980).

106 Eliav, *Autobiography*, 256.
107 Rabin, *Service Notebook*, 542–543.
108 Yesod, *Matti Peled*, 22; Goldstein and Dayan, *They Called Him Jaap*, 199; Shaham, *Zehav Ha-misholim*, 366.
109 Translation from Hebrew. Rabin, *Service Notebook*, 543.
110 UAA, Avnery to Rabin, 5 December 1976; Talks in Paris/Vienna 29 November–1 December 1976.
111 Mattityahu Peled's Archive (hereafter MPA), "The main points of the respondent number 2's argument," HCJ 650/82, 4; Interview with Yossi Amitai.
112 Goldstein and Dayan, *They Called Him Jaap*, 199; Nakdimon, "Meetings"; Eliav, *Autobiography*, 256.
113 Eliav, *Autobiography*, 256.
114 Nakdimon, "Meetings."
115 Hermann, *Israeli Peace Movement*, 86.
116 Bar-On, *In Pursuit*, 207; Shaham, *Zehav Ha-misholim*, 366–367; Interview with Sabri Jiryis.
117 S. Nakdimon, "Lova Eliav and Matti Peled met in Paris with PLO official," *Yedioth Ahronoth* (22 September 1976); S. Nakdimon, "Pierre Mendès France facilitated the meeting between Israelis and PLO offiicals," *Yedioth Ahronoth* (23 September 1976); A. Eitan, "Another confirmation for the meeting between Eliav and a PLO official," *Yedioth Ahronoth* (27 September 1976); S. Nakdimon, "Four Israelis met in Paris with PLO officials," *Yedioth Ahronoth* (20 October 1976); Goldstein and Dayan, *They Called Him Jaap*, 206.
118 Goldstein and Dayan, *They Called Him Jaap*, 202, 206–207; Avnery, *My Enemy*, 181.
119 "The Minister of Justice distinguishes between the government's position and meetings of private citizens with the PLO," *Davar* (9 November 1976); *The Knesset Plenary Records* (Divrei Haknesset), 10 November 1976; G. Reicher, "Eliav: We came to the meeting with the PLO with a Zionist platform, Lin: They should be summoned to the police," *Yedioth Ahronoth* (11 November 1976); A. Tsimuki, "Rabin: Contacts with officials from terrorist organizations are a negative phenomenon," *Yedioth Ahronoth* (8 November 1976); Goldstein and Dayan, *They Called Him Jaap*, 207–210.
120 "Foreign affairs and defense committee will discuss the topic of meetings with the PLO," *Davar* (11 November 1976); Tsimuki, "Rabin."
121 Goldstein and Dayan, *They Called Him Jaap*, 210; Avnery, *My Enemy*, 184–185.
122 Eitan: "Another confirmation"; "Another meeting of Israelis with the PLO at the end of the Month," *Davar* (12 January 1977); "Matti Peled: The PLO will change the Palestinain Charter next month," *Davar* (14 February 1977); "The Paris talks."
123 Yesod, *Matti Peled*, 24; Avnery, *My Enemy*, 187–189; Bar-On, *In Pursuit*, 208.
124 Gresh, *The PLO*, 197; Avnery, *My Enemy*, 188.
125 "Matti Peled: An agreement with the PLO on a stable framework," *Davar* (2 January 1977); "The Israeli Council for Israeli–Palestinian Peace published a joint statement with the PLO," *Davar* (3 January 1977).

126  Goldstein and Dayan, *They Called Him Jaap*, 212; Bar-On, *In Pursuit*, 208; "The PLO denied any contact with the Council for Israel–Palestine Peace," *Davar* (3 January 1977).

127  "Sartawi's bomb," *Haolam Hazeh* (22 April 1981); Shaham, *Zehav Ha-misholim*, 366; Avnery, *My Enemy*, 190.

128  Abbas, *Through Secret Channels*, 13–14; Gresh, *The PLO*, 199; "The journey of the "Rejectionist Front" continues," *Davar* (16 March 1977).

129  Abbas, *Through Secret*, 13–14; "Sartawi's bomb"; Avnery, *My Enemy*, 192; Interview with Sabri Jiryis; Yesod, *Matti Peled*, 26; Goldstein and Dayan, *They Called Him Jaap*, 218–219; Gresh, *The PLO*, 199.

130  Goldstein and Dayan, *They Called Him Jaap*, 219; Avnery, *My Enemy*, 192, 195.

131  S. Nakdimon, "The PLO is ending the contacts with the 'Council for Peace,'" *Yedioth Ahronoth* (4 July 1977); Yesod, *Matti Peled*, 26; Goldstein and Dayan, *They Called Him Jaap*, 220.

132  UAA, Meeting with Sartawi, 24 June 1977.

133  Gresh, *The PLO*, 199; Avnery, *My Enemy*, 195.

134  Avnery, *My Enemy*, 195–200.

135  UAA, Letter to Arafat, 24 June 1977; U. Avnery, "A gift for Begin," *Haolam Hazeh* (29 June 1977); Avnery, *My Enemy*, 196–200.

136  Avnery continued to meet with Sartawi in Europe, see UAA, Meeting with Sartawi, 13 May 1978; Meeting with Sartawi, 9 September 1978; Meeting with Sartawi, 13 September 1978; Meetings with Sartawi, 12–14 December 1978; Meetings with Sartawi, 5 and 9 January 1979.

137  Gresh, *The PLO*, 213–216.

138  UAA, Avnery to Arafat, 14 December 1978.

139  Avnery, *My Enemy*, 204–205; Avnery, *Optimistic 2*, 328–344; UAA, Avnery to Sadat, 8 May 1976; Avnery to Mr. Boutrus Ghali, 14 December 1978; "Uri Avnery visits Egypt," *Maariv* (26 January 1979); BKA 23, Avnery to Kreisky, 6 February 1978; Avnery to Kreisky, 9 April 1978; Avnery to Kreisky, 14 March 1980.

140  Avnery, *My Enemy*, 213, 222, 238; Szyszkowitz, *Der Friedenskämpfer*, 61; UAA, Sartawi to Avnery, 27 September 1979; Sartawi to Avnery, 26 October 1979; Sartawi to Avnery, 25 October 1980; Sartawi to Avnery, 14 March 1981; U. Avnery, "Sartawi," *Haolam Hazeh* (13 April 1983), 5–7.

141  MPA, 104-1265-70 IV, Sartawi to Peled, 28 March 1981; Peled to Sartawi, 30 October 1982; Szyszkowitz, *Der Friedenskämpfer*, 62–63; Avnery, *My Enemy*, 221, 228, 236.

142  Avnery, *My Enemy*, 207–209; U. Avnery, "The meeting: Absolutely legal," *Haolam Hazeh* (14 July 1982); Avnery, *Optimistic 2*, 342–343; T. Singer, "The police will examine the facts in the visit of Avnery to Beirut," *Yedioth Ahronoth* (12 July 1982); Meetings with Sartawi, 12–14 December 1978; Meetings with Sartawi, 5 and 9 January 1979.

143  BKA, 16, Eliav to Kreisky, 25 October 1982; Eliav to Sartawi, 25 October 1982; Eliav to Kreisky, 5 November 1982; Szyszkowitz, *Der Friedenskämpfer*, 168–172; A. Rath, "The Bruno Kreisky we did not know," *Haaretz* (22 November 2010).

144 BKA 16, Peres to Kreisky, 23 January 1985; Peres to Kreisky, 10 June 1986.
145 "The General Command asks to expel Issam Sartawi from the PNC," *Al-Safir* (22 October 1979); Avnery, *My Enemy*, 216–218; Avnery, *Optimistic 2*, 352–353; Szyszkowitz, *Der Friedenskämpfer*, 11, 121–122.
146 UUA, Meeting with Sartawi, 29 September–1 October 1980; Avnery, *My Enemy*, 223–226; Goldstein and Dayan, *They Called Him Jaap*, 225–227.
147 Goldstein and Dayan, *They Called Him Jaap*, 228–233; Avnery, *My Enemy*, 227–237, 256; A. Avnery, "The Moroccan connection," *Haolam Hazeh* (2 February 1983); UAA, Operation Dream, 29 December 1980–1 January 1981; Meeting with the King, 31 December 1980; Visit in Paris, 12–16 March 1981. Morocco was not defined in Israeli law as an "enemy state" and therefore visiting there was not against the law.
148 Avnery, *My Enemy*, 250; Goldstein and Dayan, *They Called Him Jaap*, 231.
149 "Sartawi's bomb"; "Sartawi congratulates the Council for Israel–Palestine Peace," *Davar* (14 January 1981); Avnery, *My Enemy*, 239–245; "The main points," 5; Goldstein and Dayan, *They Called Him Jaap*, 230.
150 Avnery, *My Enemy*, 242–243, 248–249; see *Yedioth Ahronoth* (12 February 1981).
151 UUA, Avnery to Arafat, 14 March 1981; Avnery, *My Enemy*, 258–261.
152 Avnery, *My Enemy*, 261; UUA, Avnery to Dajani, 15 March 1981; Avnery to Abu Jihad, 14 March 1981.
153 "Sartawi's bomb"; "Sartawi's resignation announcement," *Haolam Hazeh* (22 April 1981); Avnery, *My Enemy*, 263–264.
154 Avnery, *My Enemy*, 265; UUA, Meeting with Sartawi, 18 March 1982.
155 "Sartawi's bomb."
156 Avnery, *My Enemy*, 271, 274, 285; UUA, Meeting with Sartawi, 18 March 1982.
157 Avnery, *My Enemy*, 271–272; "Dr. Sartawi to Le-Monde: Israel is behind Abu Nidal's activity," *Davar* (22 January 1982).
158 On the Lebanon war see Z. Schiff and E. Ya'Ari, *Israel's Lebanon War* (New York: Simon and Schuster, 1985).
159 Dayan and Katz, *Media Events*, 147–187.
160 Avnery, *My Enemy*, 13–25; A. Saragusti, "We arrived with an armoured car to a house in West Beirut, and then Arafat opened the door," *Sicha Mekomit* (5 June 2014).
161 "We want peace," *Haolam Hazeh* (7 July 1982), 6.
162 Avnery, *My Enemy*, 21; U. Avnery, "The meeting," *Haolam Hazeh* (14 July 1982), 12–13.
163 "We want peace," 6–7, 72–73; B. Barzel and E. Strauch, "Arafat to Avnery: The PLO has recognized Israel for a long time," *Yedioth Ahronoth* (4 July 1982); B. Barzel, "Avnery: Arafat argued that he never wanted to destroy Israel," *Yedioth Ahronoth* (5 July 1982). Avnery was criticized for not raising the subject of Palestinian terrorism during his meeting with Arafat.
164 "We want peace," 6–7, 72.
165 S. Yishay, "Ahiaz," *Haoloam Hazeh* (7 July 1982), 13–15; Avnery, *My Enemy*, 24.

166  D. Bloch, "A source in the government: No intention to act against Avnery," *Davar* (4 July 1982).

167  A. Magen, "Avnery on his meeting with Arafat: If PLO destroyed in Beirut – it will rise somewhere else," *Davar* (5 July 1982); A. Tsimuki, "The government decided to give Habib another timeout in order to finish the negotiations," *Yedioth Ahronoth* (5 July 1982).

168  UAA, Zamir to Avnery, 17 October 1982; B. Meiri, "The Attorney General: Uri Avnery will not be prosecuted," *Davar* (20 October 1982); Singer, "The police"; G. Lior, "Avnery was questioned on his meeting with Arafat," *Yedioth Ahronoth* (30 August 1982).

169  U. Avnery, "Dear reader," *Haolam Hazeh* (7 July 1982).

170  Singer, "The police"; Lior, "Avnery was questioned."

171  "We want peace," 6–7, 72–73.

172  "The main points," 8; Yesod, *Matti Peled*, 29; UAA, Meeting with Sartawi, 13 July 1982; Press Conference, 14 July 1982; Goldstein and Dayan, *They Called Him Jaap*, 235; "PLO official and Major General (Reserves) Peled appeared together to journalists in Paris," *Yedioth Ahronoth* (21 July 1982); MPA, IV 104-1265-33; Extracts from the Press Conference in Paris, 20 July 1982; BKA, Joint Statement of General Peled and Dr. Sartawi, 20 July 1982.

173  Avnery, *My Enemy*, 302; "Stop terrorism," *Haolam Hazeh* (21 July 1982), 1, 6–7, 72–73. Avnery and al-Hassan met again in October (UAA, Meeting with Khaled, 21 October 1982).

174  UAA, Meeting with the King, 26 October 1982; Avnery, *My Enemy*, 298–306; G. Kouts, "Hasan calls on Israelis and PLO to meet in Morocco," *Davar* (26 January 1983).

175  Avnery, "The Moroccan connection."

176  Avnery, *My Enemy*, 322; Bar-On, *In Pursuit*, 212.

177  UAA, Meeting with Arafat, Abu Mazen, Sartawi, Abu Marwan and Shaqour, 18 January 1983; Avnery, *My Enemy*, 317–329; Goldstein and Dayan, *They Called Him Jaap*, 237–240; Avnery, "Uri Avnery reports," 8–11, 68; "Avnery: The meeting with Arafat in Tunis – a breakthrough," *Yedioth Ahronoth* (21 January 1983).

178  Avnery, "Uri Avnery reports," 8; Avnery, "The meeting"; UAA, Statement – January 1983.

179  Avnery, *My Enemy*, 328.

180  Avnery, "Uri Avnery reports," 10.

181  Avnery, *My Enemy*, 309; Agha et al., *Track-II*, 14.

182  "Shamir is seeking legislation to prohibit meetings with the PLO," *Davar* (27 January 1983).

183  Bar-On, *In Pursuit*, 213.

184  A. Strauch, "The PLO leadership is discussing the invitation of Israelis to the Palestinian council," *Yedioth Ahronoth* (26 January 1983).

185  Goldstein and Dayan, *They Called Him Jaap*, 241–242.

186  L. Pairs, "Abu Nidal publicly pledges to eliminate Yasser Arafat," *Davar* (28 January 1983); Gresh, *The PLO*, 235.

187  Avnery, *My Enemy*, 331, 335; UUA, Meeting with Sartawi, 25 February 1983.

188 Gresh, *The PLO*, 235; Bar-On, *In Pursuit*, 213; Avnery, *My Enemy*, 331–334; "The day of Sartawi," *Haolam Hazeh* (23 February 1983); after the 1983 PNC meeting, Avnery published a special interview with Sartawi in *Haolam Hazeh*; see "Of course the contacts will continue," *Haolam Hazeh* (23 February 1983).

189 Email interview with Tessa Szyszkowitz, 17 May 2016.

190 Translation from Hebrew. From: Avnery, *My Enemy*, 338.

191 Meeting with Sartawi, 25 February 1983; B. Rubin and J. C. Rubin, *Yasir Arafat* (London: Continuum, 2003), 93; Avnery, *My Enemy*, 339–343.

192 Avnery, *My Enemy*, 348–349; "The will," *Haolam Hazeh* (13 April 1983), 9.

193 Gresh, *The PLO*, 235; Sayigh, *Armed Struggle*, 558; Avnery, *My Enemy*, 351–354.

194 Avnery, *My Enemy*, 201, 350; Avnery, "Sartawi," 5; Interview with Yossi Amitai; Visit in Paris, 12–16 March 1981.

195 Avnery, *Optimistic 2*, 298.

196 "An event in memory of Sartawi in Tel Aviv," *Davar* (31 May 1983).

197 Y. Kroz, "An enemy you can speak to," *Yedioth Ahronoth* (11 April 1983); U. Avnery, "Alligator tears," *Haolam Hazeh* (20 April 1983).

198 P. Reina and B. Moni, "A tall man pulled a gun from his pocket, fired five bullets into Sartawi's chest – and disappeared," *Yedioth Ahronoth* (11 April 1983).

199 UUA, Visit in Turin, 4–8 May 1983 – Conversation with Imad; Avnery, *My Enemy*, 359–361.

200 UUA, Meeting with Hamed, 7 May 1983; Meeting with Hamed, 13 July 1983; Avnery, *My Enemy*, 365; Avnery, *Optimistic 2*, 399.

201 Avnery, *My Enemy*, 369–370, 397. UAA, Visit in Paris and Tunis, 18–23 April 1984; Visit in Tunis, 7 February 1985. Avnery also met with Arafat in May 1985, see UUA, Meeting with Arafat, 15 May 1984.

202 H. Siniora, "PNC: Report on the 17th session of the PNC in Amman," *Journal of Palestine Studies*, 14:3 (1985), 170.

203 Barzel: "Arafat: This Israeli is my favorite of all," *Yedioth Ahronoth* (12 February 1985); Avnery, *My Enemy*, 397; Siniora, "PNC," 170.

204 Avnery, *My Enemy*, 382, 388, 396–398. UAA, Meeting with Arafat, 21 April 1984; Meeting with Arafat, 9 February 1985.

205 UAA, The Soldiers' Families to Avnery, 3 July 1983; Avnery to Arafat, 14 July 1983; Avnery, *My Enemy*, 397–398, 362–363, 396–398; Barzel, "Arafat."

206 Goldstein and Dayan, *They Called Him Jaap*, 249–250

207 D. Zoker, "I just want to hope that they won't kill me in front of my children," *Davar* (15 April 1983).

208 MPA, File IV 104-1265-70, Peled to Sartawi, 30 October 1982; G. Kouts, "Sartawi is calling 'good-willed' Israelis to talk about possible ways for solution," *Davar* (14 July 1982); Avnery, *My Enemy*, 273, 309–310.

209 "Resolutions of the political committee of the Eighteenth Session of the PNC, 26 April 1987," *Journal of Palestine Studies*, 16:4 (1987), 200.

210 Bar-On, *In Pursuit*, 208; T. Reshef, *Peace Now* (Jerusalem: Keter, 1996), 82–84.

211 Shaham, *Zehav Ha-misholim*, 452–454.

212 Agha et al., *Track-II*, 17, 25–27; Bar-On, *In Pursit*, 209–211, 215; Abbas, *Through Secret*, 17; S. Gazit, "Kiss and tell," *NRG*, 11 June 2007.

213  Reshef, *Peace Now*, 156–161.
214  Y. Beilin, *Touching Peace* (Tel Aviv: Miskal, 1997), 37–42, 44; Abbas, *Through Secret*, 83–84.
215  See the text of "Prevention of Terrorism Ordinance (Amendment no. 2) 5746-1986": https://mfa.gov.il/mfa/mfa-archive/1900–1949/pages/prevention%20 of%20terrorism%20ordinance%20no%2033%20of%205708–19.aspx (accessed 25 March 202); Discussion on "Prevention of Terrorism Ordinance (Amendment no. 2)," *The Knesset Plenary Records* (5 August 1986).
216  Interview with Uri Avnery.
217  See Y. Hirschfeld, *Oslo* (Tel Aviv: Am Oved, 2000), 15–21, 88–117.
218  Interview with Ron Pundak.
219  S. Ben-Ami, *Battlefront without a Home Front* (Tel Aviv: Sifrei Hemed, 2004), 134.
220  Interview with Uri Avnery; Avnery, *Optimistic 2*, 464.
221  Agha et al., *Track-II*, 13.
222  Gresh, *The PLO*, 198–199.
223  Gresh, *The PLO*, 195.
224  Hirschfeld, *Oslo*, 34.
225  Bar-On, *In Pursuit*, 208–209; Yesod, *Matti Peled*, 56–57.
226  Hermann, *Israeli Peace Movement*, 86.
227  Abbas, *Through Secret*, 17–18.
228  Bar-On, *In Pursuit*, 209.
229  "The main points," 5.
230  Bar-On, *In Pursuit*, 213.
231  See "Sartawi's bomb"; "The PLO – what is it exactly?" *Haolam Hazeh* (2 March 1983); Avnery, *Optimistic 2*, 231.
232  E. Strauch, "Avnery: PLO members clarified that they gave up the secular state," *Yedioth Ahronoth* (3 October 1979).
233  Gresh, *The PLO*, 195.
234  "The Paris talks," 21.
235  Avnery, *My Enemy*, 45.
236  UUA, Begin to Avnery, 24 January 1978.
237  Interview with Sabri Jiryis.
238  U. Avnery, "The last evening," *Haolam Hazeh* (20 April 1983), 12.
239  Barzel, "Arafat"; Meeting with Arafat, 9 February 1985.
240  Avnery, *Optimistic 2*, 231.
241  Avnery, *My Enemy*, 324.
242  "The main points," 6.
243  Nakdimon, "Meetings."
244  See https://content.ecf.org.il/files/M00062_VeniceDeclaration1980English.pdf (accessed 25 March 2021).
245  A. Arian, *Security Threatened* (Cambridge: Jaffee Center, Tel Aviv University and Cambridge University Press, 1995), 105–106; G. Goldberg, G. Barzilai, and E. Inbar, *The Impact of International Conflict* (Jerusalem: Davis Institute, 1991); D. Bloch, "Public opinion survey," *Davar* (1 December 1974).

# Conclusions

The task of PPEs is a very challenging one, given that they lack the official resources enjoyed by states and international organizations, and given the dynamic, intense, and complex conditions of an ongoing conflict subject to the influence of various internal and external actors. Moreover, they often face opposition and attempts to thwart their independent activity. However, this book shows that, despite these factors, PPEs can, under certain conditions, play an important and effective role in conflict resolution processes and have a crucial impact on the official diplomatic sphere. This chapter presents a concluding discussion on PPEs' activity and their impact, building on the proposed theoretical framework and the empirical comparative analysis of the four main case studies, alongside the other cases from the broad database (see appendix). In order to examine the question of PPEs' impact, the chapter first analyzes which influence patterns were evident in the PPEs' activity and which of these were most prevalent and effective. It then examines the impact of variables at three levels: variables related to the PPE, variables related to the initiative, and external variables. The next part analyzes other questions that arise from the research regarding various aspects of the PPE phenomenon: the personality profile of the PPEs, their social characteristics, the risk of misperception and misunderstandings in their activity, PPEs as a historical phenomenon, and the potential of the study's proposed framework as a basis for future research.

## Influence patterns of the PPEs

The empirical analysis reveals three main influence patterns that PPEs succeeded in promoting and implementing in their work: mediation, crisis management, and gestures of conciliation. These patterns were more prominent and fruitful than others because they are relatively targeted and simple to execute, and do not require strategic changes and long-term commitments.

*Mediation* is a central pattern, and in all four case studies official actors used the PPEs' mediation channels to some extent. In general, decision makers prefer to use PPEs' channels for passive, rather than active, mediation, and to use the PPEs themselves as communicators or facilitators who have no active involvement in the content. In some cases, such as with Cousins and Massie, the pattern is limited to a few specific mediation missions, while in other cases, such as with Duddy, the mediation pattern can develop into a more enduring, long-term channel. Other cases that illustrate effective influence through mediation include Harry Ashmore and William Baggs, who mediated between the US State Department and North Vietnam (1967); Father Alec Reid, between Gerry Adams and John Hume in Northern Ireland (1980s); Muhammad Rabie, between the US and the PLO (1988); Bishop Jaime Gonçalves, between the Mozambican government and the Mozambican National Resistance (1990–1992); and Stella Sabiiti, between Uganda's government and the Uganda National Rescue Front II (2002).

*Crisis management* is another common pattern, one in which PPEs have a greater significant probability of exerting influence and officials are comparatively open to unofficial intervention, relative to other patterns. The pattern was implemented in all four case studies, either in an international crisis (Cousins and Massie) or during a crisis involving hostages or POWs (Avnery and Duddy). PPEs' roles in hostage or POW crises are especially prominent and effective because, under the circumstances, their activity is perceived as an ad-hoc, humanitarian effort to address an urgent need for help. This unique situation makes officials more receptive to using the PPEs' existing network of contacts. Accordingly, even in cases in which officials strongly opposed PPEs' activity, they accepted their assistance in this specific context. The Israeli government's attitude towards Avnery's and Eliav's efforts to release Israeli POWs is a good illustration. Another example is Gershon Baskin: although Israeli decision makers rejected his peace efforts over the years, they did allow him to play a role in negotiations between Israel and Hamas on the release of an Israeli soldier captured in Gaza (2011).[1]

The third main prominent pattern is *gestures of conciliation*. This is also a specific and realistic goal that many PPEs pursue, as it has a greater likelihood of implementation than do more ambitious goals. The gesture itself might be a small step, but it can serve as a significant confidence-building measure with the potential to change the dynamic of the conflict. This pattern can work both with PPEs who have good relations with leaders on their own side – such as Cousins with Kennedy – and with dissident PPEs who promote the pattern through their impact on the rival side – such as Avnery with the

PLO – without official endorsement on their side. On various occasions, PPEs have been able to convince the other party to release hostages or POWs as a gesture. For example, PPEs facilitated the release of American POWs during the Vietnam war (1960s), and Jesse Jackson engaged in efforts to release American hostages in Syria (1983) and Iraq (1990).

Two additional influence patterns are also common in PPEs' efforts but are less successful in terms of implementation. The first is *transmission of ideas*, which is more complex to achieve as it requires intervention in core matters of policy. It also difficult to detect this pattern, trace its genealogy, or ascertain the diffusion of ideas to the official sphere. Nevertheless, the case studies do reveal that certain ideas reached the official sphere, thanks to special relations that existed between PPEs and leaders. One such example was the incorporation of Cousins's proposals into Kennedy's actions and speeches. The transmission of a Russian proverb ("Trust, but verify") via Massie to the official diplomatic discourse also illustrates how a PPE's familiarity with the rival side's culture and worldview can promote this pattern. Another example is the *Hudna* (truce) initiative, led by three Israeli PPEs who brought this Islamic concept into the Israeli–Palestinian diplomatic discourse. In some cases, it took time for an idea to reach the official sphere, as illustrated by the transmission of ideas that originated with the Stockholm channel between Israeli PPEs and Palestinians in the mid-1990s and eventually reached the official negotiations in 1999–2001.

The second pattern is *influence on the public discourse*, which is also a very complex process that is difficult to measure. Avnery is the most prominent example of a PPE who devoted attention to this pattern, while Cousins combined clandestine and public activity, and Duddy and Massie focused only on efforts behind the scenes. Avnery referred to the difficulties in this pattern, explaining that "the problem in the profession that I choose for myself of influencing public opinion … is that it is an immeasurable thing. … It can always be argued that it is not you, but rather the result of something else. … You take a handful of seeds and you sow them in the minds of human beings and they can germinate or not. … It's an agricultural process, not an industry."[2] Avnery did, on certain occasions, have an impact on media and public discourse, creating "news slots," influencing the "agenda setting," and bringing about discussions in the government and the parliament.

Other examples include Staughton Lynd's public campaign around his visit to Hanoi (1965); Nahum Goldmann's public campaign after the Israeli government thwarted his plan to meet with Egypt's president (1970); Jesse Jackson's public visit to Syria (1983); and Boraine's and van Zyl Slabbert's public meeting with ANC officials in Dakar (1987).[3] As part of this pattern, PPEs become an alternative source of information for the media, creating enclaves of discourse on the possibility of negotiations during periods of conflict and warfare.

The remaining influence patterns occur more rarely and require exceptional circumstances. *Changes in institutional procedures* is an especially relevant pattern for cases involving PPE dialogue with non-state actors. Under this pattern the unofficial contacts catalyze the formation of diplomatic capabilities and the creation of relevant bodies in preparation for future official talks. The pattern emerged in the Republican movement, as a result of Duddy's channel, and within the PLO in light of contacts with Avnery and the Israeli Council for Israeli–Palestinian Peace. Similar processes took place in South Africa. According to Lieberfeld, meetings with PPEs led to the creation within the ANC of a cadre of members who specialized in negotiation and strengthened the status and influence of the "diplomats" in the ANC.[4]

*Influence through an external actor* is particularly complex, partly because it requires an international network system and the willingness of external actors to endorse PPEs' efforts. There are two examples from the main case studies: Cousins's initiative through the Vatican during the Cuban missile crisis and Avnery's efforts to involve international figures (such as Austrian chancellor Kreisky and former French prime minister Mendes-France) in his efforts with the PLO. Notably, "former official" PPEs and politician PPEs have an advantage in this regard, as they have better access to international networks. Examples include Yossi Beilin and Nimrod Novik, who used the contacts they had among American, Egyptian, and European diplomats during their efforts in the Israeli–Palestinian conflict, and Alon Liel, who used his networks with Turkish and Swiss officials in his peace efforts with Syria (2004–2006).[5]

*Official authorization* is the ultimate goal of many PPEs, but it is also the most complicated and rarest pattern, and almost impossible to achieve. It requires very special and intimate relations between the PPE and official decision makers, of the sort that make the granting of an official mandate possible. In none of the main case studies did it materialize. Indeed, when Massie proposed herself as a candidate for ambassador, she was turned down. The 1993 Oslo channel, however, involved the materialization of this pattern to a certain degree: it began as an unofficial channel between PPEs (Yair Hirschfeld and Ron Pundak) and the PLO, and became an official channel. When it turned official, two Israeli officials joined and led the talks, but the PPEs remained as part of the negotiating team.[6] Another historical example is British PPE Richard Cobden. Cobden promoted a trade agreement with France and in 1860 was granted official authorization to conduct negotiations with France on such an agreement, together with the British ambassador in Paris.[7]

## Variables related to the PPE

The research examined three types of PPE resources that play a significant role in their activity and in their ability to influence: networks, knowledge, and values.

Resources of access and networks had a crucial impact in the four case studies, and their development reveals a significant part of each story. We can identify three indicators to measure the quality of PPEs' network resources, such that the higher the degree of all three indicators, the better the conditions for the PPEs' efforts: (1) the extent to which the PPE had access to official circles on both sides; (2) the extent to which the access reached leaders and decision makers; and (3) the extent to which the contacts and interactions, with both sides, were intense, enduring, and consistent. It is difficult for PPEs to obtain good results in all the indicators. Cousins had high scores in the first and the second – good access to leaders on both sides – while in many cases, PPEs need to settle for access to low- or mid-level officials, at least on one side. Massie, for example, had contacts with mid-level Soviet officials and Duddy had access to low-level British officials. Avnery's results in these tests were poor, as for many years he could not gain access to the PLO leader, and when he managed to do so, in the 1980s, he lacked access to the Israeli leadership. But on the other hand, Avnery's contacts with the PLO were more intense and consistent than Cousins's with the Soviets.

In all four case studies, we can identify the important role of a special personal friendship that developed between PPEs and their main partner on the rival side, which went beyond the political context and served as a basis for the PPE's efforts. Examples include Avnery's, and Peled's, friendship with Sartawi, Duddy's long friendship with Oatley, Cousins's friendship with Korneichuk, and Massie's friendship with Bogdanov. The PPEs and their partners served as "brokers" between two rival network systems, and the partners helped the PPEs by assuring their colleagues that the PPEs were trustworthy, paving the PPEs' way to more access and influence on the rival side. For the partners, these relationships created a special commitment to assist the PPEs, and on some occasions they even deviated from official instructions for the sake of that goal. We can identify this element in other cases as well, such as the friendship between Willie Esterhuyse and ANC leader Thabo Mbeki, and between Gershon Baskin and Hamas official Razi Hamed. According to Baskin, these relations of trust were a key to his channel's success: "The bridges we built through human contact in inhuman circumstances created an infrastructure of trust between us. ... Razi was not my opponent, and I was not his enemy; we were partners."[8]

Another important element is gradation. The analysis of the main case studies points to a long, incremental process in which the PPEs expanded their networks, building trust and credibility, with each phase based on the previous one and the conditions for breakthroughs slowly ripening. Avnery, for example, began his efforts in the mid-1970s, at a time when the PLO was refusing to confirm the contacts publicly, and only at a later stage did it agree to acknowledge them publicly. Initially Avnery only had access to a limited circle of mid-level PLO officials, but gradually he reached the leadership. Cousins, too, started to foster contacts with Soviets in the late 1950s and only gained direct access to Khrushchev in 1962–1963. PPEs' efforts require patience and an understanding of the process, without skipping required steps. As part of this process, PPEs need to pass "credibility tests," both on the rival side and in their relations with officials on their own side, in order to move forward. Duddy's case reveals several "credibility tests" that proved to the Republicans and the British that he was trustworthy and that his channel could deliver.

The empirical analysis shows that knowledge resources are interrelated and have a reciprocal impact on resources of access and networks. On the one hand, knowledge can help in creating new access resources, as illustrated by the way Massie's expertise helped her gain access to Reagan. On the other hand, access resources can provide PPEs with new knowledge resources. For example, Avnery's contacts with PLO officials assisted him in developing expertise on the organization. It appears that on some occasions, official decision makers were more interested in the knowledge that PPEs obtained from their contacts, while in other cases they were more interested in using their contacts as channels.

The ability of PPEs to build an effective mediation system between the parties requires unique value-based resources and an ideological position that will allow them to gain the trust and respect of both parties. This is a complicated task that requires striking a delicate balance, as PPEs who wish to influence both sides need to carve out a space that both parties can accept. Under conditions of ongoing conflict, any move can "burn" the PPEs in the eyes of one of the parties. Duddy, for example, demonstrated this ability, as his support for certain Republican stances assisted him in his contacts with the Republicans, while his objection to violence and his commitment to peace helped him on the British side. Similar elements are evident in the cases of Cousins and Massie. Dissident PPEs, such as Avnery (Israel), as well as Boraine and van Zyl Slabbert (South Africa), and Tom Hayden (US), have had a more critical position towards the official policy, which hampered their acceptance as mediators by the establishment.

In South Africa, officials were more open to working with Esterhuyse than with more dissident PPEs because they viewed his ideological position as less radical. National Intelligence Service (NIS) Deputy Director Mike Louw accused various PPEs of being "naïve, uninformed … [and] prepared to kneel at the feet of the ANC," whereas, according to him, the NIS trusted Esterhuyse: "We regarded him not as someone who had a rosy view of a meeting with the ANC. ... [H]is views were balanced."[9]

Importantly, different influence patterns require different types of PPE resources. For patterns that work by influencing officials on the PPEs' side, how the officials perceive the PPEs is significant. PPEs therefore need to convince the officials that they, and their contacts, are trustworthy, and that they will maintain confidentiality and deliver reliable reports. Cousins and Massie differed in terms of character, worldview, and resources, but each was suited to the president at the time (Kennedy and Reagan, respectively), and probably would not have had the same impact with the other president. For patterns that work by influencing the rival side's officials, the latter's attitude towards the PPEs is important, as is their perception of the PPEs' resources. When the patterns depend on the media and the public, the PPEs' public image, reputation, and access to media and public platforms are central. Journalist PPEs (such as Avnery and Cousins), former-official PPEs, and politician PPEs have advantages in this context. The type of conflict also prescribes the resources that PPEs should have in order to be effective. PPEs with strong communal networks and status (such as Duddy) are needed in ethnic and internal conflicts, while PPEs with wide international networks (such as Cousins) are better suited to international conflicts.

## Variables related to the initiative

Secrecy played a key role in all four case studies. It was a central condition for Duddy's efforts, as the strict secrecy arrangements enabled the existence of his channel. Likewise, Cousins and Massie kept their role a secret at the time. Even Avnery did not reveal some of his meetings to the public, particularly when the other side requested confidentiality. We can identify this element in other cases too, such as Esterhuyse's, Reid's, and Rabie's channels. Confidentiality helped in securing the support of decision makers for an initiative, as well as the readiness of the parties to use the channel for exchanging ideas and exploring possibilities that clashed with their public position. In some cases, PPEs provided a clandestine physical location for meetings, such as Duddy's home and Father Reid's church.

In other cases, however, publicity and media exposure helped PPEs cultivate influence patterns such as influence on public discourse, gestures of conciliation, or transmission of ideas. Publicity can increase interest and attract attention, and can assist in changing public perceptions and breaking taboos. In prominent examples, such as Avnery's public meetings with Arafat (1980s),

Jackson's public visit to Syria (1983), and Carter's public visit to North Korea, the media coverage played a crucial role.

In some cases, PPEs initially worked secretly, aiming their efforts at decision makers, but after being disappointed by the establishment's reaction they decided to go public. One example is Alon Liel, who conducted secret talks with Syria (2004–2006) and reported on them to Israeli government officials. But after his efforts to transfer his initiative to the official sphere failed, he decided to disclose the story to the media.[10] Another example is that of Harry Ashmore and William Baggs, who conducted a secret channel between the US State Department and North Vietnam in 1967. When they concluded that the administration was not willing to negotiate seriously, they revealed all the details of their contacts.[11]

Notably, the disclosure of clandestine contacts is expected to impair the ability of PPEs to mobilize governmental support in future initiatives. The issue of leaks surfaced in the case studies: Meir Pa'il leaked information on the talks with the PLO in 1976, and Duddy weighed this option against the background of a stalemate. Bradley, Duddy's colleague, supported the idea, claiming that secrecy was the channel's source of power, but also a source of weakness.[12] Leaks can threaten the existence of the PPEs' channels or their ability to continue with their activity, but leaks can also encourage public conversation about peace negotiations (as happened after Pa'il's leak and after the exposure of Duddy's channel), and they can prepare the public for official talks.

Another important variable is the goal of the initiative. The empirical analysis demonstrates that the likelihood of influence increases when the goal is more specific, less sensitive, easier to implement, and does not involve long-term strategic change. As noted, PPEs are more effective in promoting patterns such as confidence-building measures or crisis management than in prompting a comprehensive peace agreement. Prominent examples are Massie's initiative on cultural exchanges, Duddy's and Avnery and Eliav's efforts for the release of hostages or POWs, and Cousins's attempt to clarify misunderstandings, as opposed to more ambitious initiatives, such as Avnery's pursuit of an Israel–PLO agreement or Cousins's nuclear disarmament efforts, which failed. In addition, process-oriented initiatives that focus on communication and facilitation are more successful than content-oriented initiatives that offer proposals and ideas.

Correlation with the official policy is a complex, non-dichotomous variable. On the one hand, there are cases in which PPEs' work correlates completely with the spirit of the government, such as the case of Cousins's initiative, which naturally enhances the probability of influence. Cousins's actions were a complementary move to Kennedy's policy, not a source of competition. On the other hand, there are cases in which PPEs' action completely clashes with official policy, such as the case of Avnery during the Begin era. In between, however, there is a wide spectrum of initiatives that are not in correlation with official policy, but which some official actors are evidently interested in or willing to consider, which in turn can have an influence on policy. Examples include the NIS's support for Esterhuyse's talks with the ANC, despite the official policy against negotiations with the ANC, or the *Hudna* initiative, which went against official policy but the underlying concept of which was eventually accepted. The discussion should also distinguish between policy that rejects the idea of negotiation with the rival side and policy that rejects specific negotiating positions or proposals. The clash with the official establishment will be more challenging in the former case.

The quality of the channels also affects the efficiency of the PPEs' efforts. Direct and intense contacts that include unmediated access to decision makers offer a significant advantage, whereas the absence of such access limits maneuverability and can lead to problems in the communication. This is illustrated by the difference between Cousins's effective initiative with the Soviet Union in 1963, based on direct contact with Khrushchev, and his failed initiative with North Vietnam in 1965, based on indirect contact through Polish mediators.[13] The use of a third party in contacts with the rival side can raise questions about deliverability, complicate and hamper the dialogue process, and result in mistakes and misunderstandings.

## External variables

PPEs operate in different types of conflicts: international conflicts between states, conflicts between states and non-state actors, and internal conflicts. They also operate during different stages, and levels of intensity, of conflicts, both under conditions of violence (Duddy and Avnery) and in conflicts without violence (Cousins and Massie).

The empirical research shows that PPEs have more potential to have an effective role in the pre-negotiation phase, or the "diagnostic phase" as Zartman and Berman termed it,[14] than in other stages. This phase includes various situations, such as negotiations with paramilitary groups (Gonçalves with the Mozambican National Resistance, Padma Ratna Tuladhar with Maoist rebels) and diplomacy in warfare (Ashmore and Baggs with North Vietnam) or with "rogue states" (Carter with North Korea). Under these conditions, PPEs serve as a "diplomatic avant-garde" that cultivates the initial contact with the rival side in the hopes of paving the way to official talks. Eliav used to draw an analogy between the contacts with the PLO and a British army tactic whereby, in order to overcome the enemy's barbed wire fences in an attack, one of the soldiers would charge ahead and prostrate himself on the fence so that the others could step on him and attack the enemy position: "It's an unpleasant job," he said, "but someone has to do it."[15] These conflict situations pose major challenges for the official diplomatic system, and official actors who seek communication are more receptive to nonconventional and unorthodox diplomacy, or "black market diplomacy" as Churchill termed it.[16]

In some of these situations, we can identify a "relay race" of sorts, in which different types of PPEs have different roles at different stages. The process shifts from radical PPEs to more central and moderate PPEs, closer to the mainstream. The dialogue between Israeli PPEs and the PLO, as presented in chapter 5, is one example. It began in the 1970s with a more radical PPE, Avnery, and eventually, in the 1990s, came to include Hirschfeld and Pundak, who were close to the political elites. Afrikaner PPEs' contacts with the ANC is another example. The process began with Hendrik van der Merwe, a pacifist Quaker, in the early 1980s, and shifted to Gavin Relly, Boraine, and van Zyl Slabbert in the mid-1980s. Eventually the torch was passed to Esterhuyse, who was close to governmental circles and a member in the Afrikaner elite organization, Broederbond.[17] Each stage represents another step in breaking the taboo on dialogue with the rival side. In the first stage, the more radical PPEs focus on the public dimension, seeking to change public perception and challenge official policy, as they see no chance of direct impact on the government. In the second stage, tending to work clandestinely, the PPEs focus on accessing and influencing the official establishment. Both stages are crucial for this process to materialize, and both types of PPEs play a significant role in reaching an official breakthrough.

During the pre-negotiation phase, in the absence of official communication, PPEs can also serve as a tool to identify and send "diplomatic signaling."[18] The reactions of the rival side to PPEs' activity can serve as a litmus paper for examining intentions and detecting strategic changes. The PLO's attitude towards Israeli PPEs was a good indicator of changes in the organization's political strategy. Similarly, the Republicans' readiness to meet with Oatley in 1991 and the British decision to appoint Fred signaled ripeness for negotiations.

An analysis of the PPEs through the prism of the ripeness theory highlights the proactive commitment of these actors to their ongoing efforts over long stretches of time, regardless of whether or not the conditions are ripe. Their role points to the complexity of the concept, as for them the assumption of ripeness for peace is a permanent perception, not one that depends on certain conditions. It is difficult to define these conditions dichotomously, as ripeness could apply to perceptions among various groups or actors, and could entail different levels, and types, of peace.

Yet the case studies show that the existence of a mutually hurting stalemate, as a central condition of ripeness, affected the outcomes of PPEs' initiatives. Cousins's 1963 initiative, for example, was aided by signs of ripeness that developed as a result of the 1962 Cuban missile crisis, and Massie's 1984 initiative was influenced by the 1983 War Scare. Likewise, Duddy's renewal of efforts in the early 1990s was based on the parties' perception that there was no military solution and that a political option should be explored. In the case of Avnery, his breakthrough in contacts with the PLO after 1982 was related to the impact of the Lebanon war on the PLO's perception. In some of these cases, public statements that signaled some indication of conciliation on the part of one of the parties led the PPEs to sense conditions of ripeness and to intensify their efforts. Examples include the article by Hammami (1973) that led to Avnery's first contact with the PLO, and the Republican prisoners' statement (1981) that sparked Duddy's mediation initiative.

Developments in the political and legal context of the contacts between the conflicting sides also had an impact on the conditions, which in turn enabled the PPEs' activity. For example, the US–USSR Cultural Exchange Agreement (1958) facilitated conditions that allowed Cousins to visit the USSR in 1959, and the establishment of the NIO in Northern Ireland (1972) created the infrastructure for the development of Duddy's channel.

The analysis attested to the importance of keeping consistent PPE channels open, whether the parties are ripe for peace or not, for two reasons: first, as a way to examine, or to prove, the existence of the second condition of the theory – the perception that there is a "way out"; second, to preserve an infrastructure of open communication lines that could be reemployed immediately when needed.

The role of political leaders, and their attitude towards the PPEs, is a significant and decisive variable. The element of leaders' perception comprises two parts: their political position on the goal of the PPE's initiative, and their attitude towards private diplomacy in general. These are two separate components. Some decision makers oppose the political goal but accept PPEs' activity (Rabin and Avnery's diplomacy), while others support the political goal but oppose involvement in diplomacy by private citizens (Shultz and Massie's diplomacy). Kennedy exemplified the best model: he supported Cousins's goal as well as the use of private diplomacy. Leaders' attitudes towards PPEs' activity are shaped by their perceptions of diplomacy, their level of trust in the bureaucratic diplomacy, and their views on civil society. In order to achieve influence patterns that work through the official leadership on their own side, PPEs need support and endorsement, but the empirical research shows that they can also be effective when their leaders are indifferent (Rabin towards Hirschfeld and Pundak, de Klerk towards Esterhuyse).

The research reveals how leadership changes can affect the outcomes of PPEs' efforts. For example, the political changes in Britain in 1974 and 1990 furthered Duddy's efforts, whereas the change in 1976 undermined them. The PPEs' efforts were also affected by domestic struggles within the establishment. For example, the internal dispute in the Reagan administration had an impact on Massie's efforts. At the same time, PPEs' initiatives can reinforce internal disputes among non-state actors, triggering political change (the Republicans after Duddy's 1975 channel), and sometimes even political assassinations (the PLO after Avnery's channels).

Another influential variable is the impact of developments in parallel channels. The analysis shows that failure, or a stalemate, in other channels or initiatives helped advance PPEs' efforts, increasing their importance and the need to use them. The collapse of the Sunningdale process in 1974 contributed to Duddy's 1975 channel, and the 1962 deadlock in the official talks on a nuclear test ban treaty catalyzed Cousins's intervention in 1963. Likewise, the stalemate in the official Israeli–Palestinian talks in Washington strengthened the unofficial talks in Oslo (1993), and the collapse of Egyptian and German mediation channels between Israel and Hamas resulted in the use of Baskin's unofficial channel (2011).

This dimension raises the question of the advantages and disadvantages of multiple channels. On the one hand, the emergence of PPE channels occasionally leads to tension and competition between channels, and to criticism by official diplomats for causing damage. Shultz claimed that private channels, such as Massie's, create confusion.[19] Competition can also exist between unofficial channels. Duddy, for example, began his efforts in the 1970s in parallel with other informal intermediaries. This competition can produce "channel shopping," such as occurred between Duddy's channel and the ICJP channel during the hunger strike (1981), or conflicting messages, as happened when Ashmore and Baggs conveyed a conciliatory message to North Vietnam from the State Department, while in parallel the president sent a firm message via Moscow (1967).

However, alternative PPE channels can also contribute to official channels and assist them in situations of deadlock. Cousins, for example, worked to solve the crisis in the official US–USSR talks, and his initiative helped revive negotiations on a test ban treaty. So, too, Albert Ballin's initiatives between Germany and Britain in 1909 and 1912 led to official talks between the parties. In certain cases, there is a division of labor between PPEs and official mediators, and while the PPEs facilitate the initial contacts, enabling a breakthrough in the dialogue, the official mediators complete the task, turning it into an official agreement. This was the case with Rabie's 1988 channel between the US and the PLO, and with Baskin's 2011 channel between Israel and Hamas: in both cases the PPE efforts had led to significant progress, but a complementary move by an official mediator – Sweden in the former case, Egypt in the latter – was needed to complete the process.

Intervention by mediators in the content of the messages, as occurred in the Duddy–Fred channel in the 1990s, points to the problem of specific mediators with full control and a monopoly over the dialogue process. To address this issue, parties sometimes use parallel channels as a means of assessing messages delivered via the main channel. Israeli prime minister Yitzhak Rabin, for example, used an alternative channel with the PLO (the Tibi–Ramon channel) to confirm the reliability of messages Israel was receiving from the PLO through the Oslo channel.[20]

The empirical analysis also emphasizes the importance of internal agents within the establishment, who serve as a critical variable by assisting PPEs from inside the official system. It points to two types of allies: political allies and governmental-bureaucratic allies. Cousins had Bundy and Sorensen to assist him, Massie was supported by McFarlane, and Oatley enabled and furthered Duddy's efforts. Support from such allies can play a crucial role in PPEs' influence, but dependence on their support can be problematic as it might come to an end once they leave their positions.

Notably, high-ranking intelligence officers served as the governmental allies of the PPEs in several cases. Oatley (MI6) and Fred (MI5) in Duddy's case, Neil Bernard (NIS) in Esterhuyse's case, and David Median (Mossad) in Baskin's case are some examples. Part of the explanation for this role being carried out by intelligence actors, rather than diplomats, lies in the fact that the former can ensure greater secrecy and distance the channels from the politicians. Intelligence officials also have a broader mandate and more room to maneuver than diplomats. This conclusion contributes to discussions in the literature regarding the potential role of intelligence services in clandestine diplomacy and peace processes.[21]

## The personality profile of the PPEs

Drawing on the study's empirical analysis, this section describes the main characteristics – in terms of personality, character, and worldview – that the PPEs have in common and which served as a basis for their activities.

*Optimism* – A prominent element in the PPEs' personality is profound optimism and belief that change is possible. "If there is one trait that has pushed me forward throughout my life," Avnery wrote, "it is optimism. I am optimistic by birth, my father was optimistic, and I think that my grandfather was too; one who does not believe in the future, cannot act for the future."[22] Likewise Cousins, in his writings, emphasized the importance of hope and spoke out against surrendering to a sense of helplessness: "No one really knows enough to be a pessimist. ... All things are possible once enough human beings realize that the whole of the human future is at stake."[23]

The optimistic approach of the PPEs took two discernible forms. The first was optimism about the possibility of transition from conflict to peace. The PPEs shared the belief that the conflict was not a predetermined destiny and that dialogue could change it. They remained committed to this view in times of crisis, deep hostility, and even violence and war. In some of the cases, this belief was part of a larger vision, at times almost utopian. Cousins, for example, believed in a federal world government and saw it as a practical plan; Avnery supported the idea of a "Semitic Union" with a federation of the Fertile Crescent states, and worked to promote this program. Alongside the element of optimism, a grave fear of the horrific scenarios that could materialize if the parties did not choose dialogue also drove the PPEs. Cousins repeatedly described the danger of nuclear war, and Duddy warned of escalation resulting in an extreme cycle of violence.

Second, the PPEs were optimistic about their ability to influence and play a role in changing the situation, believing they could promote peace through their independent activities. Avnery used the image of a small self-propelled wheel that results in the rotation of a larger wheel, which in turn rotates a larger wheel, thus ultimately bringing about significant change.[24] Cousins wrote that "big ideas in this world cannot survive unless they come to life in the individual citizen. It is what one man does in responding to his convictions that provides the forward thrust for any great movement."[25] Massie held a similar belief, saying that "each one of us can make a difference in the world. ... When it comes to human relations, nothing is impossible."[26]

*Familiarity with the other side* – Another central element concerns the PPEs' perception of the rival side. They operate under conditions of conflict that have given rise to an "enemy image" and de-humanization of the rival side, but they reject these societal beliefs. They see the human dimension of the rival side, recognize its point of view, acknowledge its interests and fears, and develop an awareness of its internal differences and the constraints it faces. The PPEs in the case studies were exposed at an early stage in life to people from the other side, took part in encounters with the rival community or state, and engaged in various types of cross-border cooperation.

Duddy grew up in a mixed neighborhood within a mixed city in Northern Ireland, and from a young age had many Protestant friends. Later, as a businessman, he was in contact with individuals from both communities. Massie was exposed to Russian culture during childhood, and over time cultivated strong friendships with Russians. Avnery grew up near the boundary between Tel Aviv and Jaffa, and after leaving school at the age of fifteen in order to work, he was frequently sent on missions to Jaffa, where he was increasingly exposed to the Arab population.[27] Later, he forged ties with

Arabs as part of his journalistic and political activities. Cousins's contact with the Soviet side came at a relatively older age, but he too integrated into frameworks that served as a basis for encounters with the opposing side.

*The importance of dialogue* – The worldview of the PPEs ascribes great importance to direct dialogue, not only as a technical tool for negotiation, but also as a process of inter-personal acquaintance between rival parties and as a prerequisite for mutual learning. Cousins believed that direct human encounters could break down barriers of mistrust and promote peace.[28] Massie also stressed the significance of direct contacts as a way to counter demonization, and believed that diplomacy "is above all about relations between people."[29] Avnery claimed that "a million written words are not equivalent to one minute of face-to-face conversation, when you look straight into your interlocutor's eyes, catch his expression, his gaze, his body language, while he watches you unaware of it."[30] The importance Duddy attached to direct encounters was also linked to the theoretical approach he adopted as a participant in Tavistock Institute workshops that followed the "group relations" model.

*Mistrust of the official diplomats* – Another common element is a deep sense of mistrust and suspicion towards the establishment, in particular the official bodies in charge of diplomacy, and a tendency to question their willingness, or ability, to promote peace. This feeling reinforced the PPEs' desire to take action. Massie was very critical of governmental bureaucracy, especially the Kremlinology specialists in the State Department and the security establishment.[31] Cousins wrote that "the enemy is a man who has a total willingness to delegate his worries about the world to officialdom. He assumes that only the people in authority are in a position to know and act."[32] Avnery claimed that the Israeli Foreign Ministry was "more belligerent than the Israel Defense Forces," and that its ambassadors "have always been the enemy of any act of peace with the Arabs."[33] This impression is evident in other PPE cases as well. Ballin, for example, saw the German Foreign Office as an arrogant closed club, preserved for "aristocratic incompetents";[34] Cobden termed the British Foreign Office "the Circumlocution Office," claiming that its entire essence was "calculated to breed and perpetuate quarrels";[35] and Rabie strongly criticized the conduct of the PLO's diplomatic staff.[36]

*Sense of mission and belief in the righteousness of their way* – Another important element is the PPEs' sense of mission and their fundamentalist belief in the righteousness of their actions and in the lofty and moral nature of the goal of resolving the conflict. In this regard they satisfy the definition of a "crusading reformer" – a term coined by Becker to describe individuals who work fervently to change rules "out of absolute ethic" and believe that their mission is holy.[37] This element also relates to the term "altruistic citizenship" coined by Rosenau to describe citizens who see a particular issue, of importance to their collectivities, as more important and urgent than their private needs, and who focus intensely on struggling for this goal, turning it into a way of life.[38] In addition, it bears resemblance to Weber's concept of a "value-rational action" that is based on "a conscious belief in a value for its own sake" – a belief that derives from obligation and conviction, regardless of the prospects of success and the possible costs.[39]

Avnery, summarizing the dialogue process with the PLO, wrote that "we suffered plenty of defeats and setbacks but we also witnessed the best human qualities – adherence to purpose, dedication to an idea, and courage in the face of hostility."[40] Judah Leon Magnes drew a parallel between his activity and the mission of the prophet Jeremiah, and Rabbi Menachem Froman also ascribed a religious significance to his actions, stating that to work for peace is to work for God.[41] Eyal Erlich, as well, underscored the sense of mission in his initiative: "Although no one appointed me, I had a sense of responsibility and mission. ... For a while I had a strange and frightening feeling that I was holding the key to changing the situation; am I going off the rails?"[42]

The combination of an optimistic belief in their ability to influence and fierce adherence to their mission helps to explain the Sisyphean dimension in the PPEs' activity. They pursued their goal over a long period of time, persistently trying over and over again even though they encountered countless objections and failures. Nimrod Novik used the image of a Weeble to describe his efforts – falling down time after time and starting from the beginning as if nothing had happened.[43] The PPEs' persistence brings to mind the image of the "hedgehog" in the human division proposed by Isaiah Berlin between the hedgehog and the fox (based on a work by the Greek poet Archilochus). It distinguishes between the hedgehog, whose thinking and feelings involve one cohesive system and one central vision, and the fox, who has many ends, sometimes even contradictory, and whose thinking and way of life are scattered and centrifugal.[44] The PPEs devote their energy and resources persistently and consistently over time. Erlich likened his efforts to "digging in the hard ground with a spoon" in order to find oil, noting that although he knew the chances of success were slim, and despite the frustrations, he felt that even a fraction of a chance of success was enough to motivate him to continue.[45] Massie also emphasized this aspect, asserting that "we, the Swiss, are very stubborn," adding that she "had to keep trying" and that she always followed Churchill's saying: "Success is going from failure to failure without loss of enthusiasm."[46]

Some of the cases indicate the influence of formative life events that shaped the PPEs' worldviews and motivated them to act. In Cousins's case, the atomic bombs dropped on Hiroshima and Nagasaki had a dramatic impact; in Avnery's case, his experience in the 1948 Israeli–Arab war affected him; and in Duddy's case, incidents of severe violence near his business increased his commitment to working for peace.

*Individualism and rowing against the tide* – The PPEs had a belief system that clashed with prevailing public and governmental perceptions, one that defied the *Zeitgeist* of the time and challenged the shared societal beliefs that formed the "conflictive ethos." The PPEs operated under conditions of tension, hostility, and, at times, violence. Cousins's and Massie's initiatives took place during peak moments in the Cold War, and Duddy and Avnery promoted their efforts in times of violence and war. Nitza Erel wrote that Avnery "did not shy away from challenging all the foundations of the Israeli consensus," and described his meeting with Arafat in the midst of the 1982 Lebanon war as "breaking all the national taboos."[47] The same was true in other cases as well: Goldmann's initiative during the War of Attrition (1970), the actions of Lynd, Ashmore, and Baggs during the Vietnam war (1965–1968), Tuladhar's efforts during the Nepalese civil war (2000s), and Erlich's during the second Intifada (2001–2003).

PPEs are aware of the clash between their activity and the hegemonic voice in their society. They realize that they are taking a personal risk that might require them to pay a personal price. Indeed, Abie Nathan was sent to prison for his meetings with PLO officials; Professor Lynd, a lecturer at Yale University, was fired after his trip to Vietnam; Boraine and Van Zyl-Slabbert encountered violent demonstrations and an orchestrated campaign of telephone harassment when they returned from the Dakar meeting with the ANC; Reverend Roy Magee was isolated by his fellow Protestant clergy for his activity; and Spanish journalist José María Portell, who promoted talks with the Basque organization ETA, paid with his life.[48] This element points to aspects of civil courage in the PPEs' profile.

The willingness to take risks was also reflected in visits to dangerous areas, such as Sayre's journey to rebel areas in Nicaragua, American PPEs' visits to Vietnam during the war, and Avnery's meeting with Arafat in Beirut. In some cases PPEs' efforts took a toll on their health: Reid remained active despite his deteriorating health, Cobden managed some of his contacts from his sickbed, and Abraham Muste, who went on a peace mission to North Vietnam at the age of eighty-two, suffered a fatal heart attack two weeks after his return.[49]

Many PPEs also exhibited independent and individualist thinking and lifestyles. The four PPEs of the case studies were independent in their professional life; they headed their own businesses and were not subordinate to anyone. Cousins and Avnery served as editors of influential weeklies created in their own image, Massie was an independent writer and lecturer, and Duddy started his own restaurant and later owned a number of businesses.

They worked independently and believed in their ability to initiate and create from scratch. Some were also founders of political organizations: Cousins was president of the World Federalist Association and chairman of SANE, and Avnery was one of the founders of Semitic Action and This World – A New Power.

## The social characteristics of the PPEs

Drawing on the empirical analysis, we can identify a number of social characteristics of the PPEs. First, PPEs are, for the most part, men. This is partly attributable to the fact that the cases relate to historical periods in which few women participated in politics and diplomacy, and this trend also permeated the space of unofficial peace initiatives. This state of affairs led to the adoption of UN Security Council Resolution 1325 (2000), calling for the inclusion of women in peace processes. However, it should be noted that throughout the twentieth century, women played an important role in peace movements in various areas (including Northern Ireland, Israel–Palestine, and the US–Vietnam war).[50] In some of these cases, women's movements either included women from both sides of the conflict or cultivated contacts with women activists on the rival side – an activity that resembled cross-national, or cross-community, peace activism or people-to-people diplomacy. For the most part, however, they did not focus on PPE activity as defined here. Notably, changes have taken place in this context, and since the end of the Cold War there has been a growing involvement of women in informal, track two, and citizen diplomacy, and this trend is expected to intensify.[51]

Second, in terms of age, PPEs were usually most active around the end of the fifth decade, or beginning of the sixth decade, of their life. Cousins promoted his main PPE initiative at age forty-seven (1962), Avnery at age fifty-two (1975), and Massie at fifty-three (1984). Duddy was relatively young at the time of the 1975 channel – thirty-nine – and fifty-five at the time of the 1991 channel. Other PPEs were of comparable ages at the time of their relevant activity: Cobden was fifty, Ashmore and Esterhuyse – fifty-one, Magnes – fifty-two, and Boraine – fifty-five. This can be explained, among other factors, by the fact that PPE activity requires a significant infrastructure of resources, networks, and reputation, acquired and accumulated over time and through life experience, and by the time they reach this age group PPEs feel more confident and capable, and freer to act.

Third, PPEs usually belong to the middle or upper socioeconomic class, and generally have a strong, stable foundation in terms of career. The PPEs' intensive activity requires free time and financial resources, and their economic status allows them to devote time and resources to their efforts. In addition, their strong socioeconomic and professional status and mature age provide PPEs with a stable basis that allows them to take personal risks that might include an economic or occupational price.

Fourth, in terms of their social status, PPEs are usually in a unique position. On the one hand they belong to, or are close to, elite circles and rub shoulders with political and economic influencers, but, on the other hand, they are anomalous, having views that are considered marginal and representing voices that are critical of the government, the establishment, and the hegemonic societal discourse. While the PPE phenomenon reflects an alternative that is fundamentally different from the mainstream outlook and poses a challenge to the establishment, PPEs actually operate near the sphere of the political elite, and to some extent their patterns of action reproduce certain traditional and official diplomatic patterns.

In addition, having some measure of democratic elements – such as freedom of expression and the presence of a civil society – provides favorable conditions for the emergence of PPEs, although the phenomenon can still occur in a variety of political regimes and systems, including nondemocratic countries. Evidently the more dissident PPEs, who are more critical of the government and more public in their actions, generally come from more democratic environments with vibrant civil societies. It also appears that in asymmetrical conflicts, PPEs usually come from the stronger side of the conflict.

## Misperception and misunderstandings

The unique and the nonconventional nature of the PPEs, and the channels they operate, can, under certain conditions, result in errors and misperceptions. One example is a misperception among officials on the rival side regarding the PPEs' status and relationship with decision makers, and, more precisely, the extent to which their activity reflects the official leadership's position. A few cases illustrate this risk. As a private citizen, Ballin promoted an initiative with Britain in 1912, but London formed the impression that he was conveying messages in the name of the German emperor, which in turn generated misunderstandings and false expectations.[52] Similarly, in the case of the Drought–Walsh mission of 1941, Japan overestimated the PPEs' status and connection to the American establishment, when in fact their initiative did not have the administration's approval.[53] In the case of Amirav's 1987 initiative, the Palestinians were certain that he was acting on behalf of the Israeli prime minister – a misperception that came to light after the initiative collapsed and was exposed in the media.[54]

Misunderstandings and communication problems might also develop if the PPEs' channels are based on a long chain of stages and intermediaries, as in the case of the Duddy–Fred channel in the 1990s. This case also illustrates the risk that, under conditions of diplomatic vacuum, PPEs or other intermediaries using an informal channel could interfere in the content of the messages, or blur the lines between assessments and reports.

In addition, PPEs are ideological players with clear political views and vision, and while this might be an advantage and a basis for strong commitment, it could also affect the way they analyze and evaluate developments and events, and in certain conditions could lead to misjudgment and misperception. In some cases, officials have argued that PPEs are influenced by being in contact with the more moderate representatives on the rival side, rather than the more hawkish and extreme forces.

## The PPE as a historical phenomenon

The theoretical scholarship on citizen and track two diplomacy that has emerged since the late twentieth century often presents the phenomenon as a new development, and focuses on recent and contemporary cases. This book, however, seeks to emphasize that PPEs represent a longstanding historical phenomenon, the origins of which preceded its conceptualization in the literature. Notable examples in this context include, among others, the activities of the Spanish bishop Bartolomé de las Casas, who mediated between the Spaniards and Native American tribes in the Spanish colonies in America in the sixteenth century; the Flemish artist Peter Paul Rubens who sought to promote negotiations during the Thirty Years' War in the seventeenth century; the American George Logan, who went on a private peace mission to France in 1789 and to Britain in 1810; William Cornell Jewett, who advanced PPE efforts during the American civil war in the nineteenth century; and the British PPE Richard Cobden, who sought to improve relations between France and England and to promote trade and arms control agreements in the mid-nineteenth century.[55]

Global processes related to democratization, globalization, and developments in the fields of technology, communications, and transportation have, over time, created more favorable conditions for the phenomenon. Against this background, PPEs have acquired new tools and encountered new opportunities, and their ability to communicate with the rival side has improved. In 1798, Logan had to embark on a long and expensive voyage to France in order to promote his initiative; Ballin relied on telegrams to London during his 1912 initiative; Avnery used the telephone as a primary means of communicating with PLO officials in 1975; and in 2011 Baskin managed a direct channel with Hamas officials in Gaza through e-mails and cellphone text messages. PPE activity has also gained more legitimacy as citizen diplomacy has become a more frequent, visible, and widespread phenomenon around the globe.

In certain respects, however, the international conditions during the early modern era were actually advantageous for activity of informal diplomacy, as the diplomatic state bureaucratic system had not yet become established and institutionalized. This allowed private individuals, such as merchants, artists, and travelers, to serve as informal intermediaries or brokers, using their mobility, languages, and networks.[56] Even though they reflect an early modern form of informal diplomacy, with different contexts and elements, some characteristics and patterns of the post-Second World War PPEs can also be traced to these cases.

The research focuses on case studies from the historical period between the post-Second World War years and the end of the Cold War, and it points to the importance of this stage in the development of the PPE phenomenon as well as its main tools and practices. During this period PPEs had a groundbreaking role in creating a model and paving the way for the expansion, institutionalization, and growing awareness of this phenomenon in later stages.

The research focuses on the lesser known and less organized and professionalized elements in the history of unofficial diplomacy. Thus it "imports" into this field a sense of the existing approaches that challenge the traditional historiographical focus on rulers and kings, seeking to expose the "unknown dimension of the past," as Hobsbawm terms it, and to explore actors and aspects that were excluded from history books.[57]

The book presents a new way of looking at the history of the US–USSR, Northern Ireland, and Israeli–Palestinian conflicts, and at the history of conflicts in general. This alternative perspective focuses on historical figures and landmarks that differ from those in the traditional narratives of history books and collective memory. The historical analysis in this work also raises new historical questions, such as questions about missed opportunities and counterfactual questions along the lines of "What would have happened if …?"[58] Thus, for example, what would history have looked like if Ballin's initiative had borne fruit and resulted in an agreement to end the naval arms race in 1912? Would this have prevented the escalation that led to the First World War? Or, how would the Israeli–Palestinian conflict have developed if Avnery had succeeded in bringing about a meeting between Rabin and Arafat in 1975?

## A framework for future research

In 1932 Albert Einstein wrote a letter to Sigmund Freud, posing the question: "Is there any way of delivering mankind from the menace of war?" Freud replied that he was surprised by the question and wrote that in his initial response he "was dumbfounded by the thought of my (of our, I almost wrote) incompetence."[59] Freud's answer reflects an approach that perceives the field of international relations and conflicts as a complex and metaphysical sphere, in which individuals are a negligible unit in the large global checkerboard, and human beings are helpless in the face of inevitable developments determined by higher power.

This book offers a different reading by focusing on the potential role of individual private citizens as players in the international arena, particularly in the field of conflict resolution. It examines the points of interface between their independent activities and official diplomacy, and between micro-level PPE initiatives and moves, on the one hand, and macro-level circumstances, changes, and processes, on the other. In this sense, the book provides a unique toolbox for analyzing the theoretical and historical phenomenon of PPEs, which hitherto has not been conceptualized as a unique phenomenon in the scholarship, and suggests a special framework for discussion of their resources, activities, relations with the establishment, and impact on the official sphere. The research offers both official actors – local and international policy makers and diplomats – and civil society actors lessons and recommendations that highlight the advantages and potential contribution of PPEs to peacemaking processes, as well as their limits and main challenges.

The proposed analytical framework can serve as a basis for further research involving additional – historical or recent – case studies of PPEs, and further examination of questions such as their typology, their resources, or the variables that determine their influence. Furthermore, the phenomenon of PPEs challenges common assumptions in the international relations literature, and therefore is a good starting point for future research on various key issues in the field, including the question of authority and representation in the international arena, the role of ideology in the diplomatic world, the opportunities and challenges of civil society's activity under conditions of intractable conflicts, and the meaning of citizenship in the age of globalization.

## Notes

1 G. Baskin, *To Release Gilad* (Or Yehuda: Kinneret Zmora Bitan, Dvir, 2013).
2 Interview with Uri Avnery.
3 Hershberger, *Traveling*, 34–50; Bar-On, *In Pursuit*, 56–58; Stanford, *Beyond the Boundaries*, 92; Lieberfeld, "Evaluating," 363–364, 367–368.
4 Lieberfeld, "Contributions," 121; Lieberfeld, "Evaluating," 359, 362, 369.
5 Interview with Nimrod Novik; Interview with Alon Liel.
6 Interview with Ron Pundak.
7 Edsall, *Richard Cobden*, 334–341.

8  Baskin, *To Release Gilad*, 268–269.
9  N. Bernard, *Secret Revolution* (Cape Town: Tafelberg, 2015), 191; D. Lieberfeld, "Promoting tractability in South Africa and Israel/Palestine: The role of semiofficial meetings," *American Behavioral Scientist*, 50:11 (2007): 1549.
10  A. Eldar, "A track to bypass Bush," *Haaretz* (30 May 2008); Interview with Alon Liel.
11  Ashmore, "An exercise," 133–139; "Chronology of events in dispute over peace feelers," *New York Times* (19 September 1967).
12  Mallie and McKittrick, *Endgame*, 119.
13  See N. Cousins, "Vietnam: The spurned peace," *Saturday Review* (26 July 1969).
14  I. W. Zartman and M. R. Berman, *The Practical Negotiator* (New Haven: Yale University Press, 1982), 86.
15  Avnery, *My Enemy*, 308; Eliav, *Autobiography*, 278–279.
16  Berridge, *Talking to the Enemy*, xiv.
17  T. Bell and D. B. Ntsebeza, *Unfinished Business* (London: Verso, 2003), 250–253, 273–275, 281; Lieberfeld, "Evaluating," 355–372.
18  See C. Jönsson, "Diplomacy, communication and signaling," in C. M. Constantinou, P. Kerr, and P. Sharp (eds), *The SAGE Handbook of Diplomacy* (London: Sage, 2016), 79–91.
19  Shultz, *Turmoil and Triumph*, 873.
20  Abbas, *Through Secret*, 72–82.
21  L. Scott, "Secret intelligence, covert action and clandestine diplomacy," *Intelligence and National Security*, 19:2 (2004), 322–341.
22  Avnery, *Optimistic*, 11.
23  Warner and Shuman, *Citizen Diplomats*, 186–188.
24  Interview with Uri Avnery; Avnery, *Optimistic 2*, 27, 448.
25  Cousins, *Present Tense*, 190, 371.
26  Massie, *Trust but Verify*, 380.
27  Avnery, *Optimistic*, 92.
28  Stewart and Saunders, "The Dartmouth," 57.
29  Massie, *Trust but Verify*, 78, 256.
30  Avnery, *My Enemy*, 21.
31  Massie, *Trust but Verify*, 295, 300, 341.
32  Warner and Shuman, *Citizen Diplomats*, 164.
33  Interview with Uri Avnery.
34  L. Cecil, *Albert Ballin* (Princeton: Princeton University Press, 1967), 123–124.
35  W. Hinde, *Richard Cobden* (New Haven: Yale University Press, 1987), 298; W. H. Dawson, *Richard Cobden and Foreign Policy* (London: Allen and Unwin, 1926), 256.
36  Rabie, *U.S.–PLO Dialogue*, 23, 25.
37  H. S. Becker, *Outsiders* (New York: Free Press, 1973), 147–148.
38  J. N. Rosenau, *Along the Domestic–Foreign Frontier* (Cambridge: Cambridge University Press, 1997), 290–292.
39  Misztal, *Intellectuals*, 84.
40  Avnery, *The Enemy*, 401.

41 J. Heller, *From Brit Shalom to Ichud* (Jerusalem: Magnes Press, 2003), 391; Little, *Peacemakers*, 345.

42 Erlich, *Hudna*, 35.

43 Interview with Nimrod Novik.

44 I. Berlin, *The Hedgehog and the Fox* (Princeton: Princeton University Press, 2013), 1–2.

45 Erlich, *Hudna*, 128–129.

46 Massie, *Trust but Verify*, 82; Interview with Suzanne Massie.

47 Erel, *Without Fear*, 98, 106–107.

48 Nathan, *Abie Nathan*, 167–179; Hershberger, *Traveling*, 52–53; Little, *Peacemakers*, 69; Clark, Negotiating *with ETA*, 85–87, 146; Lieberfeld, "Evaluating," 367; M. Levy, *From Dakar to Democracy* (Cape Town: IDASA Publishing, 2007), 7–9.

49 Moloney, *A Secret History*, 283; Edsall, *Richard Cobden*, 333, 338; Hershberger, *Traveling*, 87.

50 J. M. Powers, *Blossoms on the Olive Tree* (Westport: Praeger, 2006); M. McWilliams, "Struggling for peace and justice: Reflections on women's activism in Northern Ireland," *Journal of Women's History*, 7:1 (1995), 13–39; J. M. Frazier, "Collaborative efforts to end the war in Viet Nam: The interactions of Women Strike for Peace, the Vietnamese Women's Union, and the Women's Union of Liberation, 1965–1968," *Peace & Change*, 37:3 (2012), 339–365.

51 See R. Brenards, "Women as citizen-diplomats," *Women's Studies Quarterly*, 26:3/4 (1998), 48–56; A. Christien, *Advancing Women's Participation in Track II Peace Processes* (Washington, D. C.: Georgetown Institute for Women, Peace and Security, 2020).

52 Lehrs, "A last-minute private peace initiative," 311–317.

53 J. H. Boyle, "The Drought–Walsh mission to Japan," *Pacific Historical Review*, 34:2 (1965), 144–145.

54 Agha et al., *Track-II*, 24.

55 H. R. Wagner, *Life and Writings of Bartolome de las Casas* (Albuquerque: University of New Mexico Press, 1967); L. Duerloo and M. Smuts, *The Age of Rubens* (Turnhout: Brepols Publishers, 2016); Tolles, "Unofficial ambassador"; W. F. Spencer, "The Jewett–Greeley affair: A private scheme for French mediation in the American Civil War," *New York History*, 51:3 (1970), 238–268; Edsall, *Richard Cobden*.

56 M. Keblusek and B. Vera Noldus (eds), *Double Agents* (Leiden: Brill, 2011); T. Osborne, *Dynasty and Diplomacy in the Court of Savoy* (New York: Cambridge University Press, 2007); M. Van Gelder and T. Krstić, "Introduction: Cross-confessional diplomacy and diplomatic intermediaries in the early modern Mediterranean," *Journal of Early Modern History*, 19:2–3 (2015), 93–105; H. Cools, M. Keblusek, and B. Noldus (eds), *Your Humble Servant: Agents in Early Modern Europe* (Hilversum: Uitgeverij Verloren, 2006).

57 E. Hobsbawm, *On History* (London: Abacus, 1998), 270.

58 Larson, "Trust," 701–734; R. N. Lebow, "What's so different about a counter-factual?" *World Politics*, 52:4 (2000), 550–585; E. Podeh, *Chances for Peace* (Austin: University of Texas Press, 2015), 5–17.

59 See www.brainpickings.org/2013/05/06/why-war-einstein-freud/ (accessed 25 March 2021).

# Appendix: Private peace entrepreneurs – list of cases

| | Name | Conflict | Years | Type |
|---|---|---|---|---|
| 1 | Moshe Amirav | Israeli–Palestinian conflict | 1987 | Scholar PPE |
| 2 | Harry Ashmore and William Baggs | USA–North Vietnam | 1967–1968 | Journalist PPEs |
| 3 | Uri Avnery | Israeli–Palestinian conflict | 1970s–1980s | Journalist PPE |
| 4 | Albert Ballin | Germany–Britain | 1908–1914 | Business leader PPE |
| 5 | Gershon Baskin | Israel–Hamas | 2006–2011 | Activist PPE |
| 6 | Yossi Beilin and Nimrod Novik | Israeli–Palestinian conflict | 1990s 2000s | Politician (Beilin) and former official PPE (Novik) |
| 7 | Alex Boraine and Frederik van Zyl Slabbert | South Africa | 1980s | Politician PPEs |
| 8 | Jimmy Carter | USA–North Korea | 1994 | Former official PPE |
| 9 | Richard Cobden | Britain–France | 1859–1860 | Business leader and politician PPE |
| 10 | Norman Cousins | USA–USSR | 1959–1963 | Journalist PPE |
| 11 | Abdulwahab Darawshe | Israeli–Palestinian conflict Israel–Syria | 1980s 2001–2003 1994 | Politician and minority PPE |
| 12 | Willem de Klerk | South Africa | 1980s | Journalist PPE |
| 13 | James M. Drought and James E. Walsh | USA–Japan | 1936–1941 | Religious leader PPEs |
| 14 | Brendan Duddy | Northern Ireland | 1973–1993 | Business leader PPE |

|     | Name | Conflict | Years | Type |
| --- | --- | --- | --- | --- |
| 15 | Eyal Erlich | Israeli–Palestinian conflict | 2001–2003 | Business leader PPE |
| 16 | Willie Esterhuyse | South Africa | 1987–1990 | Scholar PPE |
| 17 | Menachem Froman | Israeli–Palestinian conflict | 1990s–2000s | Religious leader PPE |
| 18 | Joe Golan | Israel–FLN | 1954–1962 | Diaspora PPE |
| 19 | Nahum Goldmann | Israel–Egypt | 1970 | Diaspora PPE |
| 20 | Jaime Gonçalves | Mozambique | 1990–1992 | Religious leader PPE |
| 21 | Hubert Herring | USA–Mexico | 1926–1927 | Religious leader PPE |
| 22 | Yair Hirschfeld and Ron Pundak | Israeli–Palestinian conflict | 1980s–1990s | Scholar PPEs |
| 23 | Jesse Jackson | USA–Syria | 1983 | Politician PPE |
| 24 | William Cornell Jewett | American Civil War | 1860s | Activist PPE |
| 25 | Alon Liel | Israel–Syria | 2004–2006 | Former official PPE |
| 26 | George Logan | USA–France USA–UK | 1798 1810 | Politician PPE |
| 27 | Staughton Lynd | Vietnam war | 1965 | Academic PPE |
| 28 | Roy Magee | Northern Ireland | 1990s | Religious leader PPEs |
| 29 | Judah Leon Magnes | Israeli–Palestinian conflict | 1929–1947 | Scholar PPE |
| 30 | Suzanne Massie | USA–USSR | 1983–1988 | Scholar PPE |
| 31 | Abie Nathan | Israel–Egypt Israel–PLO | 1960s 1980s | Activist PPE |
| 32 | Niall O'Dowd | USA–Sinn Féin | 1992–1994 | Diaspora and journalist PPE |
| 33 | José María Portell | Spain–ETA | 1977–1978 | Journalist PPE |
| 34 | Mohamad Rabie | USA–PLO | 1988 | Diaspora and scholar PPE |
| 35 | Alec Reid | Northern Ireland | 1980s | Religious leader PPE |
| 36 | Gavin Relly and Anthony Bloom | South Africa | 1980s | Business leader PPEs |
| 37 | Stella Sabiiti | Uganda | 2002 | Activist PPE |
| 38 | John Nevin Sayre | USA–Nicaragua | 1927–1928 | Religious leader PPEs |
| 39 | Padma Ratna Tuladhar | Nepal | 1990s–2000s | Politician and activist PPE |
| 40 | Hendrik W. van der Merwe | South Africa | 1980s | Scholar PPE |

# Index

Note: page numbers in *italic* refer to figures; 'n.' after a page reference indicates the number of a note on that page

Abbas, Mahmoud (Abu Mazen) 32, 207, 214–215, 220, 226–227, 235–236, *237*, 240, 244, 247, 254n.52
Able Archer 83 (1983) 119
Abu Mazen *see* Abbas, Mahmoud
Abu Nidal Organization 221, 232, 237, 239
Adams, Gerry 164, 167–175, 178, 180, 182, 184–185, 187, 190, 192–193, 201n.173, 264
African National Congress (ANC) 21, 28, 32, 41, 43, 45, 265–267, 269, 271–272, 279
agenda setting 53, 244, 265
Allan, James 154, 158, 160, 162
American Association for the United Nations 77, 78
Amirav, Moshe 42, 44, 281
Amitai, Yossi 207, 218–219, 222
Andropov, Yuri 118, 121, 125, 137, 143n.29
Aptheker, Herbert 42
Arafat, Yasser 12, 27, 41, 45, 206–208, 213–224 *passim*, 227–248, 251, 254n.52, 259n.163, 269, 279, 283
Arbatov, Georgy 121–122, 127, 137
Arnon, Yaakov 207, 218, 222, 227, 230–231, 235–236, *237*, *238*, 241, 247

Ashmore, Harry 28, 40, 42, 264, 270–271, 274, 279, 280
Atkins, Humphrey 165–166, 168–169, 171, 192
Avnery, Uri 9, 11–12, 18, 25, 27–28, 34, 40, 45, 206–207, 209–251, 253n.46, 254n.52, 255n.83, 255n.87, 256n.90, 256n.97, 260n.173, 261n.188, 264–280, 282–283
  Arafat, Yasser, meeting in Beirut (1982) 27, 232–235, 239, 246–247, 259n.163, 279
  Hammami, Said, dialogue with (1975–1976) 213–221
  ICIPP–PLO meeting in Tunisia (1983) 235–237, *237*, *238*, 240, 244, 246
  life story and worldview 209–210
  Morocco, visit (1980) 230–231, 235, 259n.147
  Sartawi, Issam, dialogue with (1976–1977) 221–228

backchannel diplomacy 6, 11, 55, 92, 105, 130, 138, 148, 181, 184
Baggs, William 28, 42, 270–271, 274, 279
Ballin, Albert 29, 274, 277, 281–283
Baskin, Gershon 264, 267, 274–275, 282

Begin, Menachem 227–229, 234, *238*, 240–241, 246, 248–249, 251, 271
Beilin, Yossi 242, 266
Belfast Agreement *see* Good Friday Agreement
Berezhkov, Valentin 121, 124, 137, 143n.30
Bloom, Anthony 29
Bobrysheva, Alice 79–80, 85, 87, 101–102, 108
Bogdanov, Rodomir 122, 124–125, 130–131, 137, 139, 141, 267
Boraine, Alex 25, 32, 43, 45, 265, 268, 272, 279, 280
Bradley, Denis 158, 160, 163, 174–175, 177–180, 182–183, 187–188, 193, 201n.173, 270
brokers 20, 27, 154, 189, 267, 283
Brooke, Peter 172–173, 175, 181–182
Bundy, McGeorge 77, 92, 96–98, 101, 108, 275

Carlucci, Frank 130–134, 137
Carter, Jimmy 23–24, 30, 44–45, 270–271
celebrity diplomacy 25
Chernenko, Konstantin 118, 125, 140
Chilcott, John 174–176, 183
Citizens' Committee for a Nuclear Test Ban (CCNTB) 96
Cobb, Tyrus W. 121–122, 137, 141
Cobden, Richard 30–31, 44, 266, 277, 279–280, 282
Communist Party Central Committee (Soviet Union) 79–80, 90
conflictive ethos 38, 279
Cooper, Frank 154–155, 158–159, 161, 163, 165
Cousins, Norman 9, 11, 28, 71–108, 112n.68, 115n.130, 129, 139, 186, 192, 234–235, 264–271, 273–280
    Kennedy's American University speech (1963) 89–95, 97, 99
    Khrushchev, meetings with (1962–1963) 81–89
    life story and worldview 74–77

Slipyj, Archbishop Josyf, release of 83, 85–86, 99
    *see also* Dartmouth Conferences
crisis management 29, *50*, 51–52, 99, 136, 186, 245, 263–264, 270
Cuban missile crisis (1962) 73, 81–82, 87–88, 97, 99–100, 106–108, 119, 266, 273
cultural exchanges, US–USSR 79, 122–124, 138, 141, 270, 273
Curiel, Henri 212, 221–223, 243

Daniloff–Zakharov affair (1986) 129–130, 136, 139
Darawshe, Abdulwahab 34
Dartmouth Conferences 11, 79–83, 85–86, 97–98, 101–102, 104–105, 111n.46, 112n.68
de Klerk, Fredrik 43, 273
de Klerk, Willem 43
Dean–Kuznetsov talks (1962) 73, 84, 87–88
Deverell, John 173–178
diplomatic avant-garde 271
Dobrynin, Anatoly 81–82, 85, 91–92, 98, 101–102, 108, 123–125
doubting strategy 38–39, 99, 244
Drought, James M. 281
Duddy, Brendan 9, 11, 21, 148–193, 201n.173, 264–282 *passim*
    exposure of the channel 181–185
    hunger strikes (1980 and 1981) 164–171
    life story and worldview 151–152
    meetings channel (1975) 158–164
    pre–negotiation channel (1993) 175–181
Dungan, Ralph 82, 85, 90, 101

Eisenhower, Dwight D. 72–73, 75–76, 79, 105
Eliav, Arie Lova 207, 218–219, 222–225, 227, 229, 241, 243, 245, 247, 249, 264, 270–271
enemy image 38, 51, 54, 99, 120, 135, 186, 233, 235, 244, 276
Erlich, Eyal 16, 28, 278–279
Esterhuyse, Willie 21, 267–275 *passim*, 280

Euskadi Ta Askatasuna (ETA) 21, 27, 41, 279

Filin, Igor 130, 137, 141
"Fred" 173–184, 188, 193, 272, 275, 282
Froman, Menachem 21, 29, 278

Gallagher, Noel 158, 167, 174, 177–180, 182–183, 187, 190, 201n.173
gestures of conciliation 50, 53–55, 99, 136, 186, 244, 263–264, 269
Golan, Joe 33, 42, 44, 211
Goldmann, Nahum 33, 43–44, 211, 265, 279
Gonçalves, Jaime 29, 264, 271
Good Friday Agreement (Belfast Agreement) (1998) 148, 175, 185
Gorbachev, Mikhail 118–119, 125–131, 132, 135–137, 139–141, 146n.117
Gorbachev, Raisa 131, 134, 137
Gussenko, Vitaly 131, 137

Hamas 21, 29, 264, 267, 274, 282
Hammami, Said 45, 206, 213–221, 224, 230, 243–244, 247, 251, 253n.46, 254n.52, 255n.83, 256n.90, 273
*Haolam Hazeh* 11, 27, 206–207, 209, 214, 216, 227, 233, 246
Hassan II, King of Morocco 33, 230, 245
Hayden, Tom 42, 268
Herring, Hubert 25, 31
Hirschfeld, Yair 242–243, 266, 272, 273
*Hudna* initiative 16, 28, 265, 271
Hume, John 150, 153, 163, 175, 179–181, 192–193, 264
hunger strikes 11, 148, 186–187, 189, 191–192
Stagg, Frank, hunger strike (1976) 163
hunger strike (1980) 164–166
hunger strike (1981) 166–171

Institute for Democracy in Africa (IDASA) 25, 32

Irish Commission for Justice and Peace (ICJP) 168, 188, 192–193, 274
Israeli Council for Israeli–Palestinian Peace (ICIPP) 12, 25, 206–207, 218–219, 221, 236, 237, 240–241, 255n74, 256n.97, 266

Jackson, Jesse 22, 29, 32, 34, 41–42, 265, 270
Jewett, William Cornell 282
Jiryis, Sabri 207, 214–215, 222, 247, 256n.98
John XXIII, Pope 81–85, 98–100

Kelly, Gerry 174, 176–177
Kennedy, John F. 11, 71–108 *passim*, 116n.161, 129, 264–265, 269–270, 273
American University Speech (1963) 11, 89–95, 97, 99
Khouri, Razi 222, 225, 233
Khrushchev, Nikita 11, 28, 71–73, 77–108, 112n.68, 129, 234–235, 268
Korneichuk, Aleksander 80, 82, 108, 267
Kreisky, Bruno 207, 220, 223, 228–230, 245, 266

Lagan, Frank 153, 158, 187, 193
Lebanon war (1982) 27, 228–229, 232–233, 236, 240, 241, 245, 249–251, 273, 279
PPEs' efforts to release prisoners of war 229, 240, 245, 249, 251, 264, 270
Liel, Alon 30, 43, 266, 270
"local turn" in peace building 5
Logan Act 41
Logan, George 22, 29, 32, 41–43, 282
Lynd, Staughton 42, 265, 279

McFarlane, Robert 122–127, 129, 132, 135–138, 140–141, 275
McGuinness, Martin 152, 164, 167, 169, 172–179, 181–184, 186–187, 190, 192

McKee, Billy 156–158, 164, 167
Macmillan, Harold 73, 77, 84, 92
Magee, Roy 193, 279
Magnes, Judah Leon 31, 278, 280
Major, John 172, 174, 176–180,
    182–184, 190–192
Masmoudi, Mohammed 211–212
Massie, Suzanne 9, 11, 117–141,
    143n.29, 144n.75,
    145–146n.99, 146n.117, 186,
    192, 264–271, 273–280
  exchange of messages between
    Washington and Moscow 11,
    130–131, 145–146n.99
  life story and worldview 119–120
  Moscow, 1984 mission to 122–125
  "trust but verify" 129, 135, 265
  woman PPE, as a 130, 134, 136
Matlock, Jack 123, 125–127, 130,
    135
Mayhew, Patrick 173–176, 179, 181,
    184, 203n.221
Meagher, Brendan 166
media broker diplomacy 27
mediation 6, 11, 17, 21, 25–27, 29,
    36, 41, 46–49, 50, 56, 59–61,
    71, 98, 135, 148, 153, 156,
    164, 168, 181, 185–187,
    189–191, 229, 232, 245,
    263–264, 268, 273–274
Middleton, Donald 160, 163–164,
    167, 188
Morlion, Felix 81–82, 102, 104
Morrison, Danny 168, 188
Mozambican National Resistance 29,
    264, 271

Nathan, Abie 22, 41–42, 242, 279
National Committee for a Sane
    Nuclear Policy (SANE) 75, 78,
    97, 100, 104, 280
National Liberation Front (FLN) 42,
    211–213, 221, 249
Nehru, Jawaharlal 76, 97, 103
new diplomatic history 8
North Atlantic Treaty Organization
    (NATO) 76, 94, 107,
    112n.75, 119
Northern Ireland Office (NIO) 150,
    153–154, 157, 160, 164, 166,

    172, 174, 176, 178, 181–182,
    187, 273
Novik, Nimrod 30, 266, 278

Ó Brádaigh, Ruairí 149, 152–154,
    156–158, 161, 164, 167, 174,
    187, 192–193
Ó Conaill, Dáithí 152–154, 158, 187,
    192–193
O'Dowd, Niall 33, 34
O'Rawe, Richard 167, 168, 171
Oatley, Michael 154–158, 160, 163,
    165–167, 172–174, 186–188,
    193, 267, 272, 275
Oslo Accords (1993) 242–244
  *see also* Oslo channel (1993)
Oslo channel (1993) 242–244, 266,
    274–275

Pa'il, Meir 218–219, 222, 225, 227,
    270
Palestine Liberation Organization
    (PLO) 9, 11–12, 18, 27–28,
    31–34, 41–42, 45, 206–251
    *passim*, 254n.52, 256n.97,
    264–268, 270–275, 277–279,
    282
Palestinian National Council (PNC)
    208, 226, 227, 230–232, 235,
    237–241, 245, 261n.188
Partial Test Ban Treaty (PTBT) 71–72,
    94–99, 104, 115n.130
peace movements 7, 37–38, 48, 77, 280
Peled, Mattityahu 32, 206–207,
    218–219, 221–231 *passim*,
    235–236, 237, 238, 240–246
    *passim*, 249, 267
Peres, Shimon 30, 229, 239, 242
Portell, José María 21, 27, 279
pre–negotiation 36, 175, 178, 189,
    271, 272
private peace entrepreneurs (PPEs)
  action patterns 34–37
  challenges and criticism 44–46
  definition 2
  official establishment's reaction
    40–44
  patterns of influence 49–56
  personality profile 275–280
  power resources 16–27

types 27–34
 business leader PPE 28–29, 32,
  186–187, 276
 diaspora PPE 12n.3, 32–34
 former official PPE 30–31, 266,
  269
 journalist PPE 27–28, 34, 100,
  103–104, 211, 233–235, 246,
  269
 minority PPE 33–34
 politician PPE 31–32, 34, 225,
  242, 246, 266, 269
 religious leader PPE 21–22,
  29–30, 34
 scholar PPE 22, 30–31, 136
Provisional IRA Army Council (PAC)
 152, 156–157, 159–161, 163,
 165, 187
Provisional Irish Republican Army
 (PIRA) 9, 21, 148–157,
 161–164, 167, 172–179
 *passim*, 184, 187, 191,
 198n.102
Pundak, Ron 22, 34, 242, 266,
 272–274

Rabie, Mohamad 33–34, 264, 269,
 274, 277
Rabin, Yitzhak 41, 217–220, 223–225,
 242, 248–249, 251, 273, 275,
 283
Reagan, Nancy 129, 131, 134–137,
 144n.75
Reagan, Ronald 9, 11, 117–141,
 143n.50, 268–269, 274
Rees, Merlyn 155, 158–159, 162, 165
Reid, Alec 17, 29, 45, 193, 264, 269,
 279
Relly, Gavin 28, 272
Revolutionary Armed Forces of
 Colombia (FARC) 186
ripeness theory 39, 58, 59–61, 106,
 139–140, 171, 190–191, 216,
 250, 272–273
Royal Ulster Constabulary (RUC) 153,
 160, 162, 187
Rusk, Dean 85, 88, 96, 105

Sabiiti, Stella 21, 264
Salinger, Pierre 77, 82

Sartawi, Issam 45, 206–207, 214–215,
 220–233, 235–241, 243–247,
 251, 254n.52, 256n.98,
 261n.188, 267
*Saturday Review* 11, 28, 74, 76
Sayre, John Nevin 42, 279
Schlesinger, Arthur M. 94, 96
Schweitzer, Albert 75–76, 97, 103
Semitic Action 210–211, 280
Shaham, David 207, 218–219
Shaqour, Imad 214, 235–236, 237,
 240–241, 247
Shultz, George 117–118, 123, 125,
 129–131, 136–137, 139,
 140–141, 273–274
Sinn Féin 41, 45, 152, 164, 172, 174,
 181–182, 184, 192
Social Democratic and Labour Party
 (SDLP) 45, 150, 153, 163,
 168, 174–175, 190, 192
Sorensen, Ted 81, 90–91, 93, 96–97,
 101, 106, 108, 275
Soviet Peace Committee 79, 80, 87,
 130, 137, 141
special envoy 6–7, 36
Steele, Frank 150, 153–154, 187
Stowe, Ken 166
Strategic Defense Initiative (SDI)
 118–119, 128, 139

Tavistock Institute 152, 277
Thatcher, Margaret 135, 165–166,
 168–170, 172, 191–192
track two diplomacy 3–5, 39–40,
 46–49, 130, 243, 280, 282
transnational civil society 7, 18, 21,
 30, 39–40, 48
transnational moral entrepreneur 7, 38
truce, Britain and the Provisional IRA
 (1975) 11, 148, 160–164, 189
Tuladhar, Padma Ratna 21, 32, 41,
 271, 279
two-level game 36

Uganda National Rescue Front II 21,
 264
United Nations (UN) 75, 77, 81, 83,
 93, 103, 105, 107, 112n.75,
 121, 129, 208–209, 211, 219,
 240, 242, 250, 280

United Nations Security Council
        Resolution 242 (1967) 209,
        219, 242, 250–251
United World Federalists 75, 100
USA Institute 121, 124, 130, 137, 141,
        143n.28

van der Merwe, Hendrik W. 30–31,
        272
van Zyl Slabbert, Frederik 25, 32, 265,
        268, 272, 279
Vietnam war 229, 265, 279–280
    PPEs' efforts during the war 41–42,
        229, 264–265, 270–271, 274,
        279

Walsh, James E. 281
Warsaw Pact 94, 107, 112n.75
Whitelaw, William 150–151, 169
Wilson, Harold 150, 154–155,
        159–160, 163, 190–191

Zhukov, Yuri 81–82
Zhurkin, Vitaly 121, 124

EU authorised representative for GPSR:
Easy Access System Europe, Mustamäe tee 50,
10621 Tallinn, Estonia
gpsr.requests@easproject.com

www.ingramcontent.com/pod-product-compliance
Lightning Source LLC
Chambersburg PA
CBHW051953270326
41929CB00015B/2642